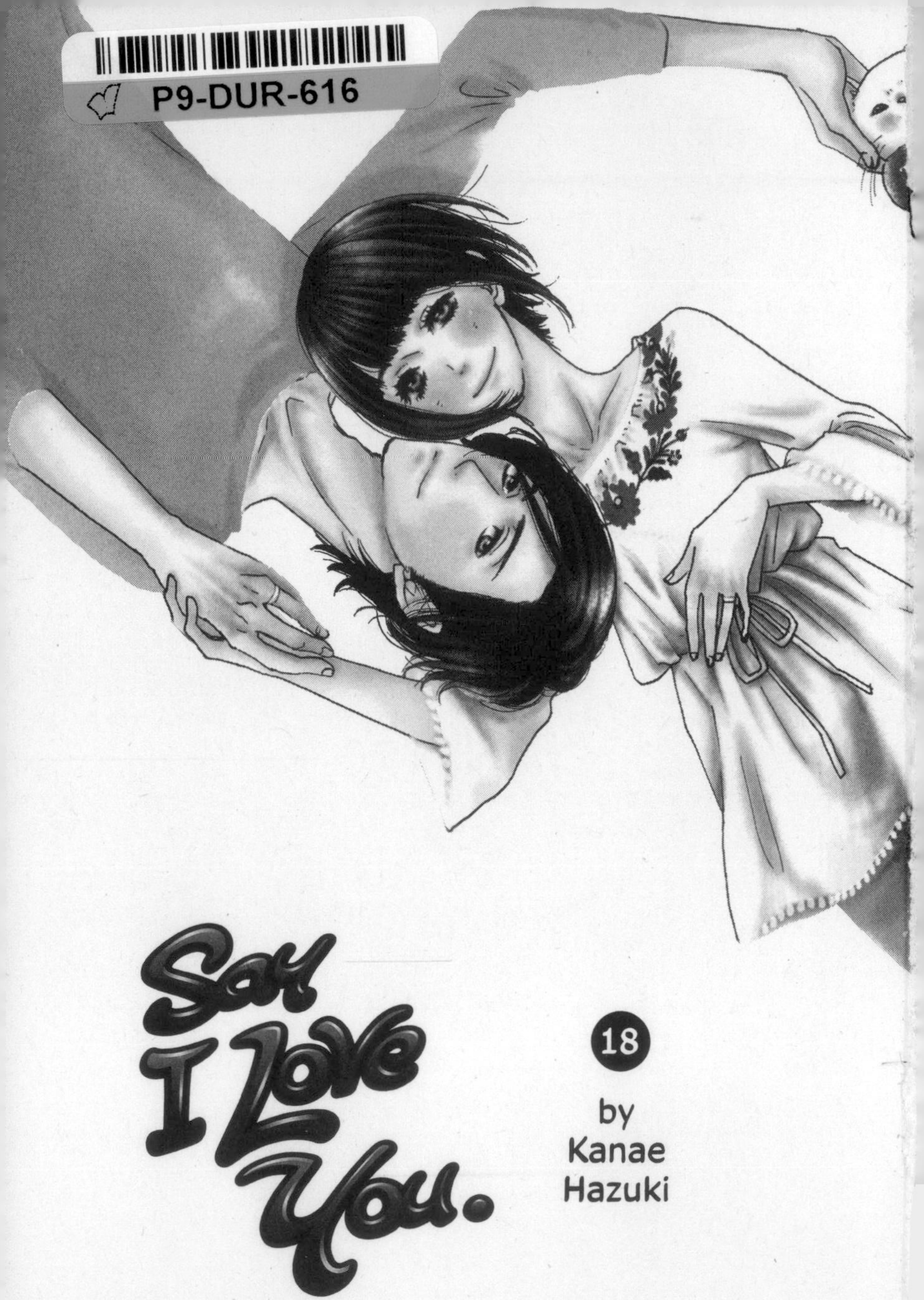

Say I Love You.

18

by
Kanae
Hazuki

Kanae Hazuki
presents

Say I Love You.

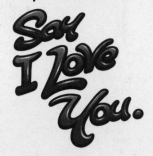

CHARACTER

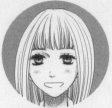

Mei Tachibana

A girl who hadn't had a single friend, let alone boyfriend, for sixteen years, but then started dating Yamato and was able to grow as a woman! Currently, she is working her dream job as a preschool teacher.

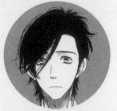

Yamato Kurosawa

The most popular boy at school. He was taken in by the charms of the brooding weirdo Mei, and they are now dating. After graduating college, he is struggling to make a career for himself as a photographer.

Asami Oikawa

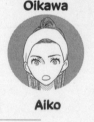

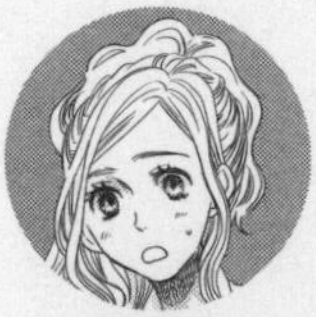

An amiable girl, and Mei's first friend. Encouraged by Mei, she started dating Yamato's friend Nakanishi. She has found a job as a preschool teacher.

Megumi Kitagawa

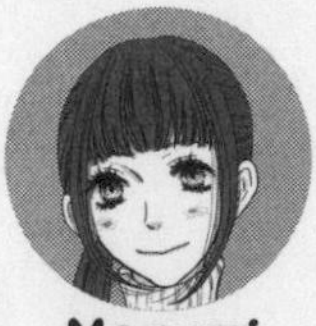

A popular amateur model who was once extremely aggressive in her pursuit of Yamato. After he dumped her, she got serious about her career. Since graduating high school, she has been working her own way through the modeling world of Paris.

Aiko

Mei's first rival in love. She had been living with her ever-devoted boyfriend Masashi, and when they learned she was pregnant, they decided to get married.

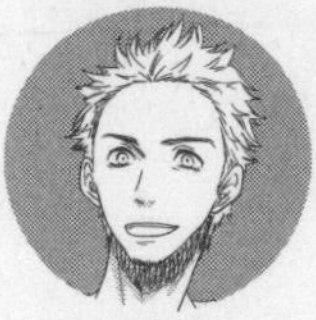

Kai Takemura

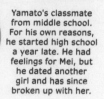

Yamato's classmate from middle school. For his own reasons, he started high school a year late. He had feelings for Mei, but he dated another girl and has since broken up with her.

STORY

Mei has been concerned that Yamato might be cheating on her, but when she opens up to him about her fears, the bond between them grows even stronger. Soon Mei begins work as a preschool teacher, and Yamato takes a job at a photo studio in the hopes of one day being able to work for himself. As all of her friends join the work force, Aiko gets pregnant and marries Masashi. Meanwhile, Megumi has been struggling to make it as a model in Paris, and now that she's broken up with her French boyfriend, she's having an even harder time getting work...?!

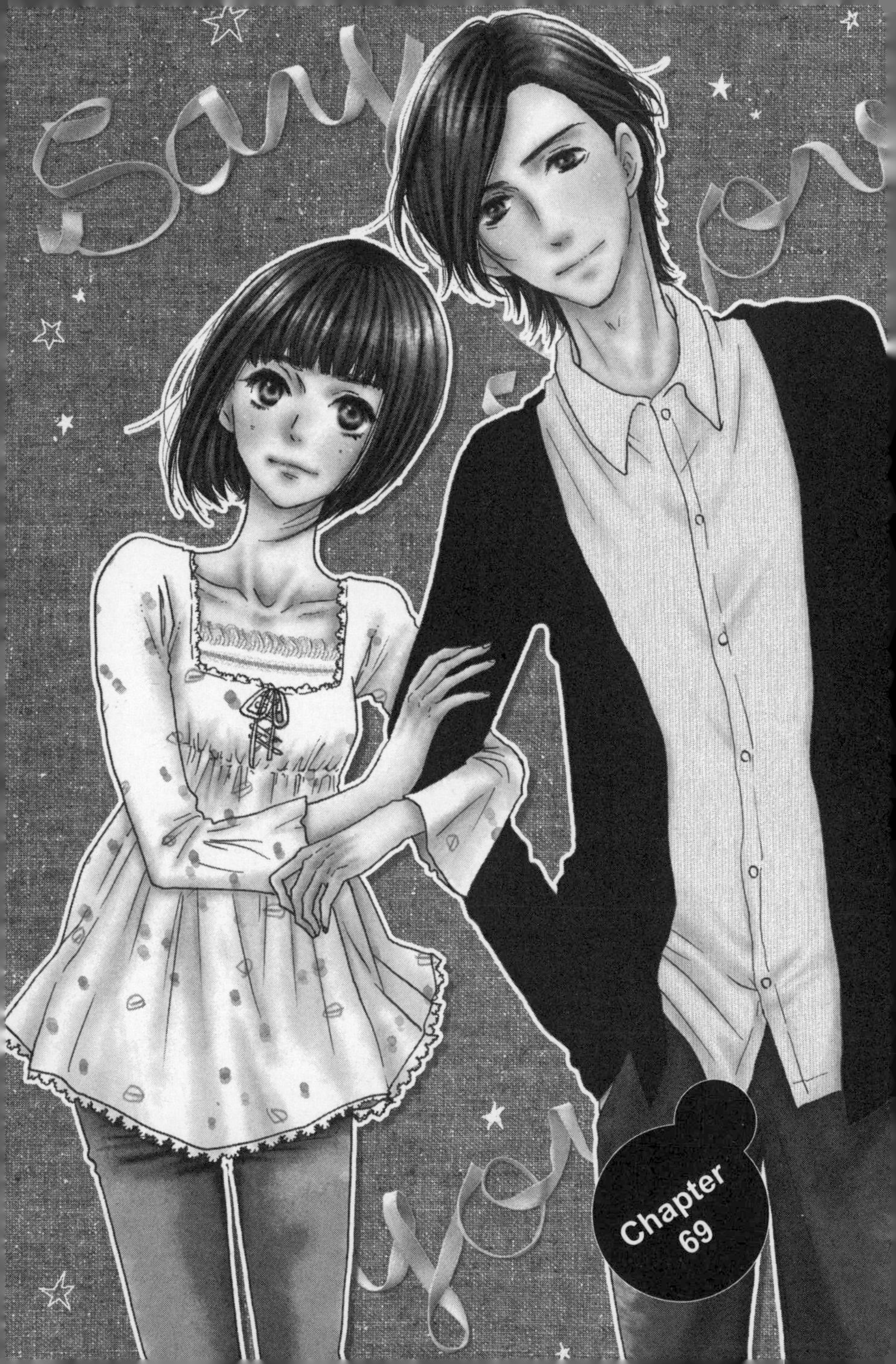
Chapter 69

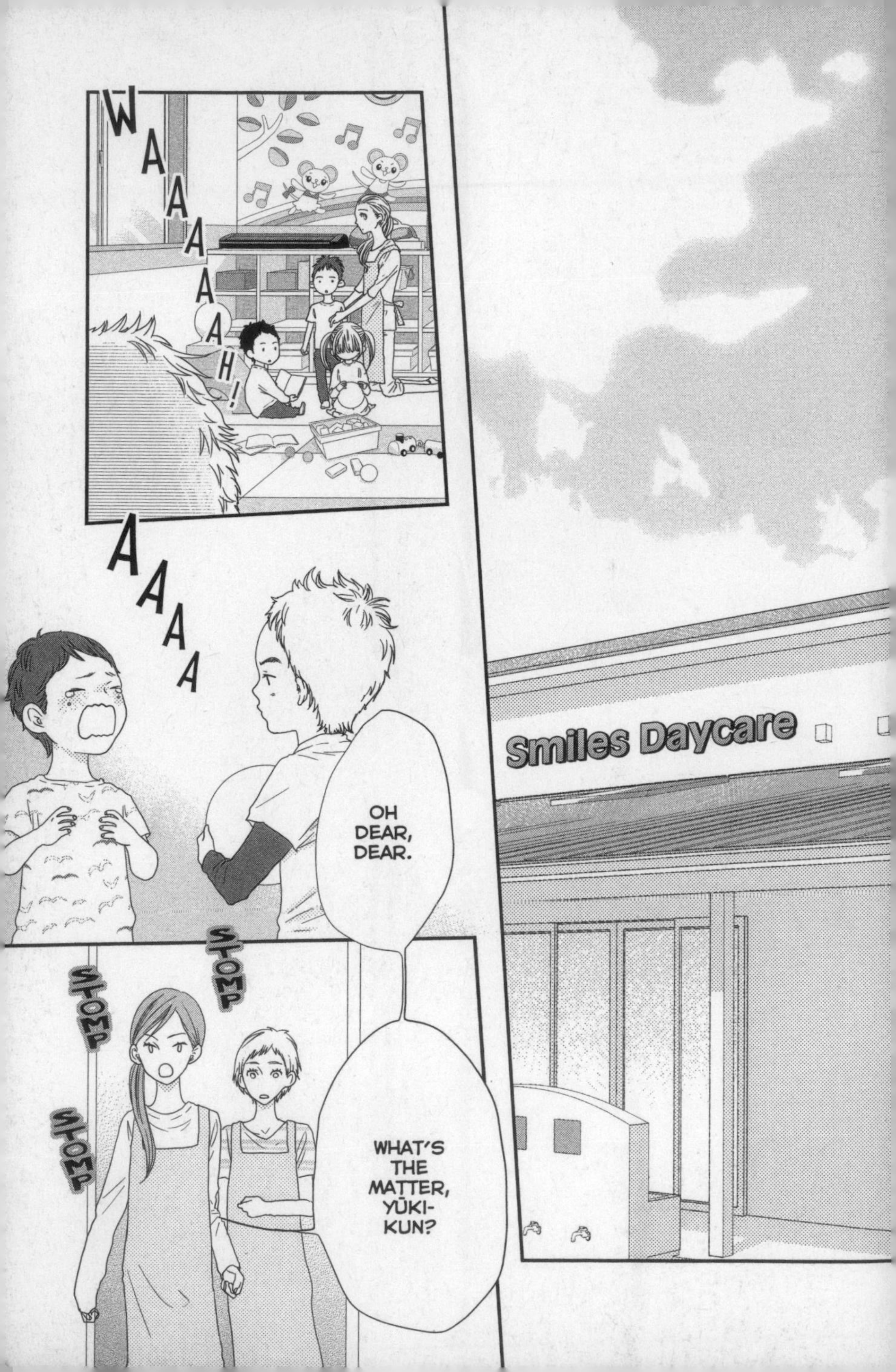
Smiles Daycare
WAAAAAH!
AAAA
OH DEAR, DEAR.
STOMP
STOMP
STOMP
WHAT'S THE MATTER, YŪKI-KUN?

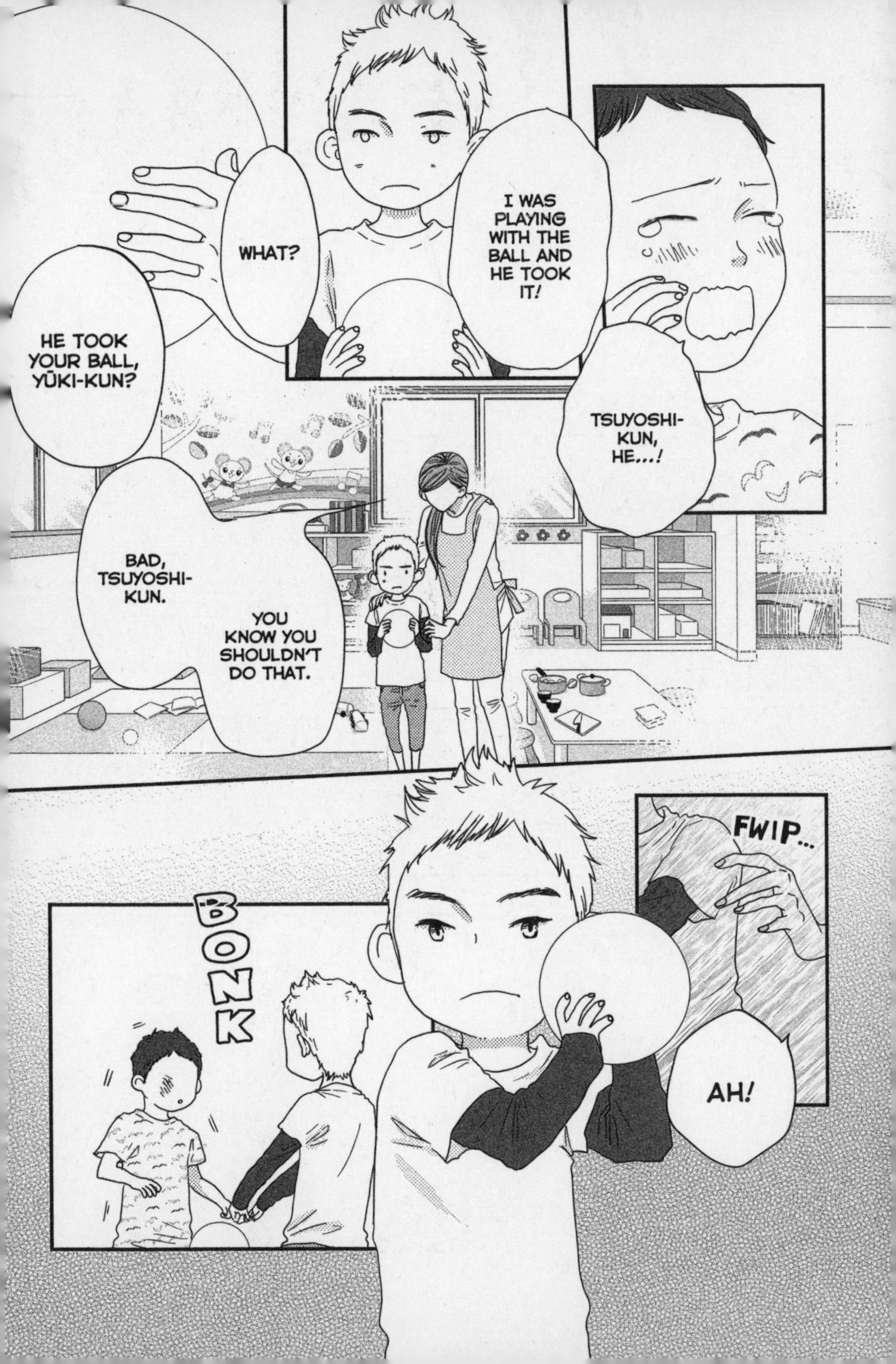
I WAS PLAYING WITH THE BALL AND HE TOOK IT!
TSUYOSHI-KUN, HE...!
WHAT?
HE TOOK YOUR BALL, YŪKI-KUN?
BAD, TSUYOSHI-KUN.
YOU KNOW YOU SHOULDN'T DO THAT.
FWIP...
AH!
BONK

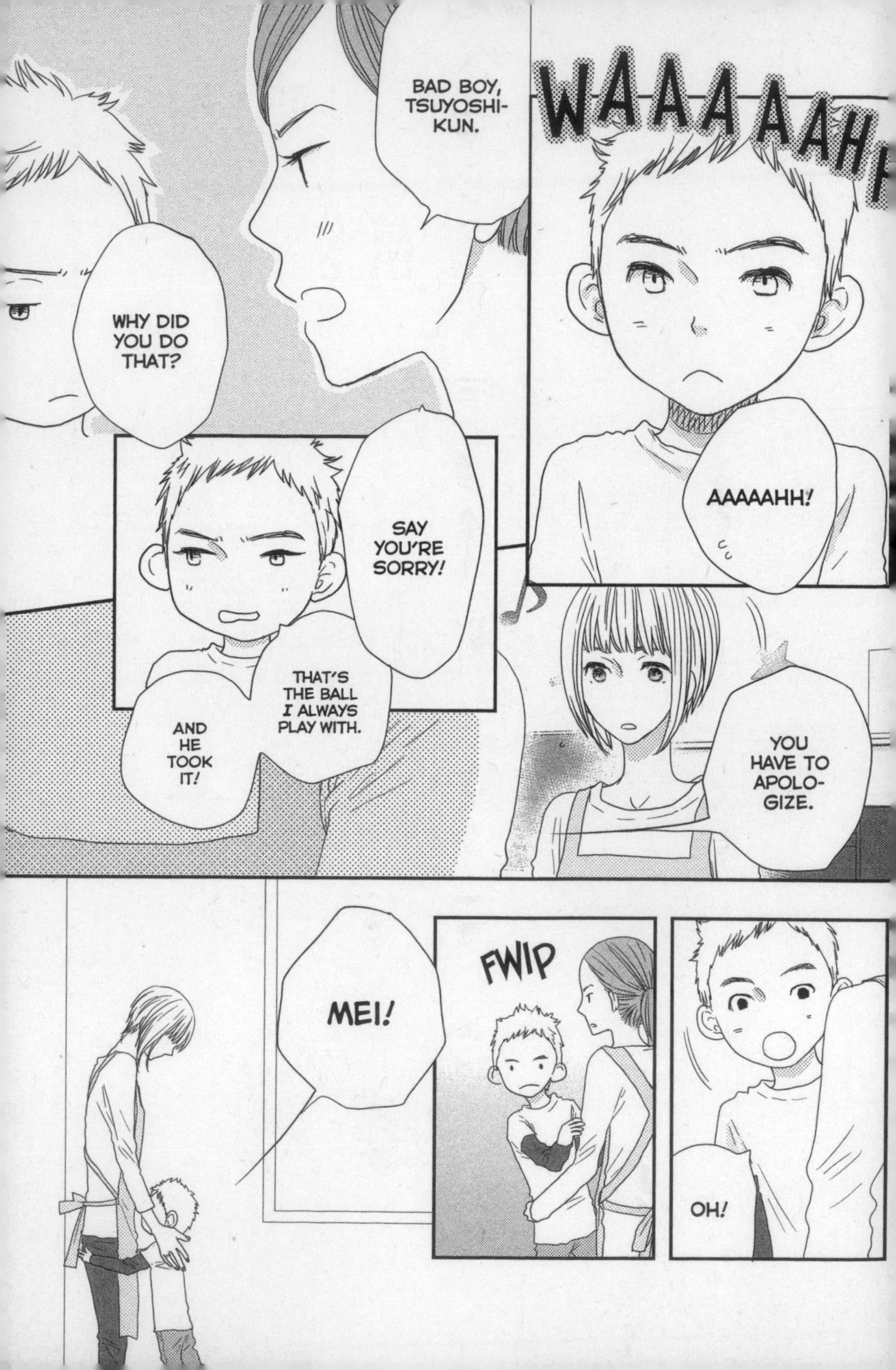
WAAAAAAHH
AAAAAHH!
YOU HAVE TO APOLOGIZE.
BAD BOY, TSUYOSHI-KUN.
WHY DID YOU DO THAT?
SAY YOU'RE SORRY!
THAT'S THE BALL *I* ALWAYS PLAY WITH.
AND HE TOOK IT!
OH!
FWIP
MEI!

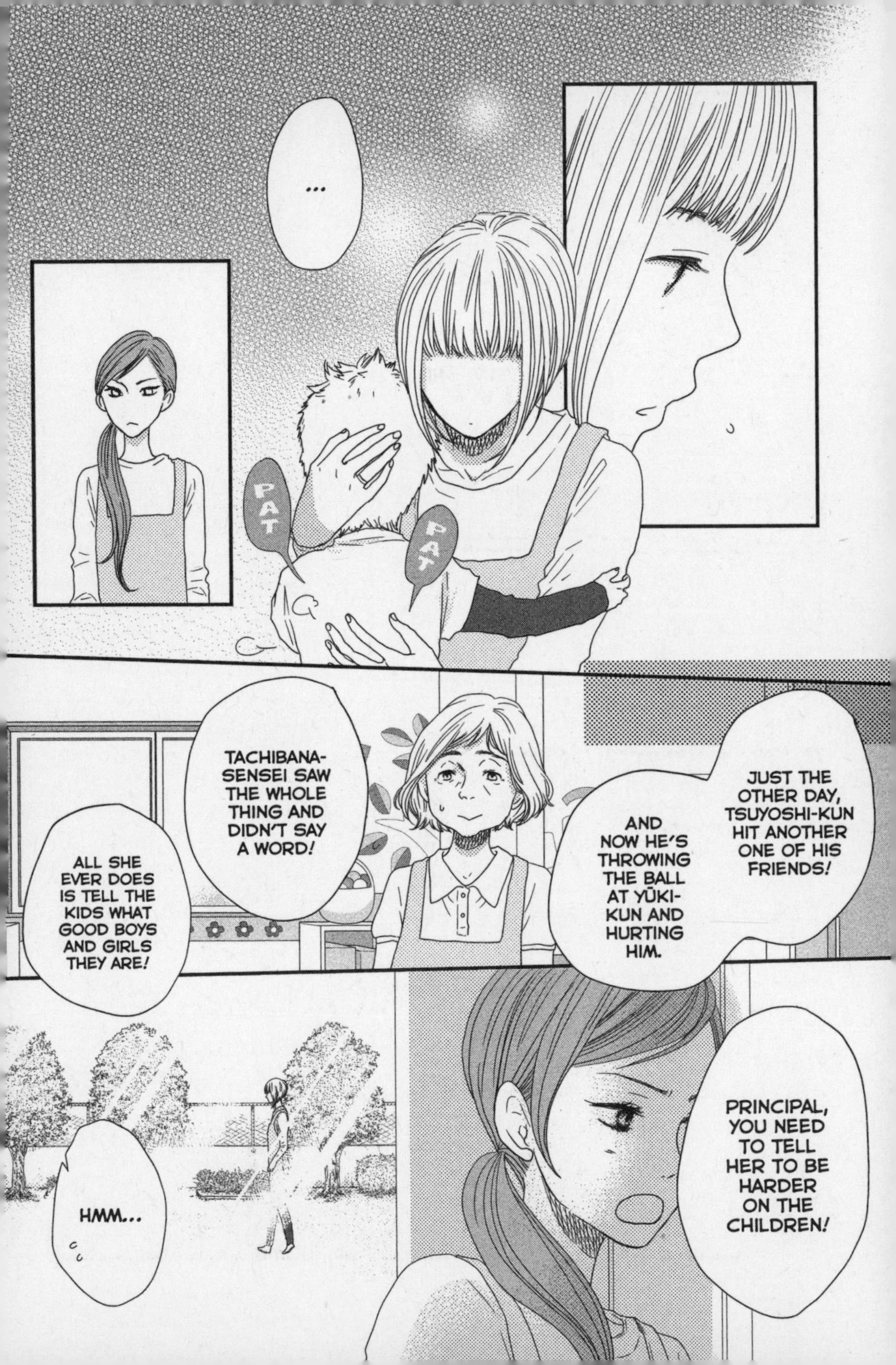
...
PAT
PAT
JUST THE OTHER DAY, TSUYOSHI-KUN HIT ANOTHER ONE OF HIS FRIENDS!
AND NOW HE'S THROWING THE BALL AT YŪKI-KUN AND HURTING HIM.
TACHIBANA-SENSEI SAW THE WHOLE THING AND DIDN'T SAY A WORD!
ALL SHE EVER DOES IS TELL THE KIDS WHAT GOOD BOYS AND GIRLS THEY ARE!
PRINCIPAL, YOU NEED TO TELL HER TO BE HARDER ON THE CHILDREN!
HMM...

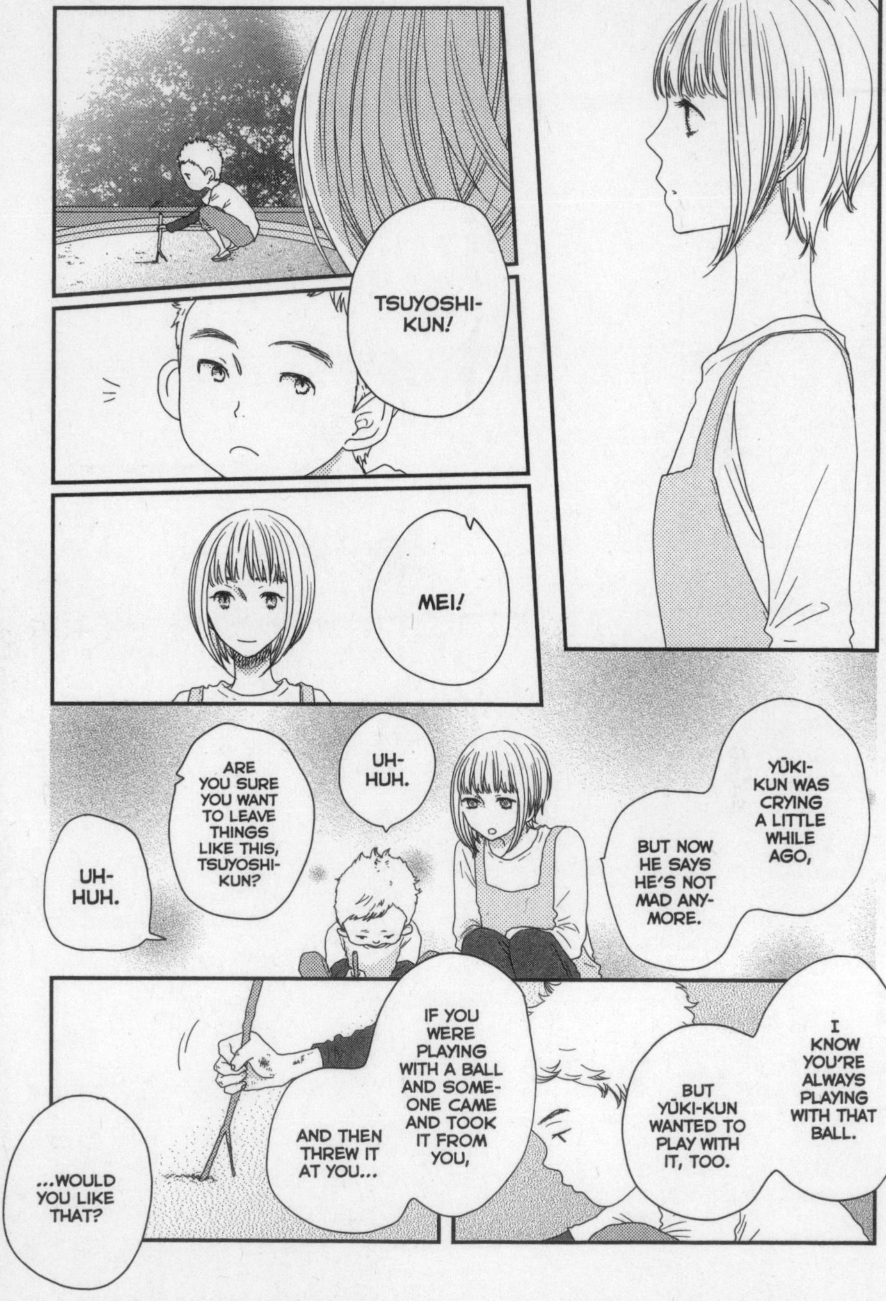
TSUYOSHI-KUN!
MEI!
YŪKI-KUN WAS CRYING A LITTLE WHILE AGO,
BUT NOW HE SAYS HE'S NOT MAD ANYMORE.
UH-HUH.
ARE YOU SURE YOU WANT TO LEAVE THINGS LIKE THIS, TSUYOSHI-KUN?
UH-HUH.
I KNOW YOU'RE ALWAYS PLAYING WITH THAT BALL.
BUT YŪKI-KUN WANTED TO PLAY WITH IT, TOO.
IF YOU WERE PLAYING WITH A BALL AND SOMEONE CAME AND TOOK IT FROM YOU,
AND THEN THREW IT AT YOU...
...WOULD YOU LIKE THAT?

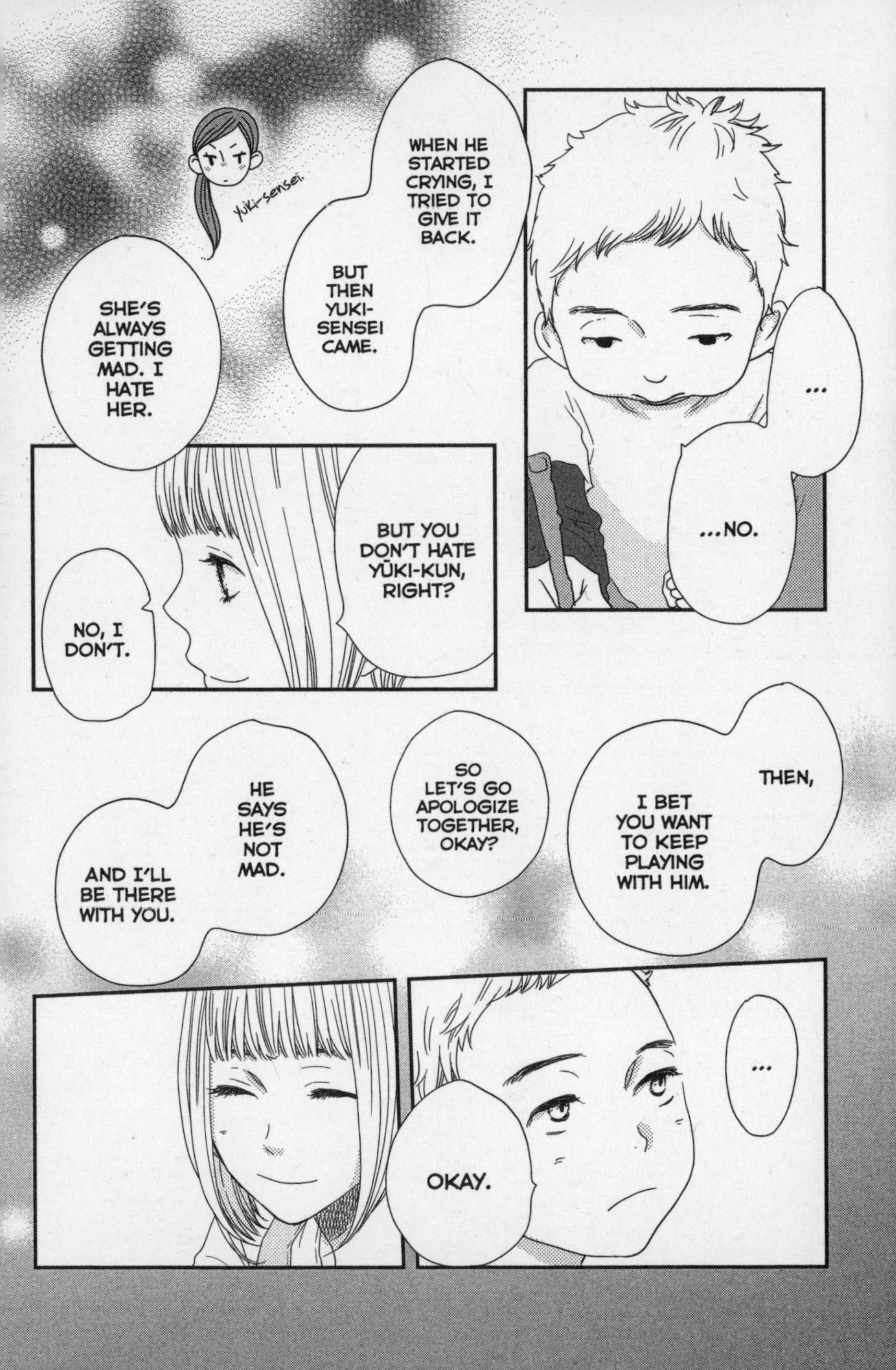
WHEN HE STARTED CRYING, I TRIED TO GIVE IT BACK.
BUT THEN YUKI-SENSEI CAME.
YUKI-SENSEI.
SHE'S ALWAYS GETTING MAD. I HATE HER.
...
...NO.
BUT YOU DON'T HATE YŪKI-KUN, RIGHT?
NO, I DON'T.
THEN,
I BET YOU WANT TO KEEP PLAYING WITH HIM.
SO LET'S GO APOLOGIZE TOGETHER, OKAY?
HE SAYS HE'S NOT MAD.
AND I'LL BE THERE WITH YOU.
...
OKAY.

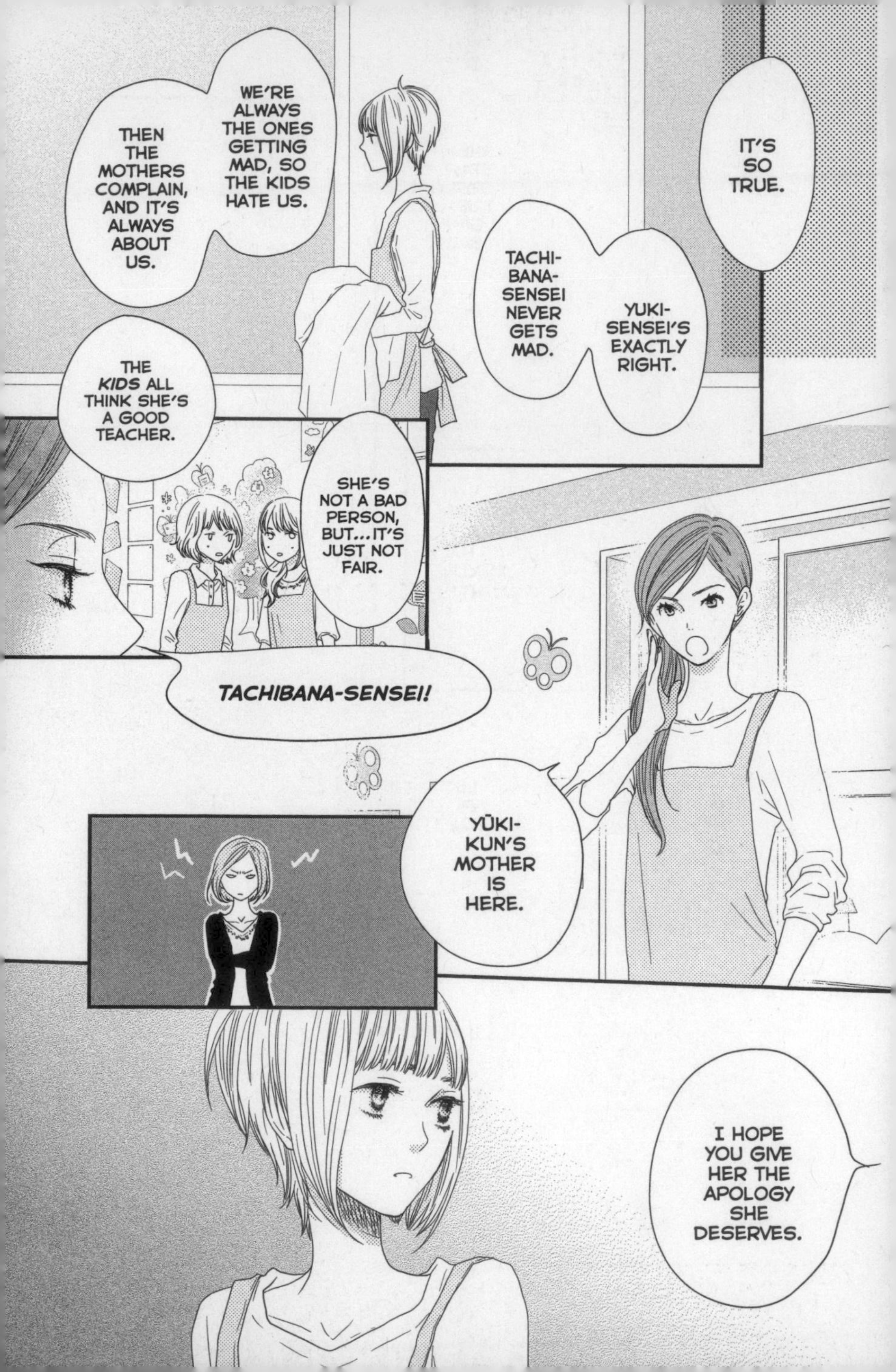
IT'S SO TRUE.
YUKI-SENSEI'S EXACTLY RIGHT.
TACHIBANA-SENSEI NEVER GETS MAD.
WE'RE ALWAYS THE ONES GETTING MAD, SO THE KIDS HATE US.
THEN THE MOTHERS COMPLAIN, AND IT'S ALWAYS ABOUT US.
THE *KIDS* ALL THINK SHE'S A GOOD TEACHER.
SHE'S NOT A BAD PERSON, BUT...IT'S JUST NOT FAIR.
TACHIBANA-SENSEI!
YŪKI-KUN'S MOTHER IS HERE.
I HOPE YOU GIVE HER THE APOLOGY SHE DESERVES.

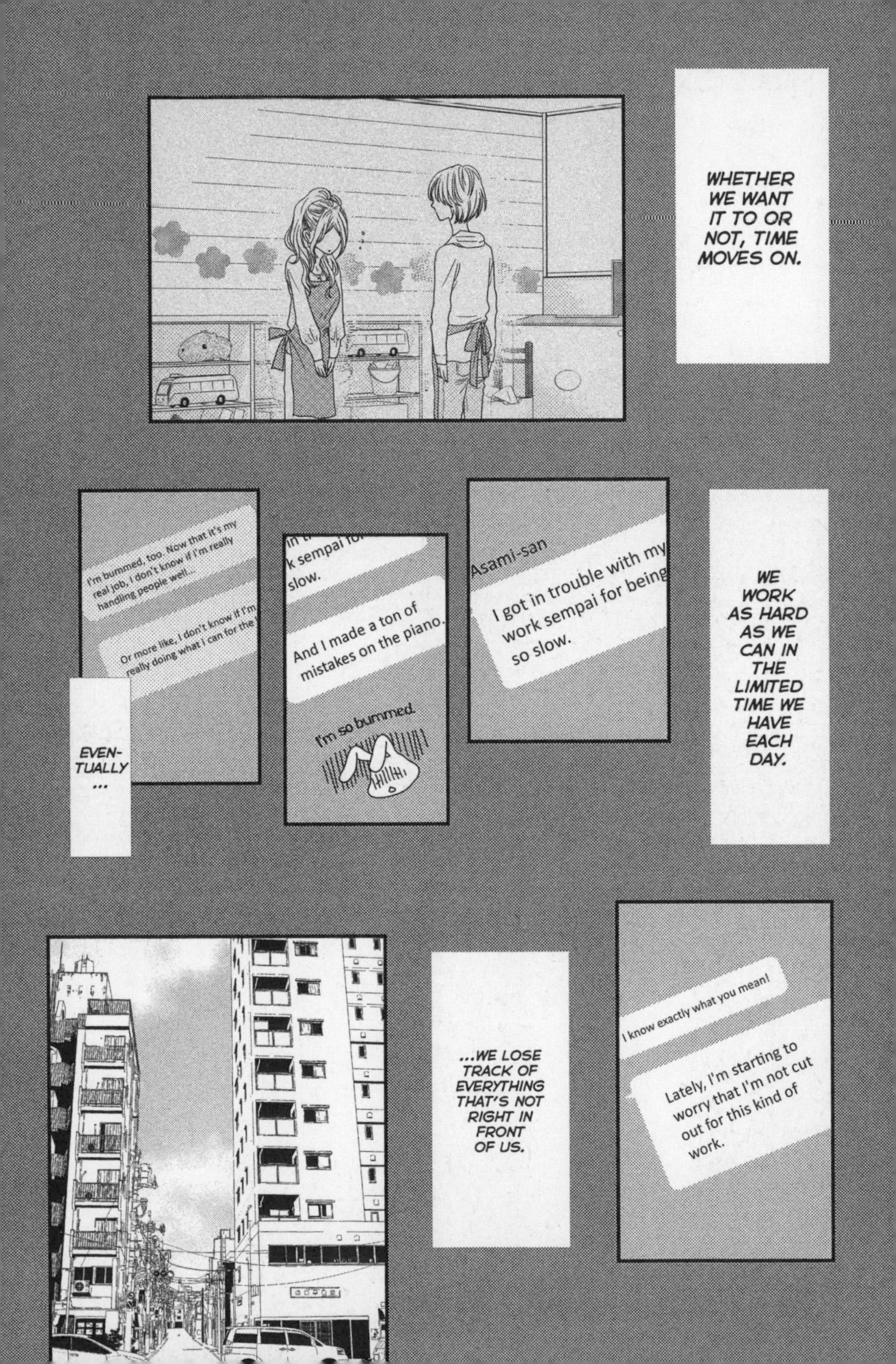
WHETHER WE WANT IT TO OR NOT, TIME MOVES ON.
WE WORK AS HARD AS WE CAN IN THE LIMITED TIME WE HAVE EACH DAY.
Asami-san
I got in trouble with my work sempai for being so slow.
slow.
And I made a ton of mistakes on the piano.
I'm so bummed.
I'm bummed, too. Now that it's my real job, I don't know if I'm really handling people well...
Or more like, I don't know if I'm really doing what I can for the
EVEN-TUALLY...
I know exactly what you mean!
Lately, I'm starting to worry that I'm not cut out for this kind of work.
...WE LOSE TRACK OF EVERYTHING THAT'S NOT RIGHT IN FRONT OF US.

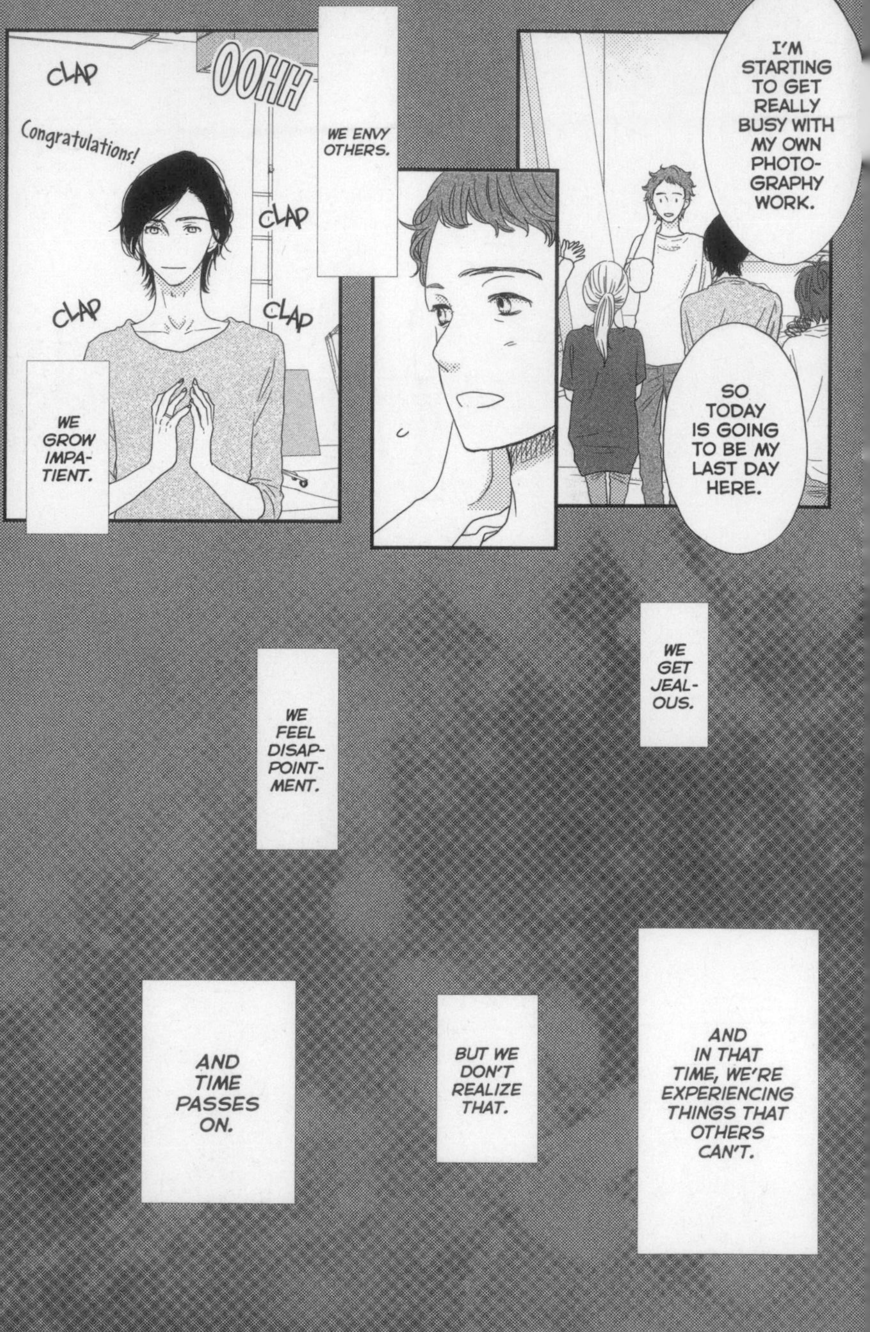
I'M STARTING TO GET REALLY BUSY WITH MY OWN PHOTOGRAPHY WORK.
SO TODAY IS GOING TO BE MY LAST DAY HERE.
WE ENVY OTHERS.
OOHH
CLAP
Congratulations!
CLAP
CLAP
CLAP
WE GROW IMPATIENT.
WE GET JEALOUS.
WE FEEL DISAPPOINTMENT.
AND TIME PASSES ON.
BUT WE DON'T REALIZE THAT.
AND IN THAT TIME, WE'RE EXPERIENCING THINGS THAT OTHERS CAN'T.

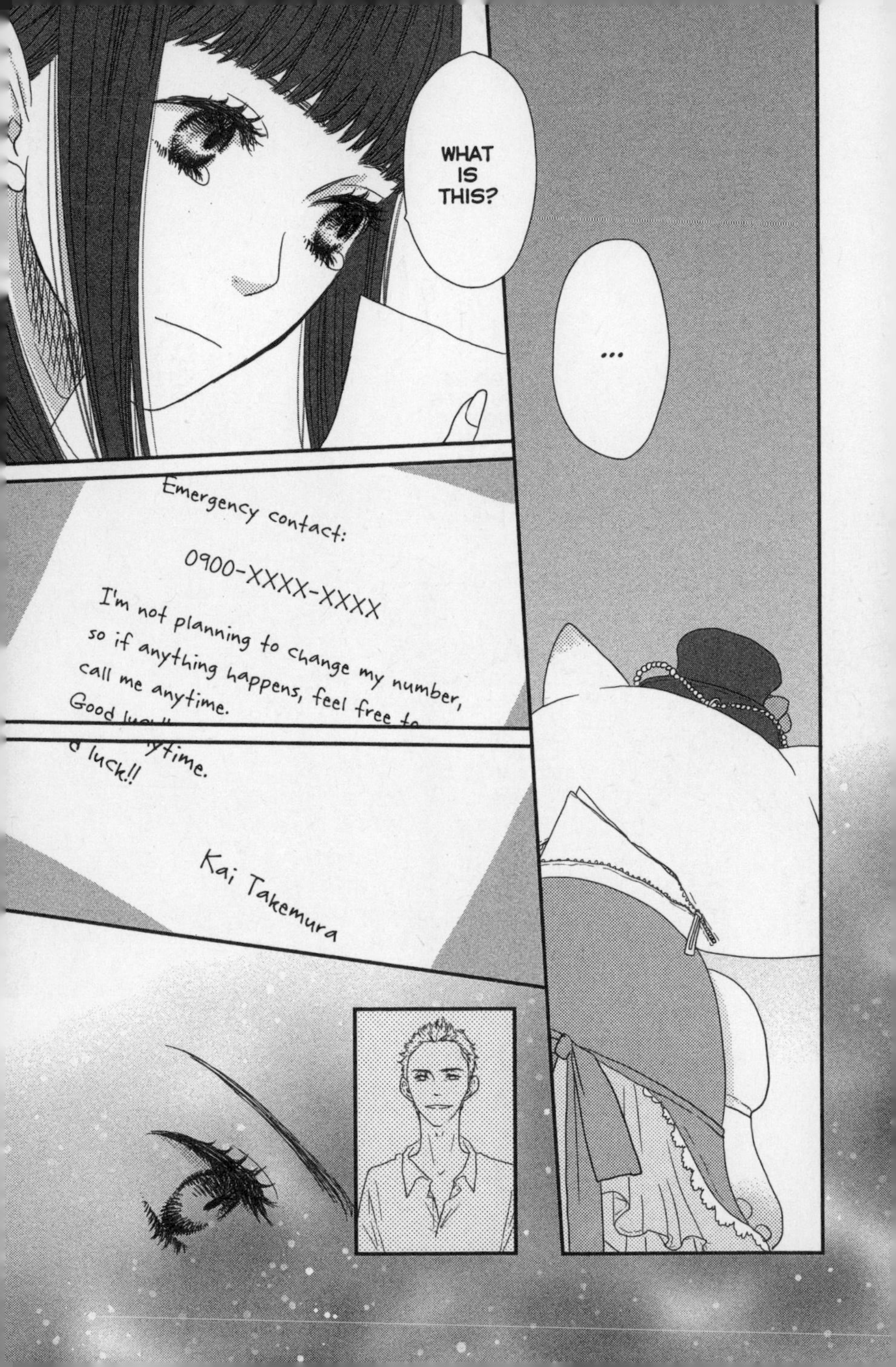
...
WHAT IS THIS?
Emergency contact:
0900-XXXX-XXXX
I'm not planning to change my number,
so if anything happens, feel free to
call me anytime.
ytime.
luck!!
Kai Takemura

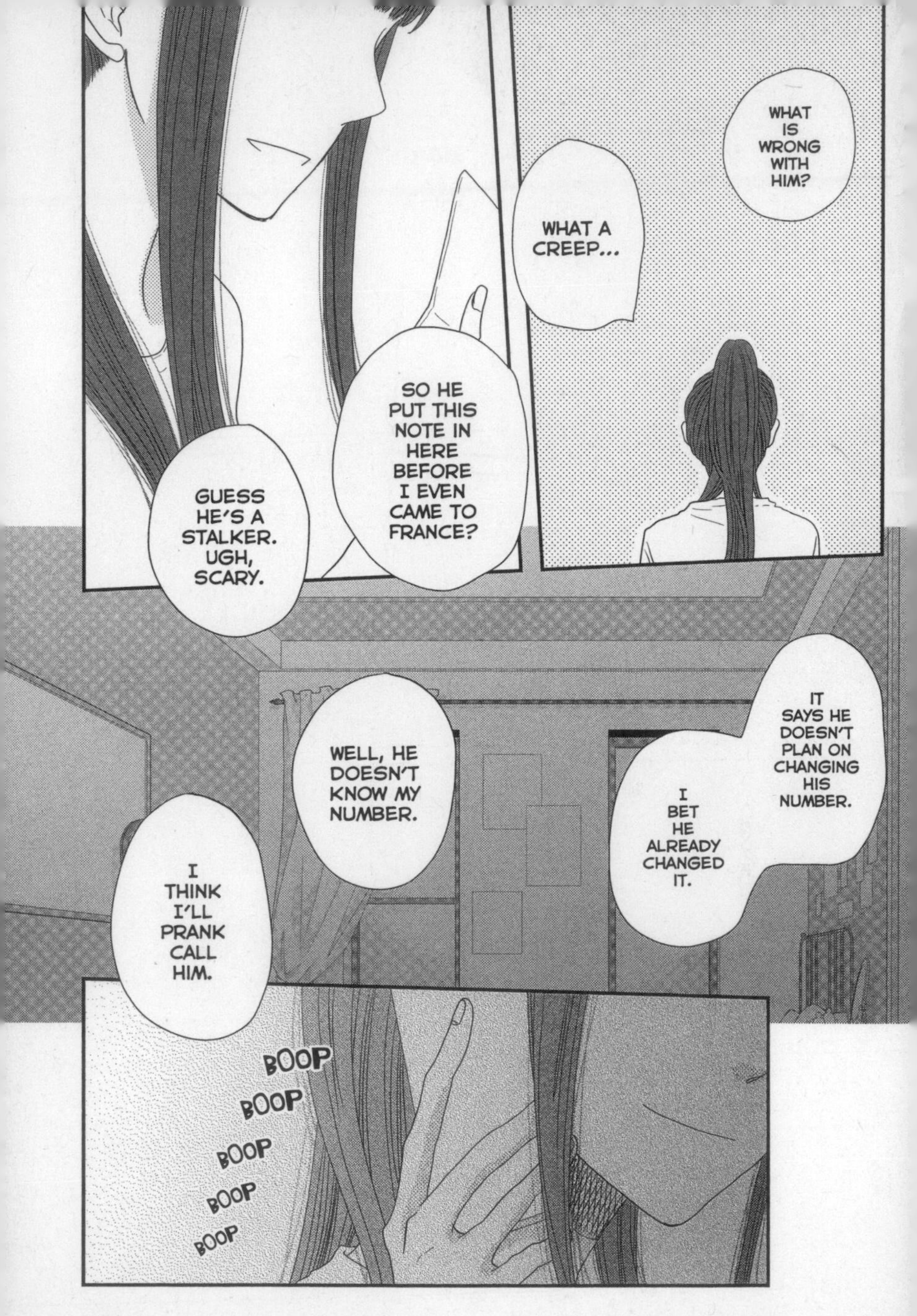
WHAT IS WRONG WITH HIM?
WHAT A CREEP...
SO HE PUT THIS NOTE IN HERE BEFORE I EVEN CAME TO FRANCE?
GUESS HE'S A STALKER. UGH, SCARY.
IT SAYS HE DOESN'T PLAN ON CHANGING HIS NUMBER.
I BET HE ALREADY CHANGED IT.
WELL, HE DOESN'T KNOW MY NUMBER.
I THINK I'LL PRANK CALL HIM.
BOOP
BOOP
BOOP
BOOP
BOOP

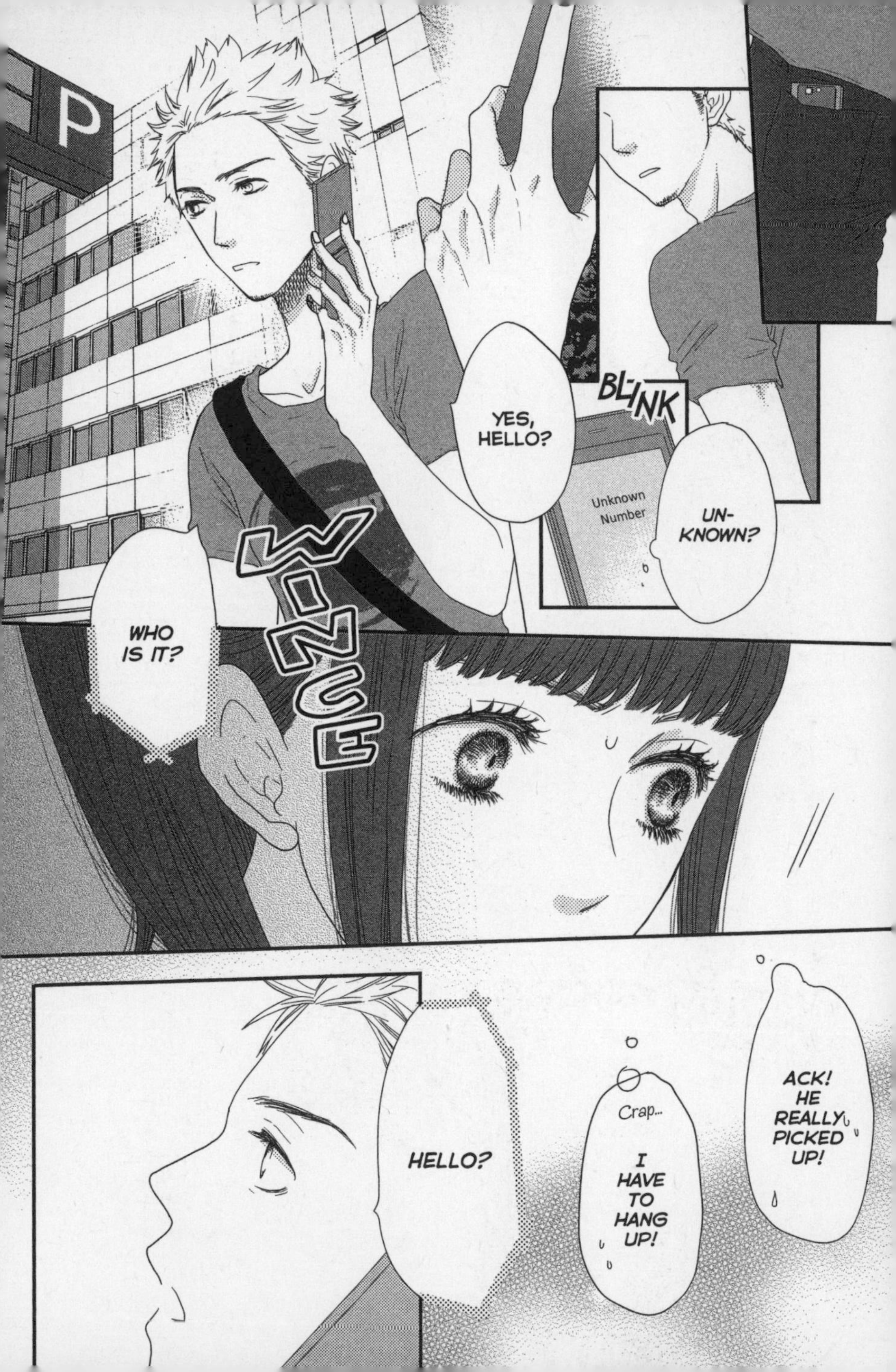
BLINK
Unknown Number
UN-KNOWN?
YES, HELLO?
WHO IS IT?
WINCE
ACK! HE REALLY PICKED UP!
Crap...
I HAVE TO HANG UP!
HELLO?

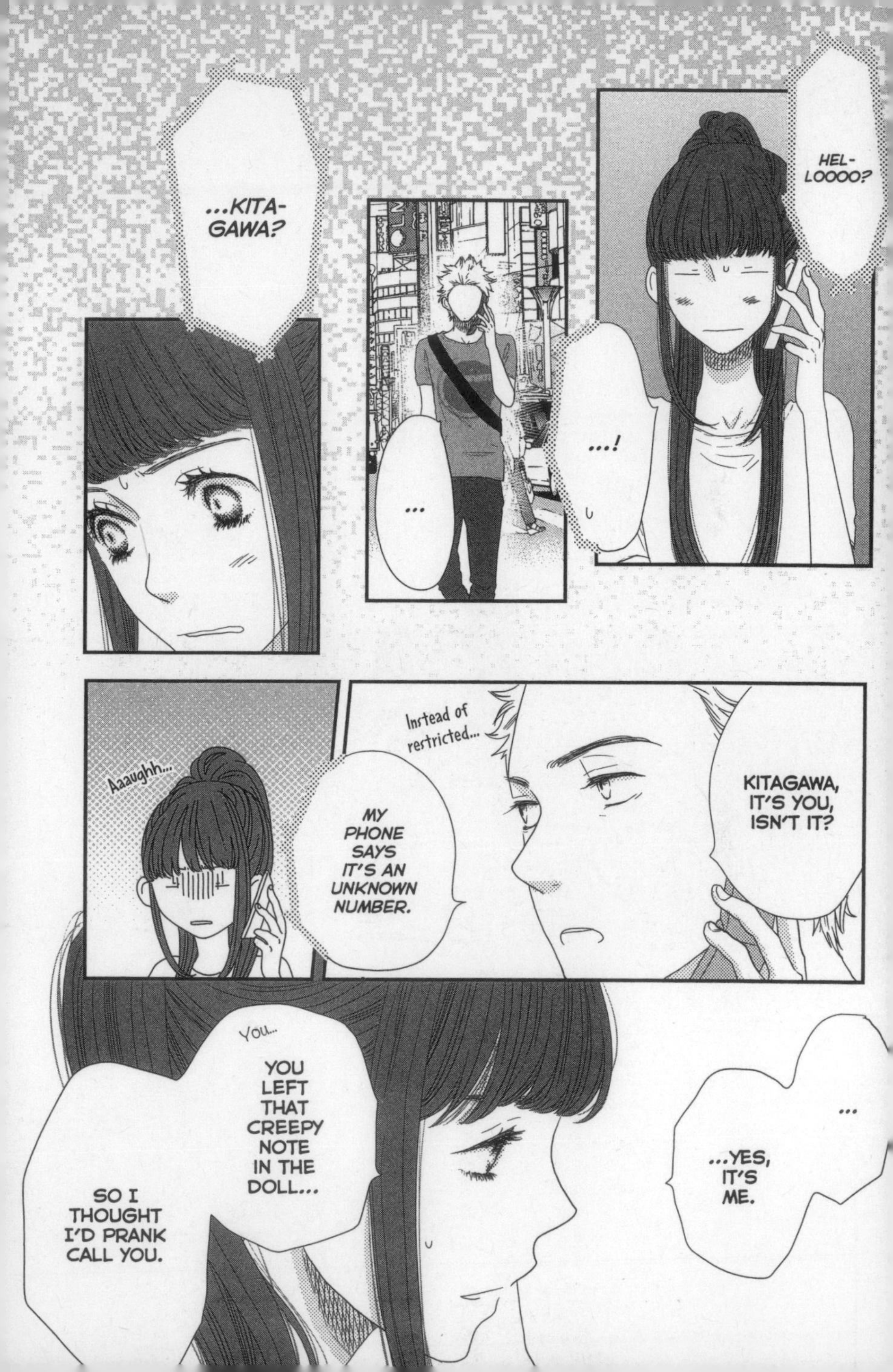
HEL-LOOOO?
...!
...
...KITA-GAWA?
KITAGAWA, IT'S YOU, ISN'T IT?
Instead of restricted...
MY PHONE SAYS IT'S AN UNKNOWN NUMBER.
Aaaughh...
...
...YES, IT'S ME.
YOU...
YOU LEFT THAT CREEPY NOTE IN THE DOLL...
SO I THOUGHT I'D PRANK CALL YOU.

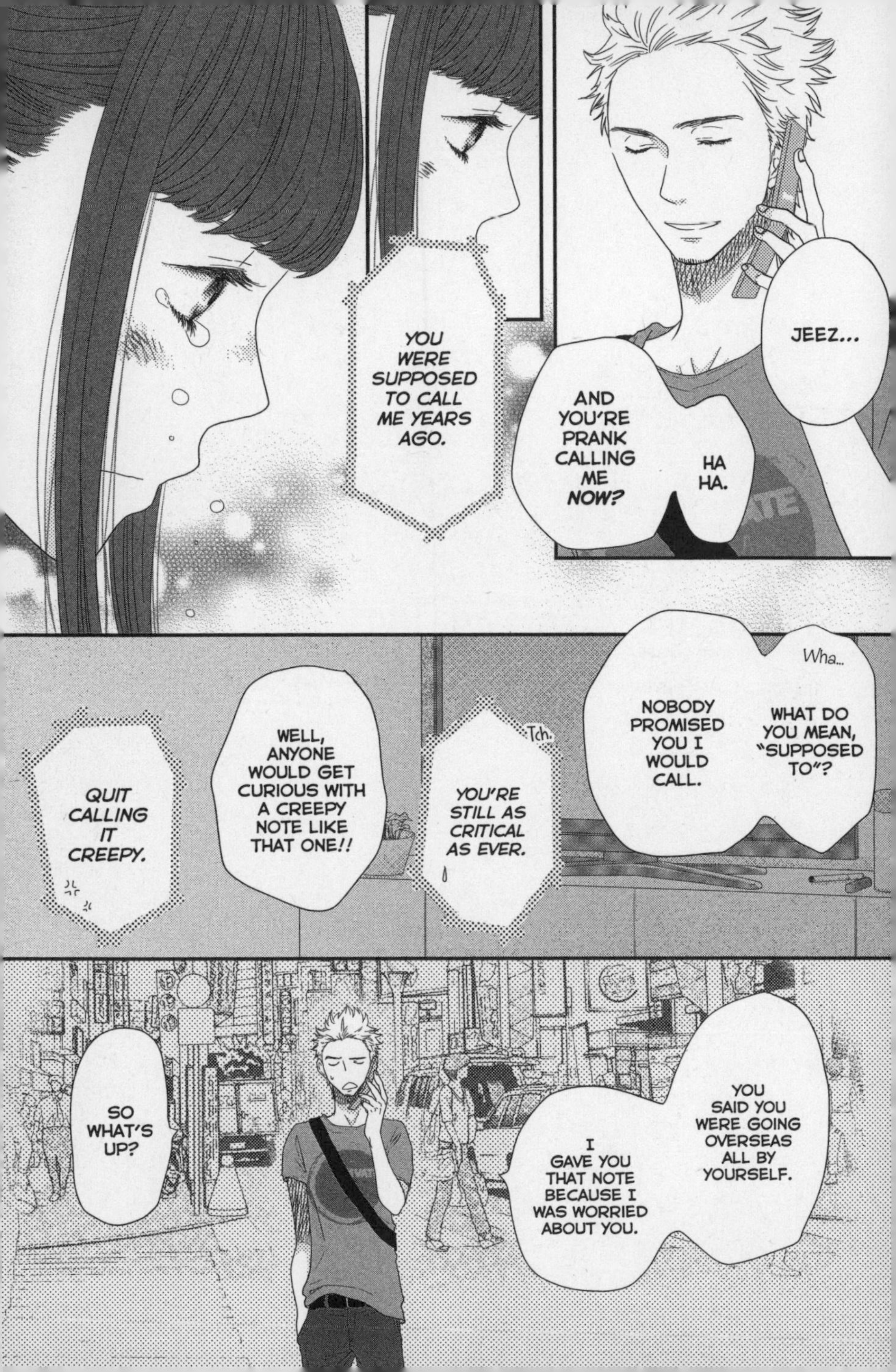
JEEZ...
AND YOU'RE PRANK CALLING ME NOW?
HA HA.
YOU WERE SUPPOSED TO CALL ME YEARS AGO.
Wha...
WHAT DO YOU MEAN, "SUPPOSED TO"?
NOBODY PROMISED YOU I WOULD CALL.
Tch.
YOU'RE STILL AS CRITICAL AS EVER.
WELL, ANYONE WOULD GET CURIOUS WITH A CREEPY NOTE LIKE THAT ONE!!
QUIT CALLING IT CREEPY.
YOU SAID YOU WERE GOING OVERSEAS ALL BY YOURSELF.
I GAVE YOU THAT NOTE BECAUSE I WAS WORRIED ABOUT YOU.
SO WHAT'S UP?

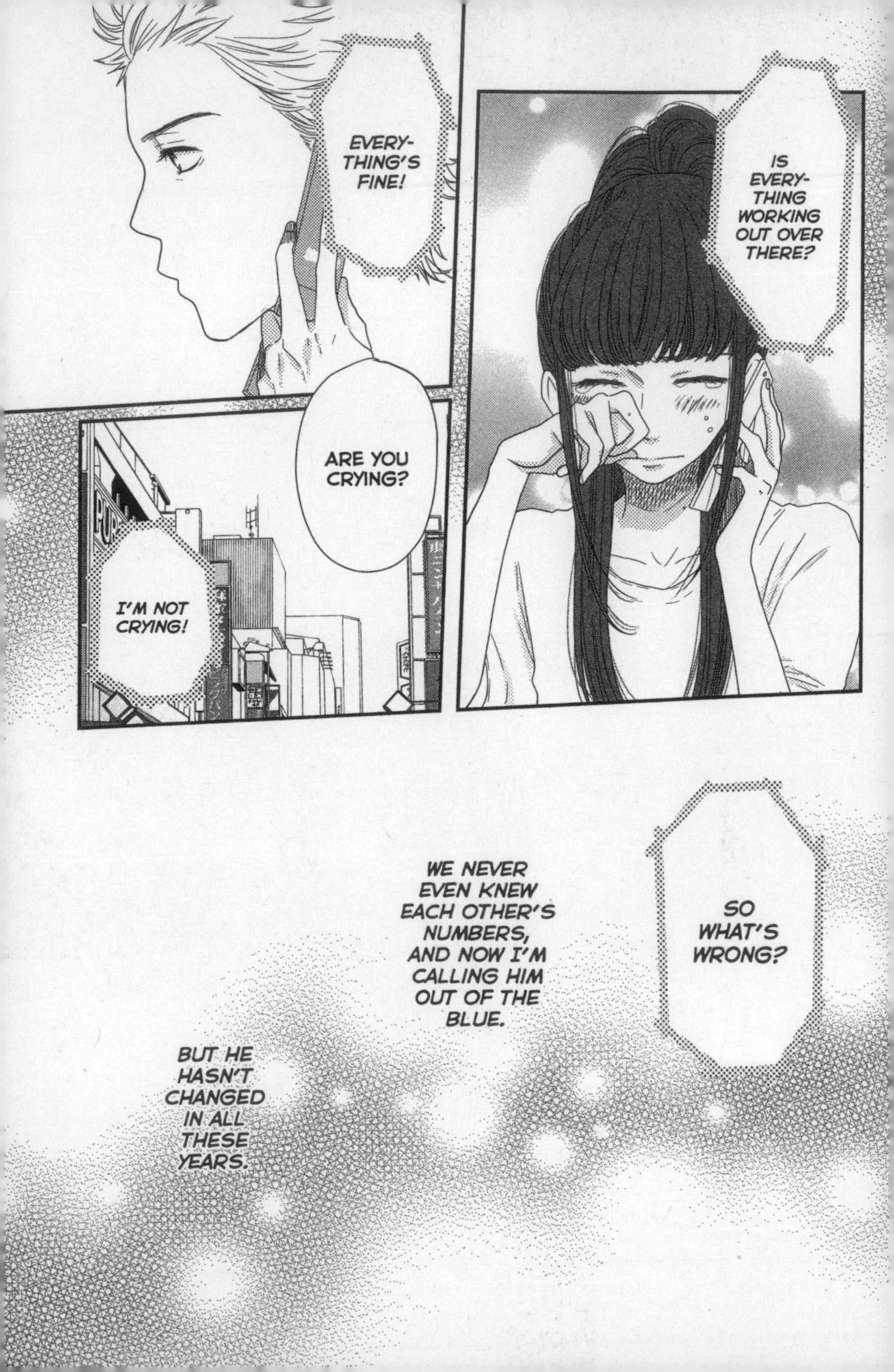
IS EVERYTHING WORKING OUT OVER THERE?
EVERYTHING'S FINE!
ARE YOU CRYING?
I'M NOT CRYING!
SO WHAT'S WRONG?
WE NEVER EVEN KNEW EACH OTHER'S NUMBERS, AND NOW I'M CALLING HIM OUT OF THE BLUE.
BUT HE HASN'T CHANGED IN ALL THESE YEARS.

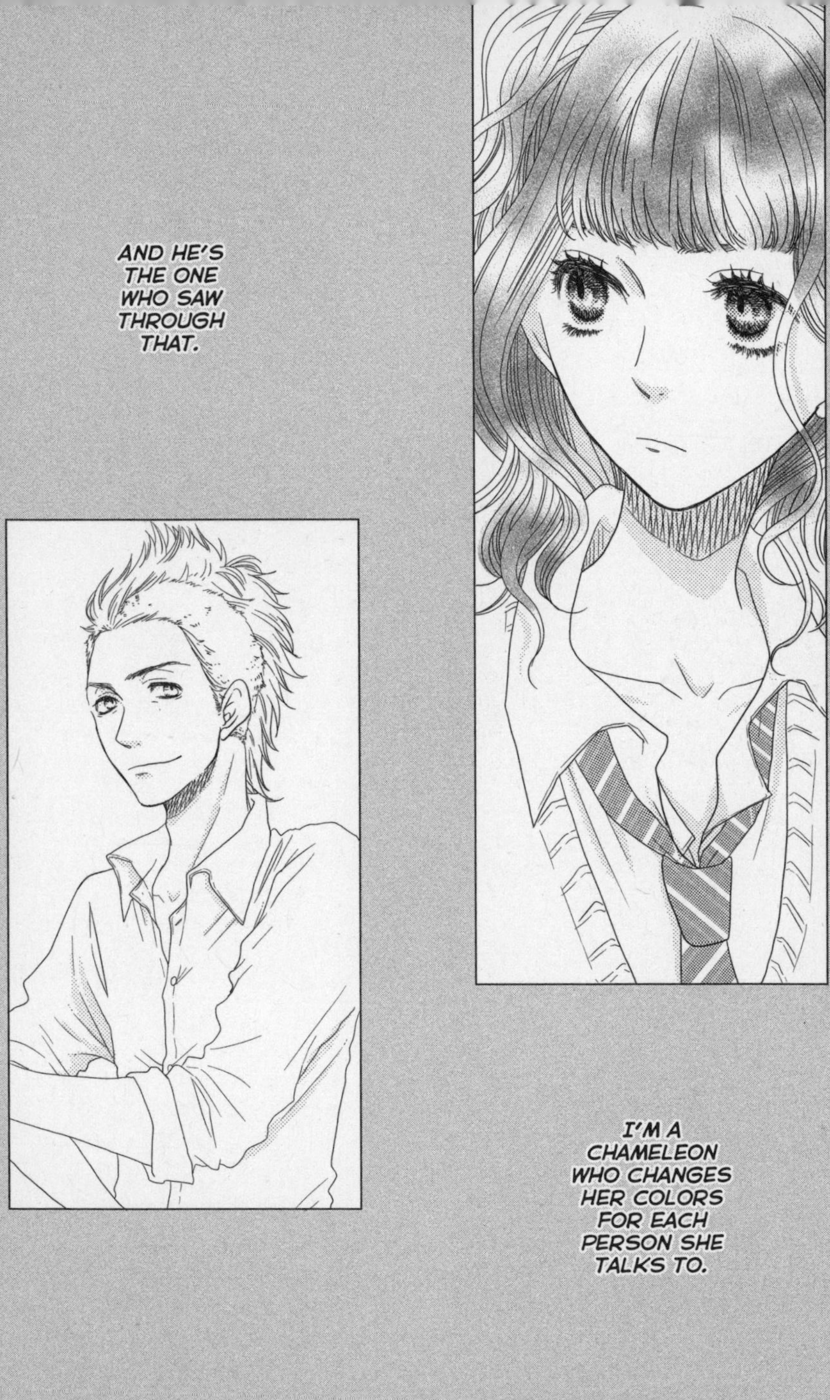
I'M A CHAMELEON WHO CHANGES HER COLORS FOR EACH PERSON SHE TALKS TO.
AND HE'S THE ONE WHO SAW THROUGH THAT.

HE'S THE ONLY ONE I CAN BE MYSELF WITH.

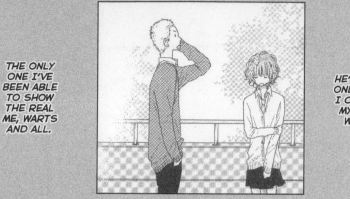

THE ONLY ONE I'VE BEEN ABLE TO SHOW THE REAL ME, WARTS AND ALL.

I'M A SLOB.

I LIE.

I DISCRIMINATE.

I DON'T SUGAR-COAT THINGS.

JUST THE OPPOSITE—I'M CONSTANTLY SAYING WHATEVER'S MOST HURTFUL.

I HAVE VERY FEW FRIENDS.

BUT THAT'S EXACTLY WHY I WAS ABLE TO ACCEPT THE LAST THING HE TOLD ME...

"BUT WORK HARD IN FRANCE, TOO, OKAY!"

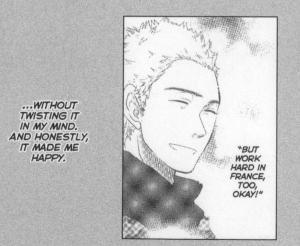

...WITHOUT TWISTING IT IN MY MIND. AND HONESTLY, IT MADE ME HAPPY.

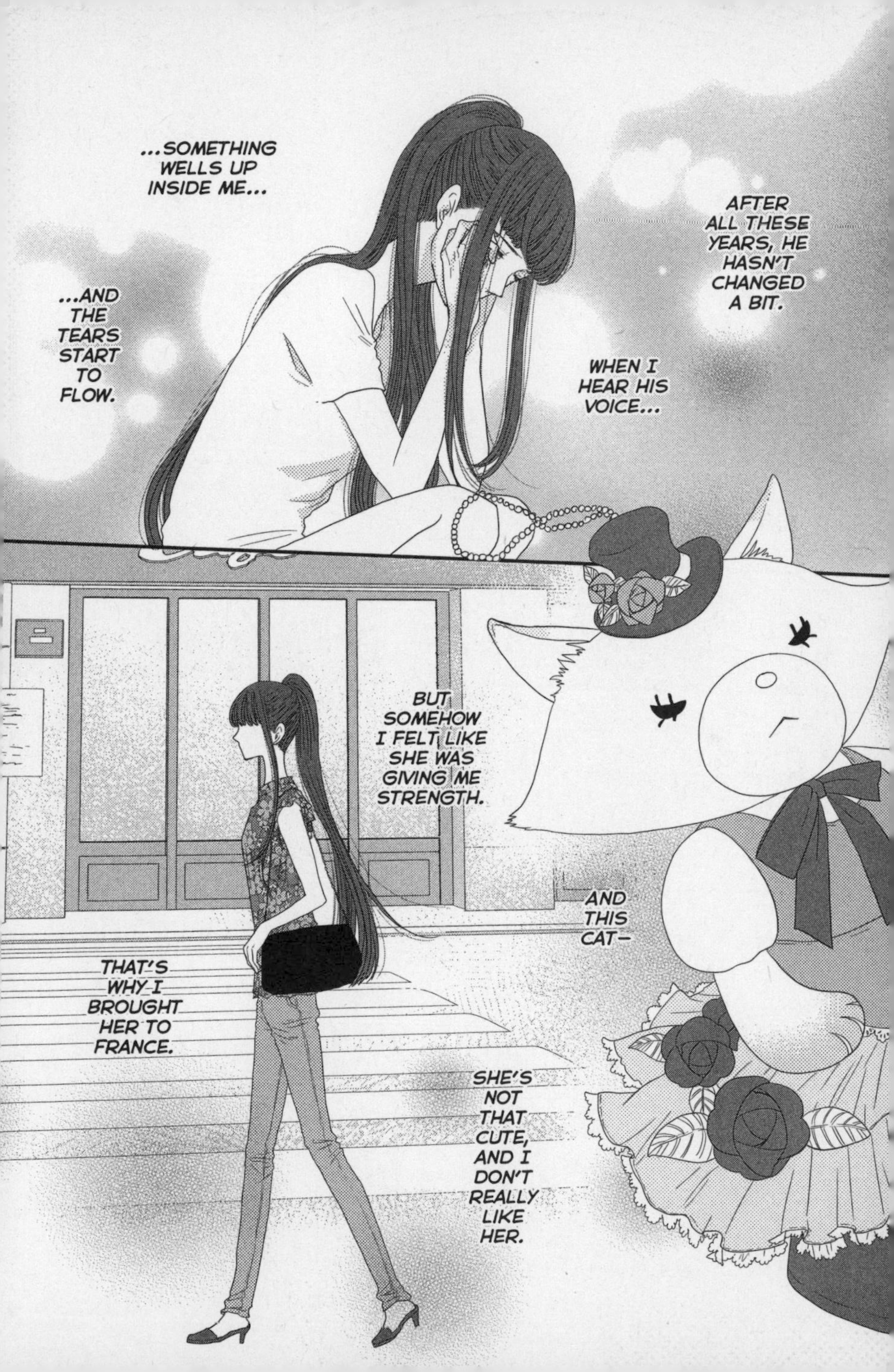
AFTER ALL THESE YEARS, HE HASN'T CHANGED A BIT.
WHEN I HEAR HIS VOICE...
...SOMETHING WELLS UP INSIDE ME...
...AND THE TEARS START TO FLOW.
AND THIS CAT—
SHE'S NOT THAT CUTE, AND I DON'T REALLY LIKE HER.
BUT SOMEHOW I FELT LIKE SHE WAS GIVING ME STRENGTH.
THAT'S WHY I BROUGHT HER TO FRANCE.

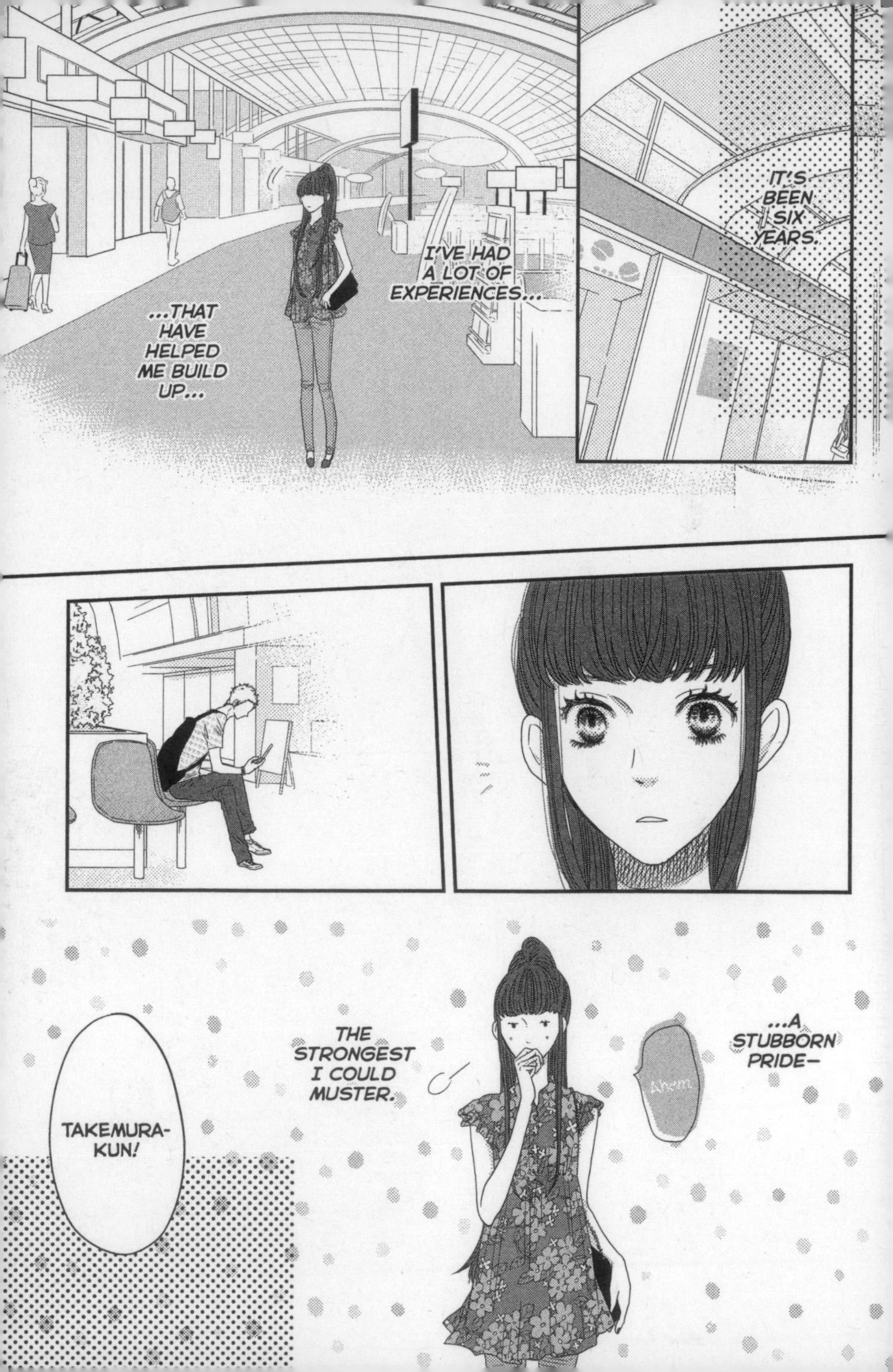
IT'S BEEN SIX YEARS.
I'VE HAD A LOT OF EXPERIENCES...
...THAT HAVE HELPED ME BUILD UP...
...A STUBBORN PRIDE—
Ahem.
THE STRONGEST I COULD MUSTER.
TAKEMURA-KUN!

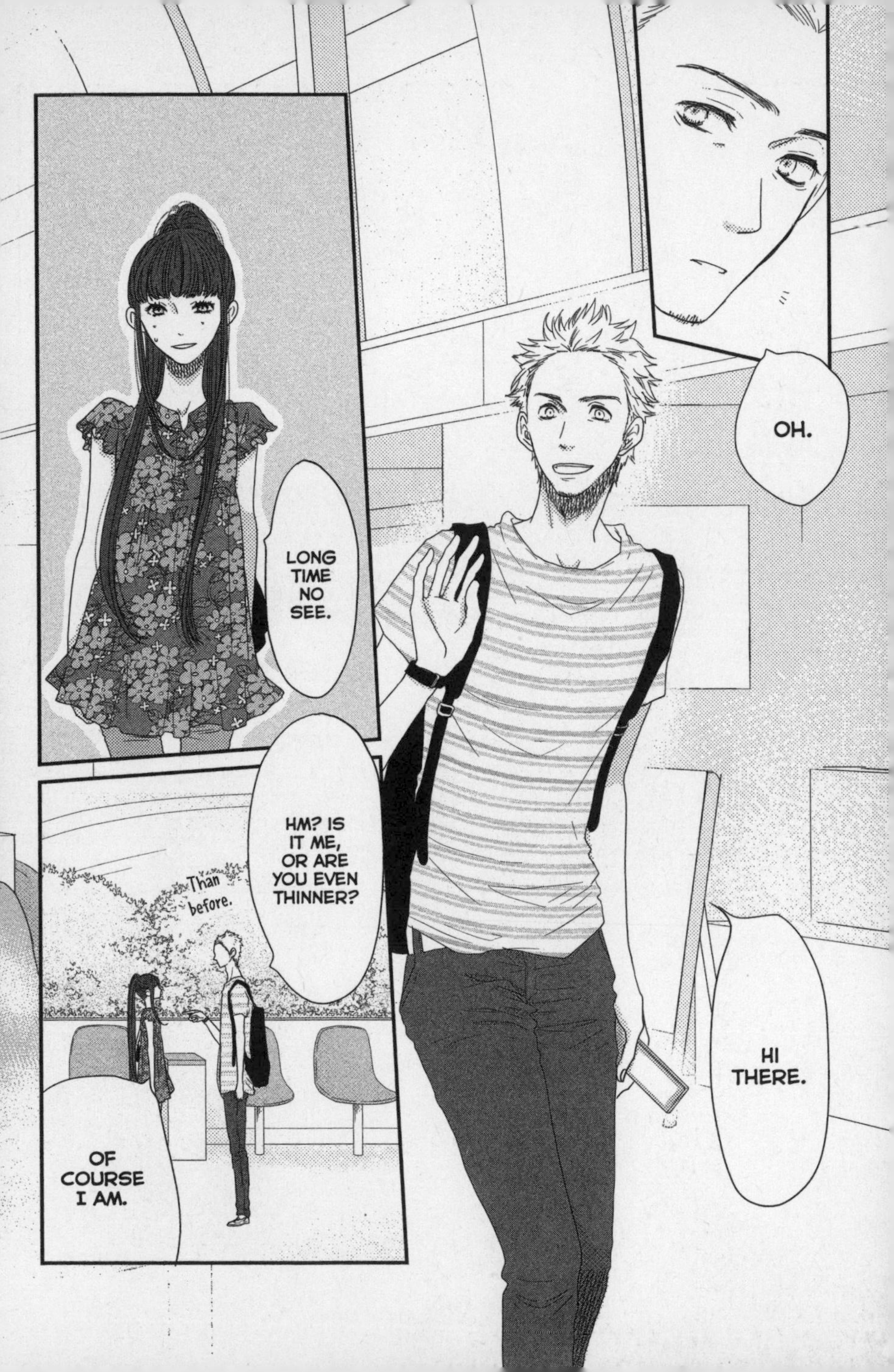
OH.
HI THERE.
LONG TIME NO SEE.
HM? IS IT ME, OR ARE YOU EVEN THINNER?
Than before.
OF COURSE I AM.

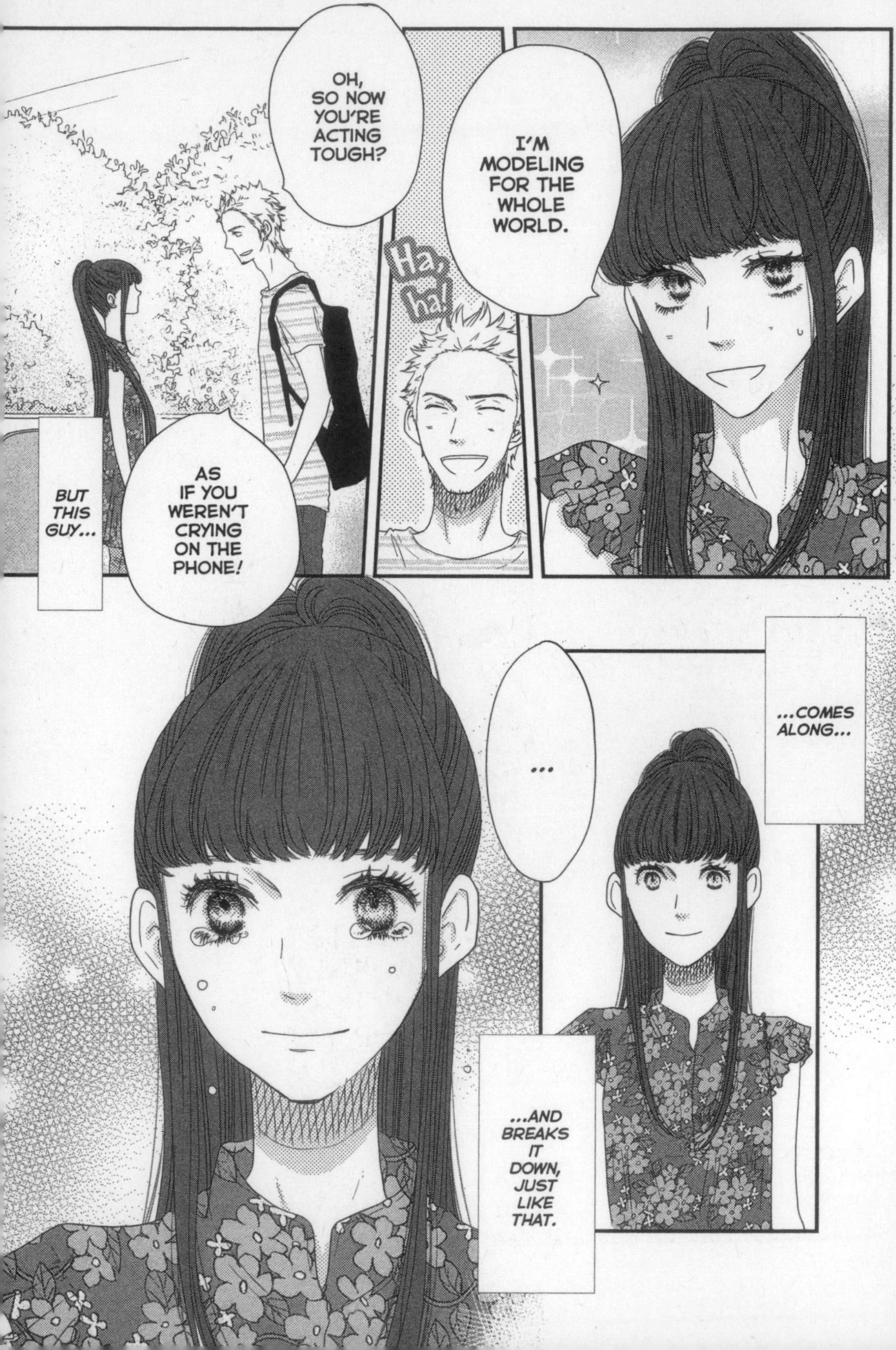
I'M MODELING FOR THE WHOLE WORLD.
Ha, ha!
OH, SO NOW YOU'RE ACTING TOUGH?
AS IF YOU WEREN'T CRYING ON THE PHONE!
BUT THIS GUY...
...COMES ALONG...
...
...AND BREAKS IT DOWN, JUST LIKE THAT.

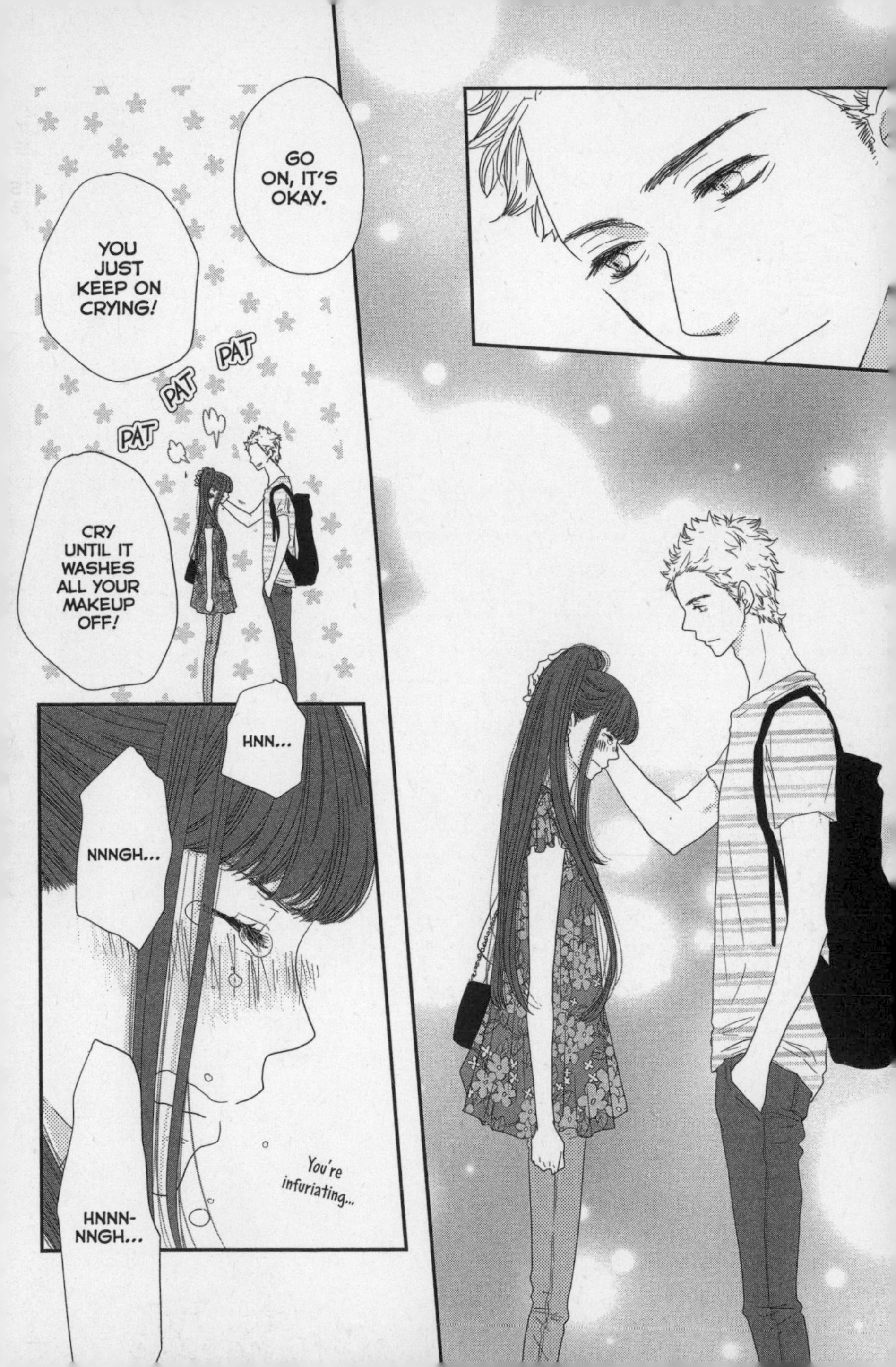
GO ON, IT'S OKAY.
YOU JUST KEEP ON CRYING!
PAT
PAT
PAT
CRY UNTIL IT WASHES ALL YOUR MAKEUP OFF!
HNN...
NNNGH...
You're infuriating...
HNNN-NNGH...

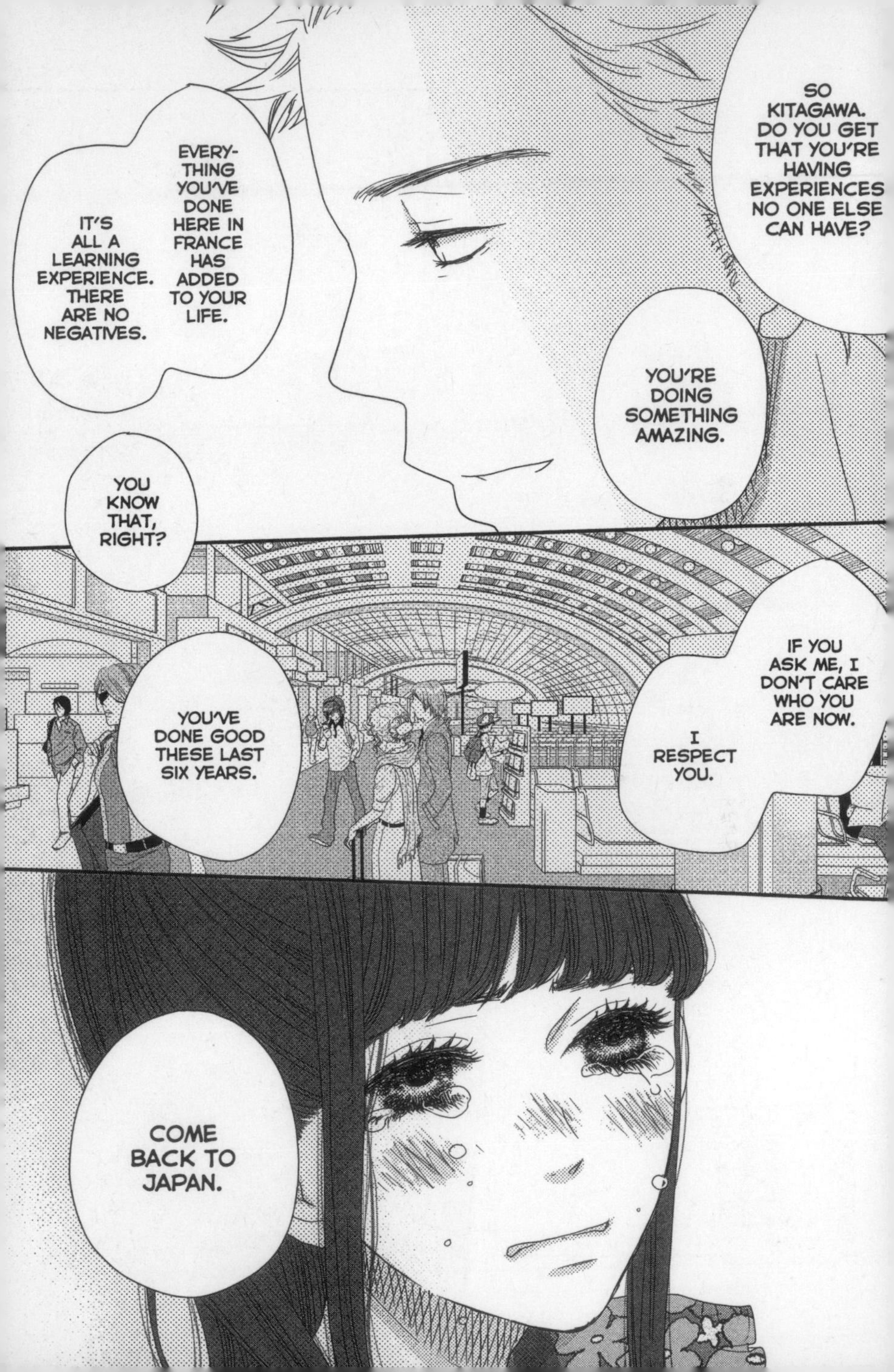
SO KITAGAWA. DO YOU GET THAT YOU'RE HAVING EXPERIENCES NO ONE ELSE CAN HAVE?
YOU'RE DOING SOMETHING AMAZING.
EVERY-THING YOU'VE DONE HERE IN FRANCE HAS ADDED TO YOUR LIFE.
IT'S ALL A LEARNING EXPERIENCE. THERE ARE NO NEGATIVES.
YOU KNOW THAT, RIGHT?
IF YOU ASK ME, I DON'T CARE WHO YOU ARE NOW.
I RESPECT YOU.
YOU'VE DONE GOOD THESE LAST SIX YEARS.
COME BACK TO JAPAN.

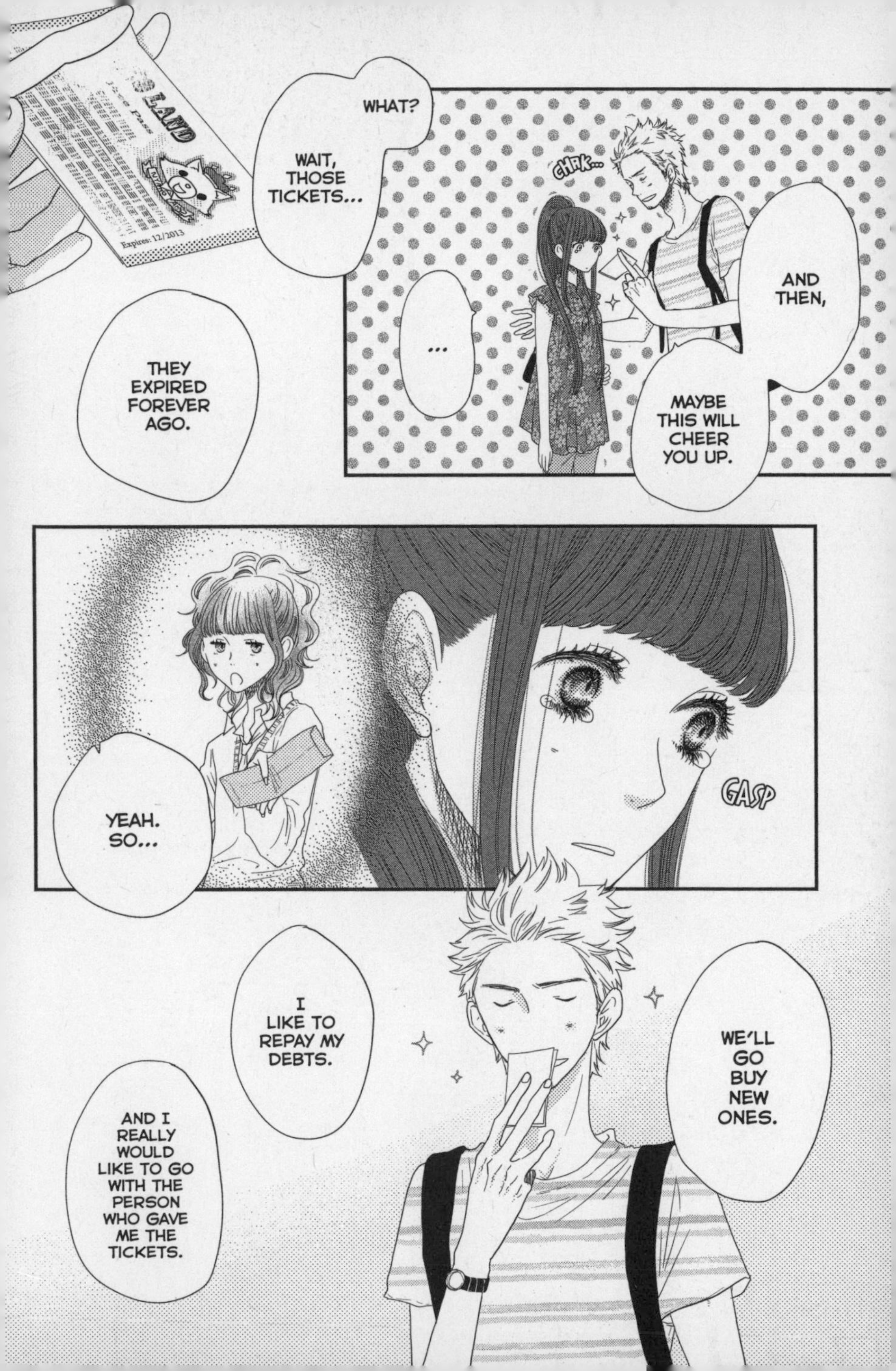
CHAK...
AND THEN,
MAYBE THIS WILL CHEER YOU UP.
...
LAND
Expires: 12/2013
WHAT?
WAIT, THOSE TICKETS...
THEY EXPIRED FOREVER AGO.
GASP
YEAH. SO...
WE'LL GO BUY NEW ONES.
I LIKE TO REPAY MY DEBTS.
AND I REALLY WOULD LIKE TO GO WITH THE PERSON WHO GAVE ME THE TICKETS.

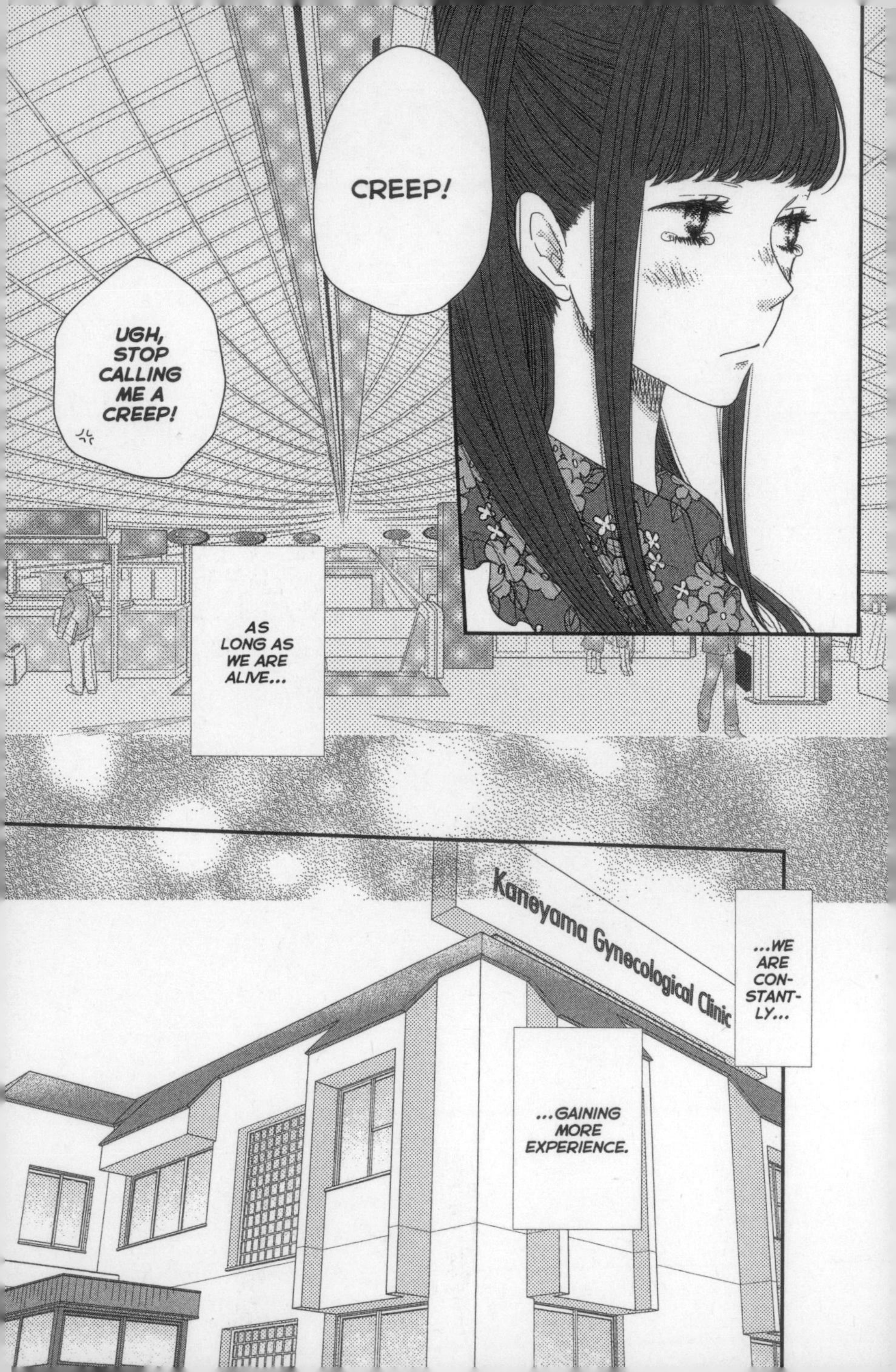
CREEP!
UGH, STOP CALLING ME A CREEP!
AS LONG AS WE ARE ALIVE...
Kaneyama Gynecological Clinic
...WE ARE CON-STANT-LY...
...GAINING MORE EXPERIENCE.

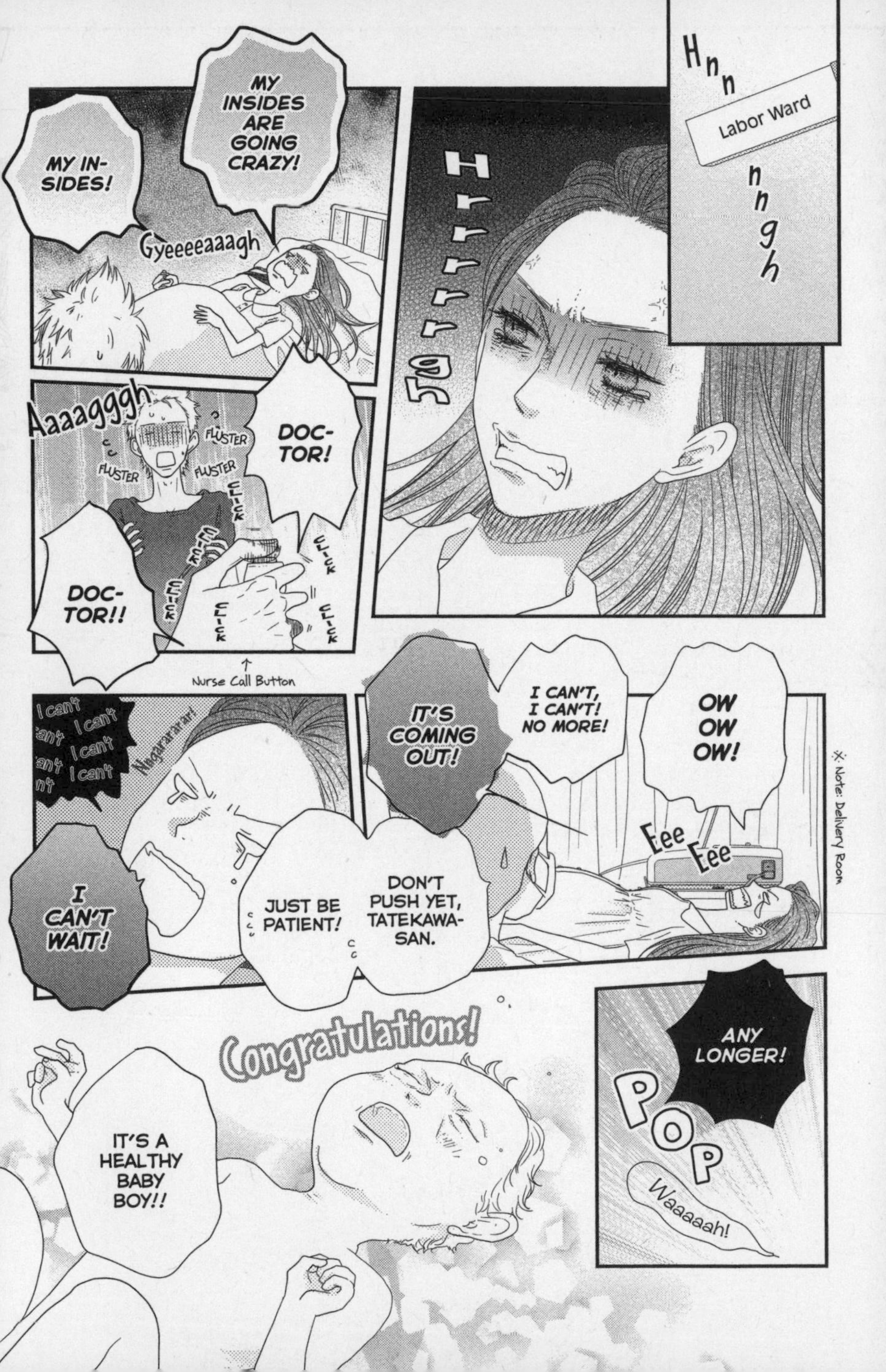
Hnn nngh
Labor Ward
Hrrrrrgh
MY INSIDES ARE GOING CRAZY!
MY IN-SIDES!
Gyeeeeaaagh
DOC-TOR!
Aaaagggh
FLUSTER
FLUSTER
FLUSTER
CLICK
CLICK
CLICK
CLICK
CLICK
CLICK
DOC-TOR!!
Nurse Call Button
OW OW OW!
I CAN'T, I CAN'T! NO MORE!
IT'S COMING OUT!
Eee Eee
DON'T PUSH YET, TATEKAWA-SAN.
JUST BE PATIENT!
I can't I can't I can't I can't
Nngararararar!
I CAN'T WAIT!
ANY LONGER!
POP
Waaaaah!
Congratulations!
IT'S A HEALTHY BABY BOY!!

※ Note: Delivery Room

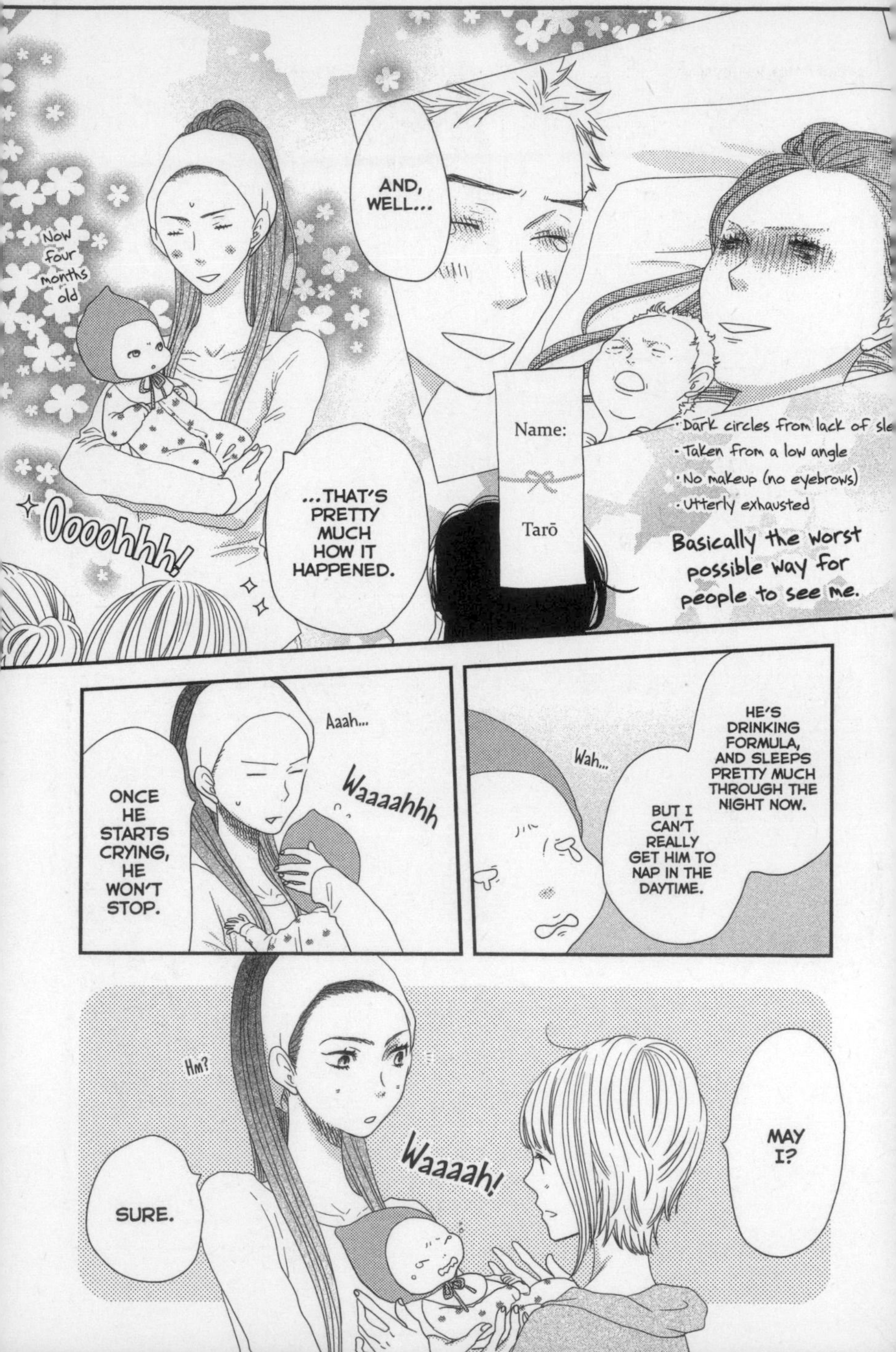
AND, WELL...
· Dark circles from lack of sle
· Taken from a low angle
· No makeup (no eyebrows)
· Utterly exhausted
Basically the worst possible way for people to see me.
Name:
Tarō
Now four months old
...THAT'S PRETTY MUCH HOW IT HAPPENED.
Ooooohhh!
HE'S DRINKING FORMULA, AND SLEEPS PRETTY MUCH THROUGH THE NIGHT NOW.
Wah...
BUT I CAN'T REALLY GET HIM TO NAP IN THE DAYTIME.
Aaah...
Waaaahhh
ONCE HE STARTS CRYING, HE WON'T STOP.
MAY I?
Waaaah!
Hm?
SURE.

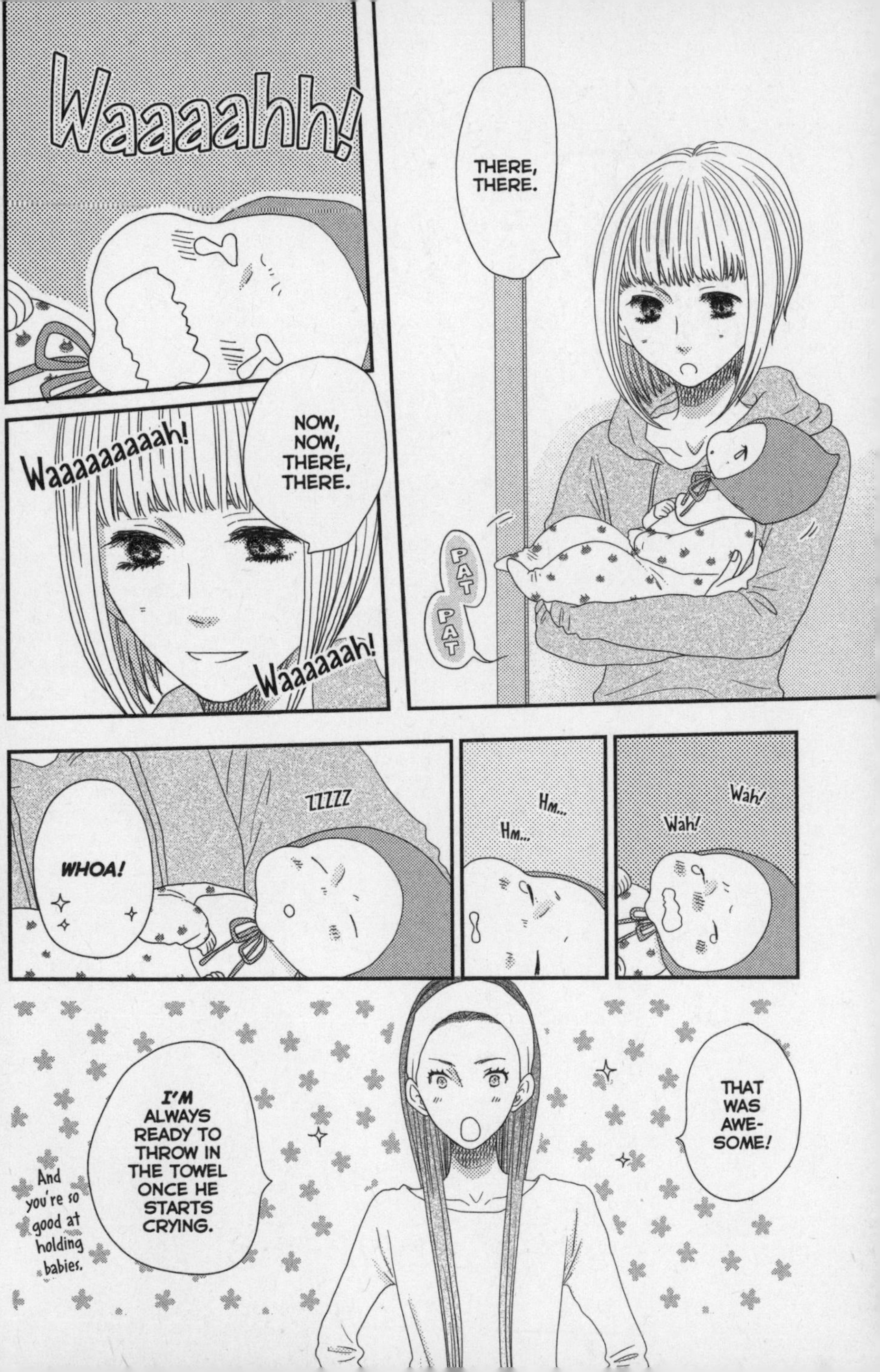

THERE, THERE.
PAT PAT
Waaaaahh!
NOW, NOW, THERE, THERE.
Waaaaaaaaah!
Waaaaaah!
Wah!
Wah!
Hm...
Hm...
ZZZZZ
WHOA!
THAT WAS AWE-SOME!
I'M ALWAYS READY TO THROW IN THE TOWEL ONCE HE STARTS CRYING.
And you're so good at holding babies.

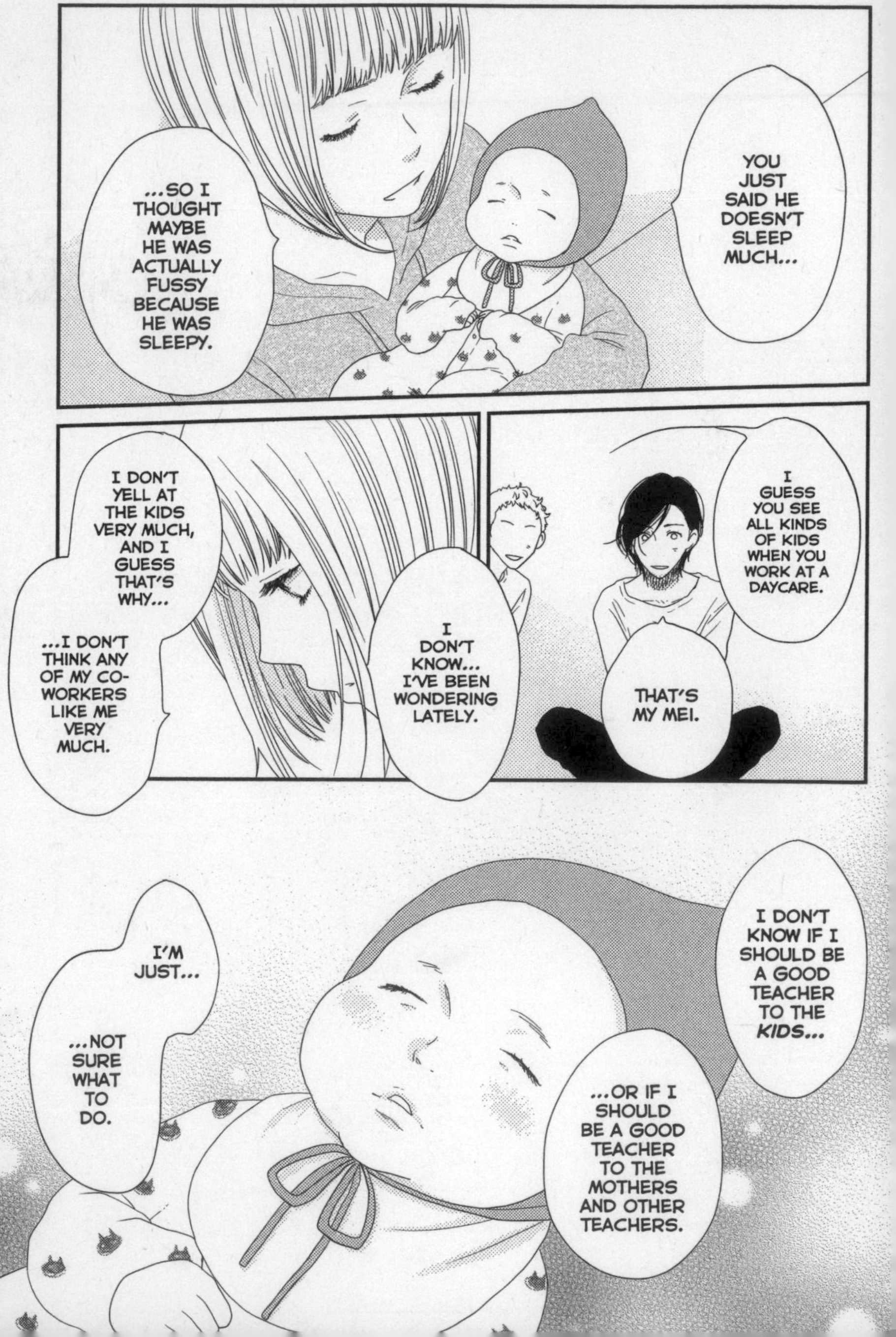
YOU JUST SAID HE DOESN'T SLEEP MUCH...
...SO I THOUGHT MAYBE HE WAS ACTUALLY FUSSY BECAUSE HE WAS SLEEPY.
I GUESS YOU SEE ALL KINDS OF KIDS WHEN YOU WORK AT A DAYCARE.
THAT'S MY MEI.
I DON'T KNOW... I'VE BEEN WONDERING LATELY.
I DON'T YELL AT THE KIDS VERY MUCH, AND I GUESS THAT'S WHY...
...I DON'T THINK ANY OF MY CO-WORKERS LIKE ME VERY MUCH.
I DON'T KNOW IF I SHOULD BE A GOOD TEACHER TO THE ***KIDS...***
...OR IF I SHOULD BE A GOOD TEACHER TO THE MOTHERS AND OTHER TEACHERS.
I'M JUST...
...NOT SURE WHAT TO DO.

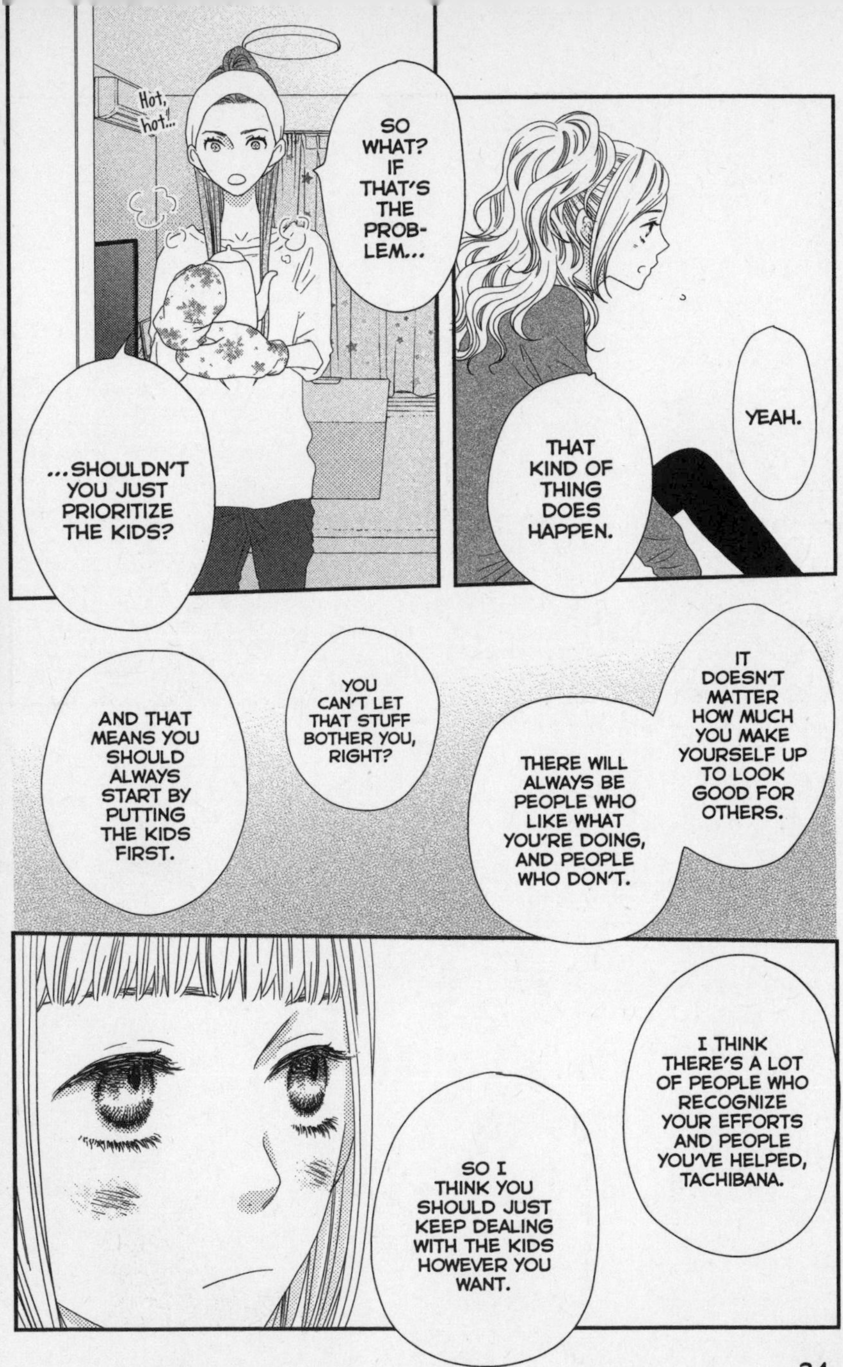
YEAH.
THAT KIND OF THING DOES HAPPEN.
SO WHAT? IF THAT'S THE PROB-LEM...
Hot, hot!..
...SHOULDN'T YOU JUST PRIORITIZE THE KIDS?
IT DOESN'T MATTER HOW MUCH YOU MAKE YOURSELF UP TO LOOK GOOD FOR OTHERS.
THERE WILL ALWAYS BE PEOPLE WHO LIKE WHAT YOU'RE DOING, AND PEOPLE WHO DON'T.
YOU CAN'T LET THAT STUFF BOTHER YOU, RIGHT?
AND THAT MEANS YOU SHOULD ALWAYS START BY PUTTING THE KIDS FIRST.
I THINK THERE'S A LOT OF PEOPLE WHO RECOGNIZE YOUR EFFORTS AND PEOPLE YOU'VE HELPED, TACHIBANA.
SO I THINK YOU SHOULD JUST KEEP DEALING WITH THE KIDS HOWEVER YOU WANT.

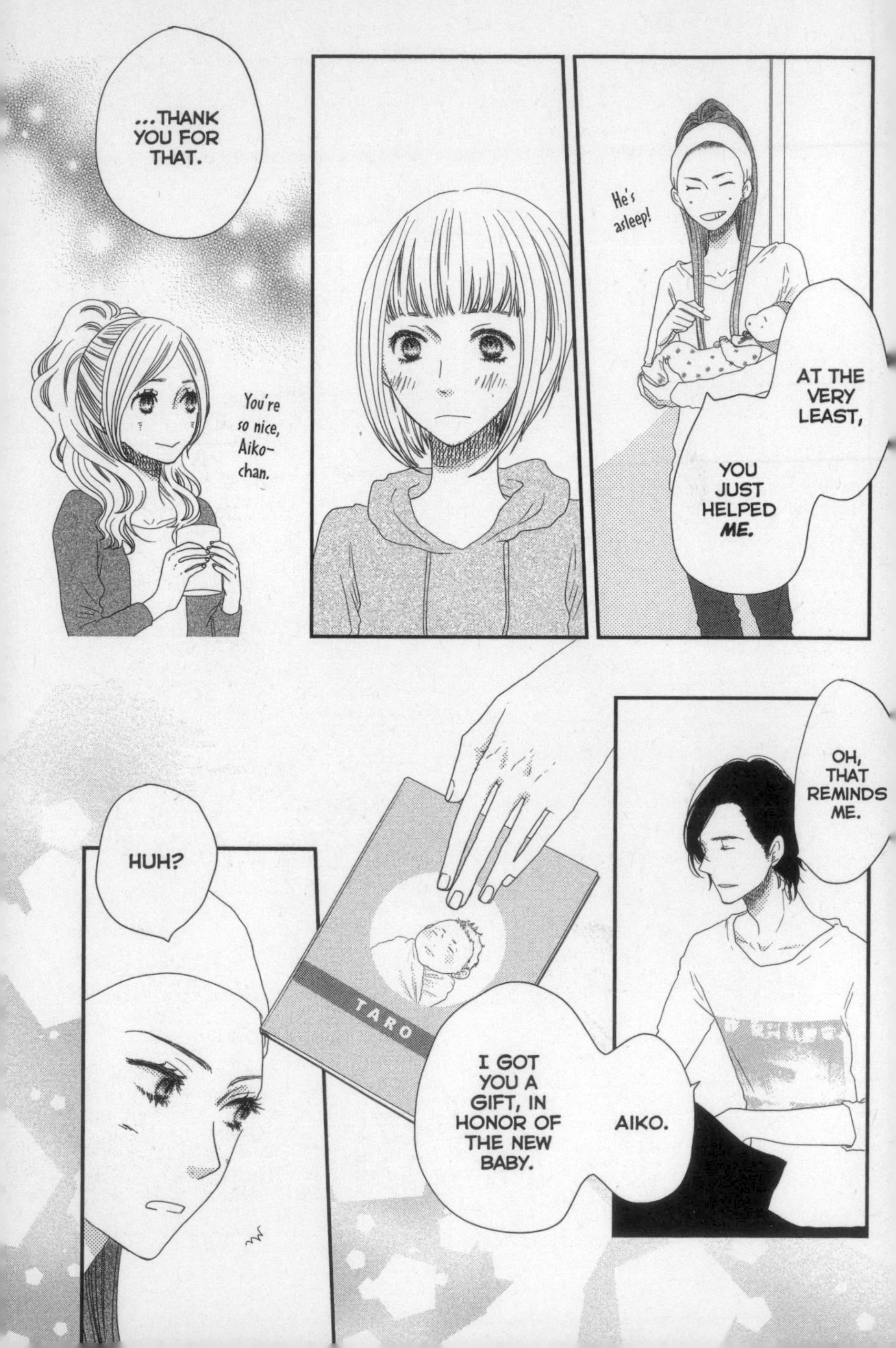
He's asleep!
AT THE VERY LEAST, YOU JUST HELPED *ME.*
...THANK YOU FOR THAT.
You're so nice, Aiko-chan.
OH, THAT REMINDS ME.
AIKO.
I GOT YOU A GIFT, IN HONOR OF THE NEW BABY.
TARO
HUH?

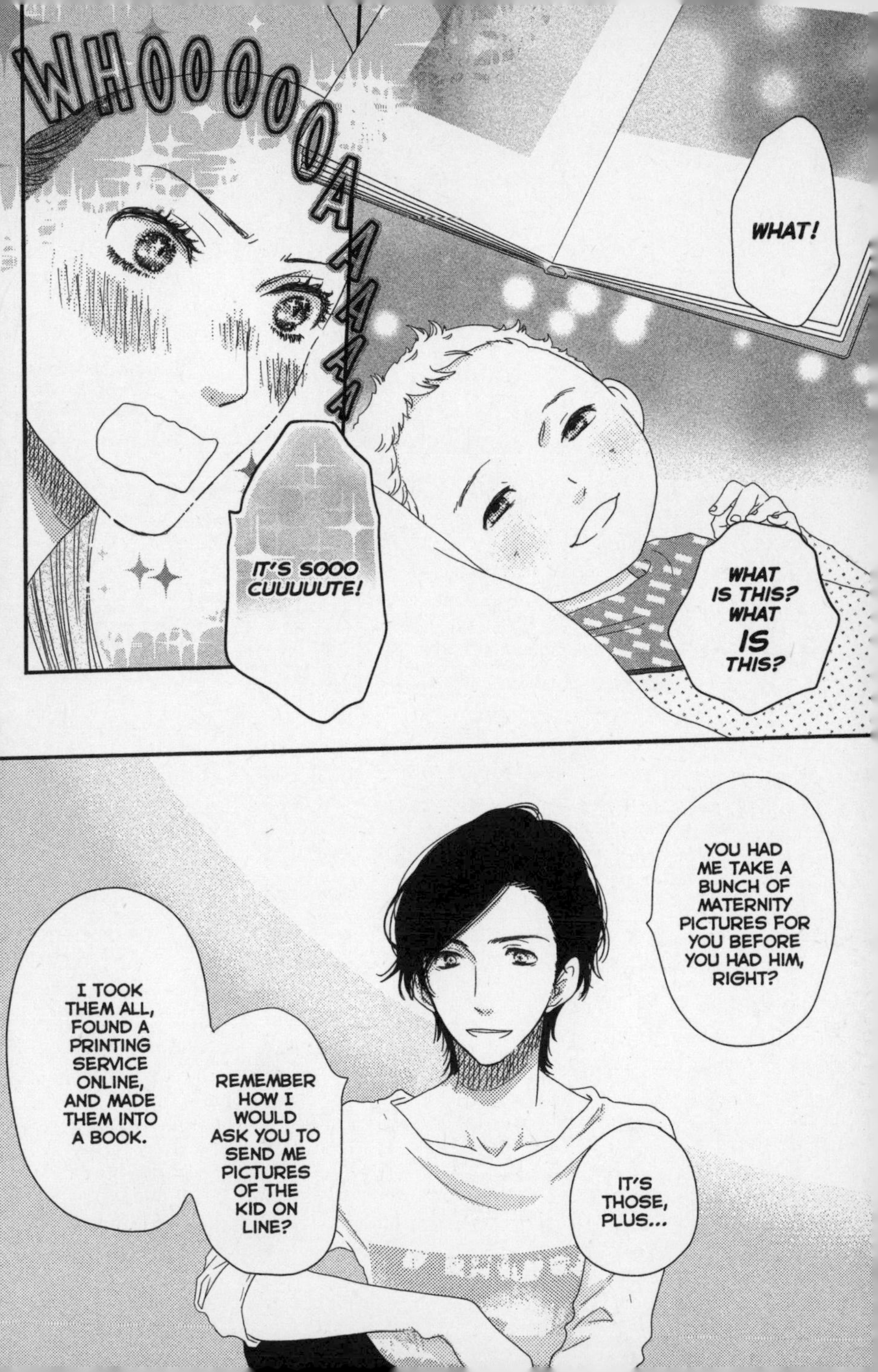
WHAT!
WHAT IS THIS? WHAT IS THIS?
WHOOOOOOAAAAAA
IT'S SOOO CUUUUUTE!
YOU HAD ME TAKE A BUNCH OF MATERNITY PICTURES FOR YOU BEFORE YOU HAD HIM, RIGHT?
IT'S THOSE, PLUS...
REMEMBER HOW I WOULD ASK YOU TO SEND ME PICTURES OF THE KID ON LINE?
I TOOK THEM ALL, FOUND A PRINTING SERVICE ONLINE, AND MADE THEM INTO A BOOK.

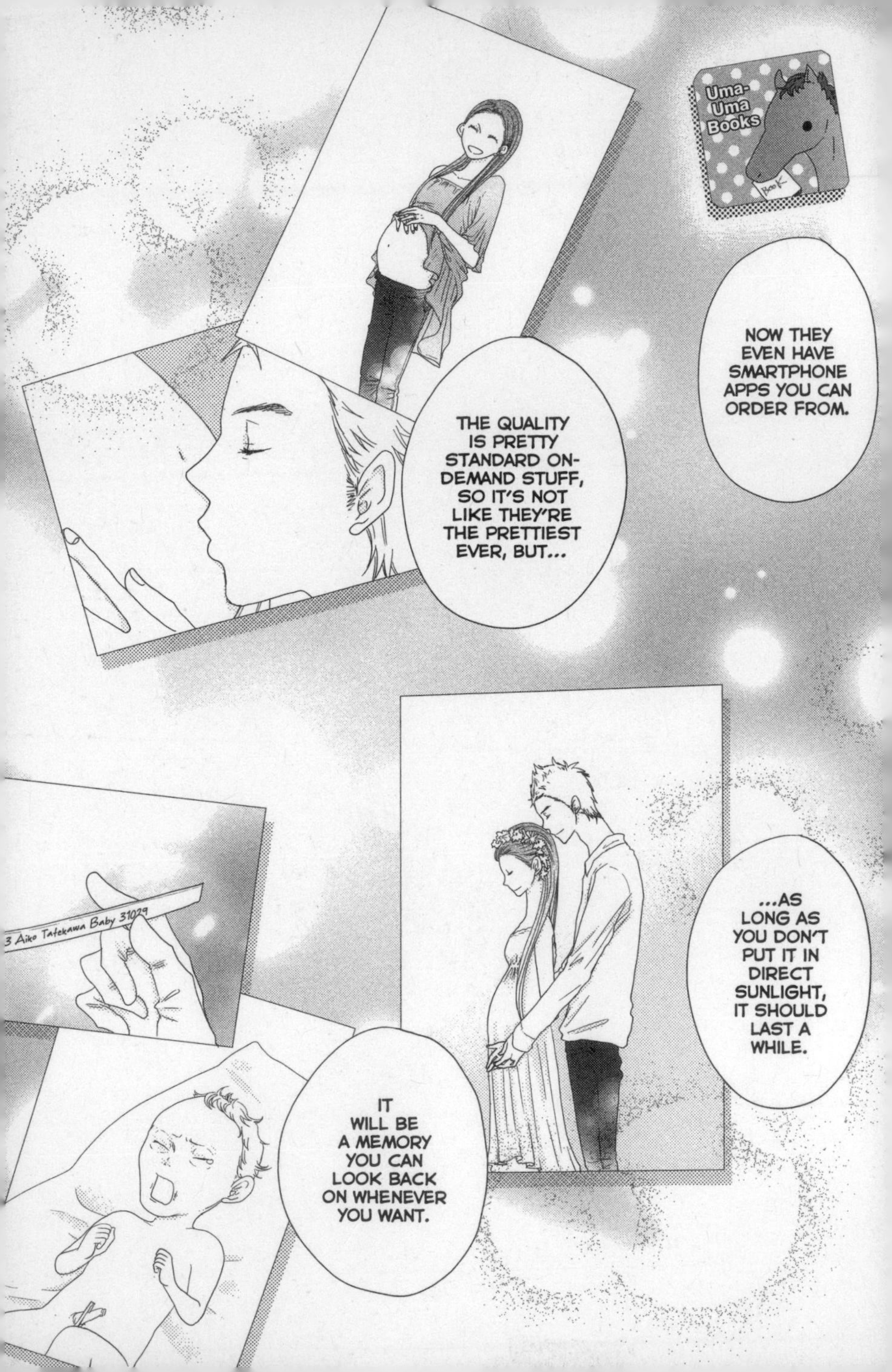
Uma-Uma Books
Book
NOW THEY EVEN HAVE SMARTPHONE APPS YOU CAN ORDER FROM.
THE QUALITY IS PRETTY STANDARD ON-DEMAND STUFF, SO IT'S NOT LIKE THEY'RE THE PRETTIEST EVER, BUT...
...AS LONG AS YOU DON'T PUT IT IN DIRECT SUNLIGHT, IT SHOULD LAST A WHILE.
3 Aiko Tatekawa Baby 31029
IT WILL BE A MEMORY YOU CAN LOOK BACK ON WHENEVER YOU WANT.

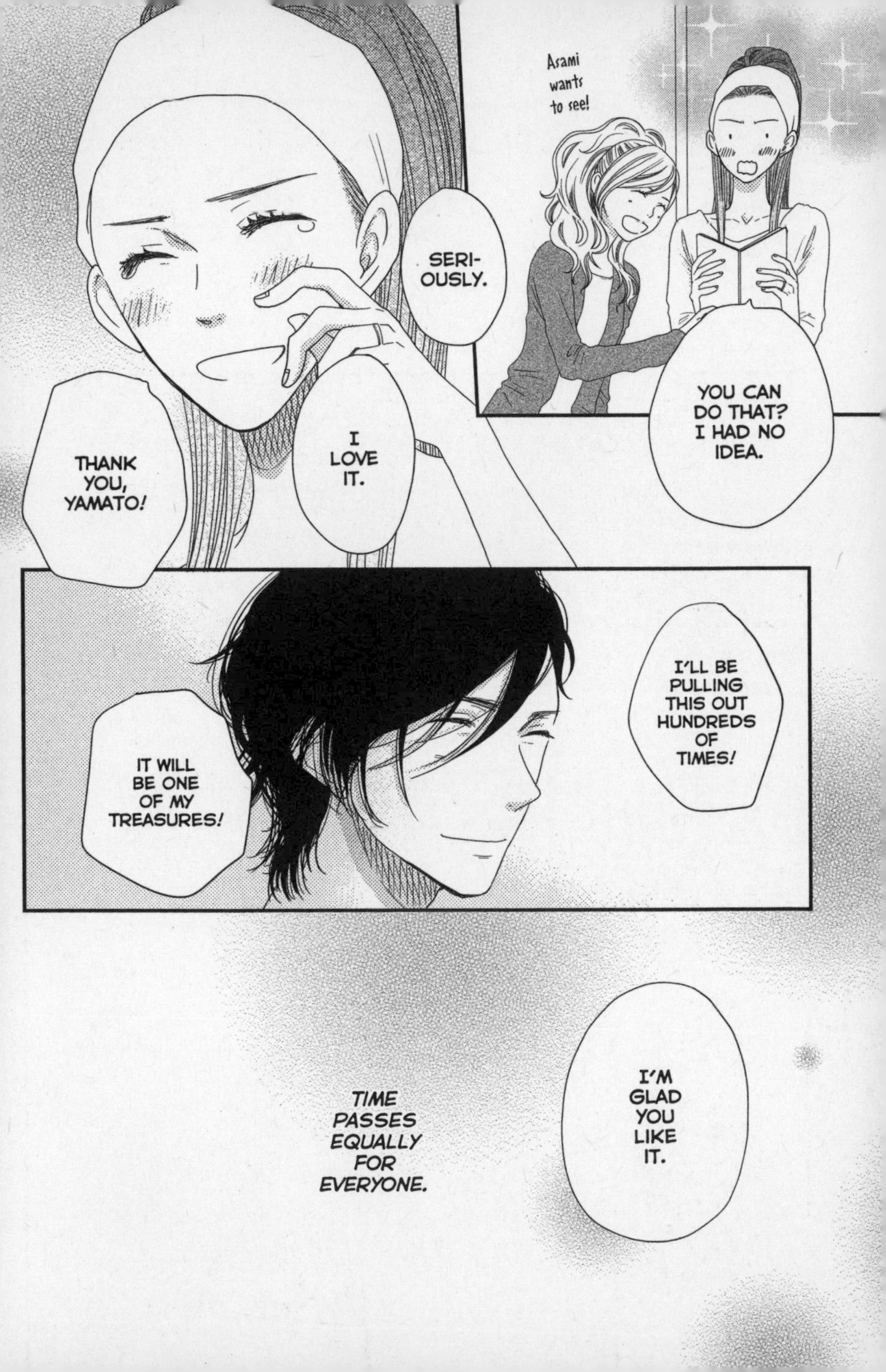
Asami wants to see!
YOU CAN DO THAT? I HAD NO IDEA.
SERI-OUSLY.
I LOVE IT.
THANK YOU, YAMATO!
I'LL BE PULLING THIS OUT HUNDREDS OF TIMES!
IT WILL BE ONE OF MY TREASURES!
I'M GLAD YOU LIKE IT.
TIME PASSES EQUALLY FOR EVERYONE.

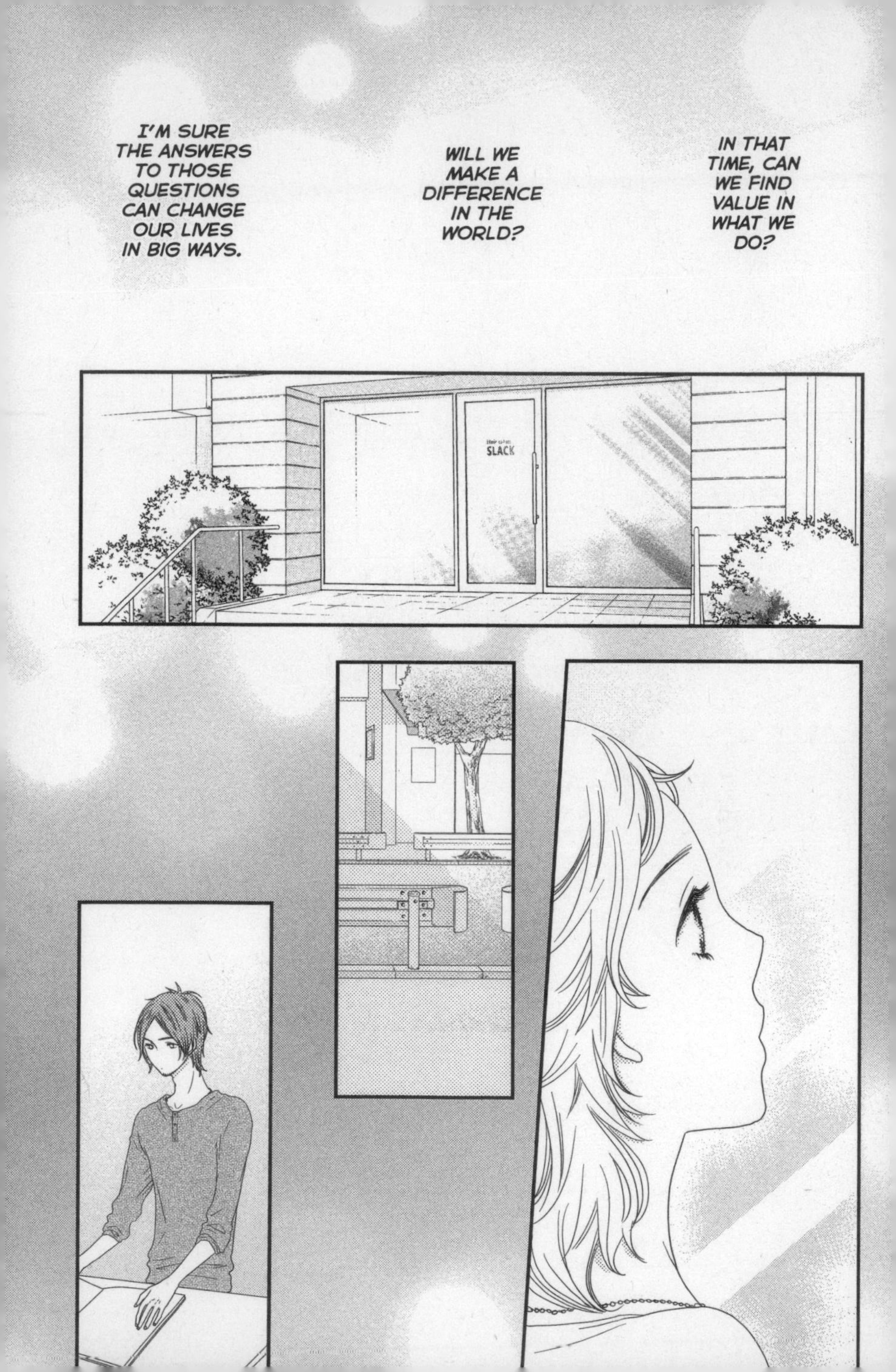
IN THAT TIME, CAN WE FIND VALUE IN WHAT WE DO?
WILL WE MAKE A DIFFERENCE IN THE WORLD?
I'M SURE THE ANSWERS TO THOSE QUESTIONS CAN CHANGE OUR LIVES IN BIG WAYS.
SLACK

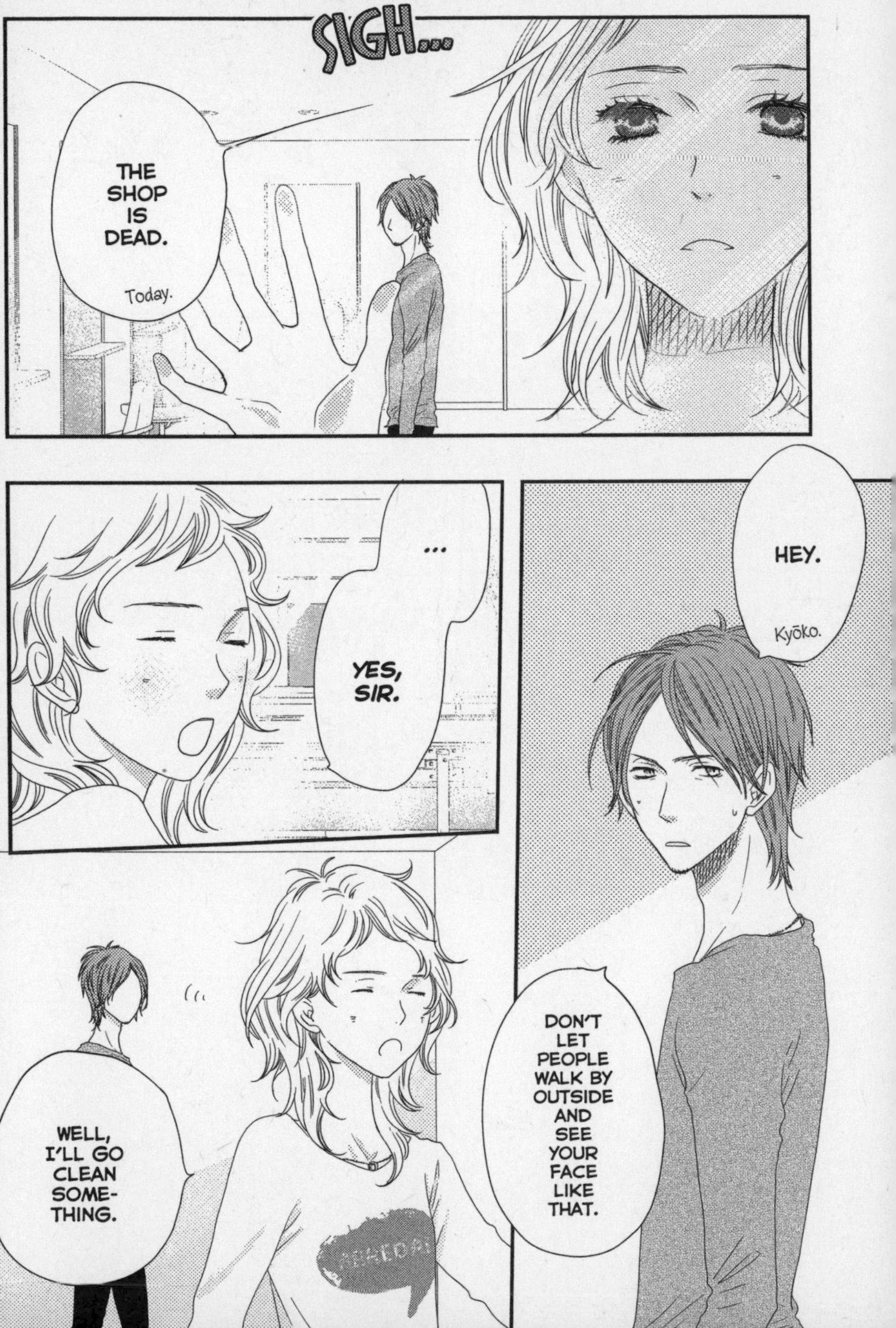
SIGH...
THE SHOP IS DEAD.
Today.
HEY.
Kyōko.
DON'T LET PEOPLE WALK BY OUTSIDE AND SEE YOUR FACE LIKE THAT.
...
YES, SIR.
WELL, I'LL GO CLEAN SOMETHING.

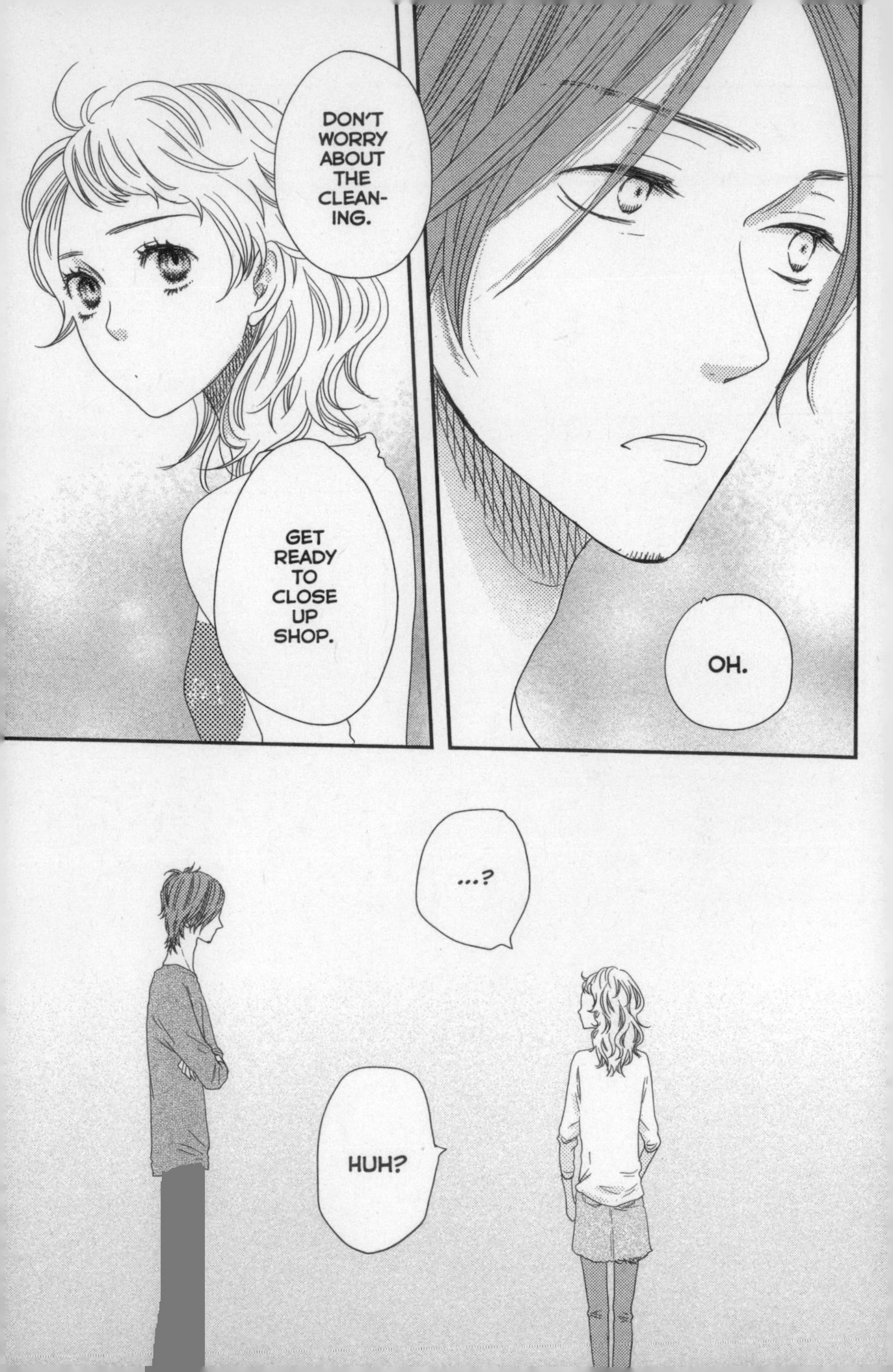
OH.
DON'T WORRY ABOUT THE CLEAN-ING.
GET READY TO CLOSE UP SHOP.
...?
HUH?

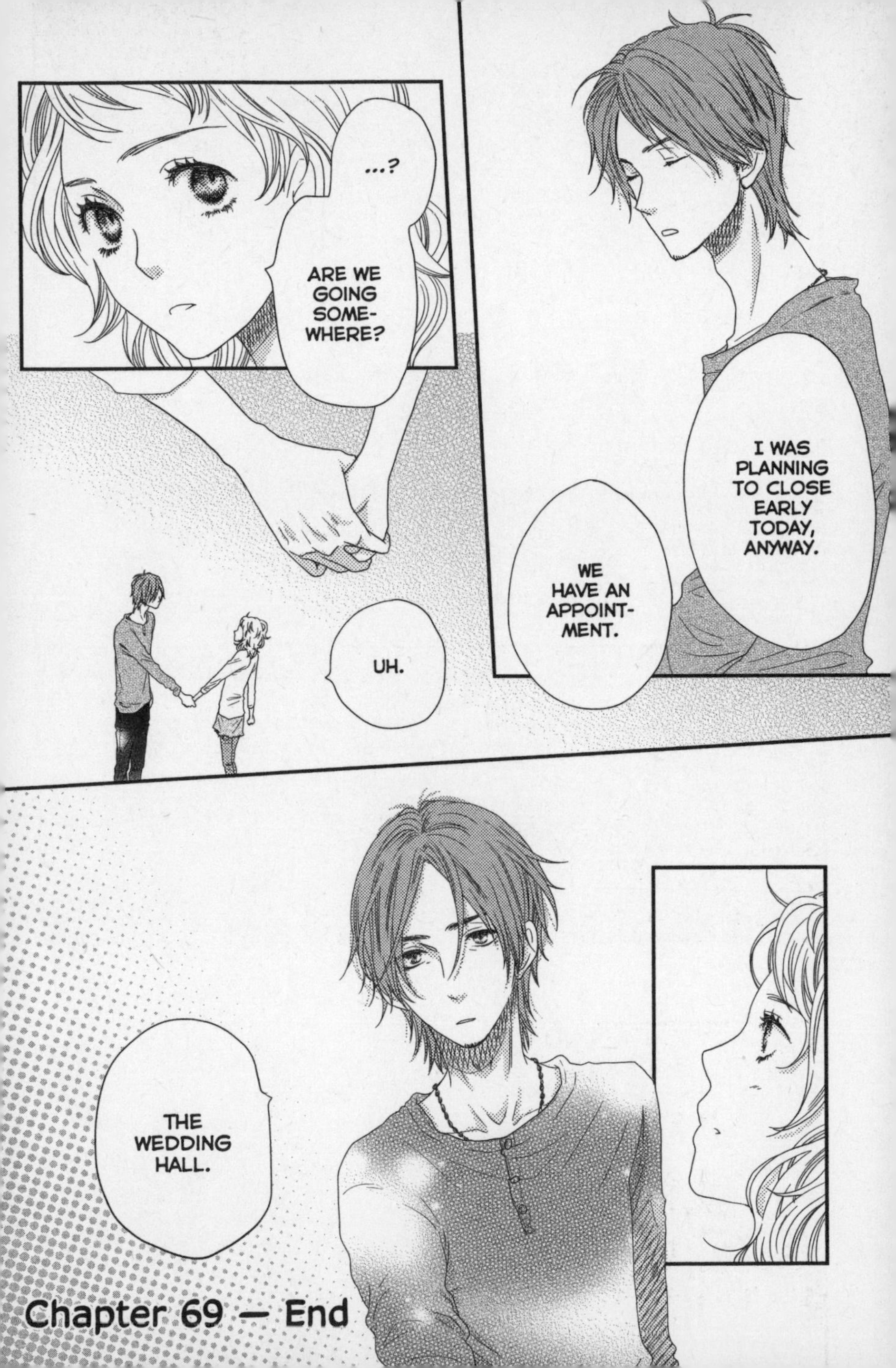
I WAS PLANNING TO CLOSE EARLY TODAY, ANYWAY.
WE HAVE AN APPOINTMENT.
...?
ARE WE GOING SOMEWHERE?
UH.
THE WEDDING HALL.
Chapter 69 — End

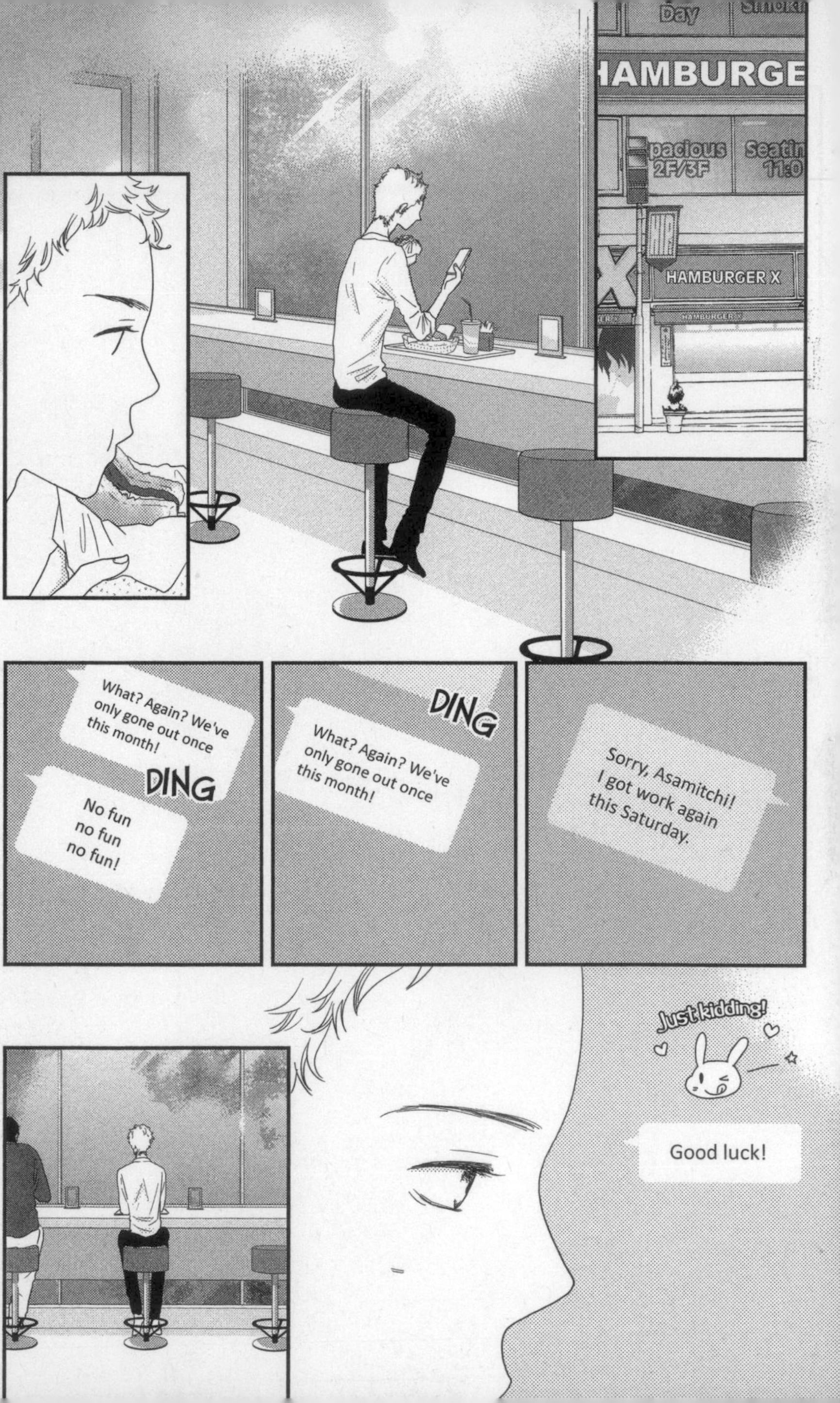
Day
HAMBURGE
2F/3F
HAMBURGER X
Sorry, Asamitchi! I got work again this Saturday.
DING
What? Again? We've only gone out once this month!
What? Again? We've only gone out once this month!
DING
No fun no fun no fun!
Just kidding!
Good luck!

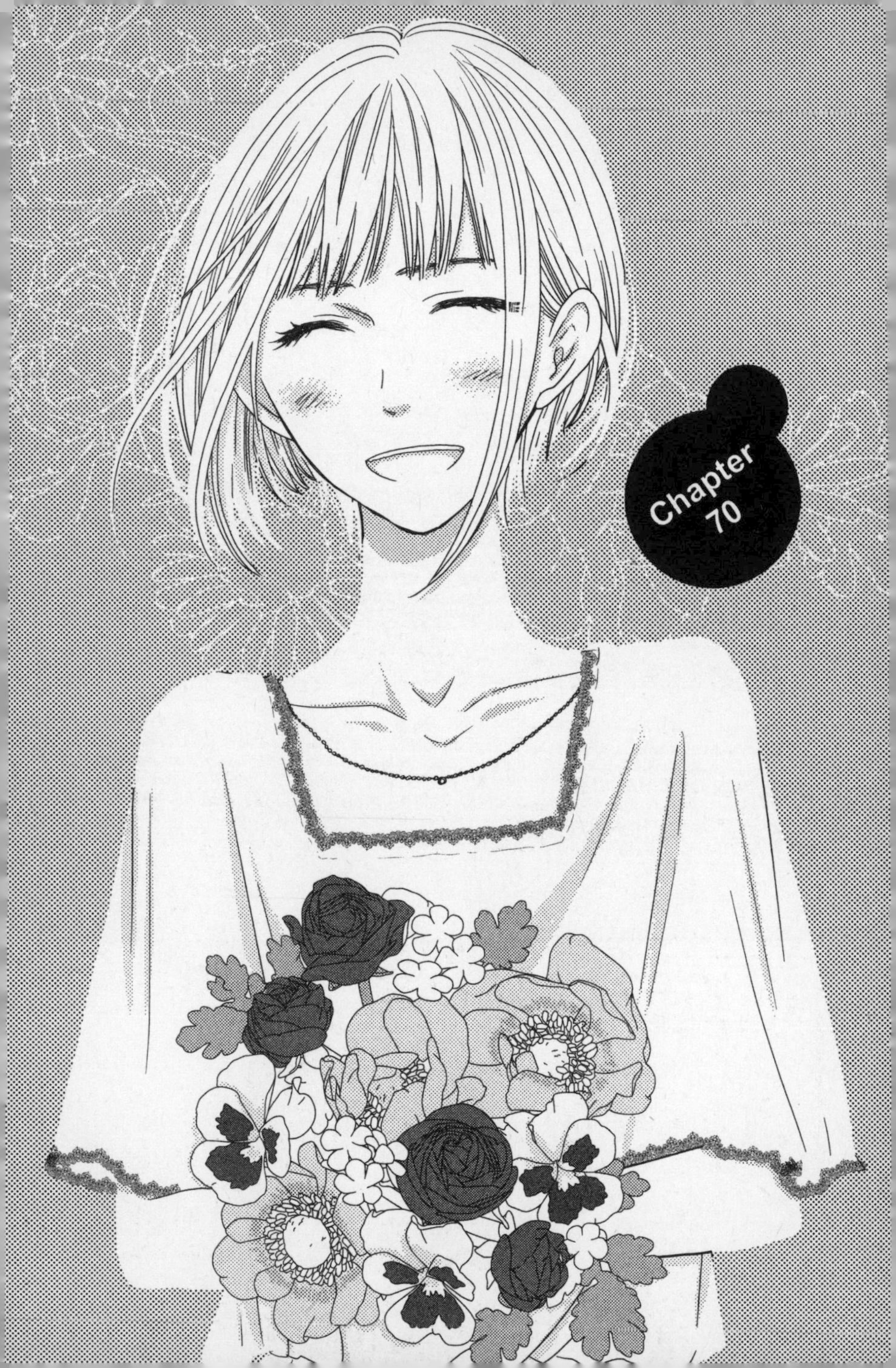
Chapter
70

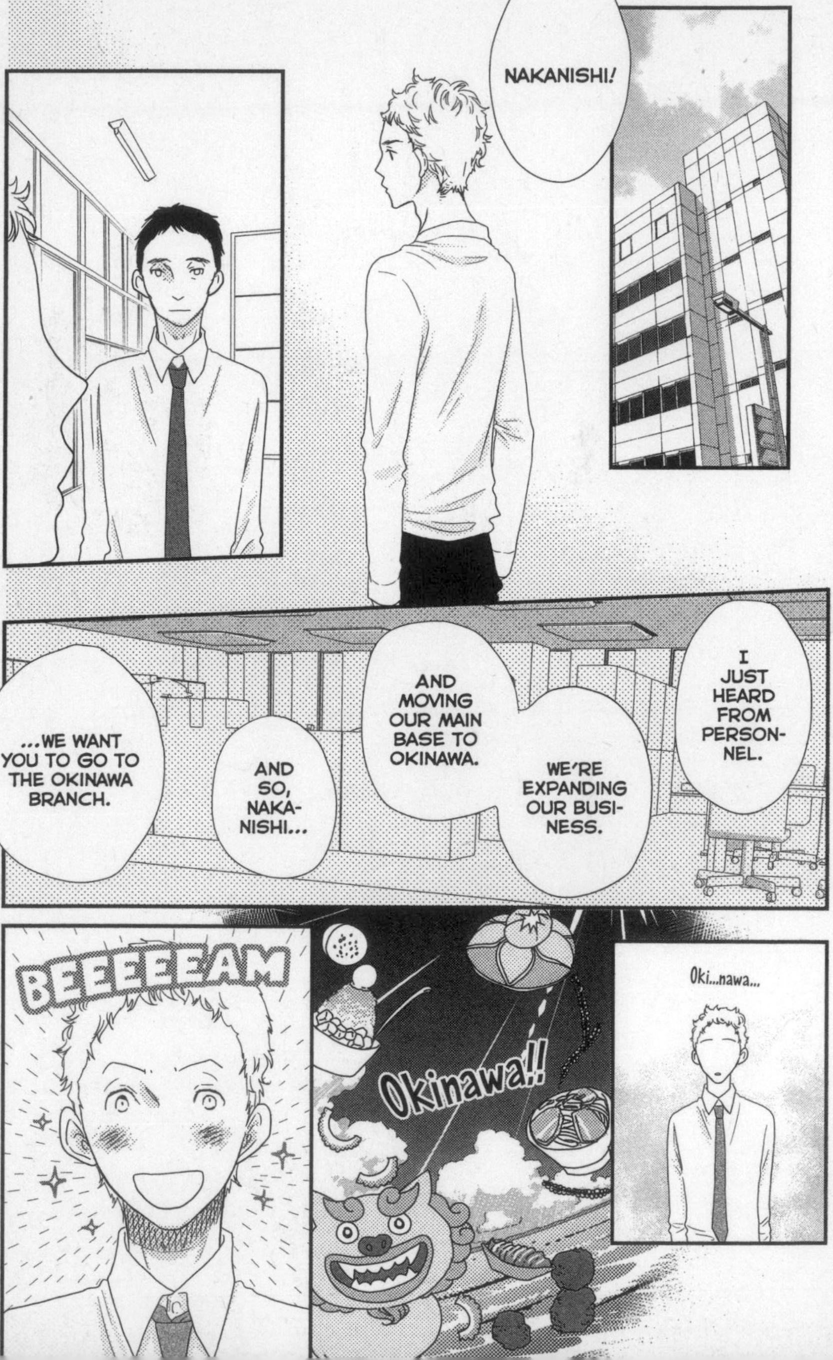
NAKANISHI!
I JUST HEARD FROM PERSON-NEL.
WE'RE EXPANDING OUR BUSI-NESS.
AND MOVING OUR MAIN BASE TO OKINAWA.
AND SO, NAKA-NISHI...
...WE WANT YOU TO GO TO THE OKINAWA BRANCH.
Oki...nawa...
Okinawa!!
BEEEEEEAM

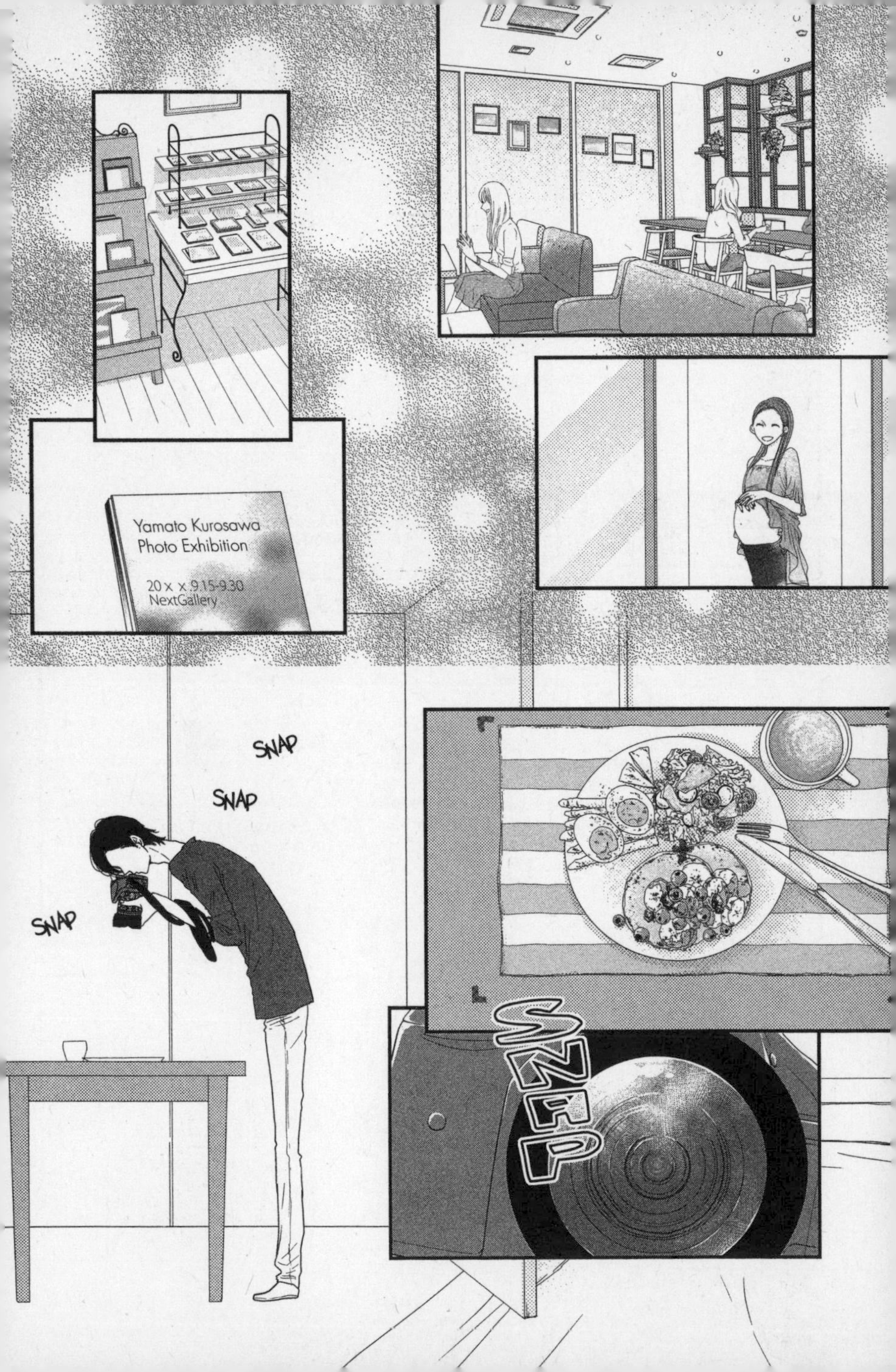
Yamato Kurosawa
Photo Exhibition
20xx 9.15-9.30
NextGallery
SNAP
SNAP
SNAP
SNAP

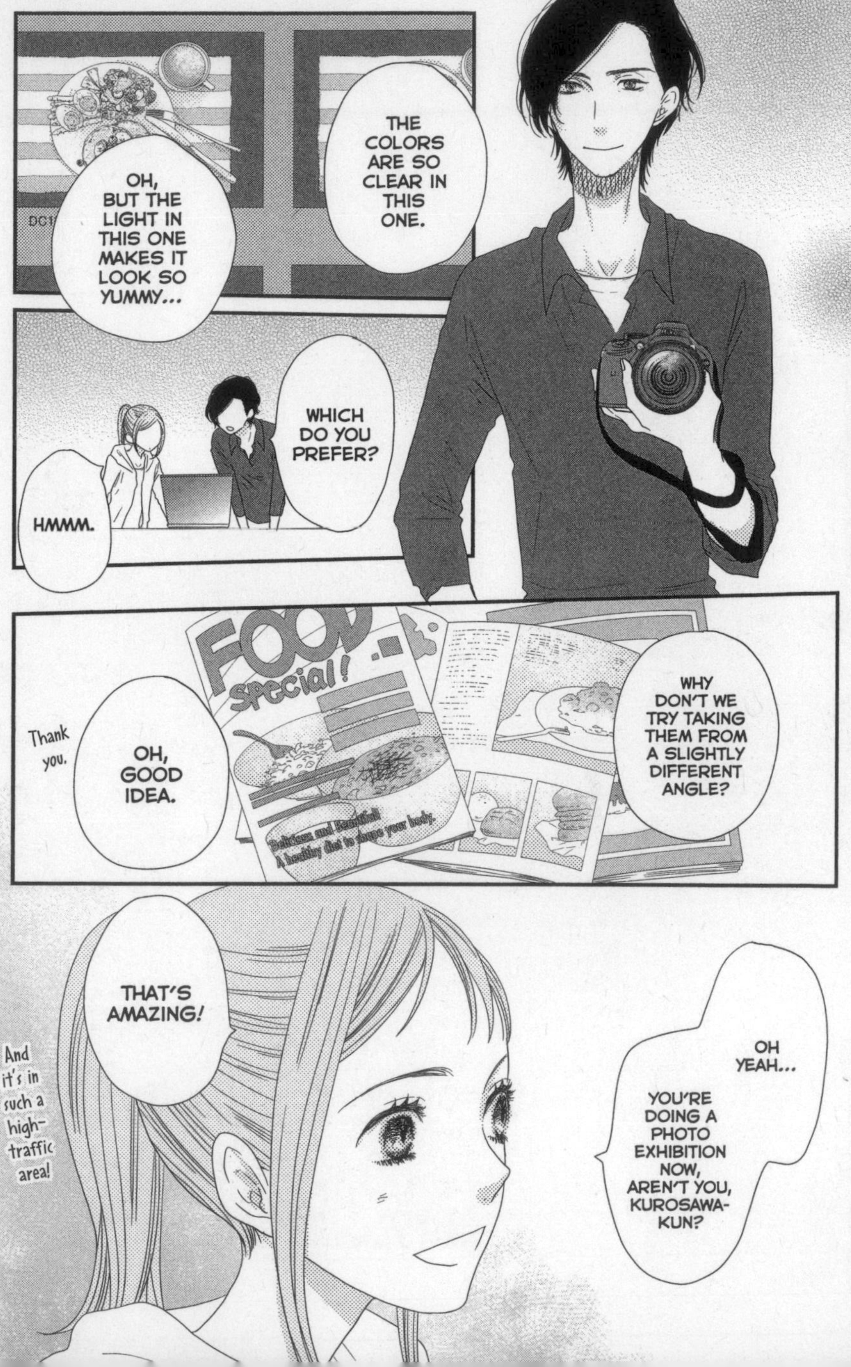
THE COLORS ARE SO CLEAR IN THIS ONE.
OH, BUT THE LIGHT IN THIS ONE MAKES IT LOOK SO YUMMY...
WHICH DO YOU PREFER?
HMMM.
WHY DON'T WE TRY TAKING THEM FROM A SLIGHTLY DIFFERENT ANGLE?
OH, GOOD IDEA.
Thank you.
OH YEAH... YOU'RE DOING A PHOTO EXHIBITION NOW, AREN'T YOU, KUROSAWA-KUN?
THAT'S AMAZING!
And it's in such a high-traffic area!

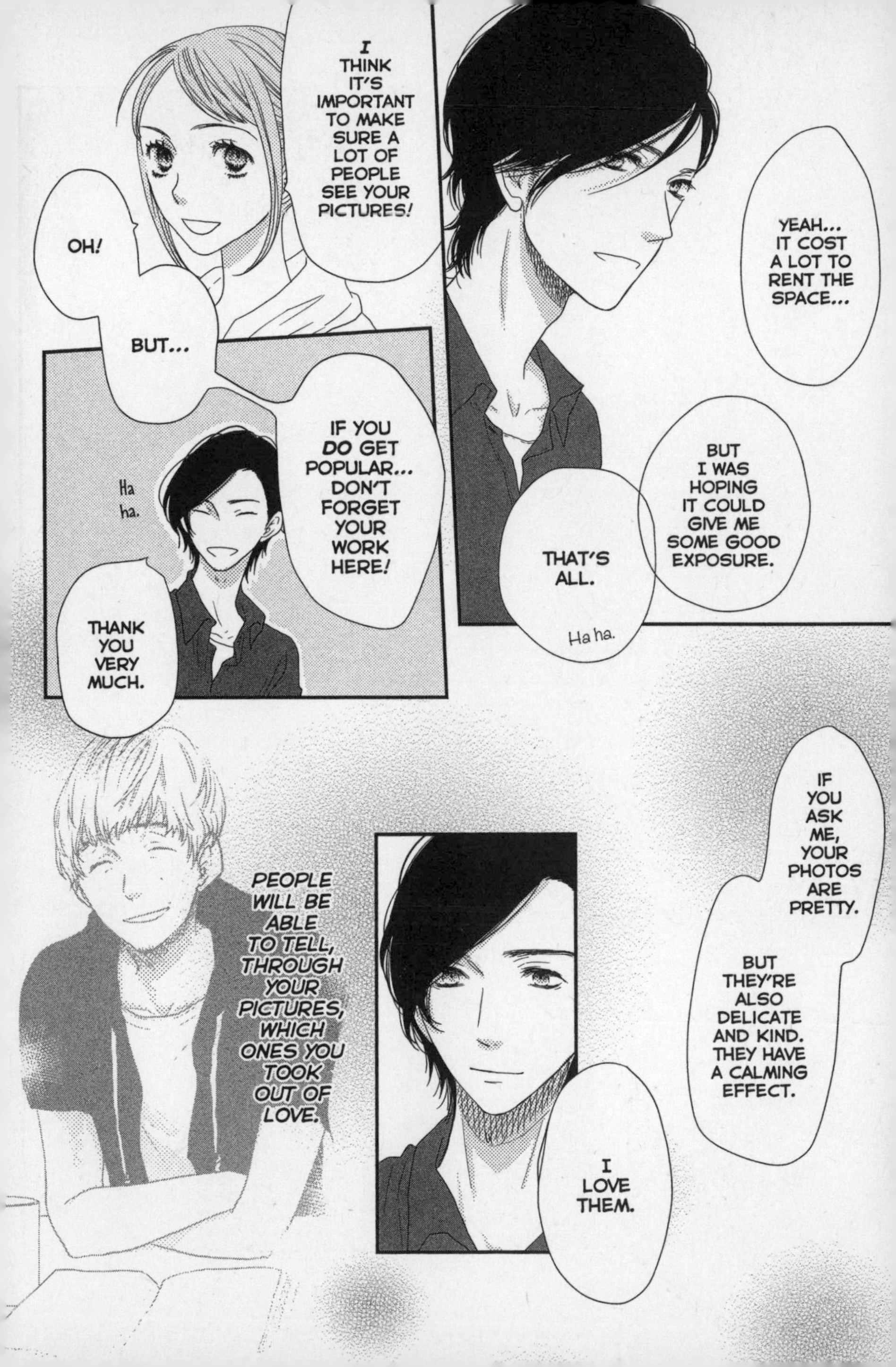
YEAH... IT COST A LOT TO RENT THE SPACE...
BUT I WAS HOPING IT COULD GIVE ME SOME GOOD EXPOSURE.
THAT'S ALL.
Ha ha.
I THINK IT'S IMPORTANT TO MAKE SURE A LOT OF PEOPLE SEE YOUR PICTURES!
OH!
BUT...
IF YOU *DO* GET POPULAR... DON'T FORGET YOUR WORK HERE!
Ha ha.
THANK YOU VERY MUCH.
IF YOU ASK ME, YOUR PHOTOS ARE PRETTY.
BUT THEY'RE ALSO DELICATE AND KIND. THEY HAVE A CALMING EFFECT.
I LOVE THEM.
PEOPLE WILL BE ABLE TO TELL, THROUGH YOUR PICTURES, WHICH ONES YOU TOOK OUT OF LOVE.

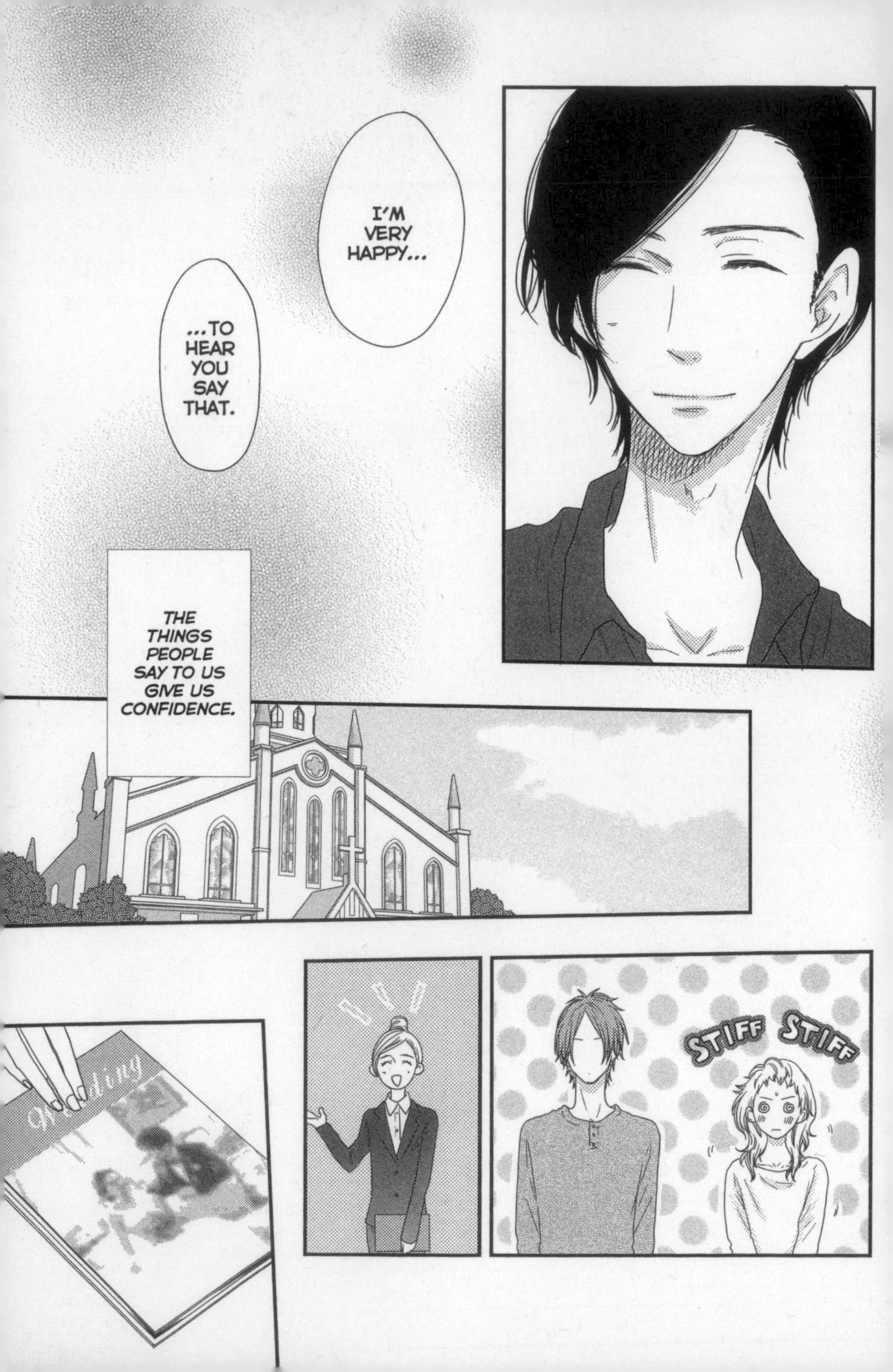
I'M VERY HAPPY...
...TO HEAR YOU SAY THAT.
THE THINGS PEOPLE SAY TO US GIVE US CONFIDENCE.
STIFF STIFF

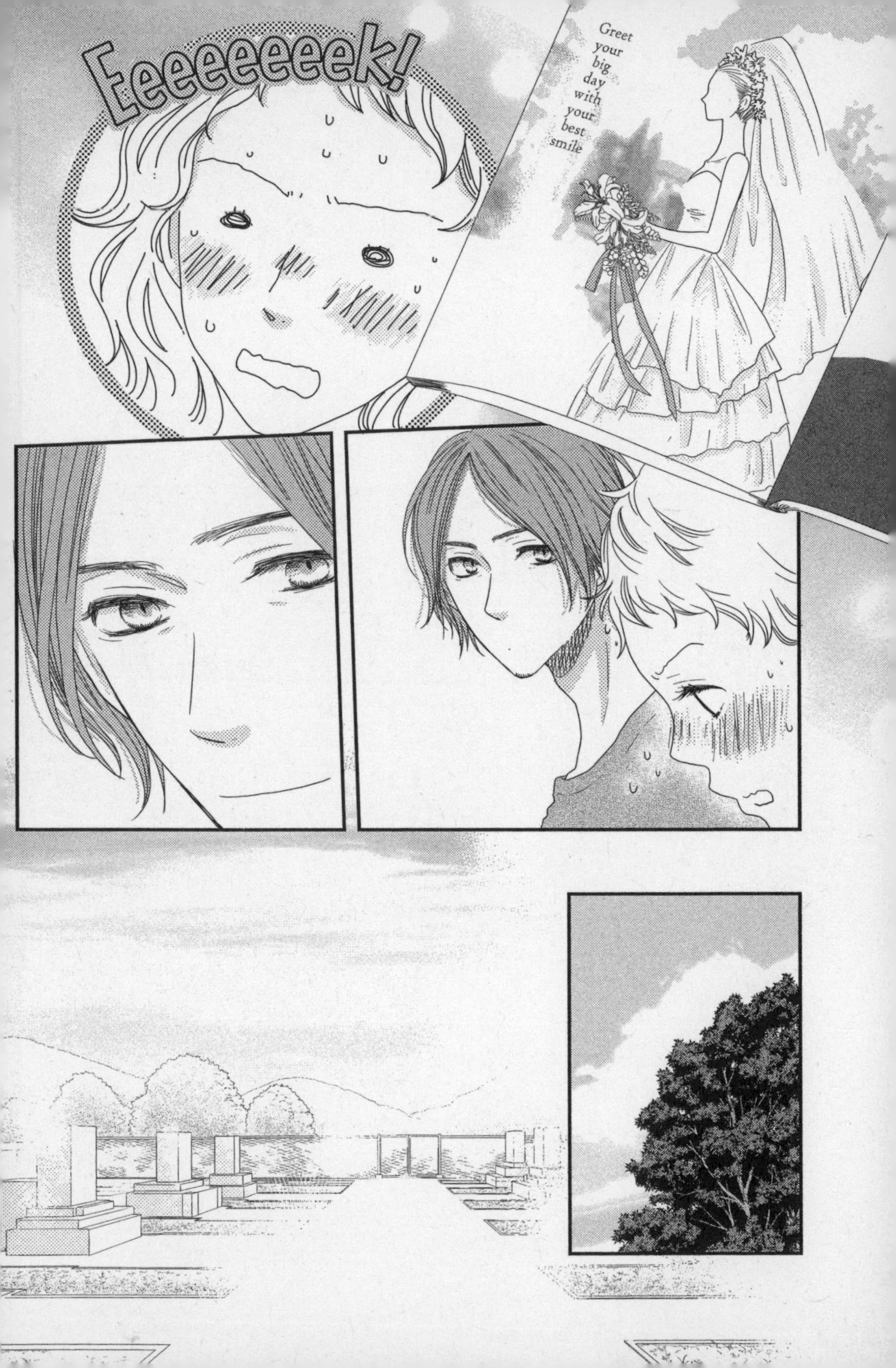
Greet your big day with your best smile
Eeeeeeeek!

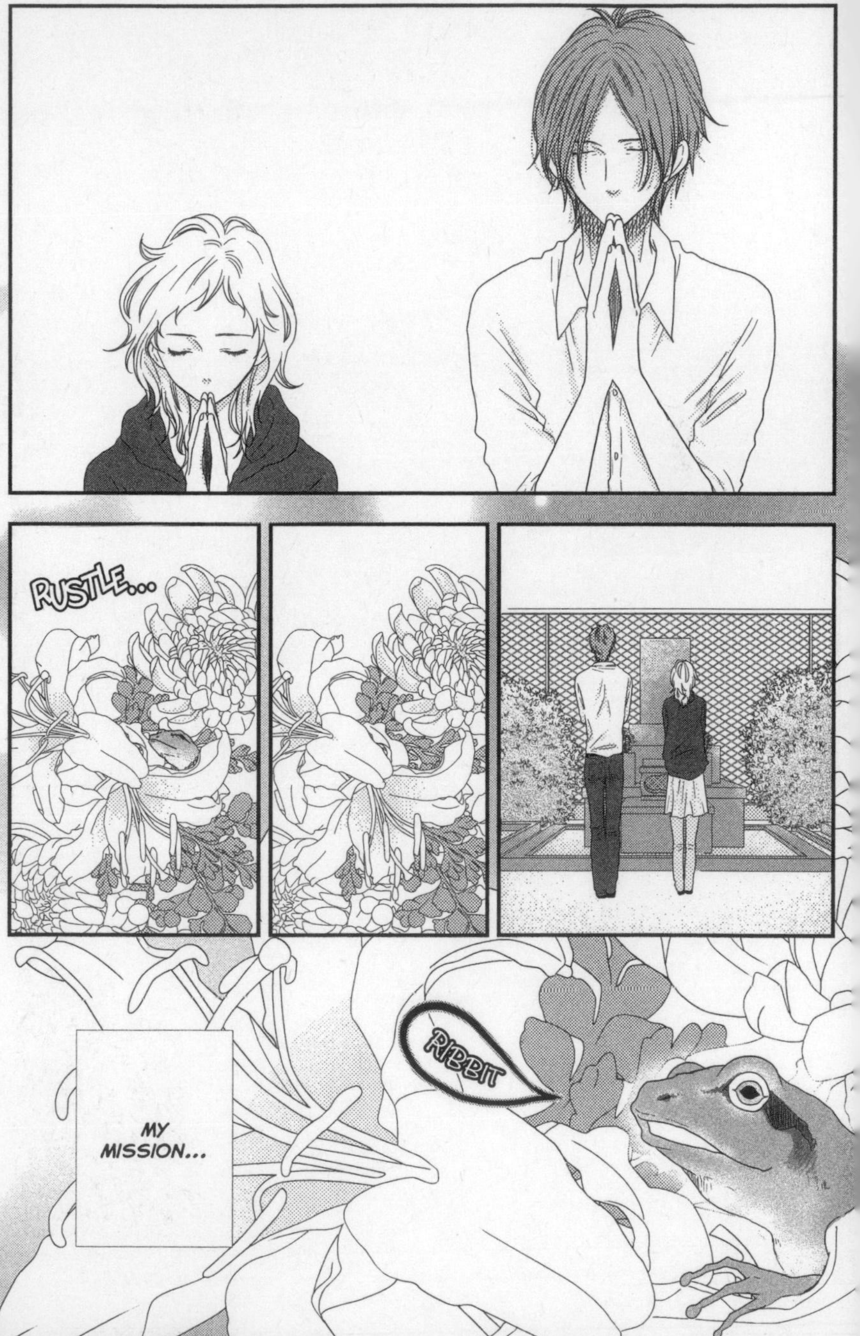
RUSTLE...
RIBBIT
MY MISSION...

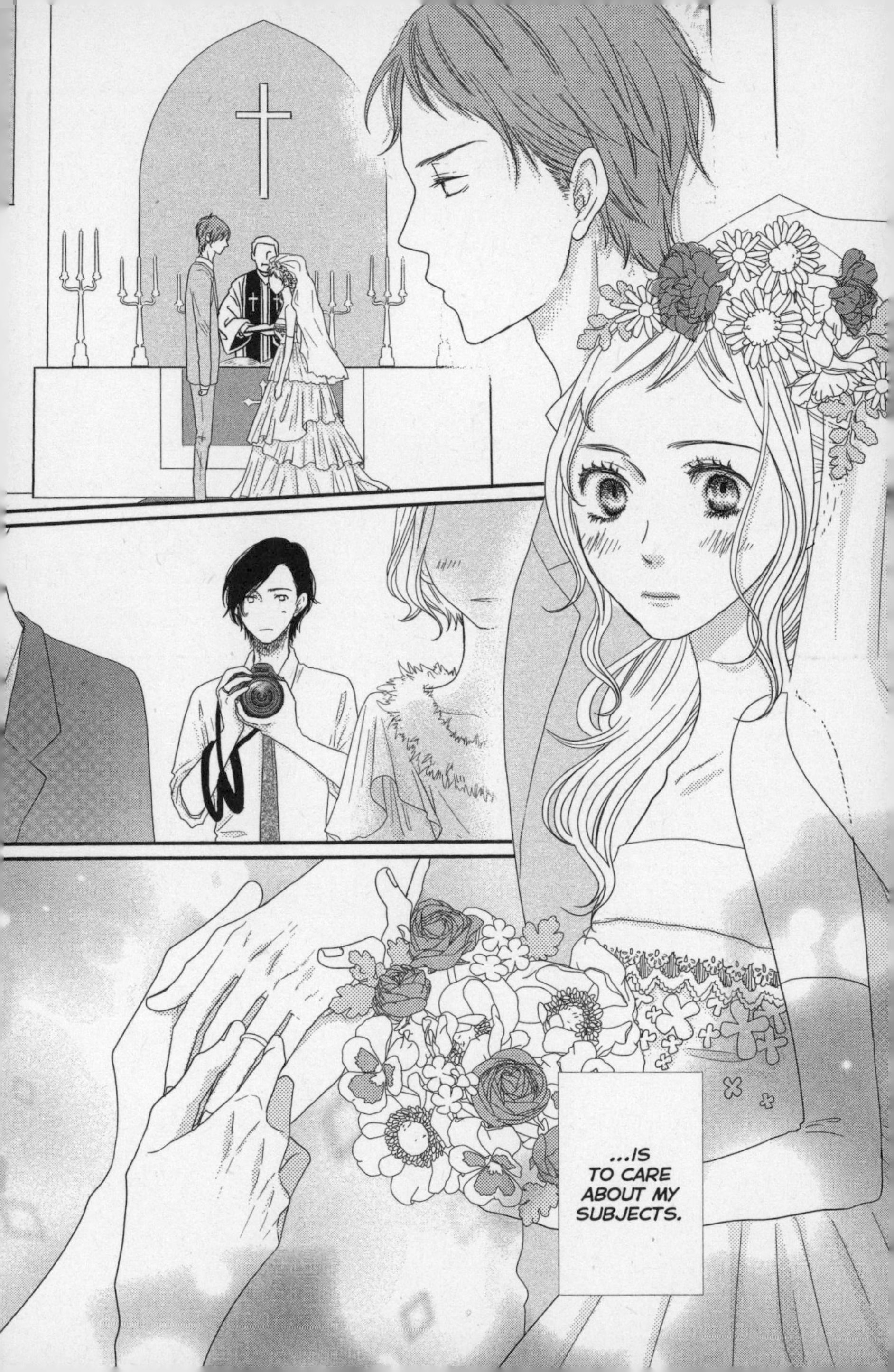
...IS
TO CARE
ABOUT MY
SUBJECTS.

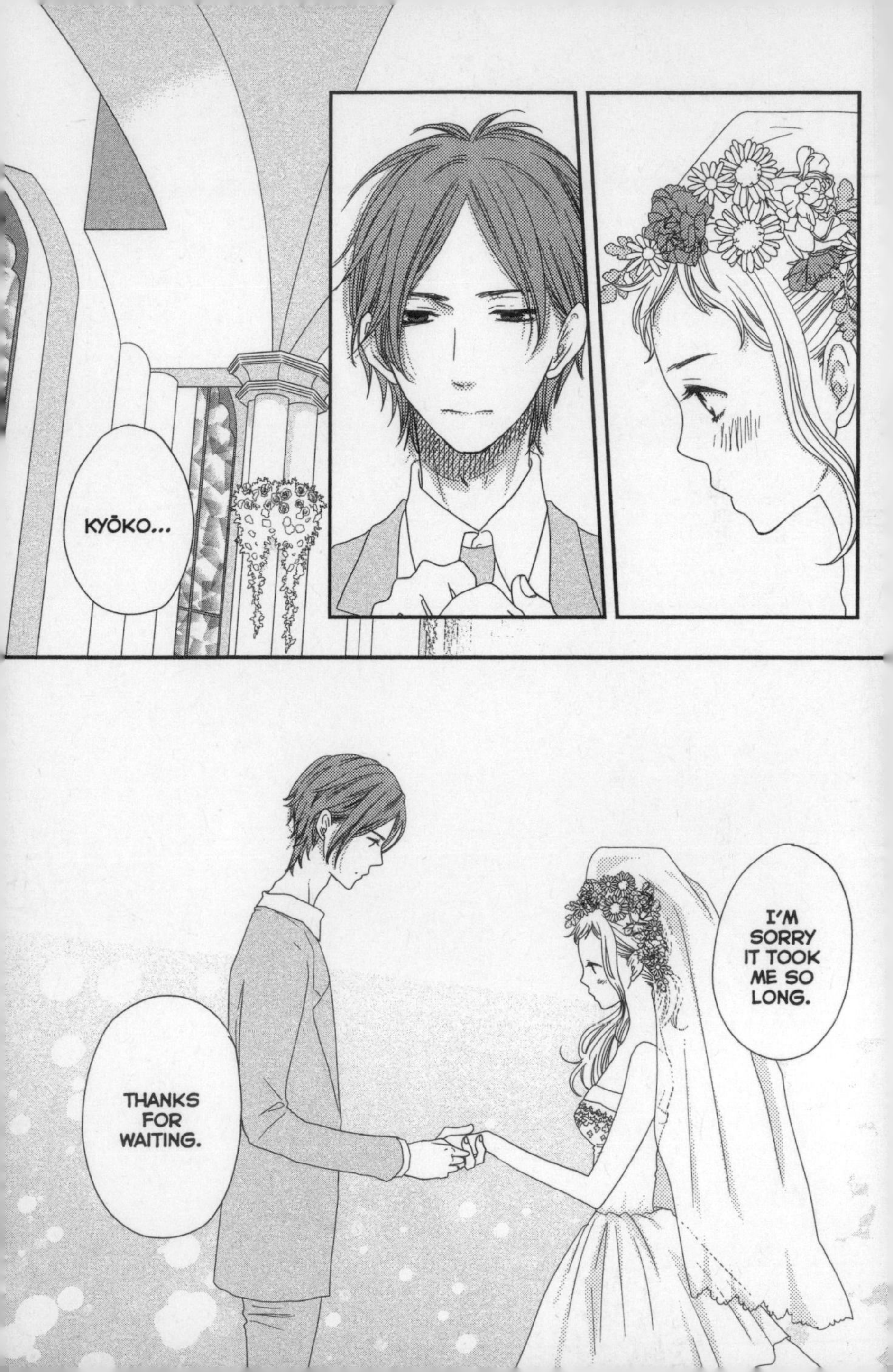
KYŌKO...
I'M SORRY IT TOOK ME SO LONG.
THANKS FOR WAITING.

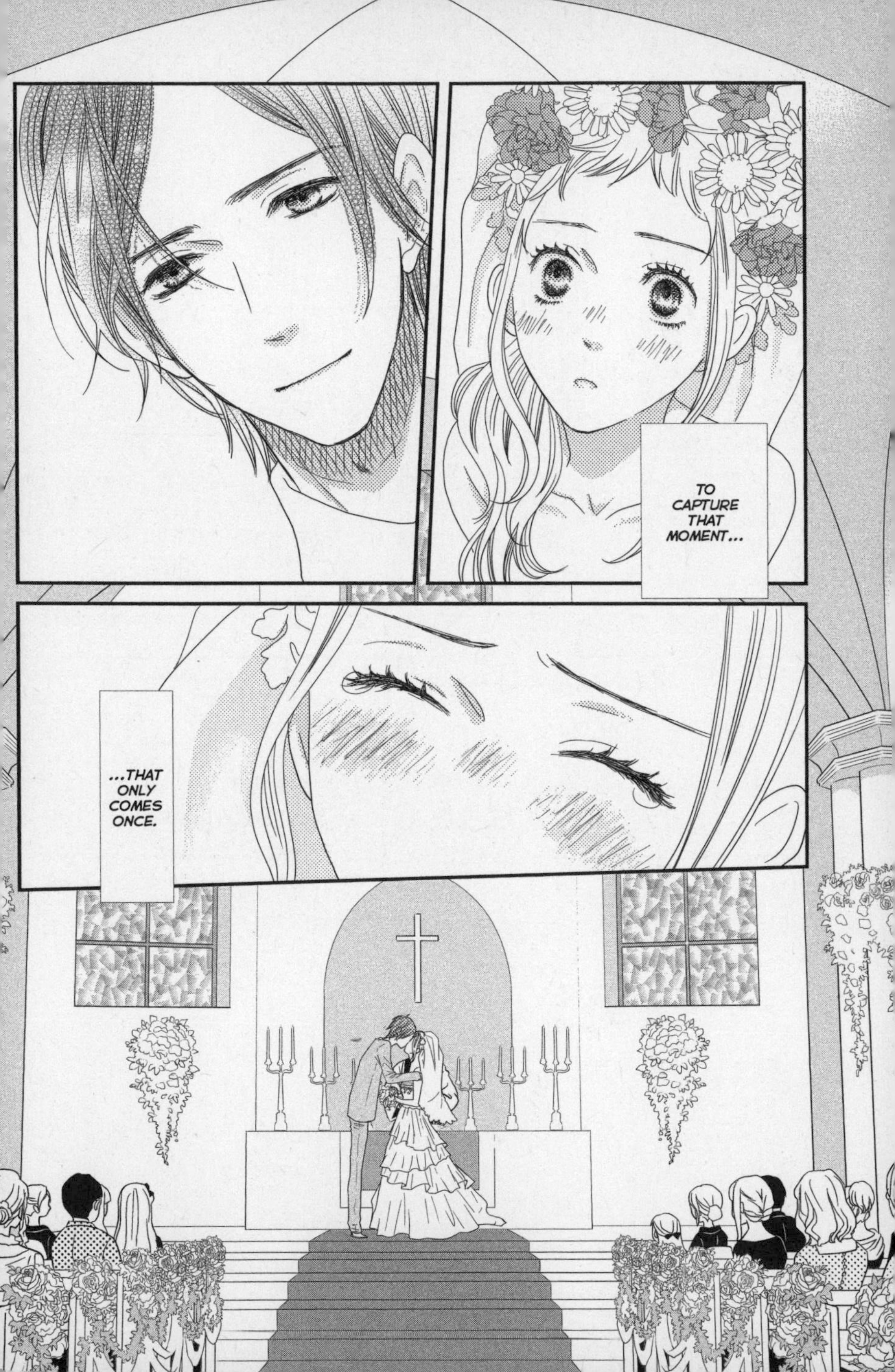
TO CAPTURE THAT MOMENT...
...THAT ONLY COMES ONCE.

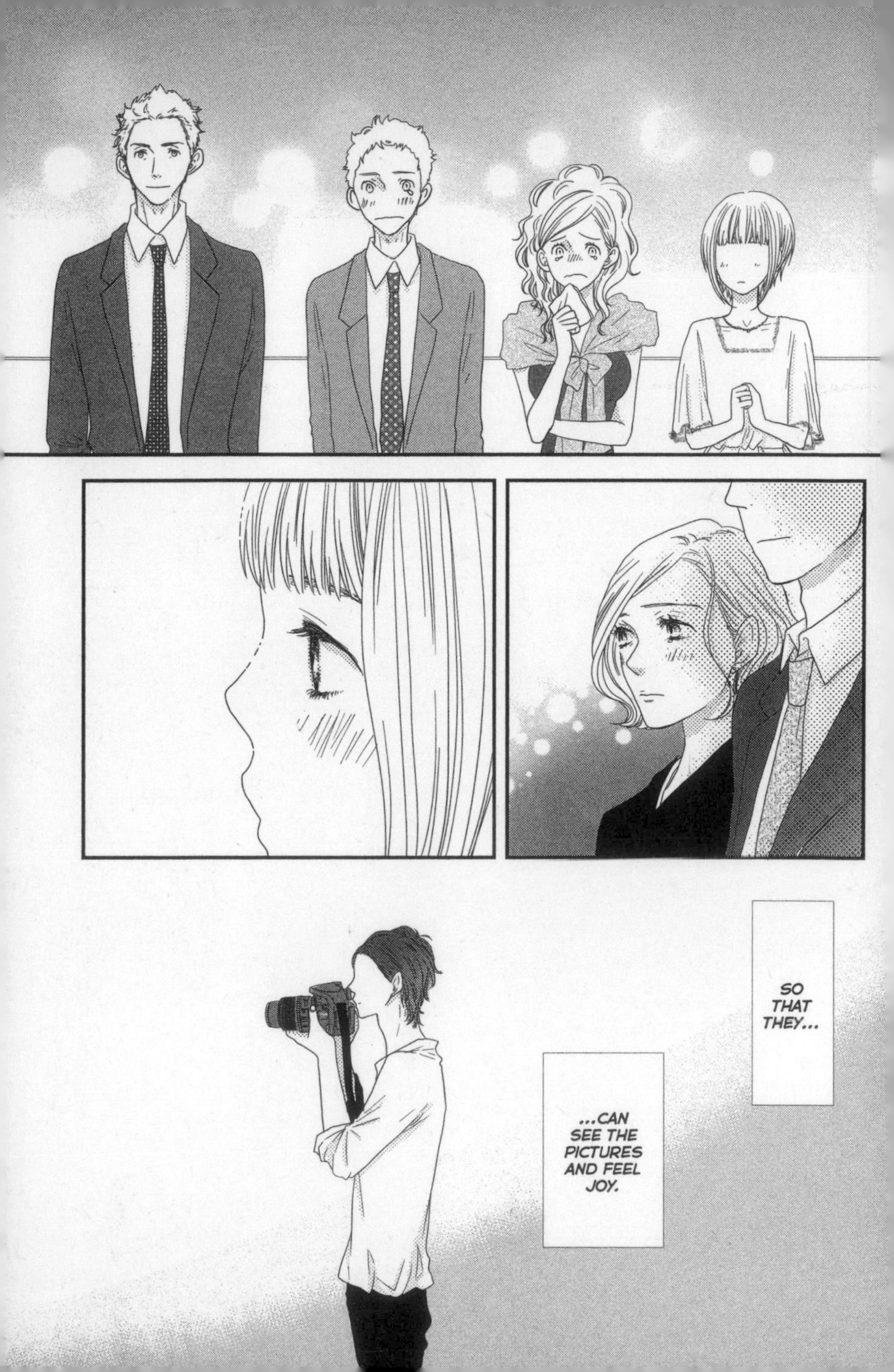
SO THAT THEY...
...CAN SEE THE PICTURES AND FEEL JOY.

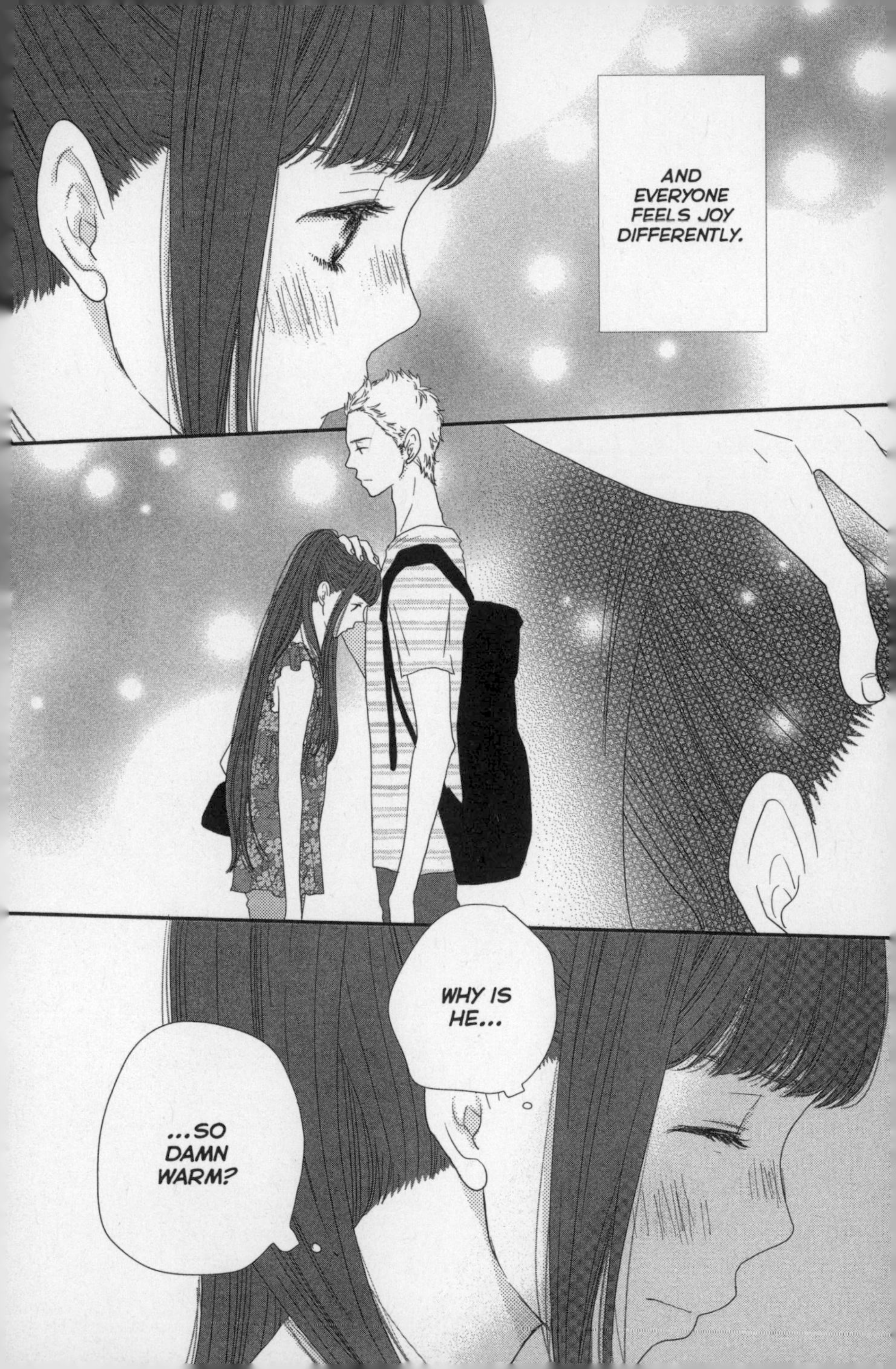
AND EVERYONE FEELS JOY DIFFERENTLY.
WHY IS HE...
...SO DAMN WARM?

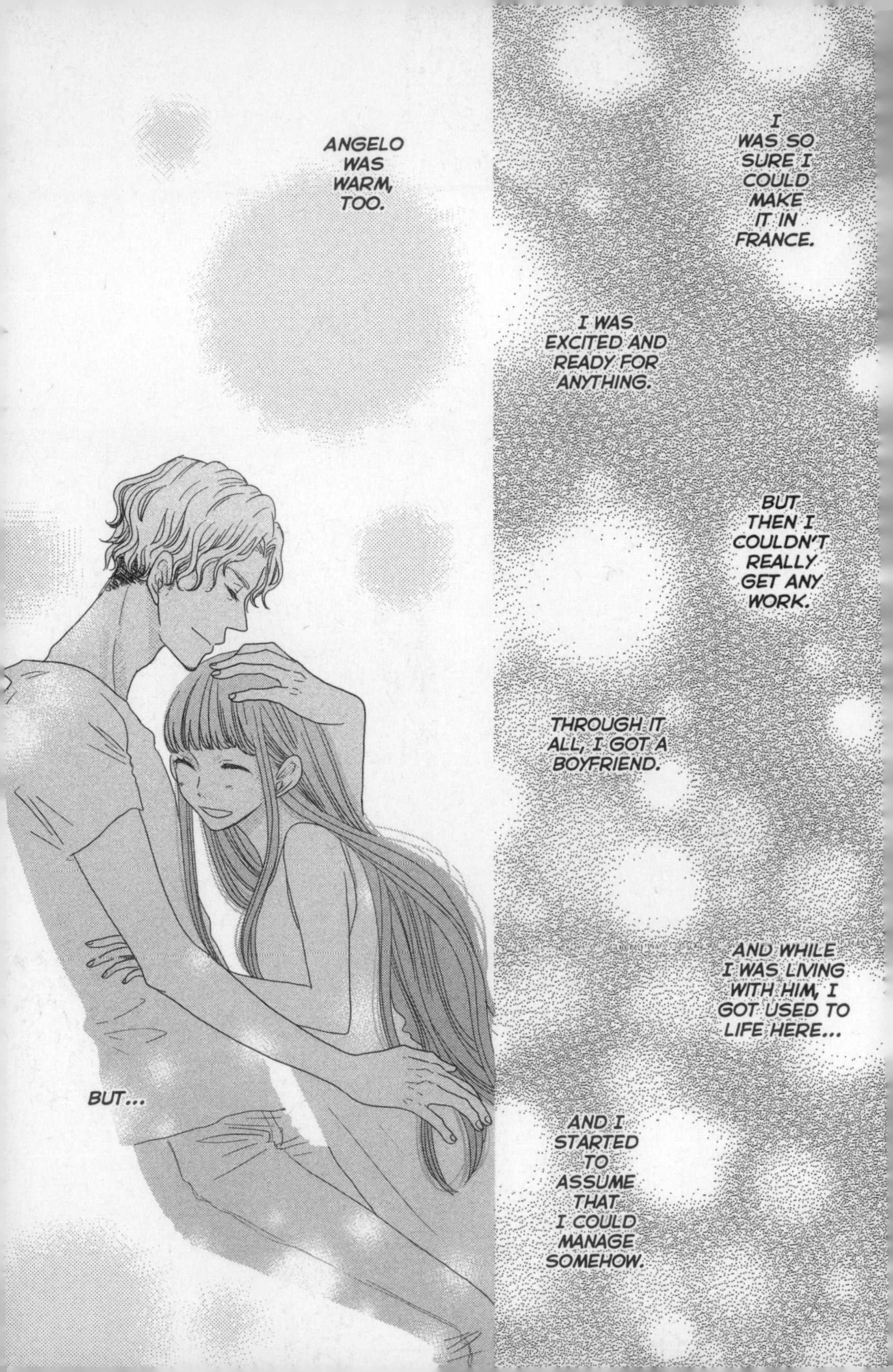
I WAS SO SURE I COULD MAKE IT IN FRANCE.
I WAS EXCITED AND READY FOR ANYTHING.
BUT THEN I COULDN'T REALLY GET ANY WORK.
THROUGH IT ALL, I GOT A BOYFRIEND.
AND WHILE I WAS LIVING WITH HIM, I GOT USED TO LIFE HERE...
AND I STARTED TO ASSUME THAT I COULD MANAGE SOMEHOW.
ANGELO WAS WARM, TOO.
BUT...

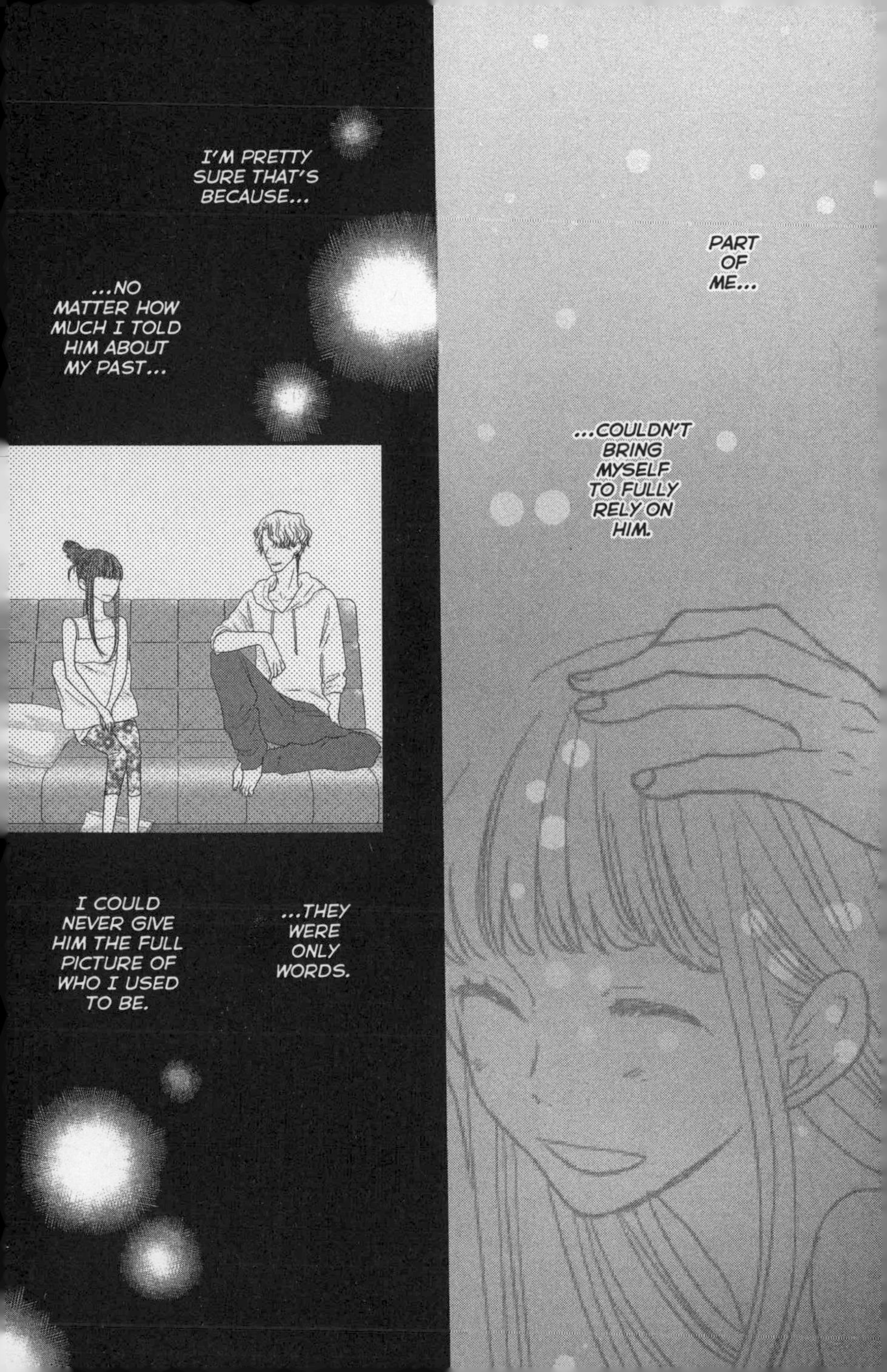
PART OF ME...
...COULDN'T BRING MYSELF TO FULLY RELY ON HIM.
I'M PRETTY SURE THAT'S BECAUSE...
...NO MATTER HOW MUCH I TOLD HIM ABOUT MY PAST...
...THEY WERE ONLY WORDS.
I COULD NEVER GIVE HIM THE FULL PICTURE OF WHO I USED TO BE.

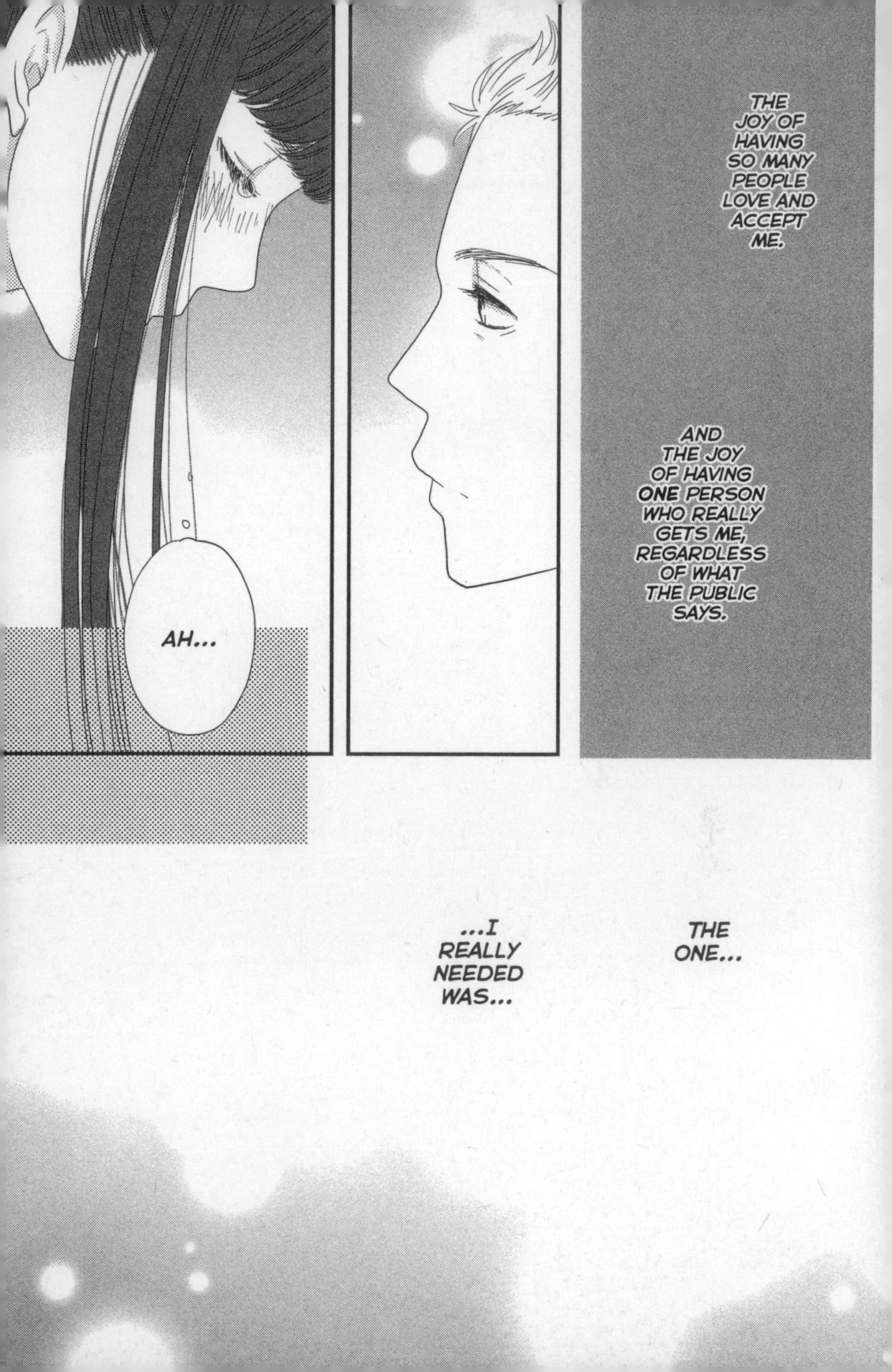
THE JOY OF HAVING SO MANY PEOPLE LOVE AND ACCEPT ME.
AND THE JOY OF HAVING ONE PERSON WHO REALLY GETS ME, REGARDLESS OF WHAT THE PUBLIC SAYS.
AH...
THE ONE...
...I REALLY NEEDED WAS...

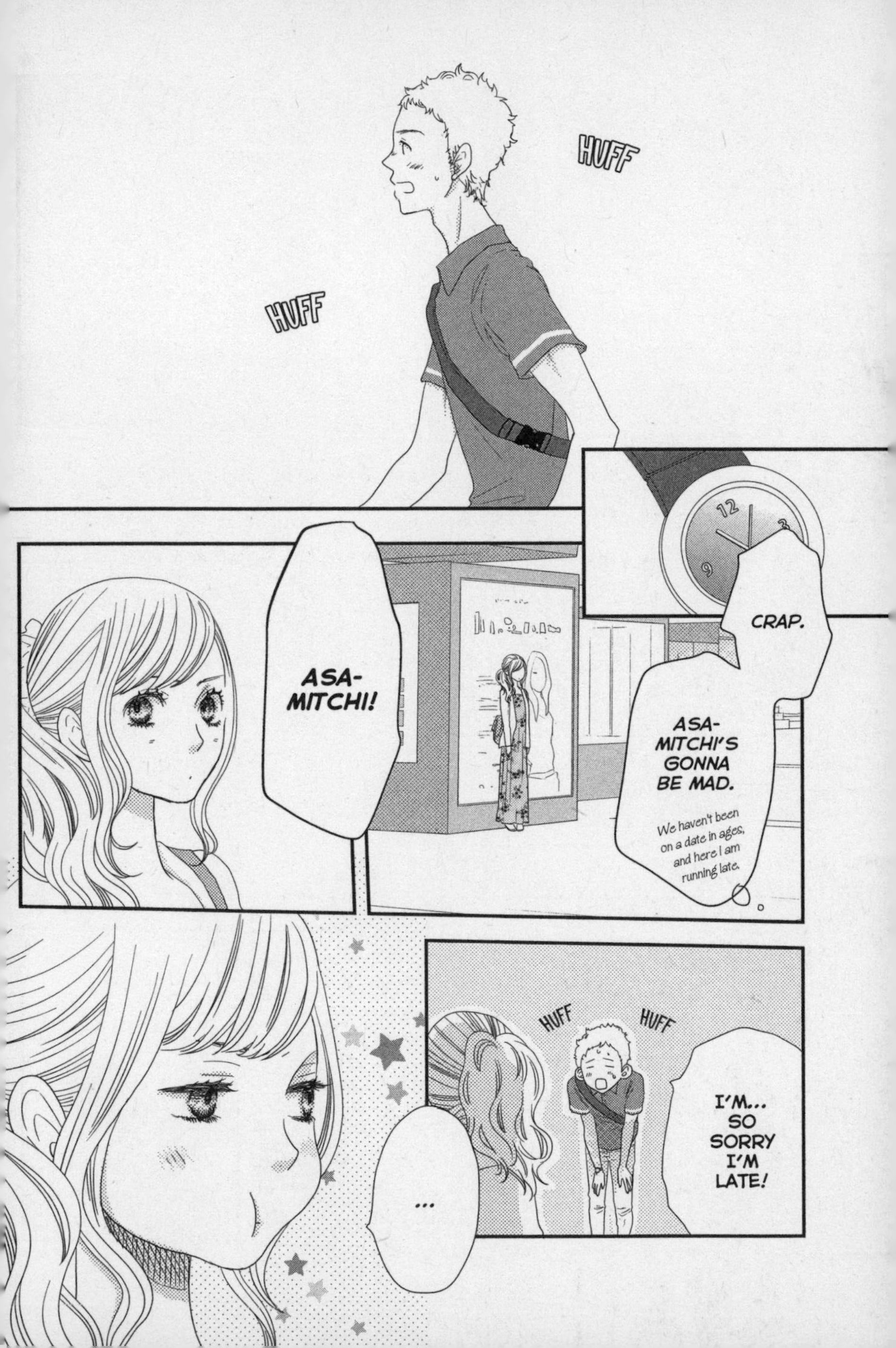
HUFF
HUFF
CRAP.
ASA-MITCHI'S GONNA BE MAD.
We haven't been on a date in ages, and here I am running late.
ASA-MITCHI!
HUFF
HUFF
I'M... SO SORRY I'M LATE!
...

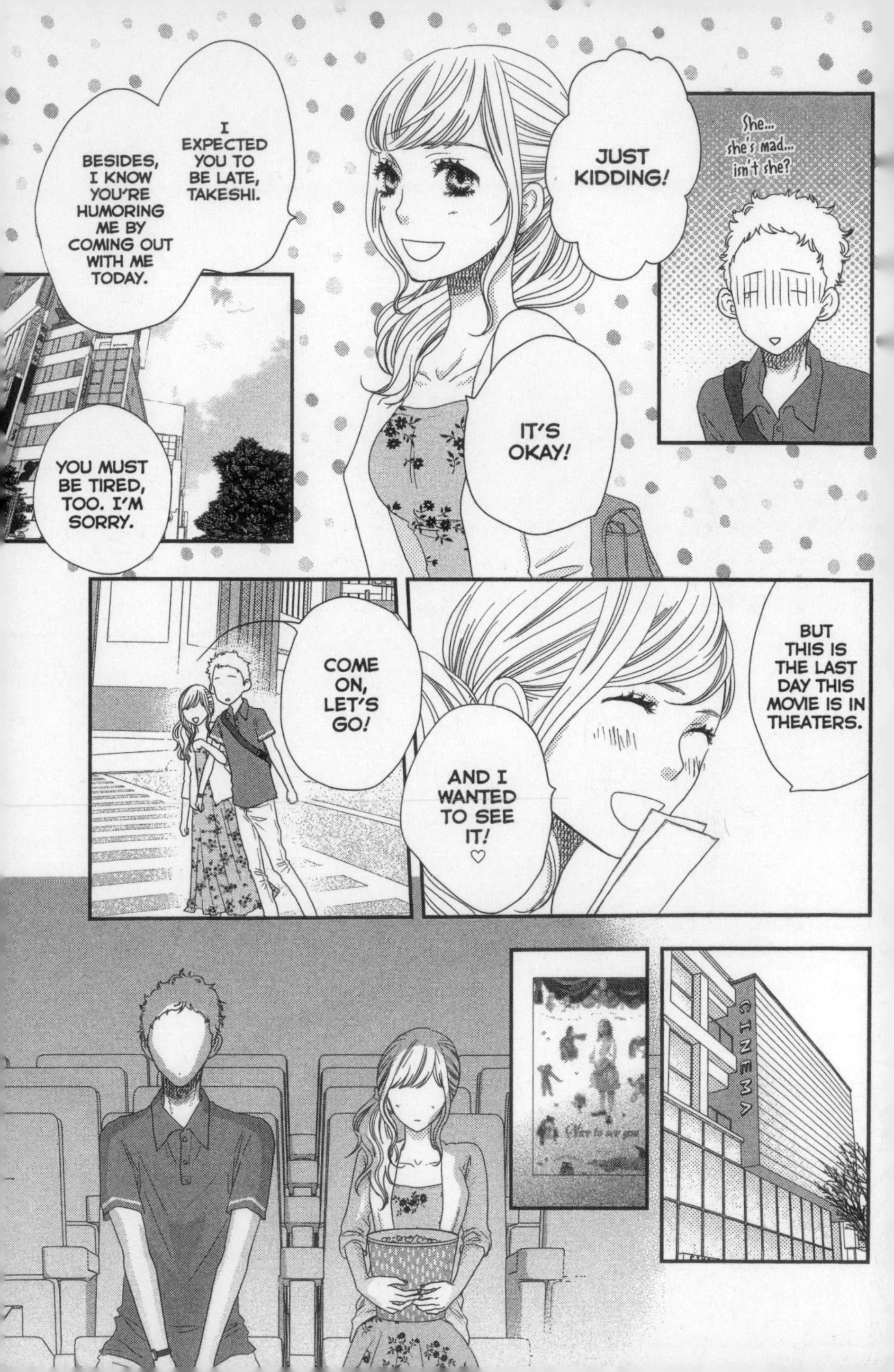
She... she's mad... isn't she?
JUST KIDDING!
I EXPECTED YOU TO BE LATE, TAKESHI.
BESIDES, I KNOW YOU'RE HUMORING ME BY COMING OUT WITH ME TODAY.
IT'S OKAY!
YOU MUST BE TIRED, TOO. I'M SORRY.
BUT THIS IS THE LAST DAY THIS MOVIE IS IN THEATERS.
AND I WANTED TO SEE IT! ♡
COME ON, LET'S GO!
CINEMA

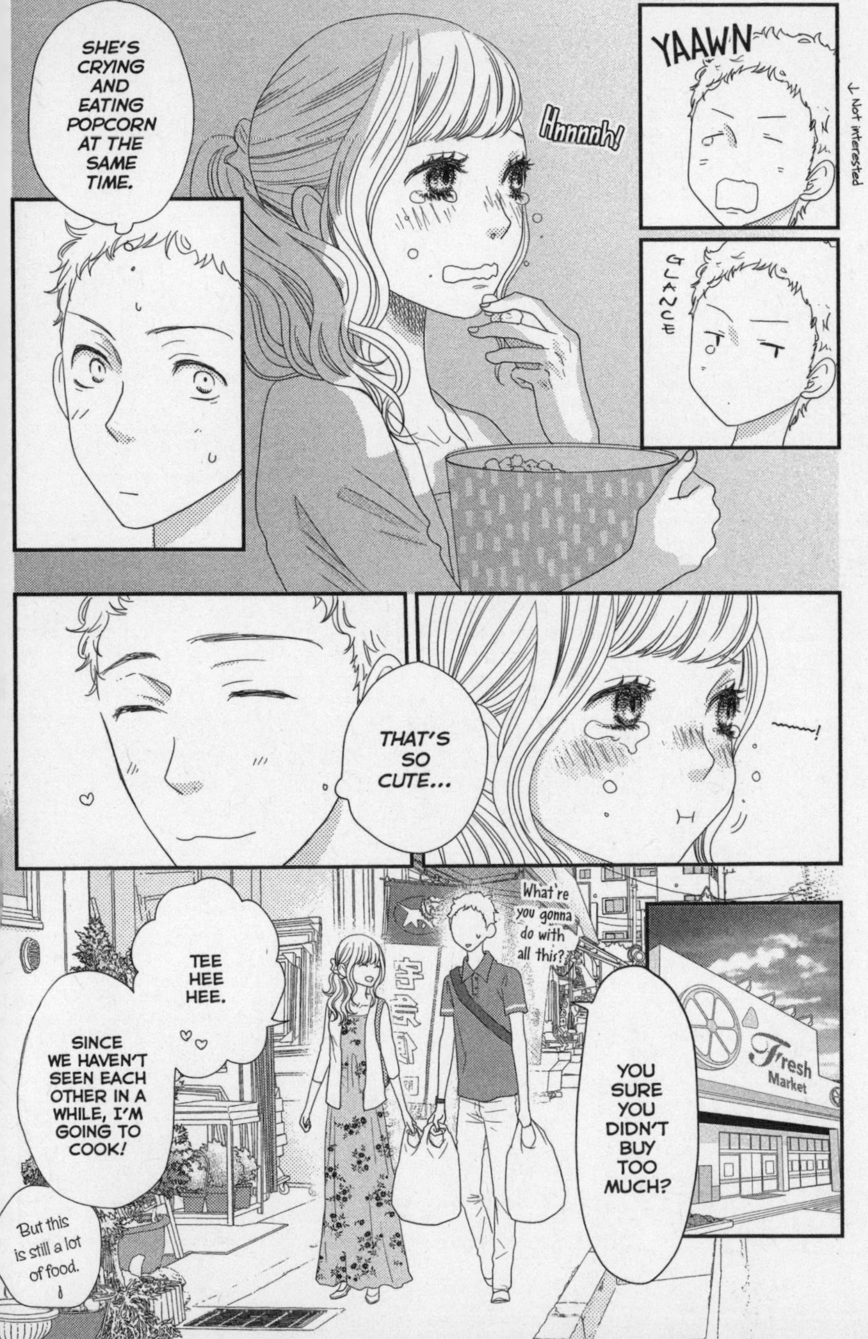
YAAWN
↓ Not interested
GLANCE
Hnnnnh!
SHE'S CRYING AND EATING POPCORN AT THE SAME TIME.
~~~~!
THAT'S SO CUTE...
What're you gonna do with all this?
YOU SURE YOU DIDN'T BUY TOO MUCH?
TEE HEE HEE.
SINCE WE HAVEN'T SEEN EACH OTHER IN A WHILE, I'M GOING TO COOK!
But this is still a lot of food.
Fresh Market
~~~~

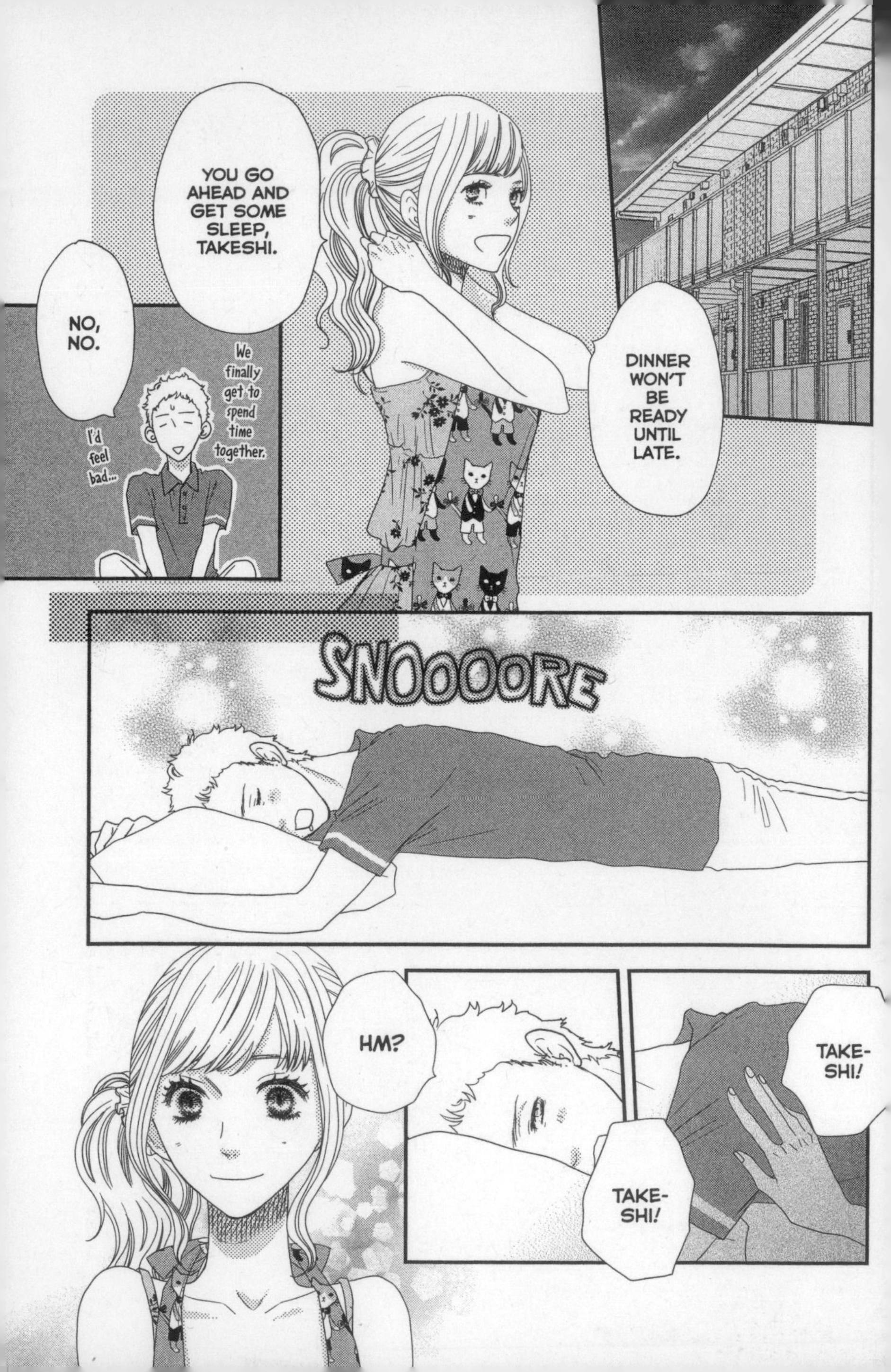
DINNER WON'T BE READY UNTIL LATE.
YOU GO AHEAD AND GET SOME SLEEP, TAKESHI.
NO, NO.
We finally get to spend time together.
I'd feel bad...
SNOOOORE
TAKE-SHI!
TAKE-SHI!
HM?

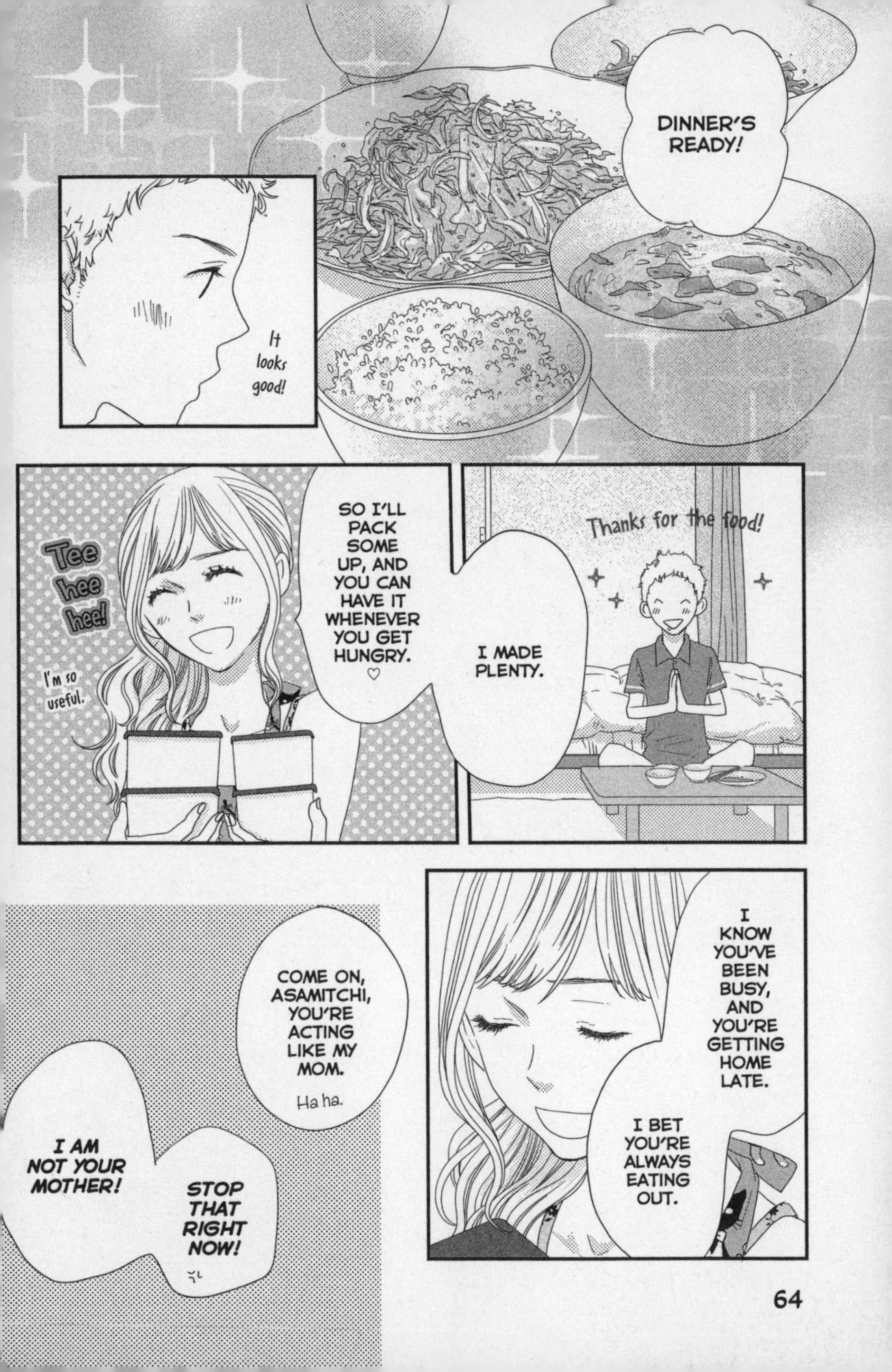
DINNER'S READY!
It looks good!
Thanks for the food!
I MADE PLENTY.
SO I'LL PACK SOME UP, AND YOU CAN HAVE IT WHENEVER YOU GET HUNGRY. ♡
Tee hee hee!
I'm so useful.
I KNOW YOU'VE BEEN BUSY, AND YOU'RE GETTING HOME LATE.
I BET YOU'RE ALWAYS EATING OUT.
COME ON, ASAMITCHI, YOU'RE ACTING LIKE MY MOM.
Ha ha.
I AM NOT YOUR MOTHER!
STOP THAT RIGHT NOW!

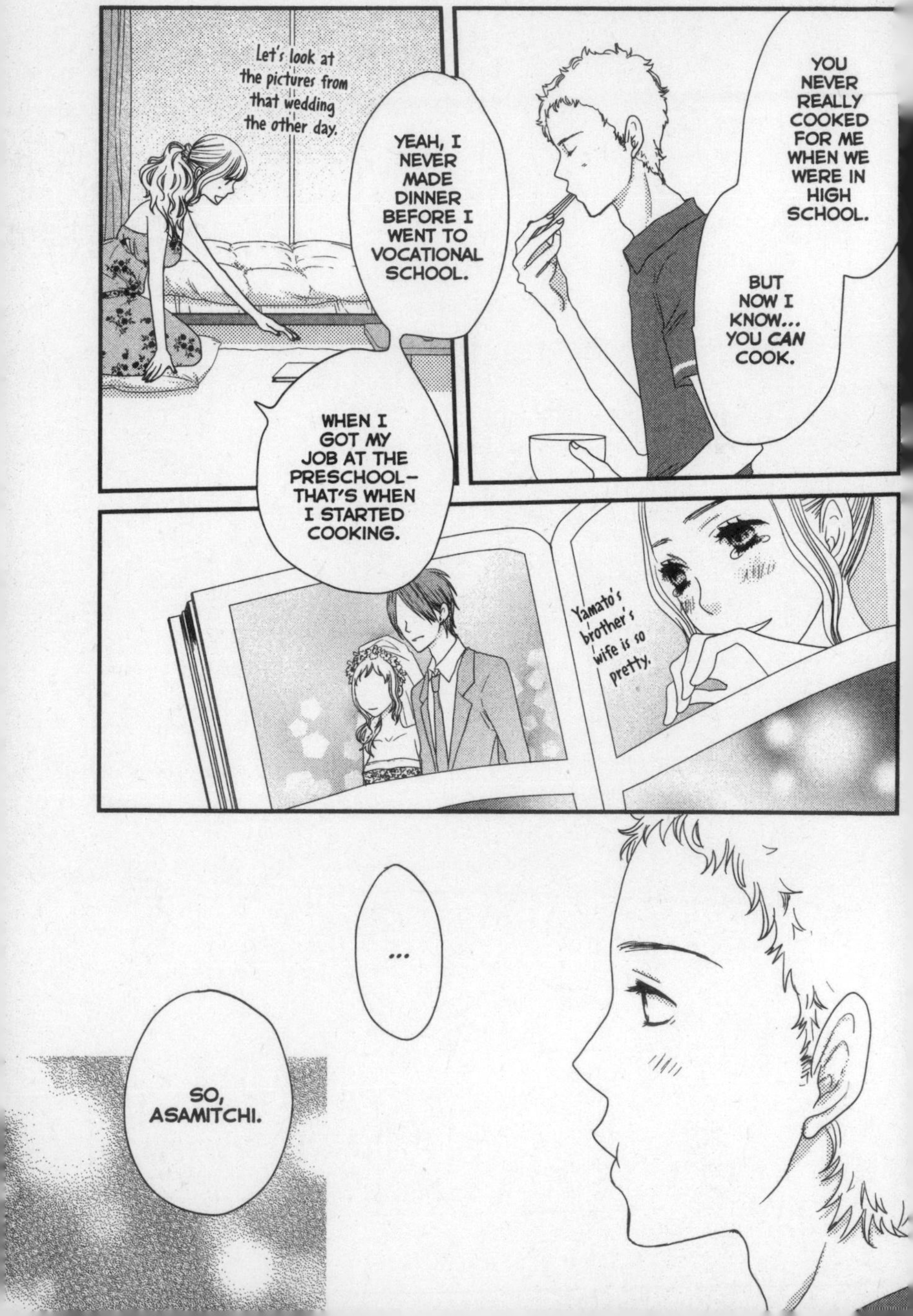
YOU NEVER REALLY COOKED FOR ME WHEN WE WERE IN HIGH SCHOOL.
BUT NOW I KNOW... YOU CAN COOK.
YEAH, I NEVER MADE DINNER BEFORE I WENT TO VOCATIONAL SCHOOL.
WHEN I GOT MY JOB AT THE PRESCHOOL— THAT'S WHEN I STARTED COOKING.
Let's look at the pictures from that wedding the other day.
Yamato's brother's wife is so pretty.
...
SO, ASAMITCHI.

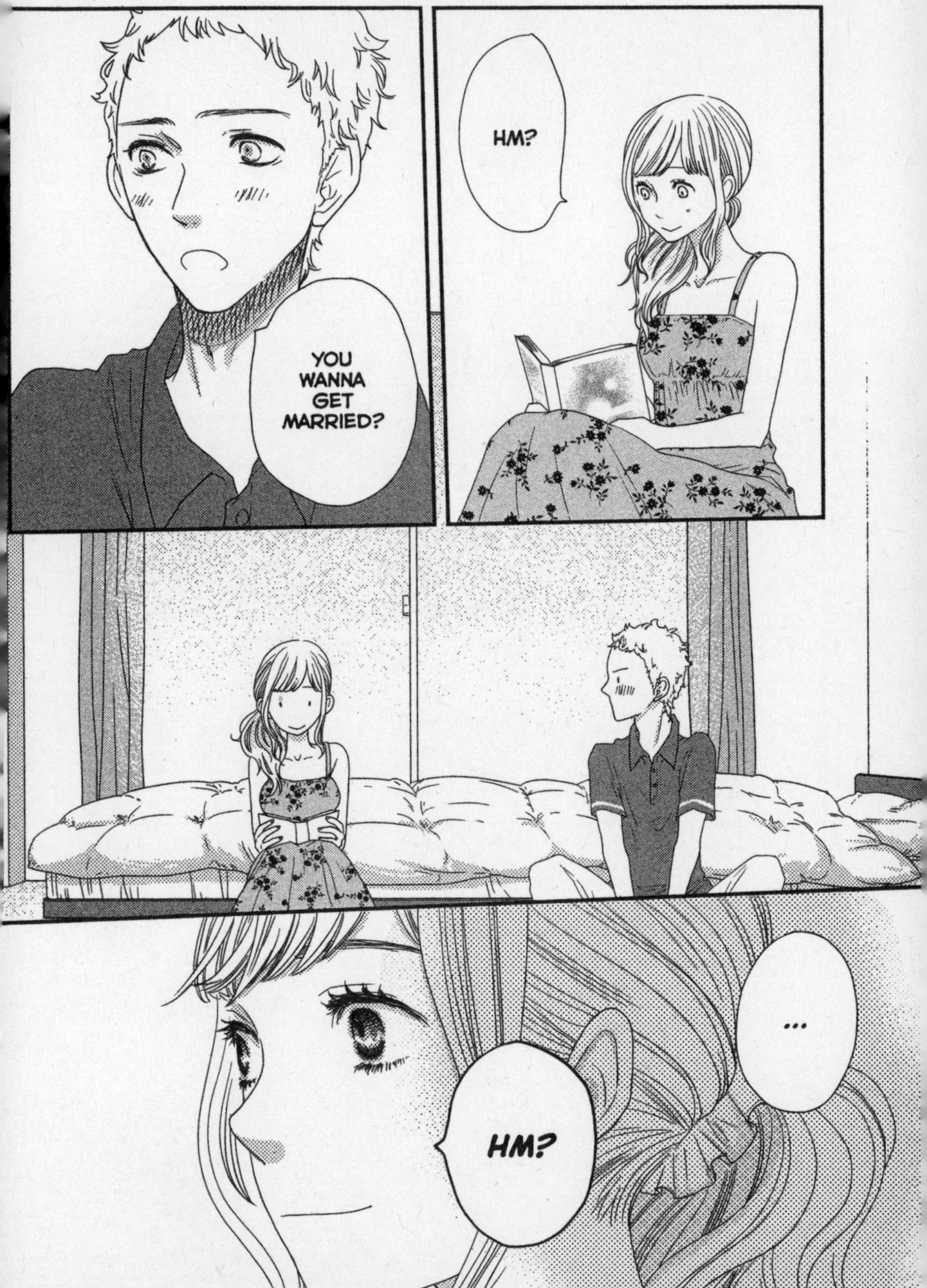
HM?
YOU WANNA GET MARRIED?
...
HM?

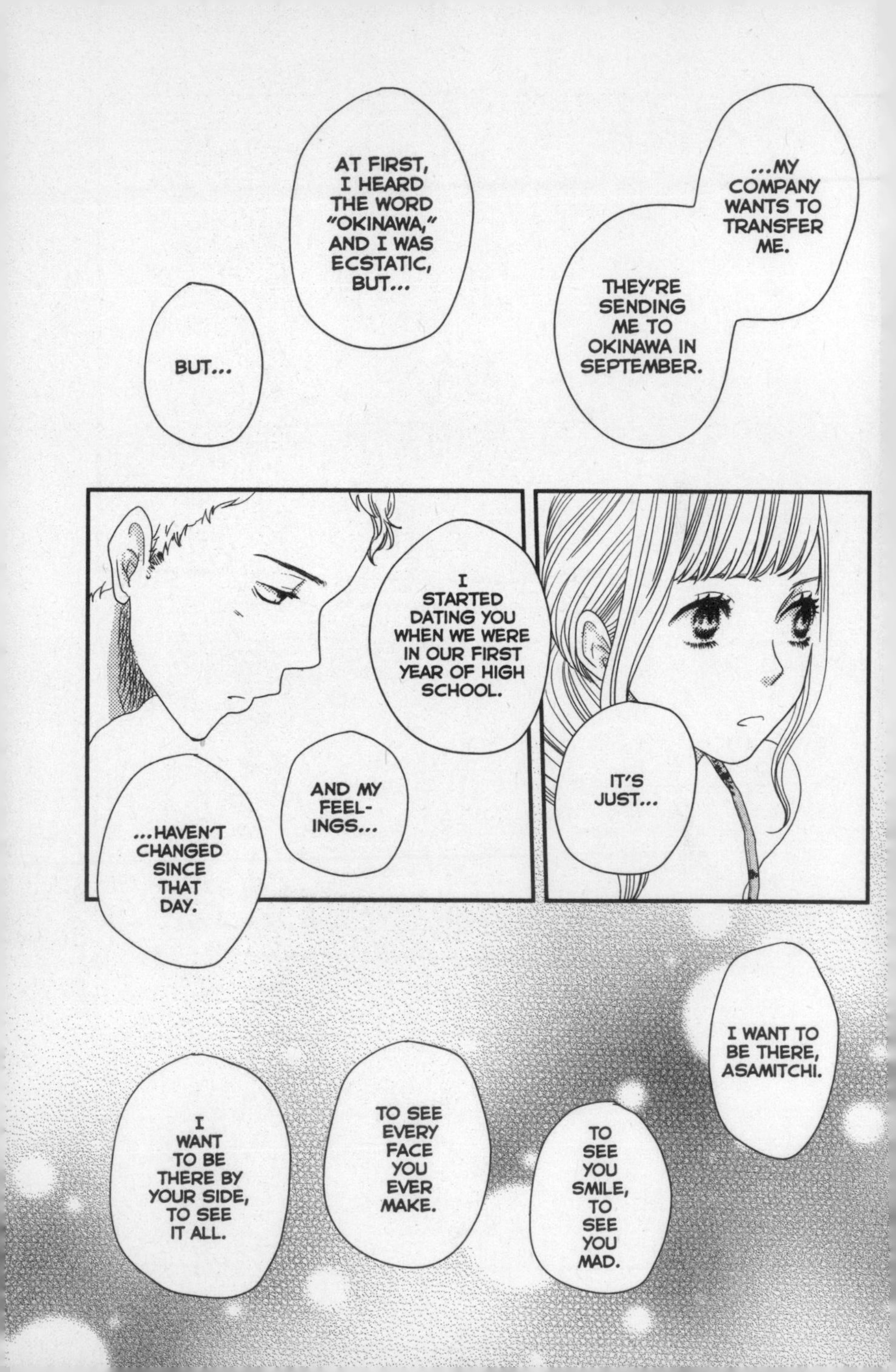
...MY COMPANY WANTS TO TRANSFER ME.
THEY'RE SENDING ME TO OKINAWA IN SEPTEMBER.
AT FIRST, I HEARD THE WORD "OKINAWA," AND I WAS ECSTATIC, BUT...
BUT...
IT'S JUST...
I STARTED DATING YOU WHEN WE WERE IN OUR FIRST YEAR OF HIGH SCHOOL.
AND MY FEEL-INGS...
...HAVEN'T CHANGED SINCE THAT DAY.
I WANT TO BE THERE, ASAMITCHI.
TO SEE YOU SMILE, TO SEE YOU MAD.
TO SEE EVERY FACE YOU EVER MAKE.
I WANT TO BE THERE BY YOUR SIDE, TO SEE IT ALL.

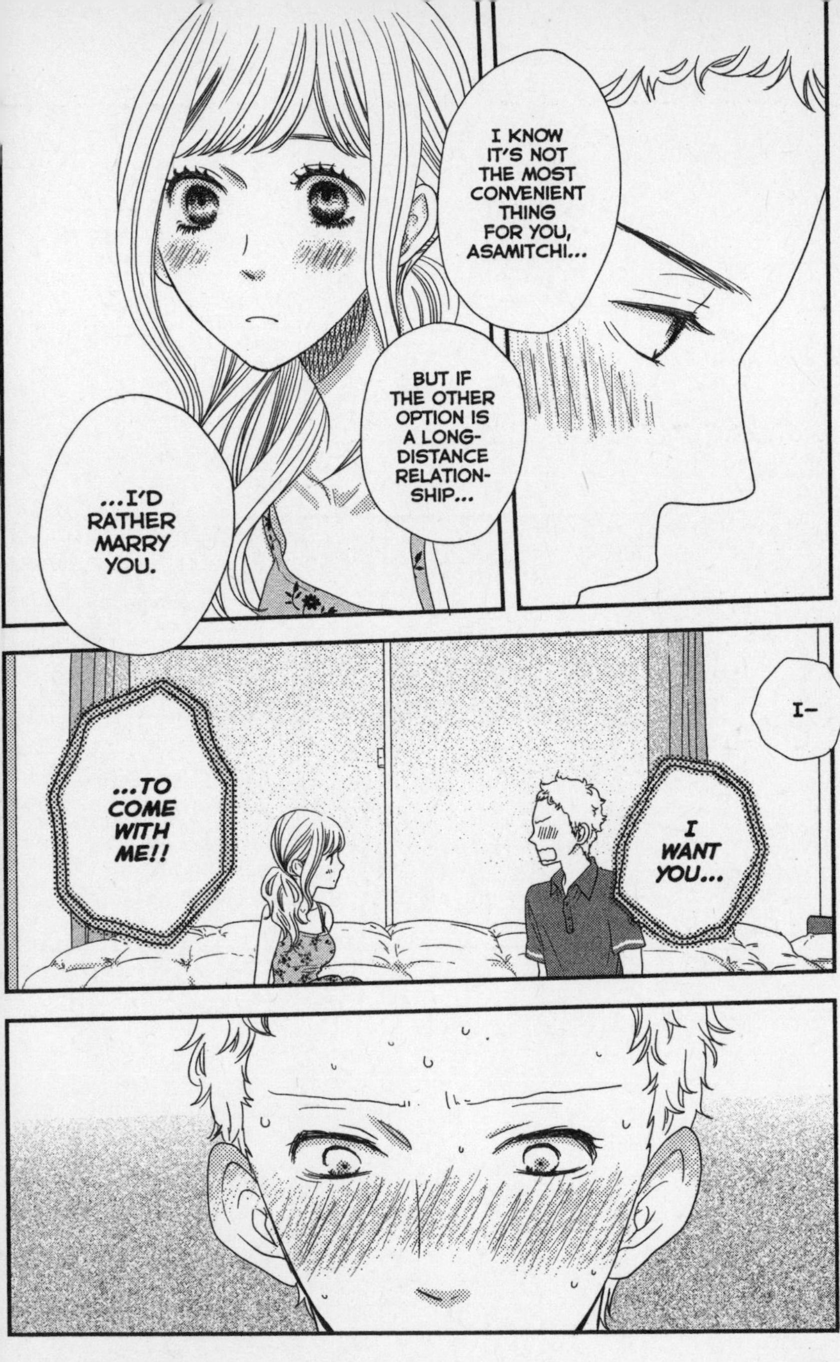
I KNOW IT'S NOT THE MOST CONVENIENT THING FOR YOU, ASAMITCHI...
BUT IF THE OTHER OPTION IS A LONG-DISTANCE RELATION-SHIP...
...I'D RATHER MARRY YOU.
I-
I WANT YOU...
...TO COME WITH ME!!

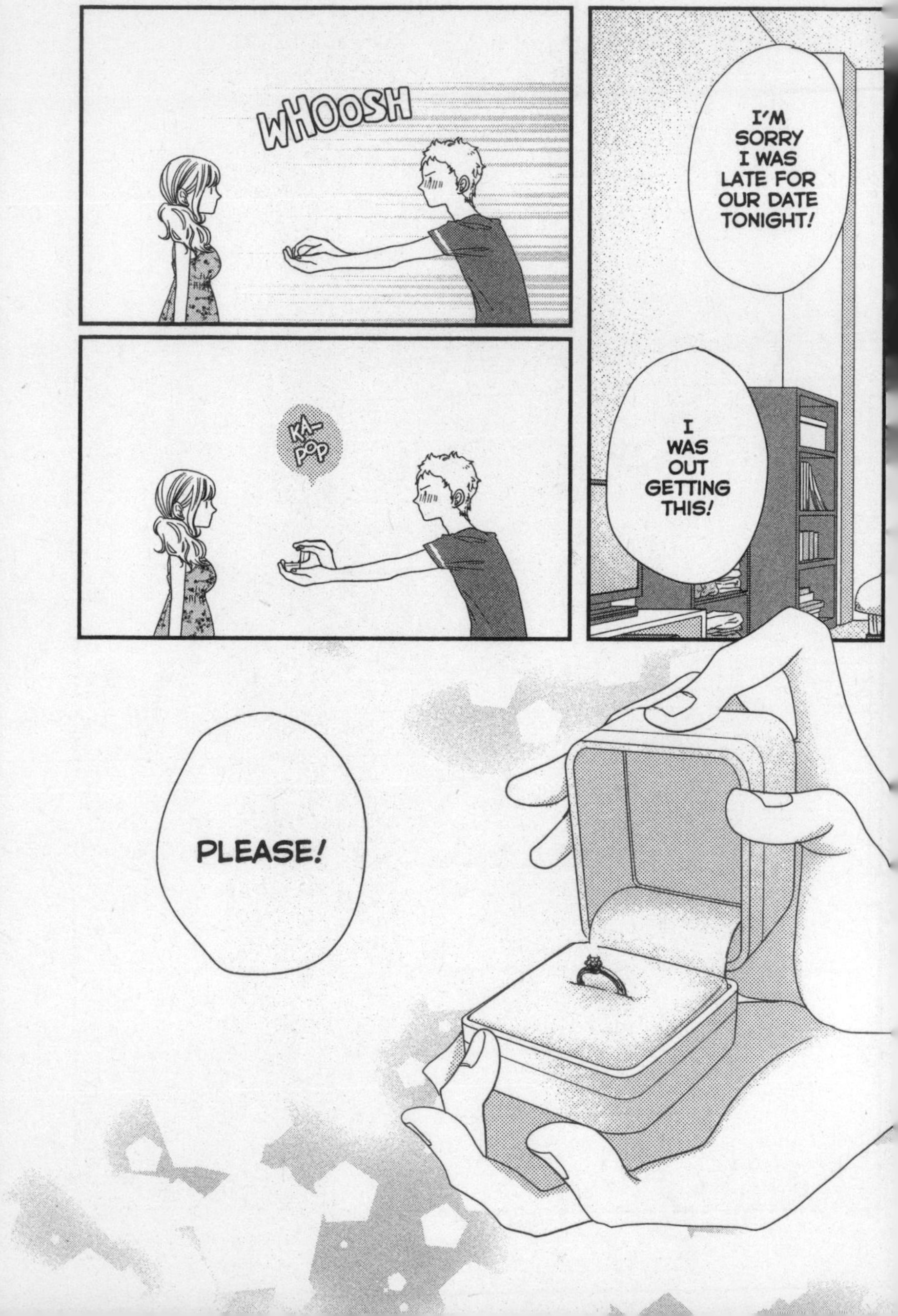
I'M SORRY I WAS LATE FOR OUR DATE TONIGHT!
I WAS OUT GETTING THIS!
WHOOSH
KA-POP
PLEASE!

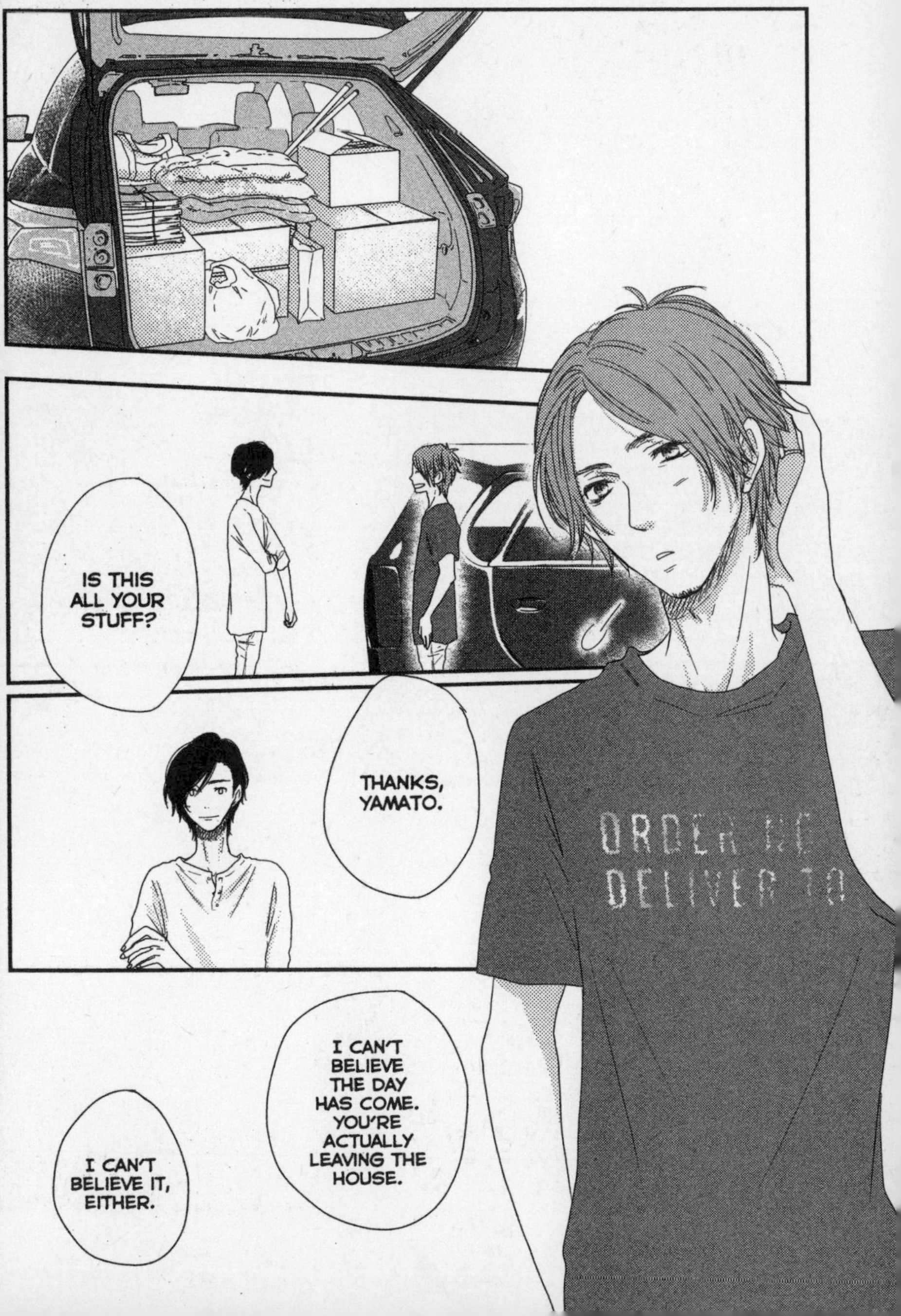
IS THIS ALL YOUR STUFF?
THANKS, YAMATO.
I CAN'T BELIEVE THE DAY HAS COME. YOU'RE ACTUALLY LEAVING THE HOUSE.
I CAN'T BELIEVE IT, EITHER.

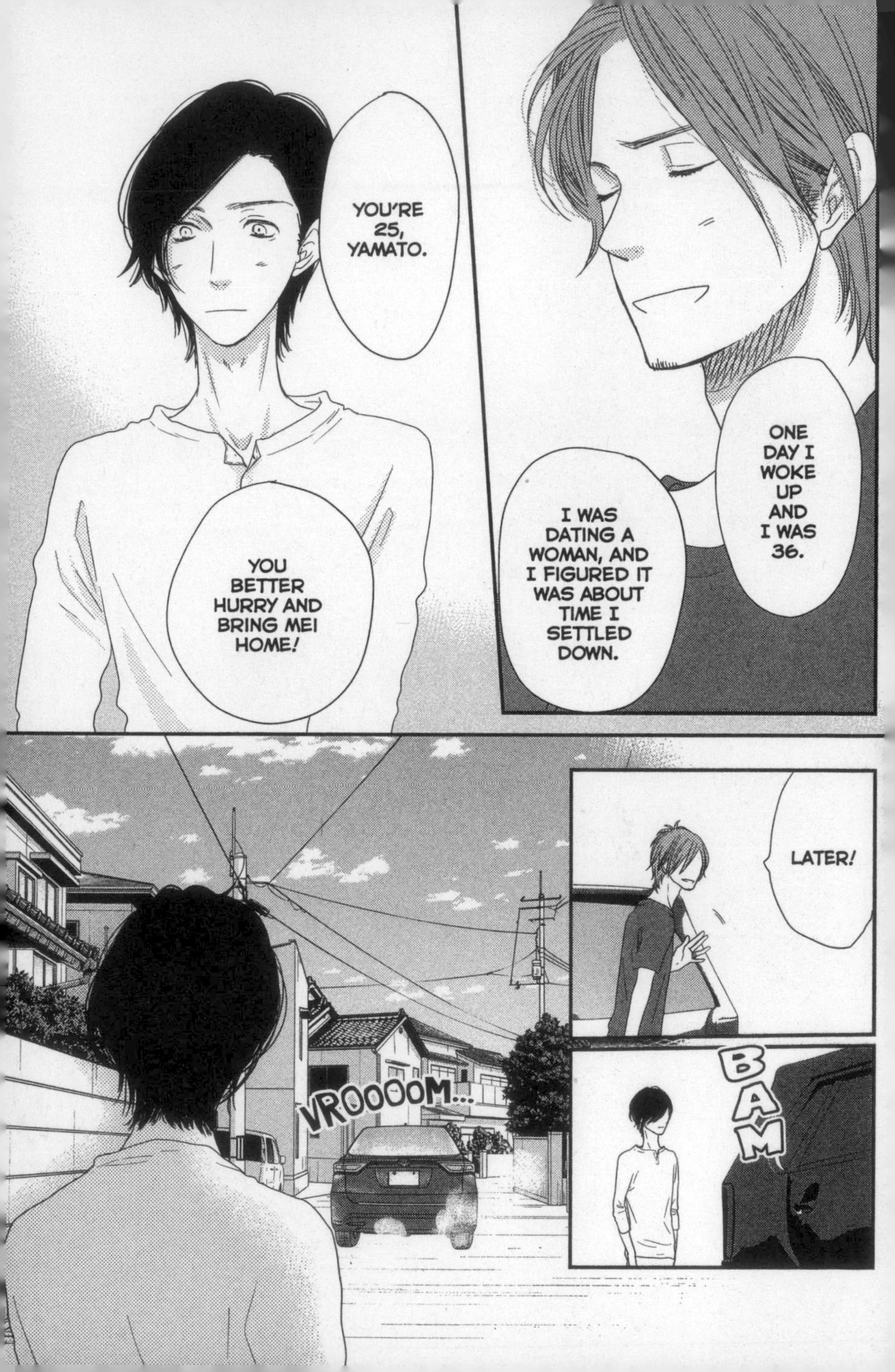
ONE DAY I WOKE UP AND I WAS 36.
I WAS DATING A WOMAN, AND I FIGURED IT WAS ABOUT TIME I SETTLED DOWN.
YOU'RE 25, YAMATO.
YOU BETTER HURRY AND BRING MEI HOME!
LATER!
BAM
VROOOOM...

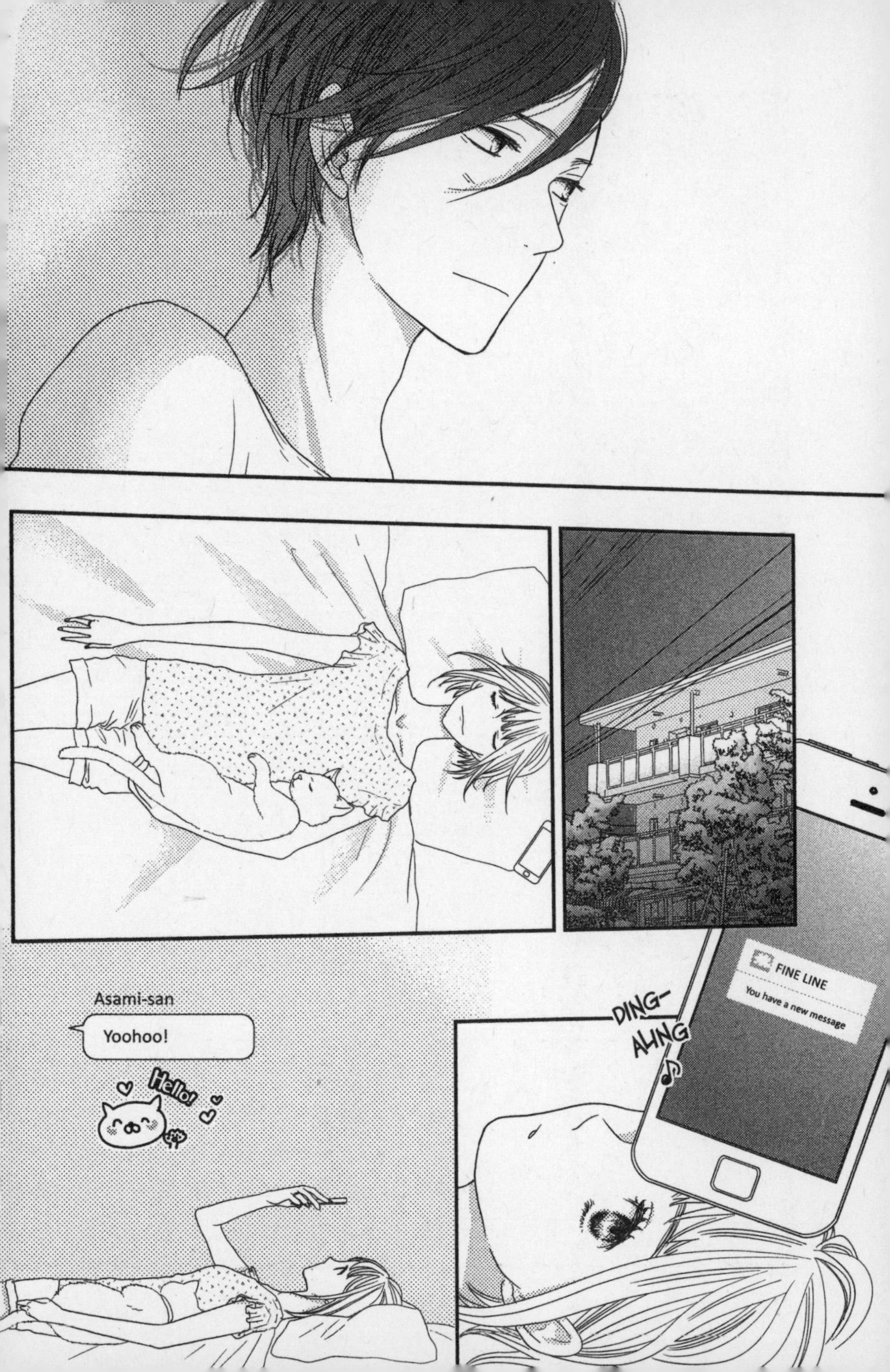

FINE LINE
You have a new message
DING-ALING
Asami-san
Yoohoo!
Hello!

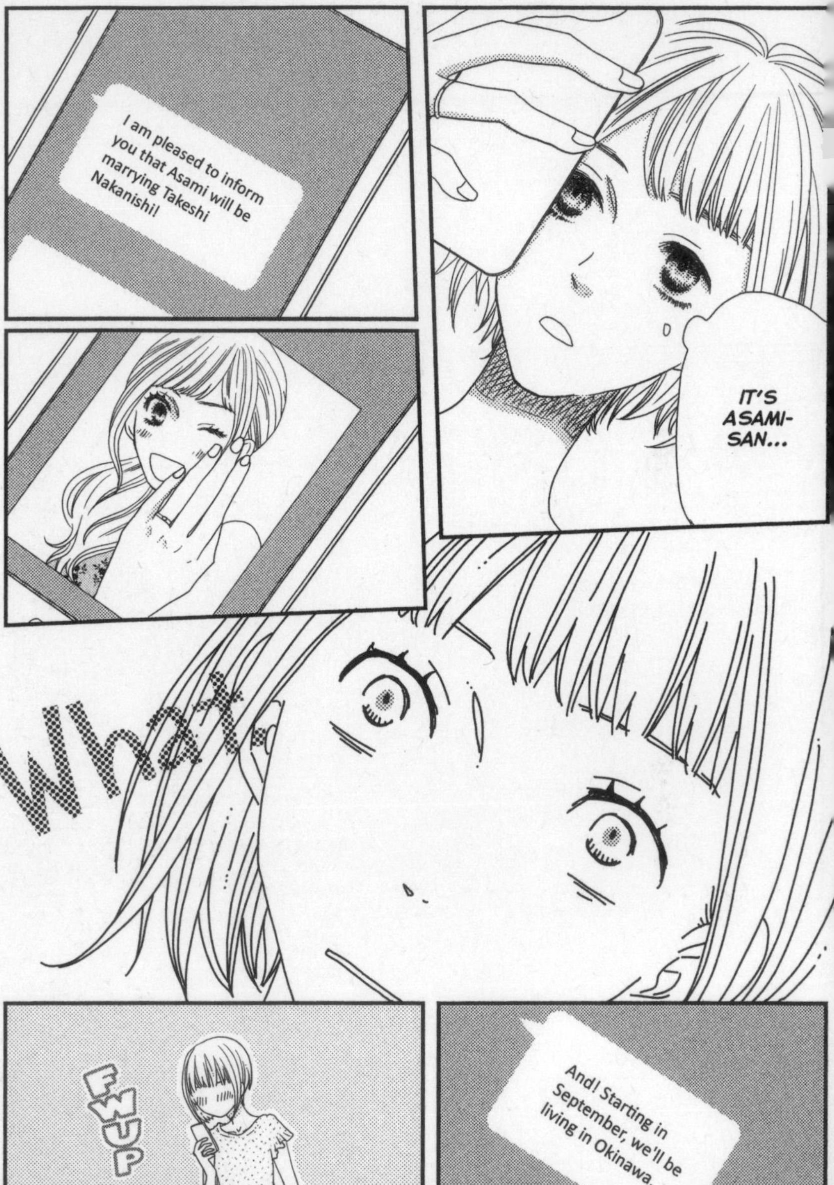
IT'S ASAMI-SAN...
I am pleased to inform you that Asami will be marrying Takeshi Nakanishi!
What
And! Starting in September, we'll be living in Okinawa.
FWUP

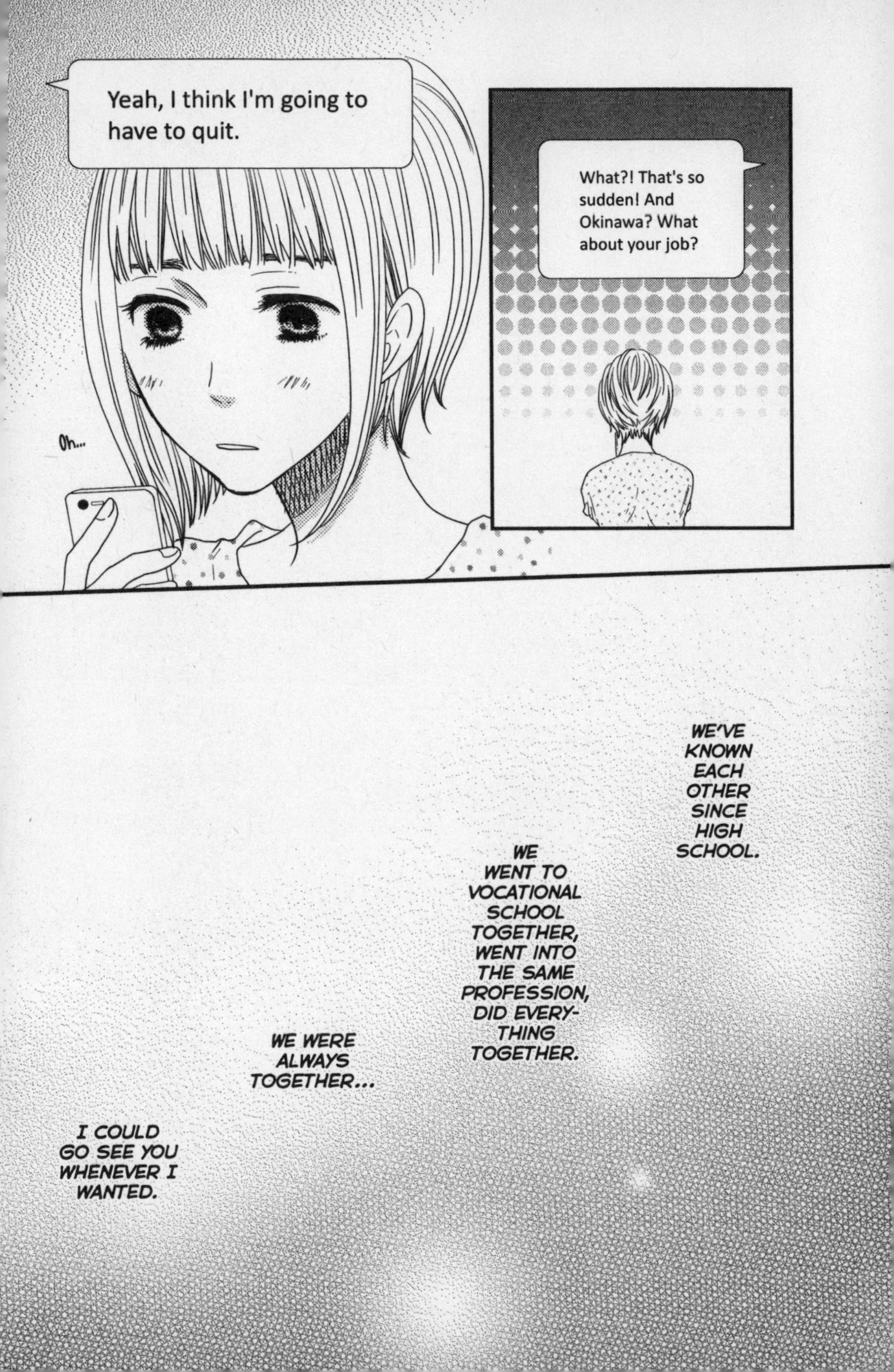
What?! That's so sudden! And Okinawa? What about your job?
Yeah, I think I'm going to have to quit.
Oh...
WE'VE KNOWN EACH OTHER SINCE HIGH SCHOOL.
WE WENT TO VOCATIONAL SCHOOL TOGETHER, WENT INTO THE SAME PROFESSION, DID EVERY-THING TOGETHER.
WE WERE ALWAYS TOGETHER...
I COULD GO SEE YOU WHENEVER I WANTED.

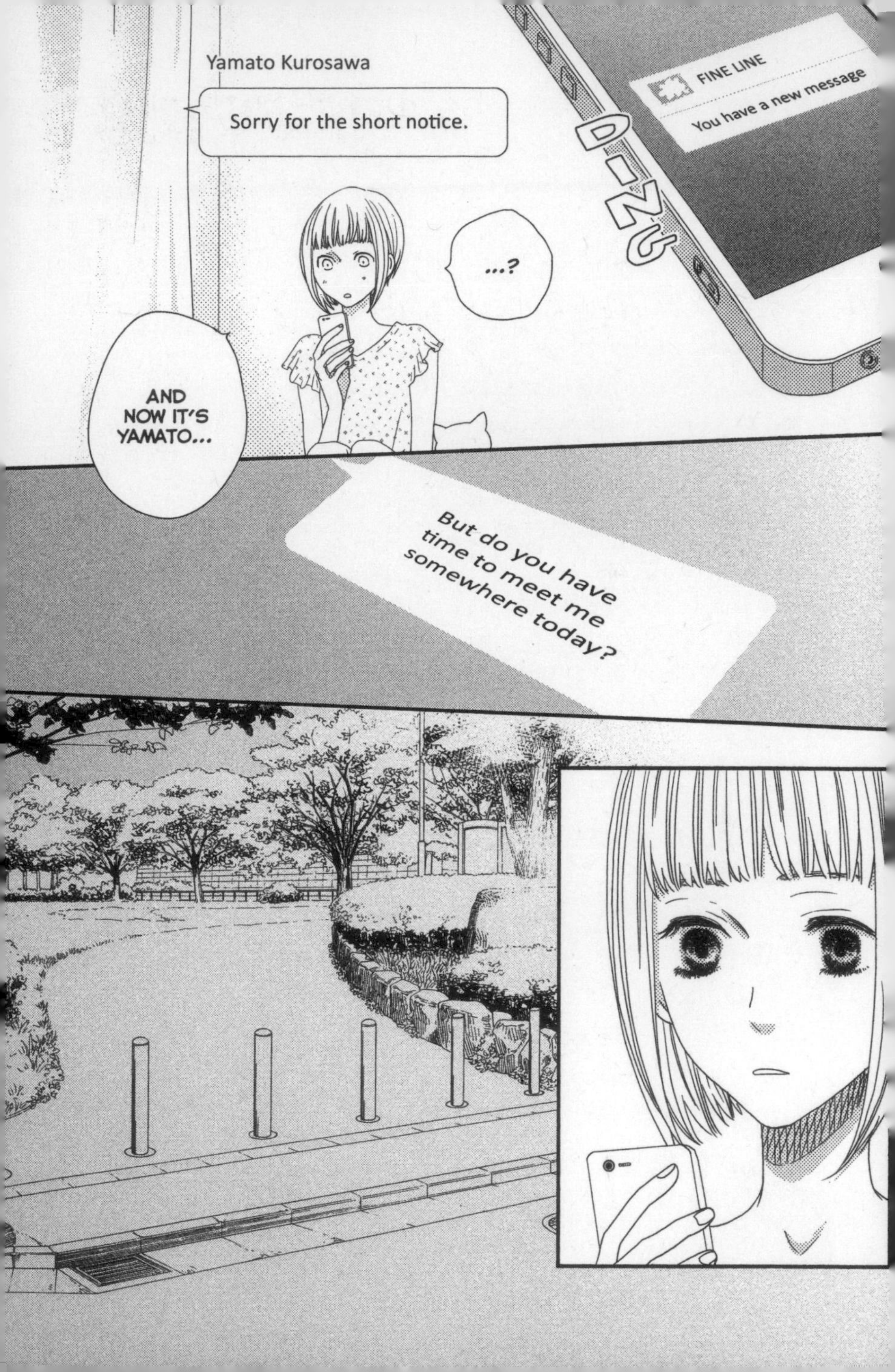
FINE LINE
You have a new message
DING
Yamato Kurosawa
Sorry for the short notice.
...?
AND NOW IT'S YAMATO...
But do you have time to meet me somewhere today?

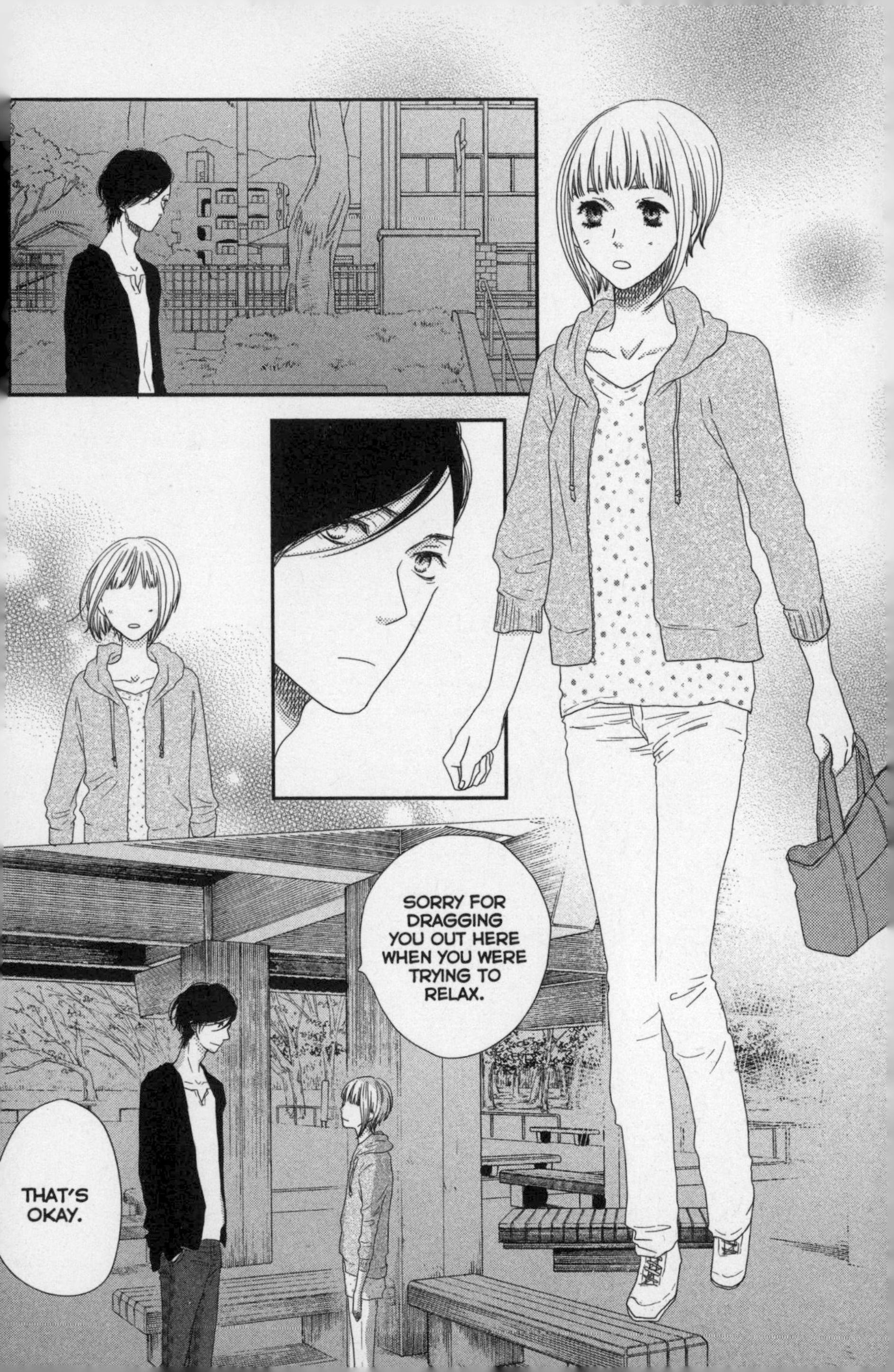
SORRY FOR DRAGGING YOU OUT HERE WHEN YOU WERE TRYING TO RELAX.
THAT'S OKAY.

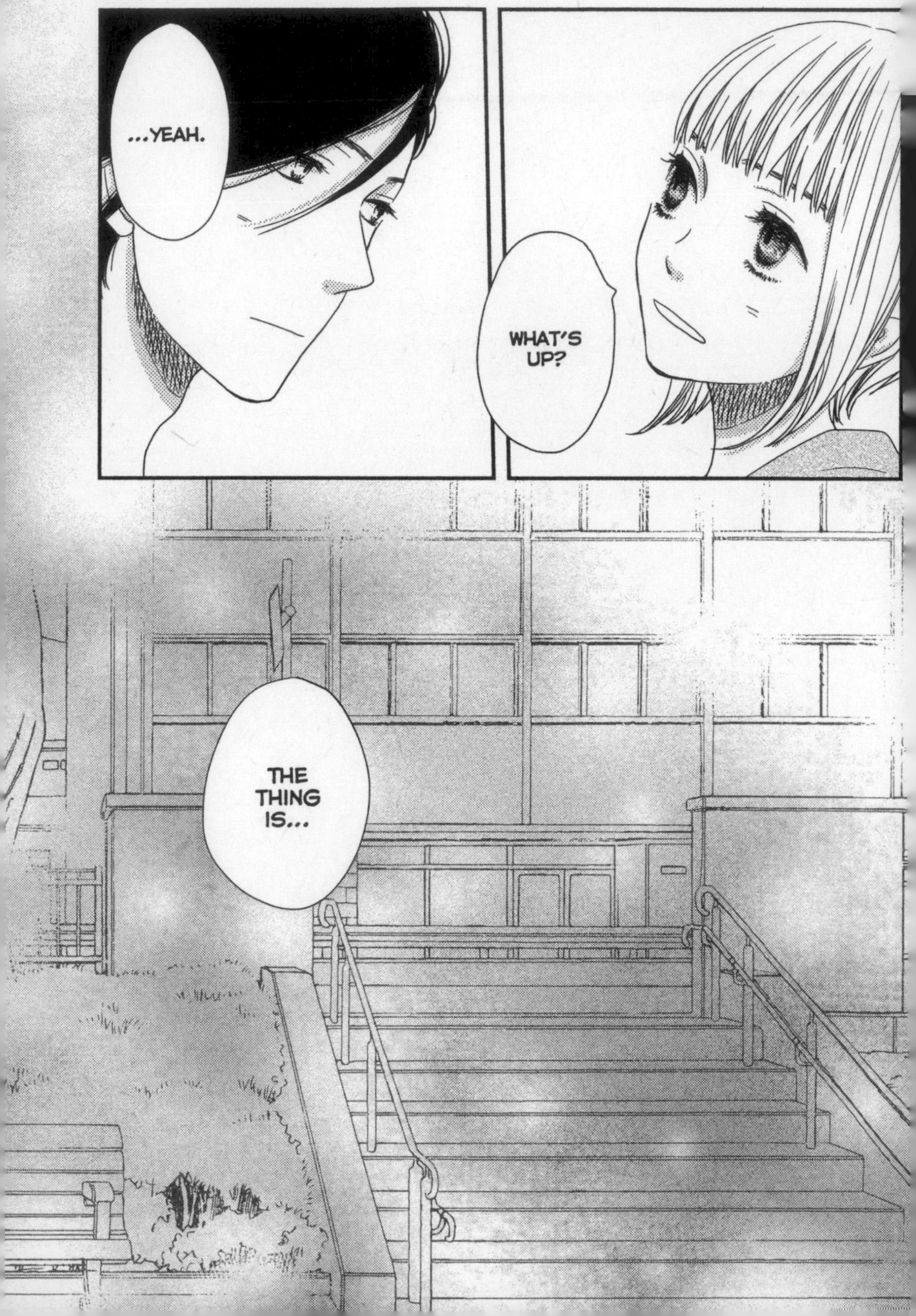
WHAT'S UP?
...YEAH.
THE THING IS...

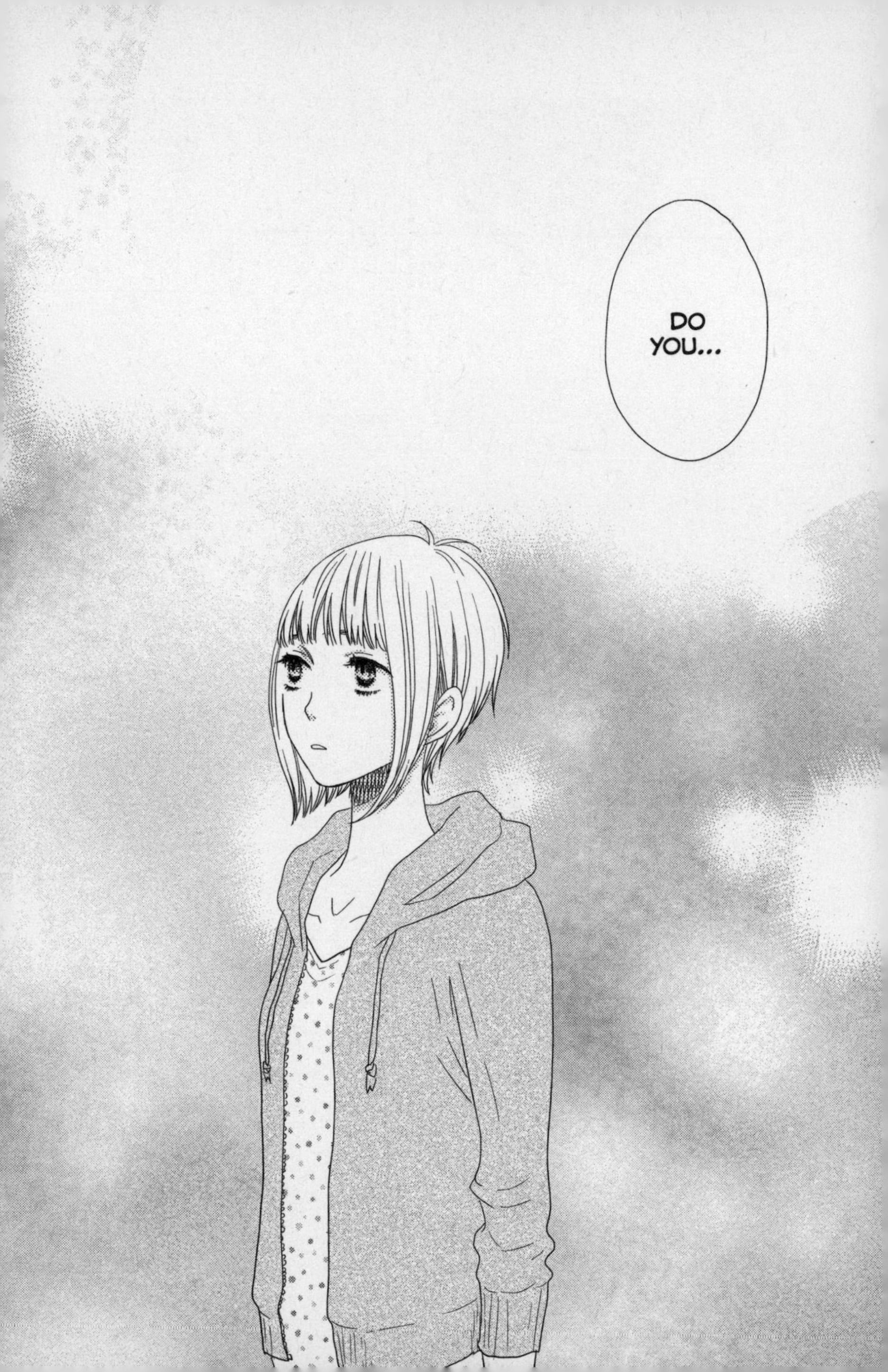
DO YOU...

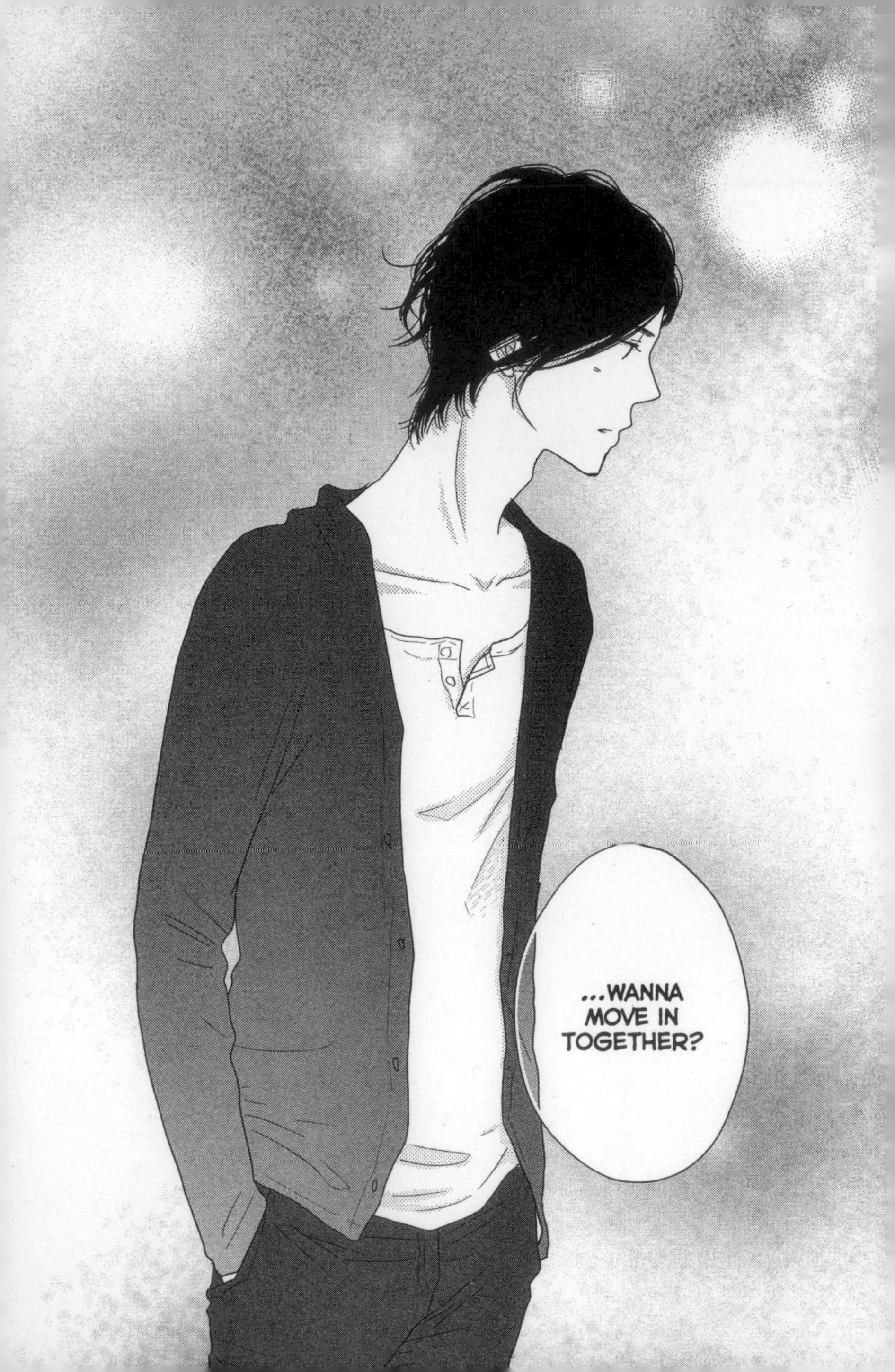
...WANNA MOVE IN TOGETHER?

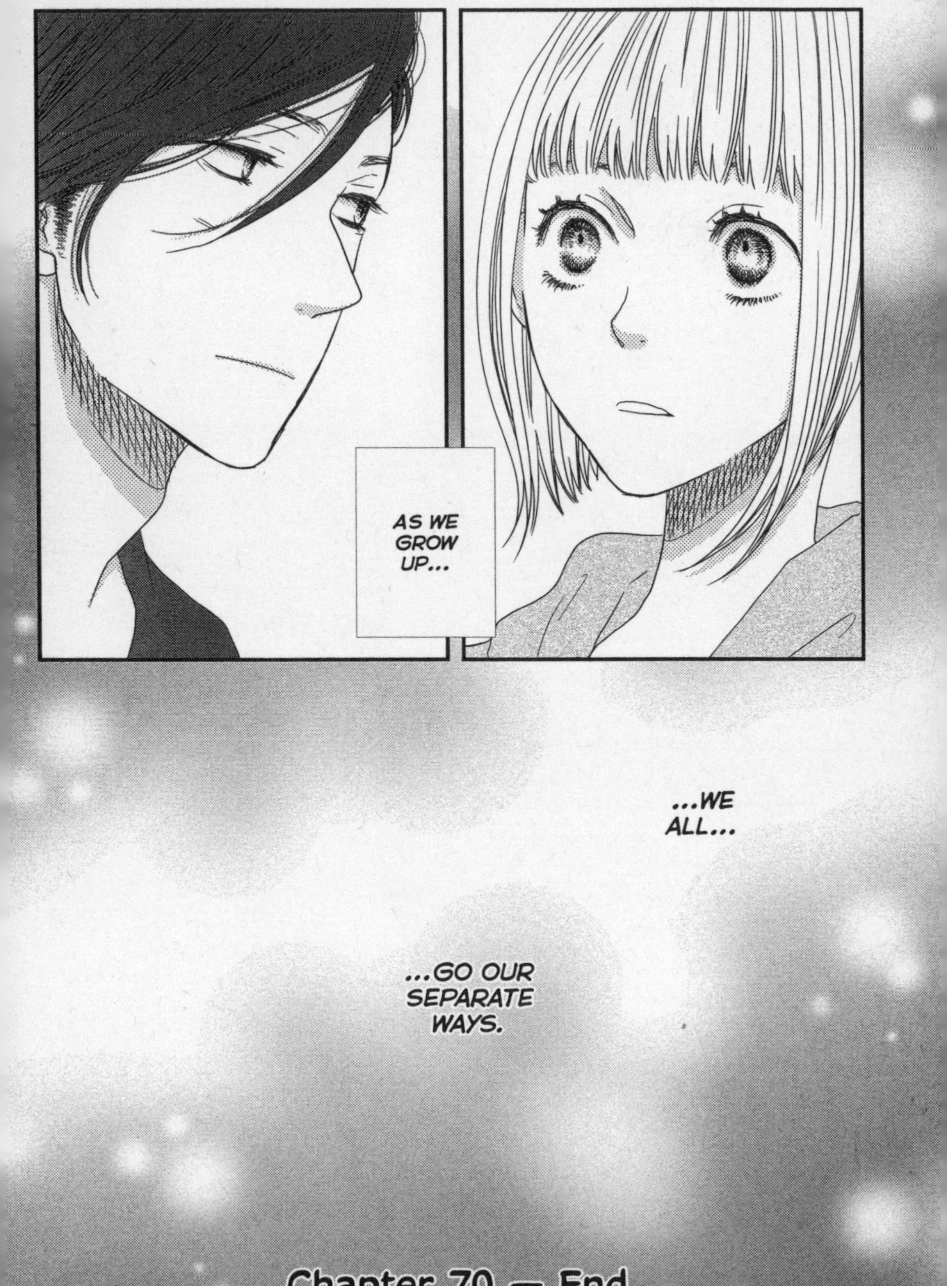
AS WE GROW UP...
...WE ALL...
...GO OUR SEPARATE WAYS.

Chapter 70 — End

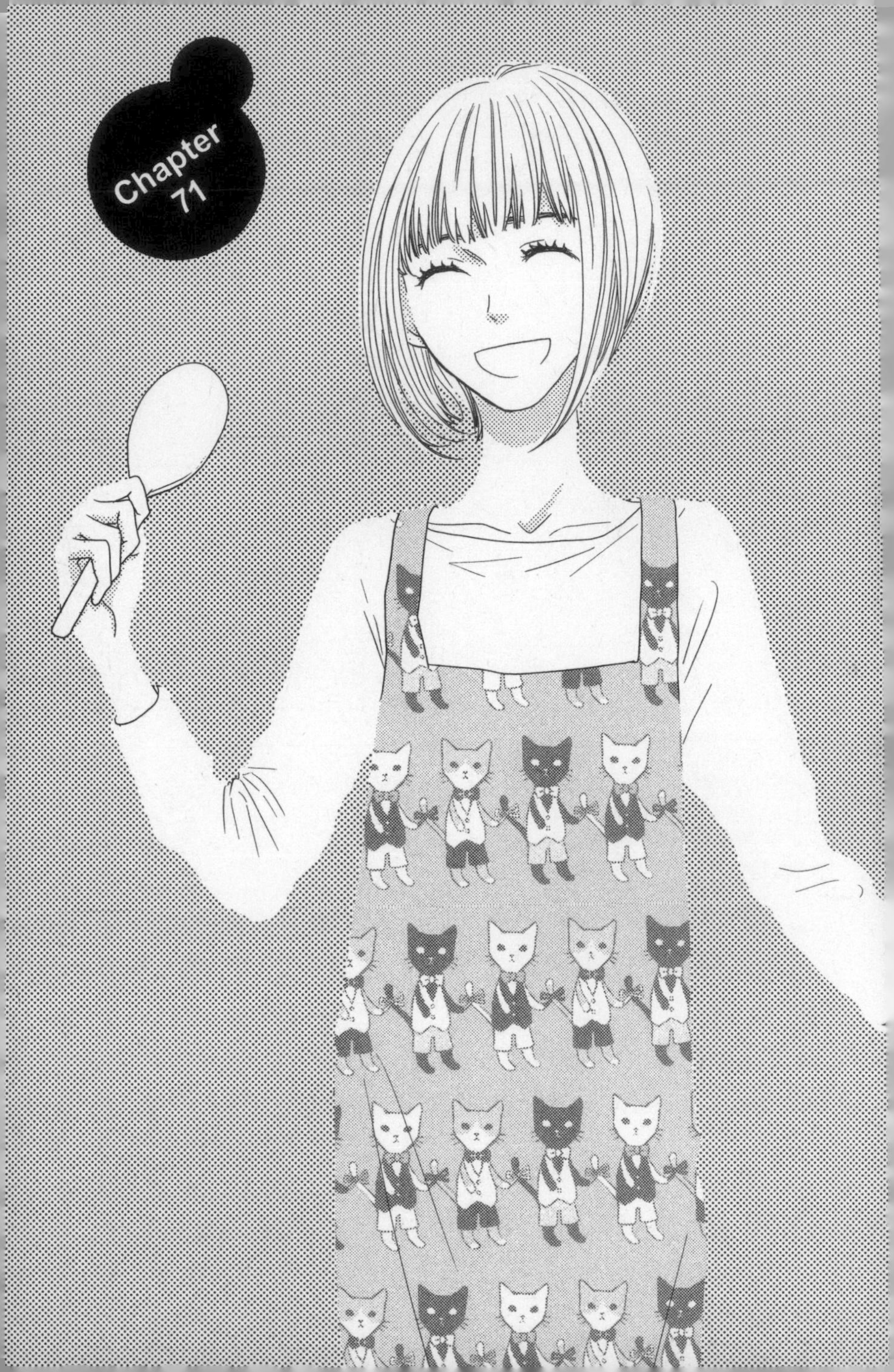
Chapter
71

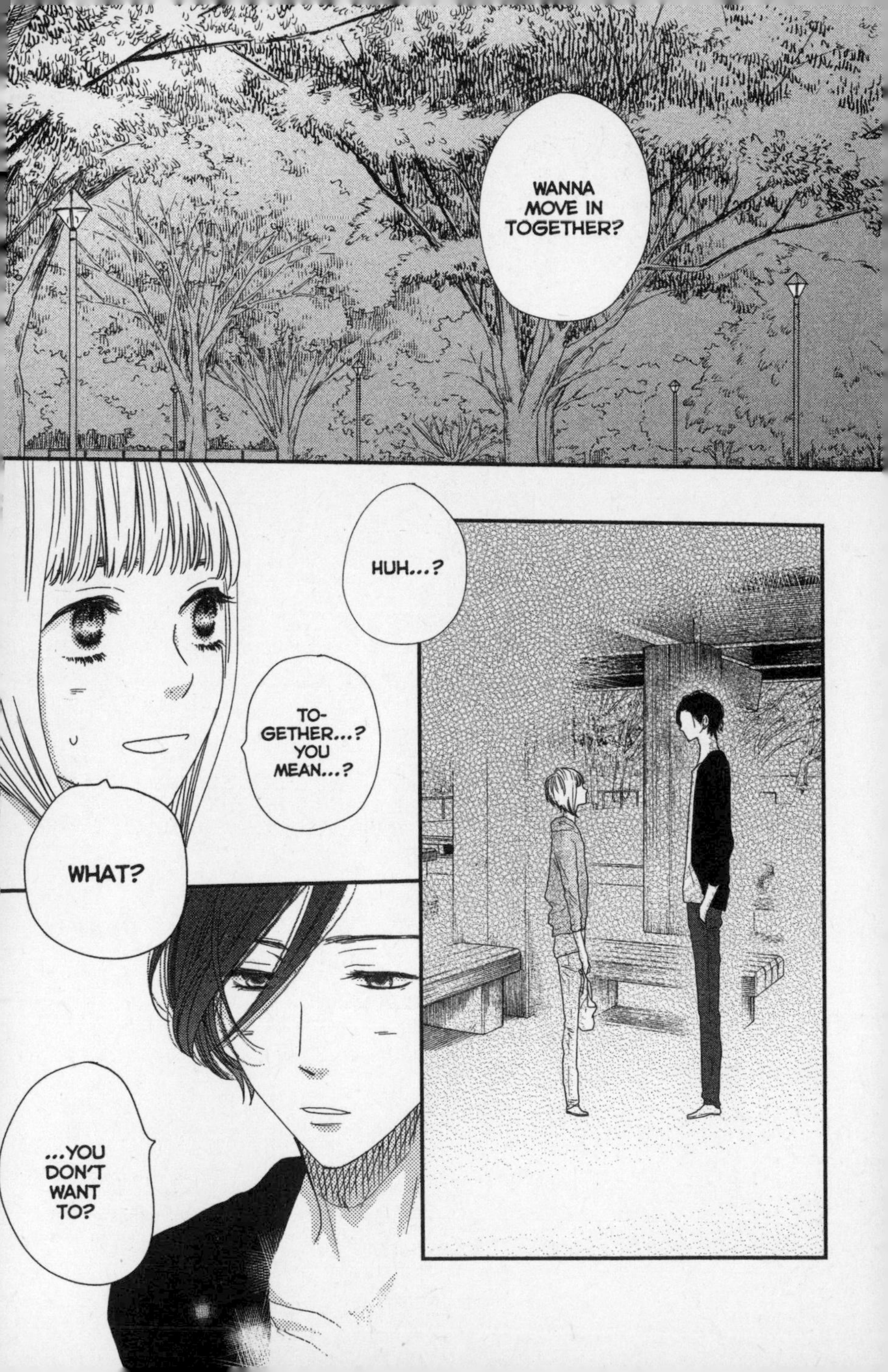
WANNA MOVE IN TOGETHER?
HUH...?
TO-GETHER...? YOU MEAN...?
WHAT?
...YOU DON'T WANT TO?

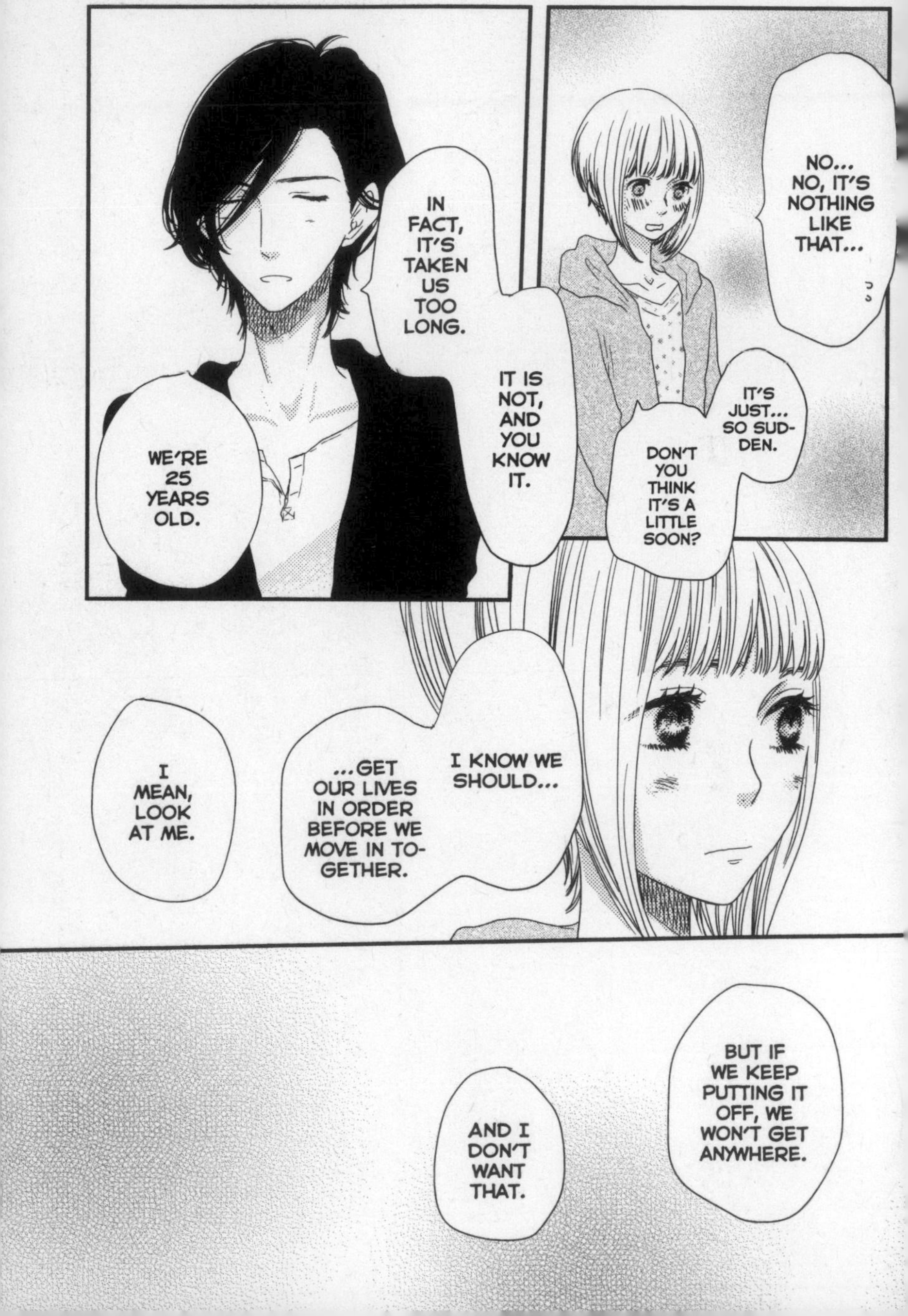
NO... NO, IT'S NOTHING LIKE THAT...
IT'S JUST... SO SUD-DEN.
DON'T YOU THINK IT'S A LITTLE SOON?
IT IS NOT, AND YOU KNOW IT.
IN FACT, IT'S TAKEN US TOO LONG.
WE'RE 25 YEARS OLD.
I KNOW WE SHOULD...
...GET OUR LIVES IN ORDER BEFORE WE MOVE IN TO-GETHER.
I MEAN, LOOK AT ME.
BUT IF WE KEEP PUTTING IT OFF, WE WON'T GET ANYWHERE.
AND I DON'T WANT THAT.

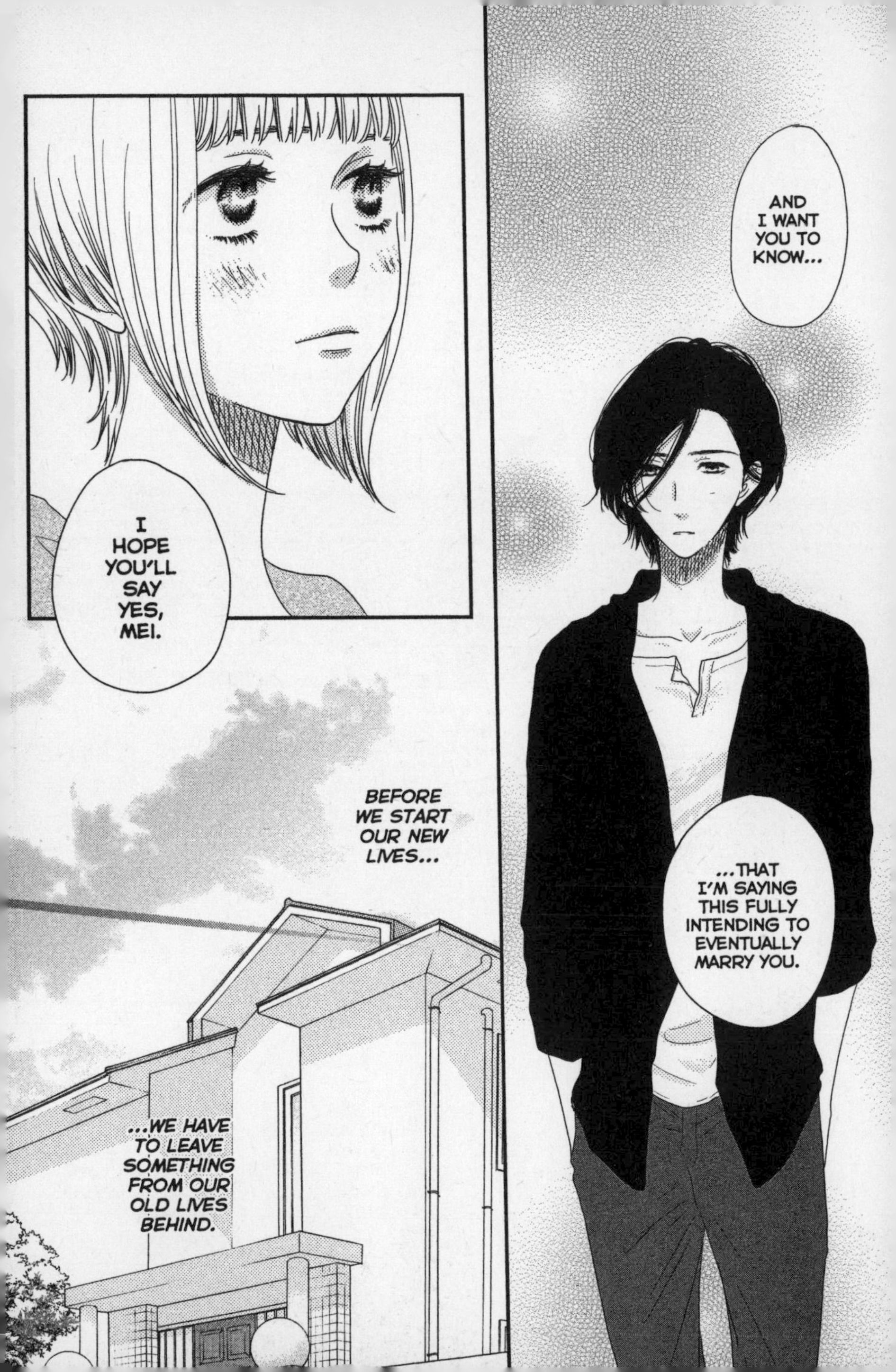
AND I WANT YOU TO KNOW...
...THAT I'M SAYING THIS FULLY INTENDING TO EVENTUALLY MARRY YOU.
I HOPE YOU'LL SAY YES, MEI.
BEFORE WE START OUR NEW LIVES...
...WE HAVE TO LEAVE SOMETHING FROM OUR OLD LIVES BEHIND.

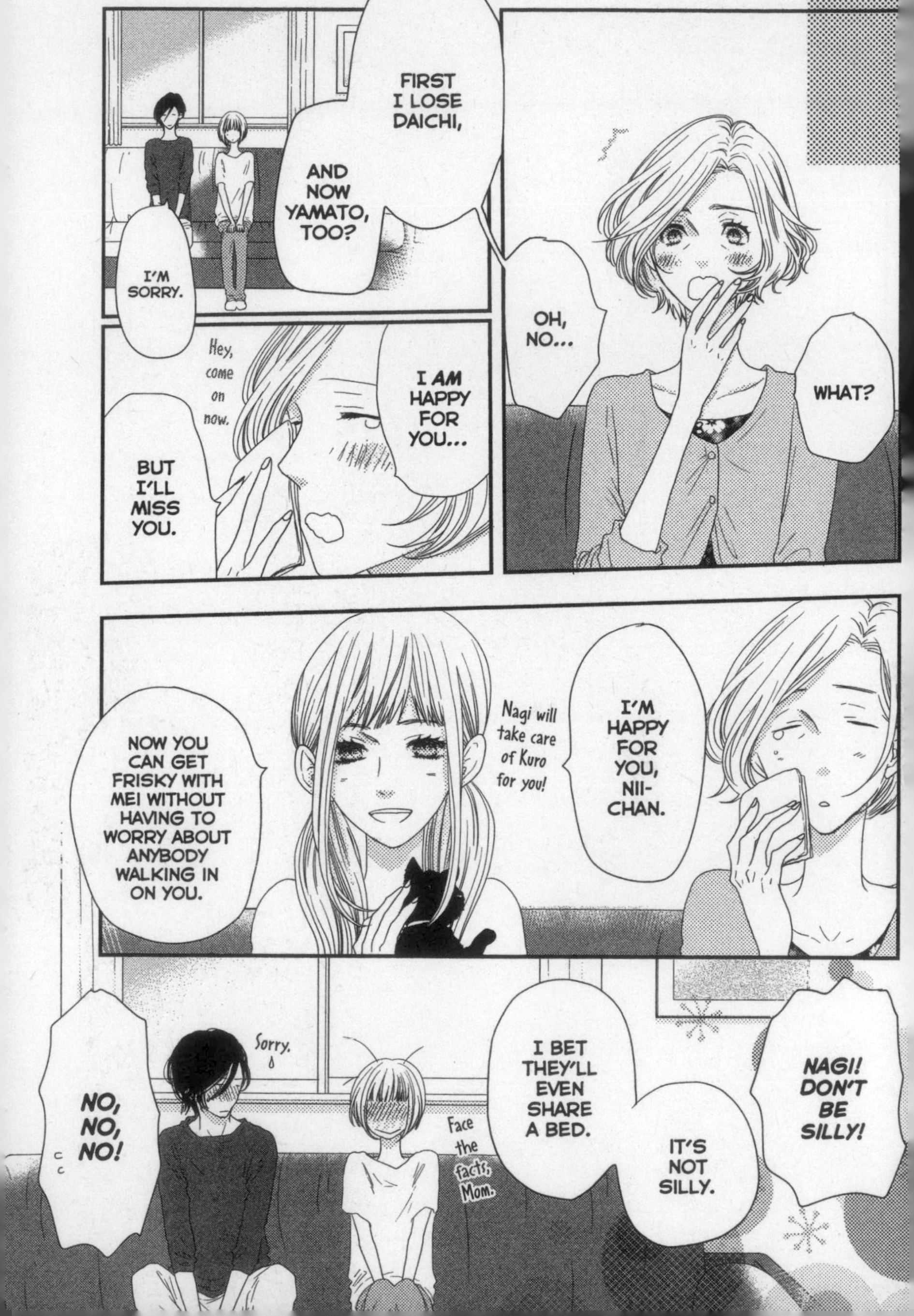
WHAT?
OH, NO...
FIRST I LOSE DAICHI,
AND NOW YAMATO, TOO?
I'M SORRY.
I *AM* HAPPY FOR YOU...
Hey, come on now.
BUT I'LL MISS YOU.
I'M HAPPY FOR YOU, NII-CHAN.
Nagi will take care of Kuro for you!
NOW YOU CAN GET FRISKY WITH MEI WITHOUT HAVING TO WORRY ABOUT ANYBODY WALKING IN ON YOU.
NAGI! DON'T BE SILLY!
I BET THEY'LL EVEN SHARE A BED.
IT'S NOT SILLY.
Face the facts, Mom.
Sorry.
NO, NO, NO!

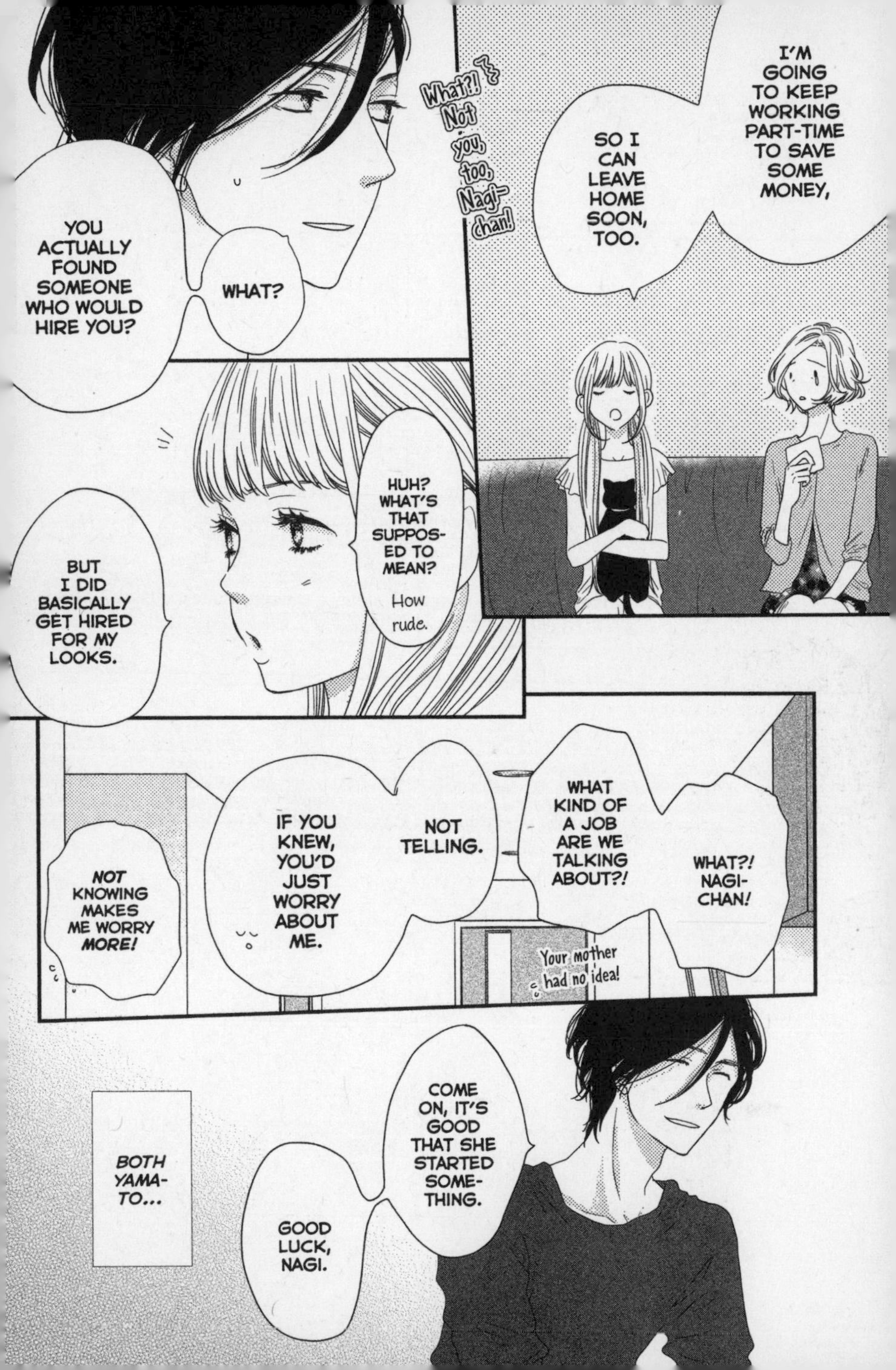
I'M GOING TO KEEP WORKING PART-TIME TO SAVE SOME MONEY,
SO I CAN LEAVE HOME SOON, TOO.
What?! Not you, too, Nagi-chan!
WHAT?
YOU ACTUALLY FOUND SOMEONE WHO WOULD HIRE YOU?
HUH? WHAT'S THAT SUPPOS-ED TO MEAN? How rude.
BUT I DID BASICALLY GET HIRED FOR MY LOOKS.
WHAT?! NAGI-CHAN!
WHAT KIND OF A JOB ARE WE TALKING ABOUT?!
Your mother had no idea!
NOT TELLING.
IF YOU KNEW, YOU'D JUST WORRY ABOUT ME.
NOT KNOWING MAKES ME WORRY MORE!
COME ON, IT'S GOOD THAT SHE STARTED SOME-THING.
GOOD LUCK, NAGI.
BOTH YAMA-TO...

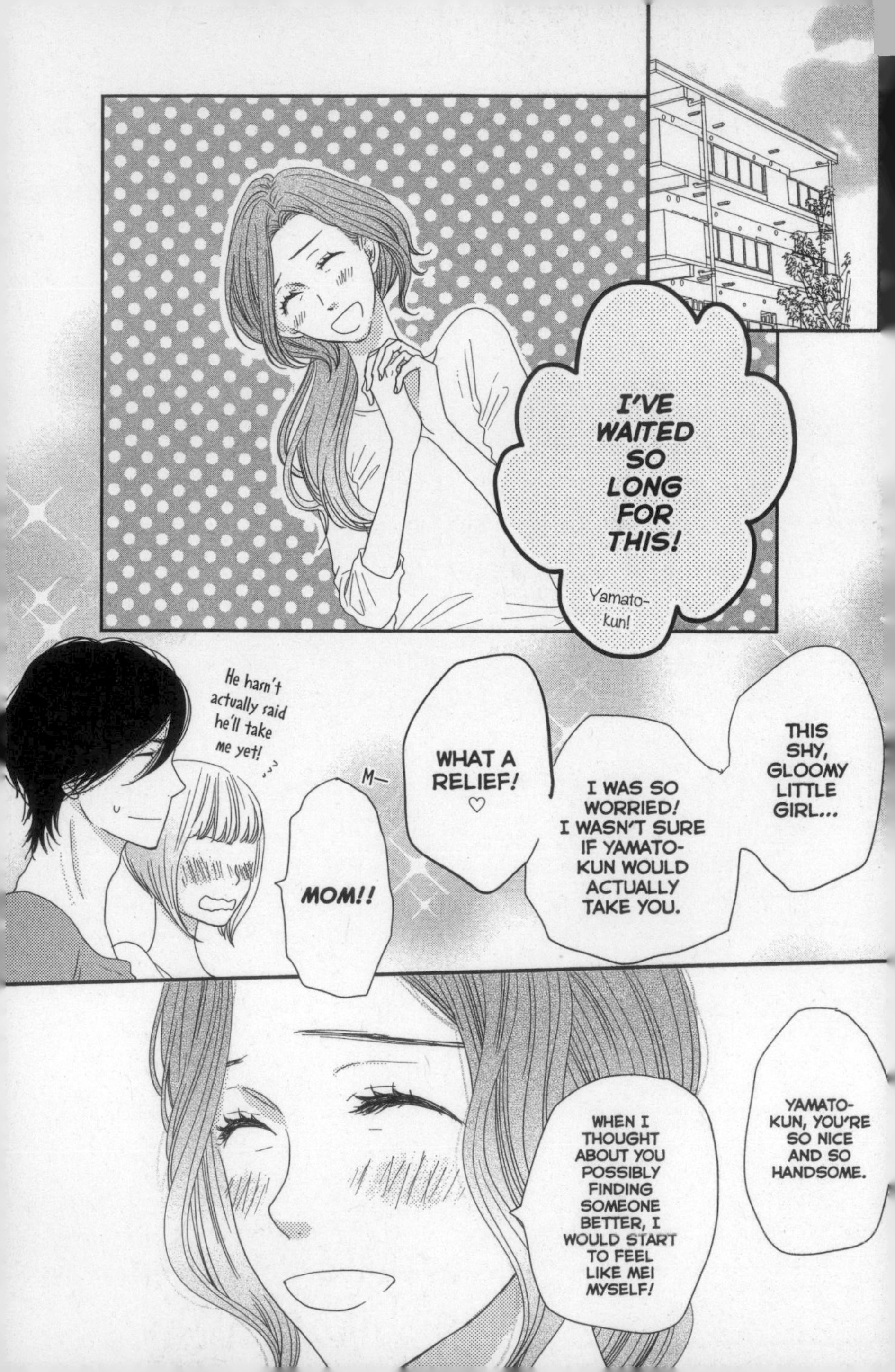
I'VE WAITED SO LONG FOR THIS!
Yamato-kun!
THIS SHY, GLOOMY LITTLE GIRL...
I WAS SO WORRIED! I WASN'T SURE IF YAMATO-KUN WOULD ACTUALLY TAKE YOU.
WHAT A RELIEF! ♡
M— MOM!!
He hasn't actually said he'll take me yet!
YAMATO-KUN, YOU'RE SO NICE AND SO HANDSOME.
WHEN I THOUGHT ABOUT YOU POSSIBLY FINDING SOMEONE BETTER, I WOULD START TO FEEL LIKE MEI MYSELF!

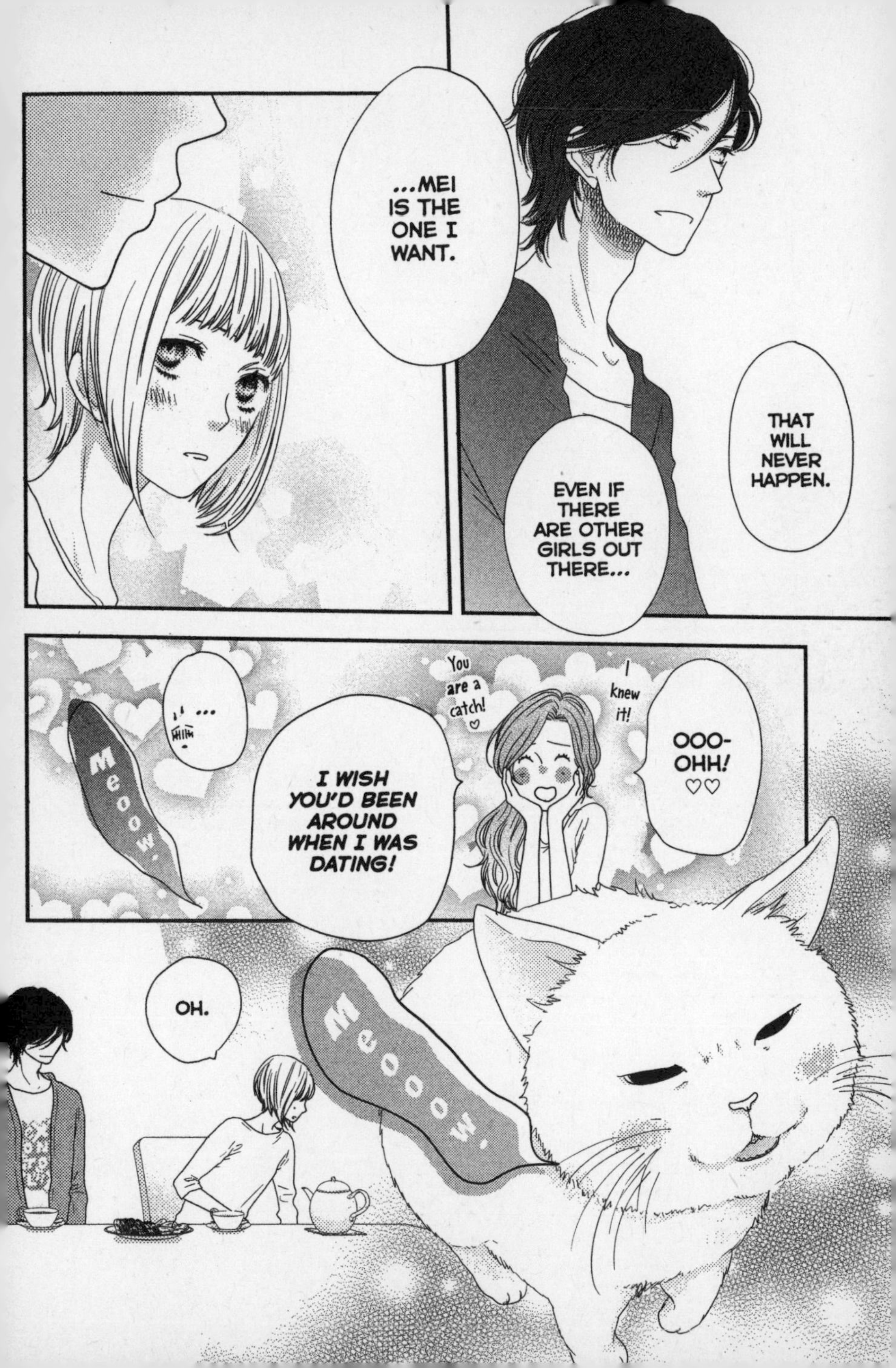

THAT WILL NEVER HAPPEN.
EVEN IF THERE ARE OTHER GIRLS OUT THERE...
...MEI IS THE ONE I WANT.
I knew it!
OOO-OHH! ♡♡
You are a catch! ♡
I WISH YOU'D BEEN AROUND WHEN I WAS DATING!
...
Meoow.
Meooow.
OH.

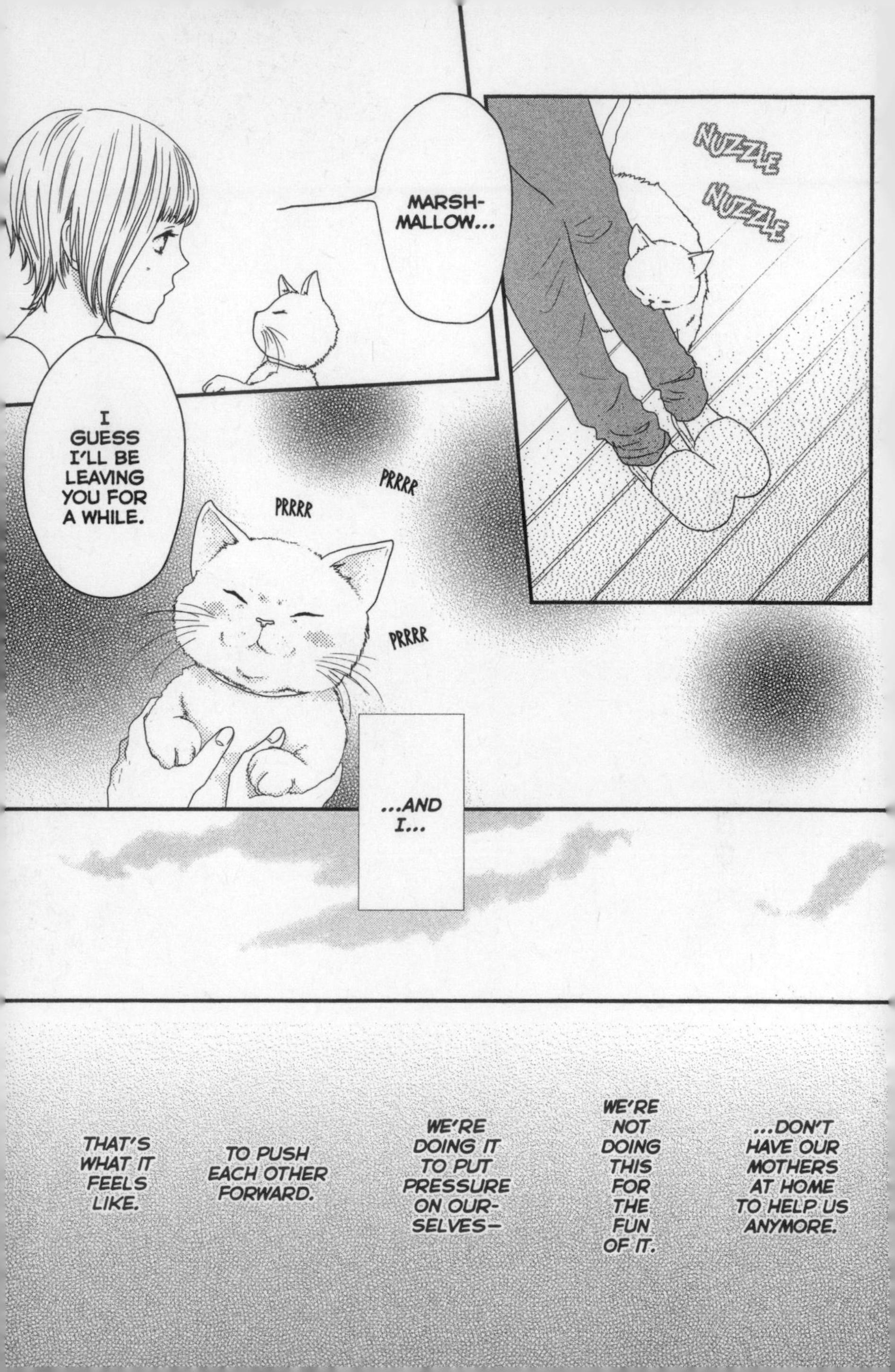
NUZZLE
NUZZLE
MARSH-MALLOW...
PRRRR
PRRRR
I GUESS I'LL BE LEAVING YOU FOR A WHILE.
PRRRR
...AND I...
...DON'T HAVE OUR MOTHERS AT HOME TO HELP US ANYMORE.
WE'RE NOT DOING THIS FOR THE FUN OF IT.
WE'RE DOING IT TO PUT PRESSURE ON OUR-SELVES—
TO PUSH EACH OTHER FORWARD.
THAT'S WHAT IT FEELS LIKE.

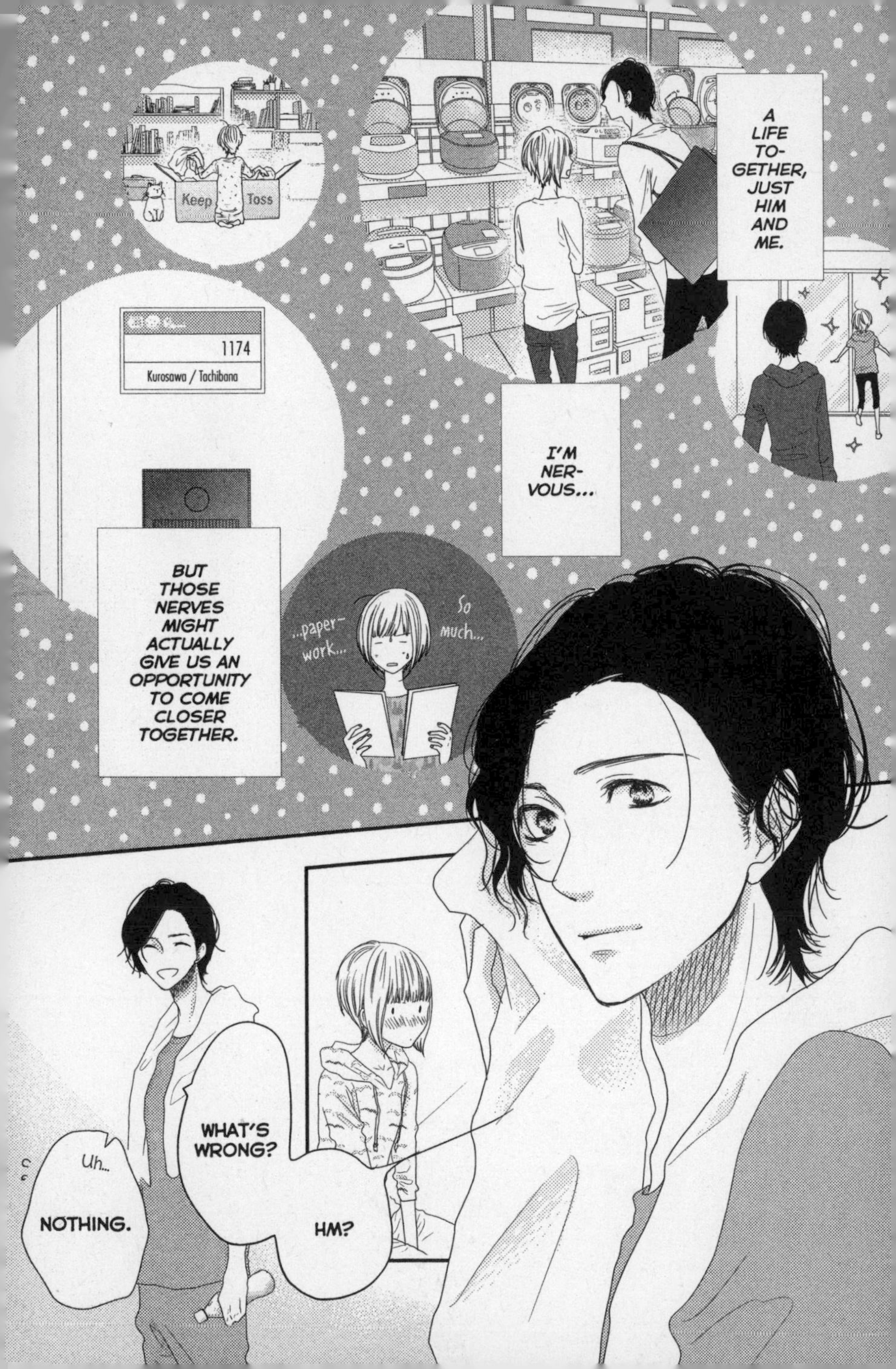
A LIFE TO-GETHER, JUST HIM AND ME.
Keep
Toss
I'M NER-VOUS...
1174
Kurosawa / Tachibana
So much...
...paper-work...
BUT THOSE NERVES MIGHT ACTUALLY GIVE US AN OPPORTUNITY TO COME CLOSER TOGETHER.
HM?
WHAT'S WRONG?
Uh...
NOTHING.

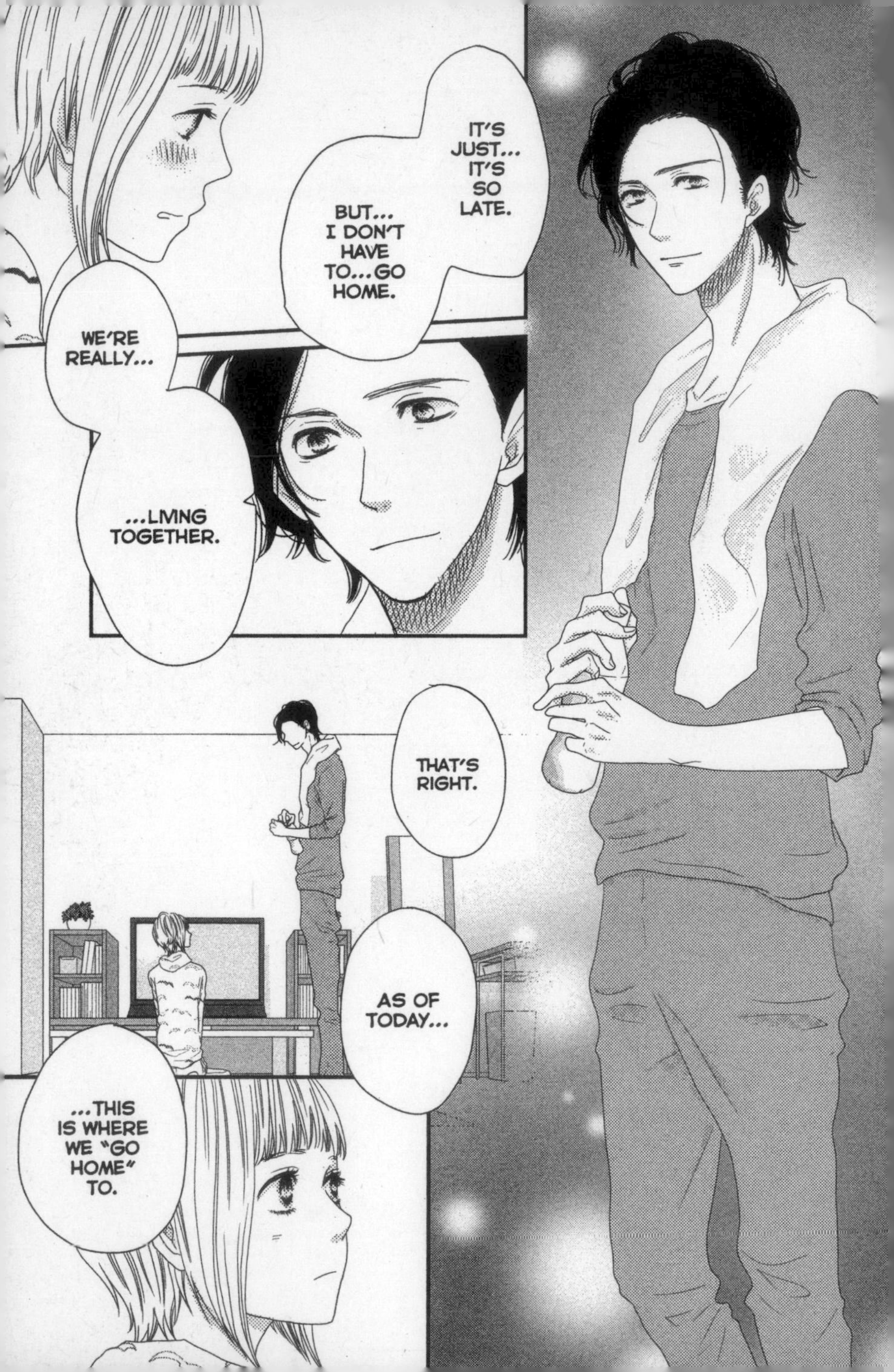
IT'S JUST... IT'S SO LATE.
BUT... I DON'T HAVE TO...GO HOME.
WE'RE REALLY...
...LIVING TOGETHER.
THAT'S RIGHT.
AS OF TODAY...
...THIS IS WHERE WE "GO HOME" TO.

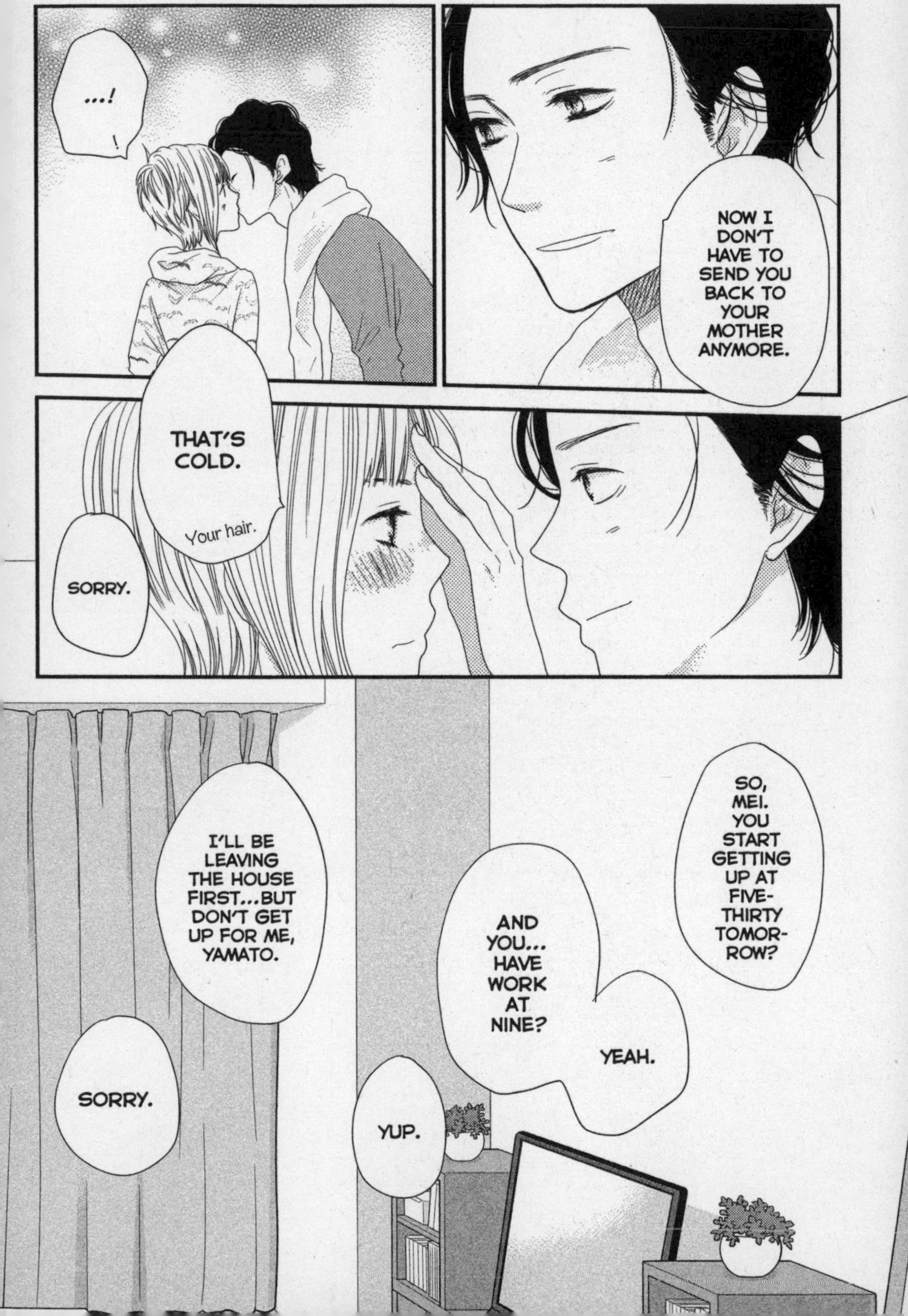
NOW I DON'T HAVE TO SEND YOU BACK TO YOUR MOTHER ANYMORE.
...!
!
THAT'S COLD.
Your hair.
SORRY.
SO, MEI. YOU START GETTING UP AT FIVE-THIRTY TOMOR-ROW?
AND YOU... HAVE WORK AT NINE?
YEAH.
YUP.
I'LL BE LEAVING THE HOUSE FIRST...BUT DON'T GET UP FOR ME, YAMATO.
SORRY.

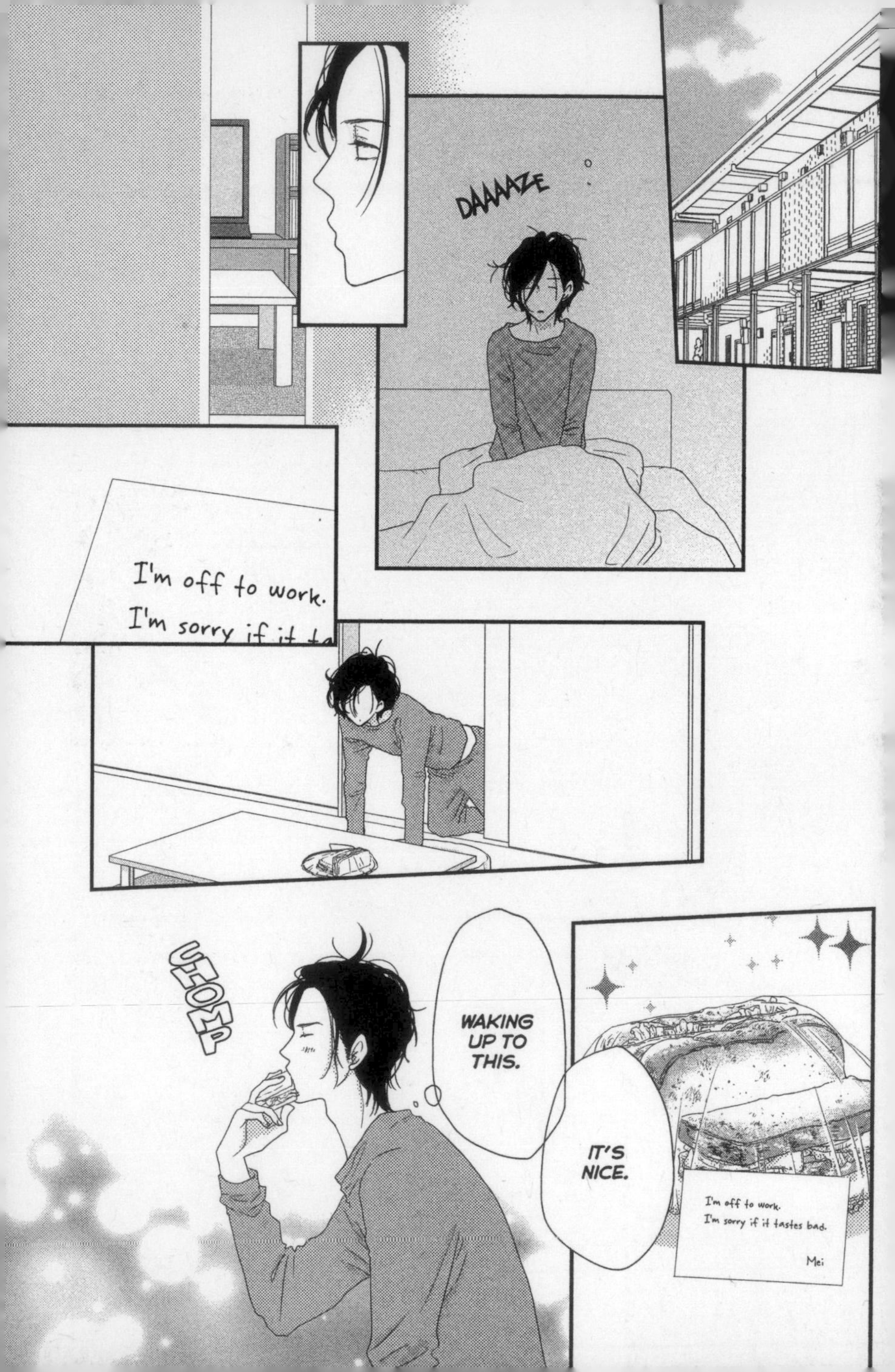
DAAAAZE
I'm off to work.
I'm sorry if it ta
WAKING UP TO THIS.
IT'S NICE.
I'm off to work.
I'm sorry if it tastes bad.
Mei
CHOMP

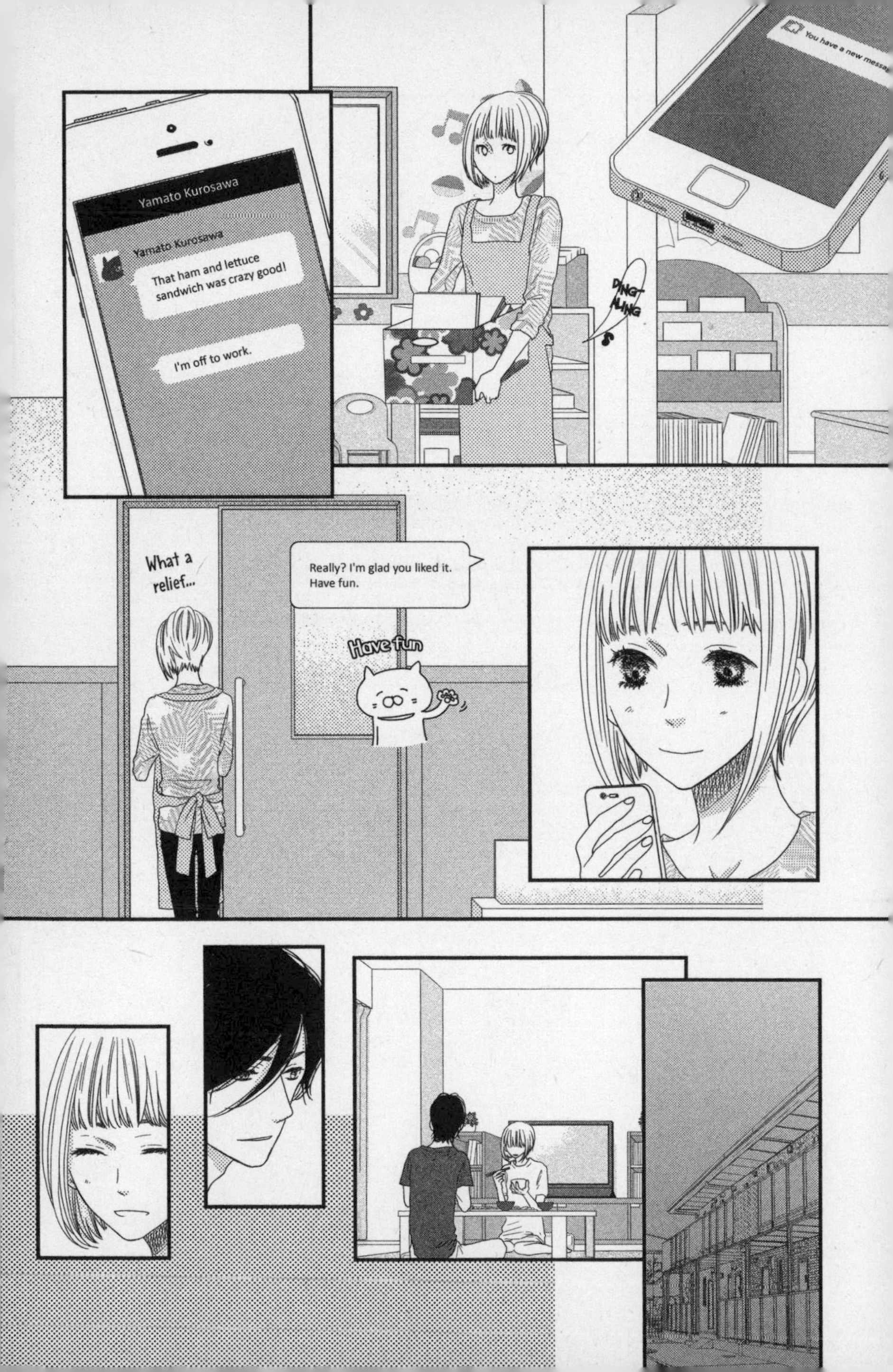
You have a new messa
DING ALING
Yamato Kurosawa
Yamato Kurosawa
That ham and lettuce sandwich was crazy good!
I'm off to work.
Really? I'm glad you liked it. Have fun.
What a relief...
Have fun

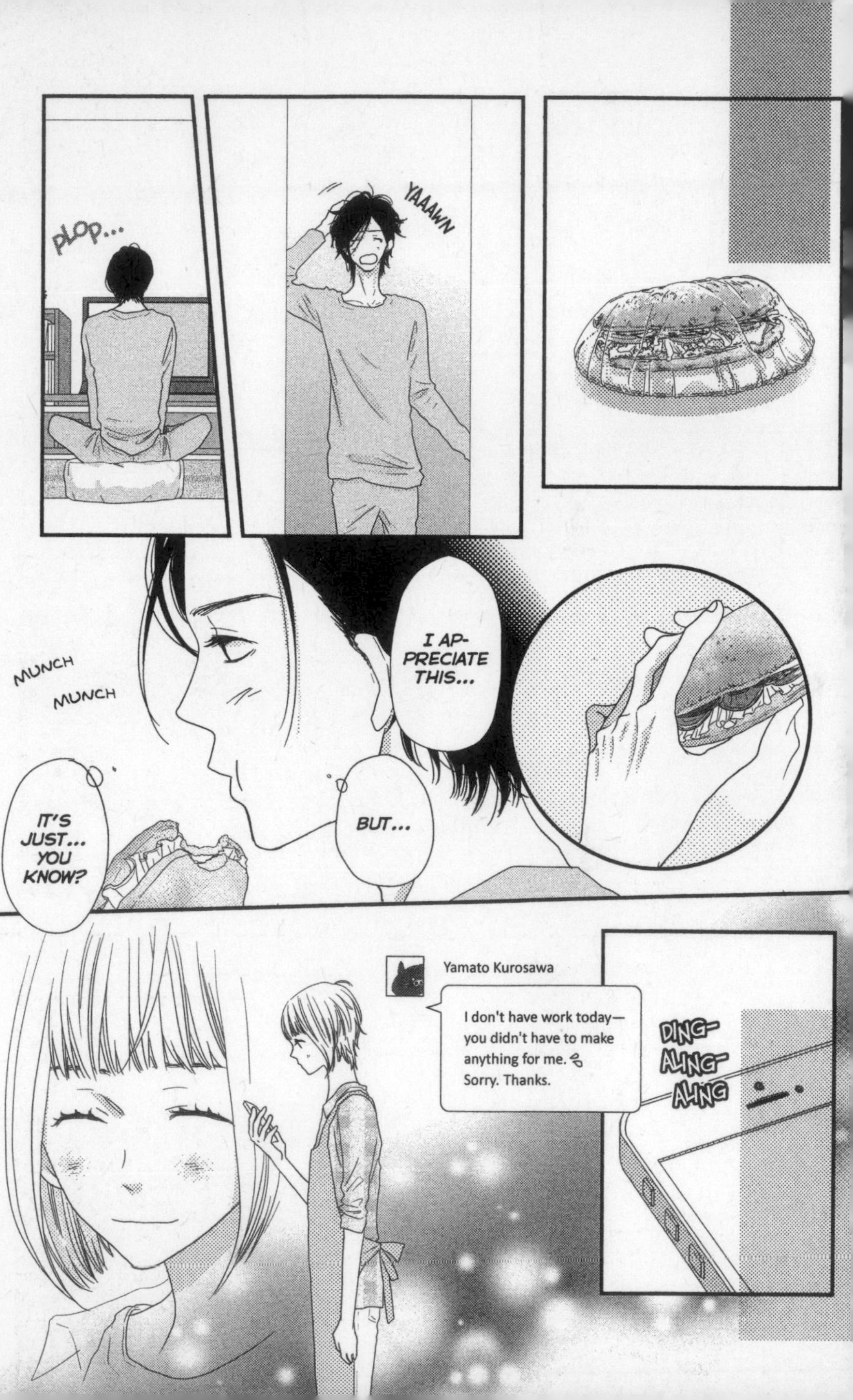
YAAAWN
PLOP...
I AP-PRECIATE THIS...
MUNCH MUNCH
BUT...
IT'S JUST... YOU KNOW?
DING-ALING-ALING
Yamato Kurosawa
I don't have work today—you didn't have to make anything for me.
Sorry. Thanks.

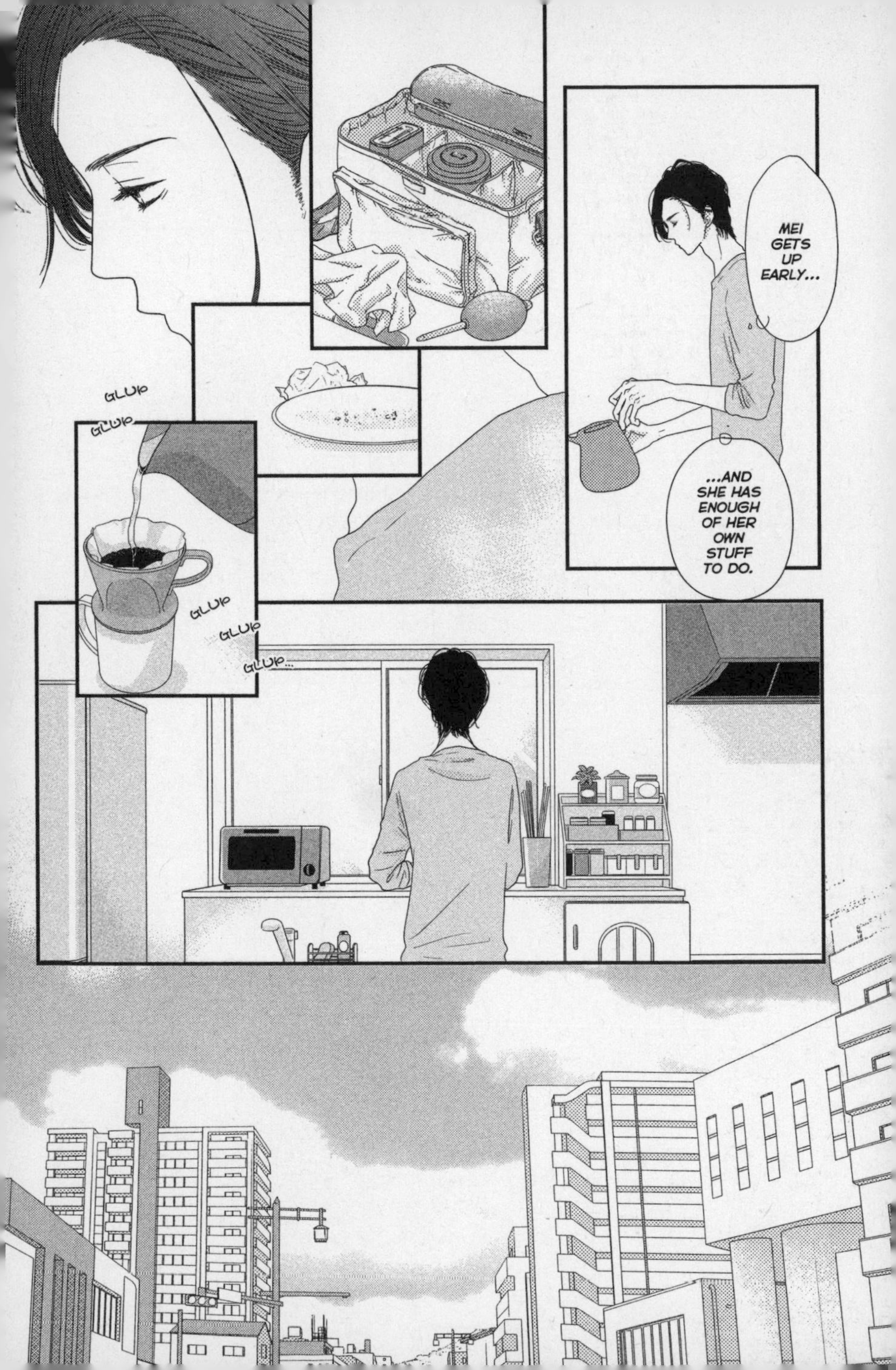

MEI GETS UP EARLY...
...AND SHE HAS ENOUGH OF HER OWN STUFF TO DO.
GLUP
GLUP
GLUP
GLUP
GLUP...

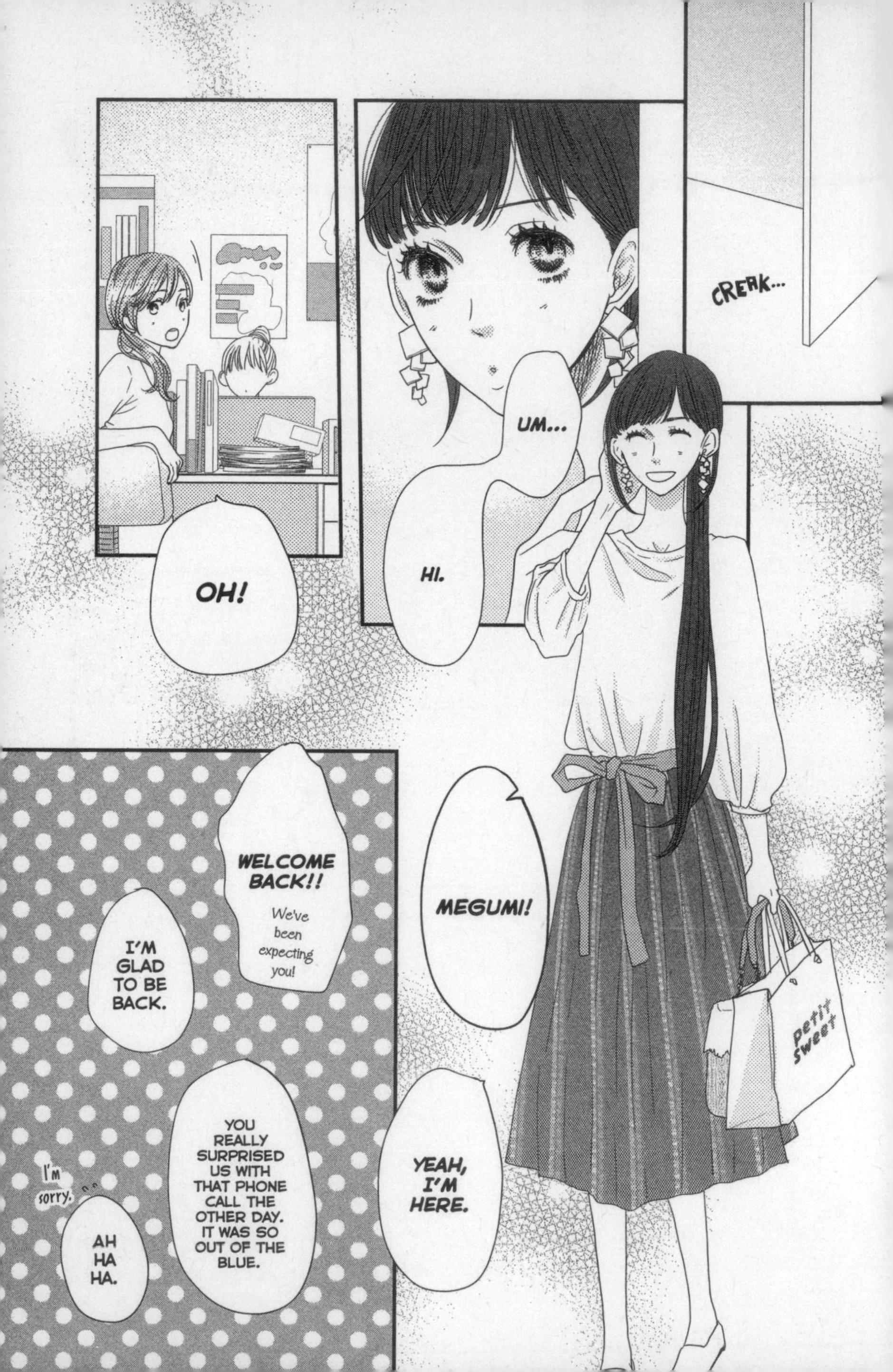
CREAK...
UM...
HI.
OH!
MEGUMI!
YEAH, I'M HERE.
WELCOME BACK!!
We've been expecting you!
I'M GLAD TO BE BACK.
YOU REALLY SURPRISED US WITH THAT PHONE CALL THE OTHER DAY. IT WAS SO OUT OF THE BLUE.
I'm sorry.
AH HA HA.
petit sweet

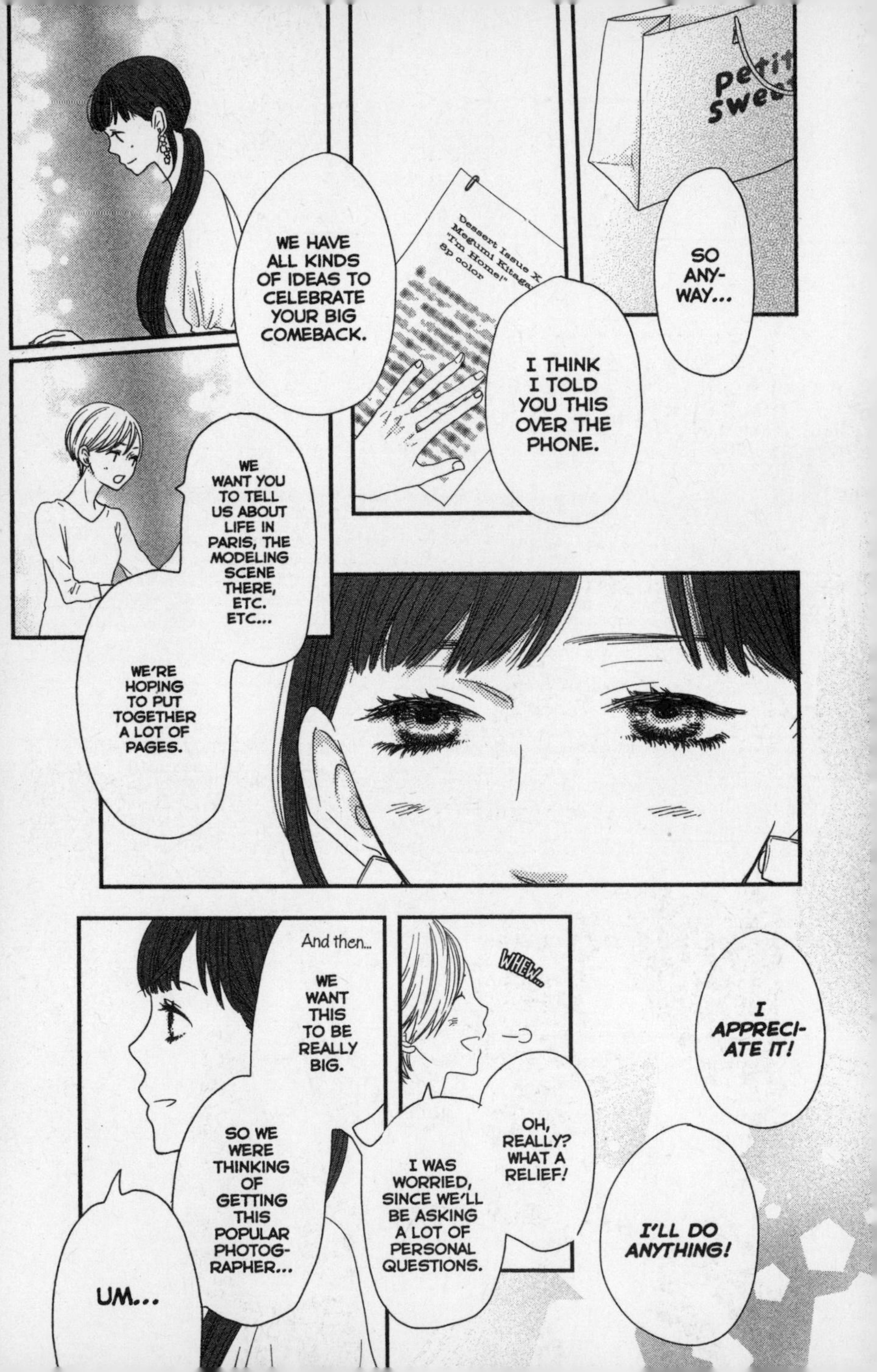
SO ANYWAY...
Dessert Issue X
8p color
I THINK I TOLD YOU THIS OVER THE PHONE.
WE HAVE ALL KINDS OF IDEAS TO CELEBRATE YOUR BIG COMEBACK.
WE WANT YOU TO TELL US ABOUT LIFE IN PARIS, THE MODELING SCENE THERE, ETC. ETC...
WE'RE HOPING TO PUT TOGETHER A LOT OF PAGES.
I APPRECIATE IT!
I'LL DO ANYTHING!
WHEW...
OH, REALLY? WHAT A RELIEF!
I WAS WORRIED, SINCE WE'LL BE ASKING A LOT OF PERSONAL QUESTIONS.
And then...
WE WANT THIS TO BE REALLY BIG.
SO WE WERE THINKING OF GETTING THIS POPULAR PHOTOGRAPHER...
UM...

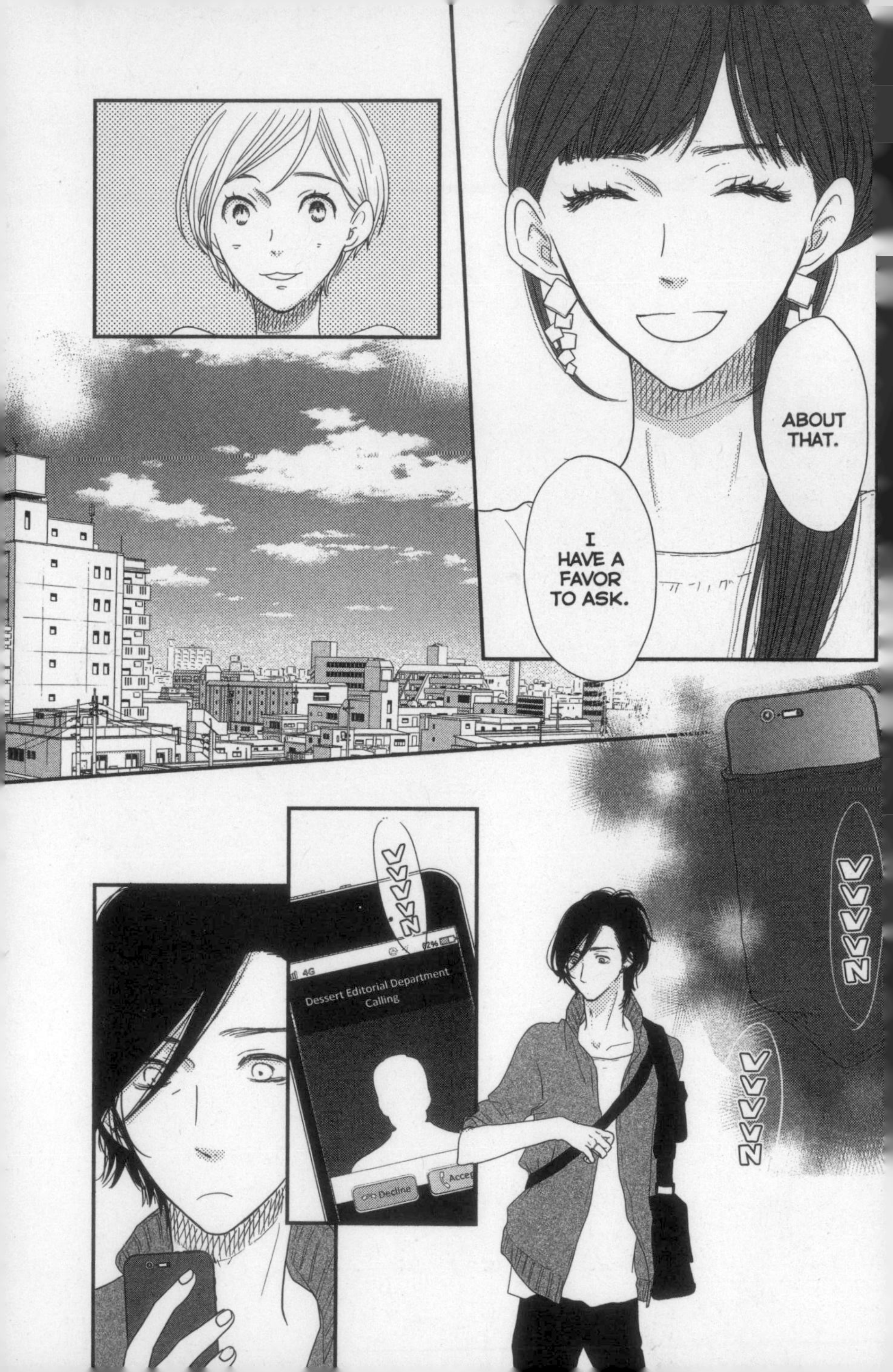
ABOUT THAT.
I HAVE A FAVOR TO ASK.
VVVVN
VVVVN
VVVVN
Dessert Editorial Department Calling
Decline

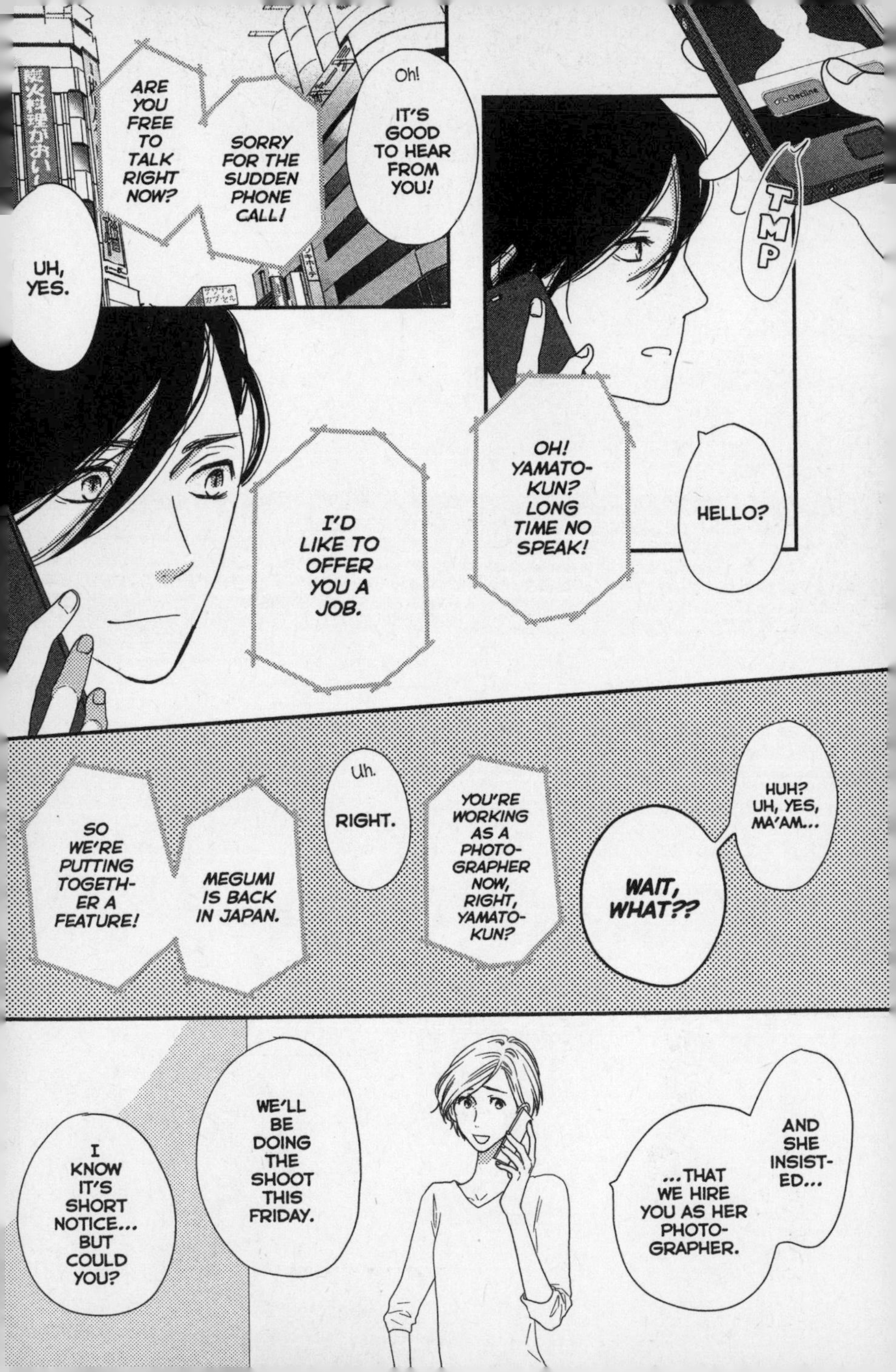
Decline
TMP
HELLO?
OH! YAMATO-KUN? LONG TIME NO SPEAK!
Oh! IT'S GOOD TO HEAR FROM YOU!
SORRY FOR THE SUDDEN PHONE CALL!
ARE YOU FREE TO TALK RIGHT NOW?
UH, YES.
I'D LIKE TO OFFER YOU A JOB.
HUH? UH, YES, MA'AM...
WAIT, WHAT??
YOU'RE WORKING AS A PHOTOGRAPHER NOW, RIGHT, YAMATO-KUN?
Uh. RIGHT.
MEGUMI IS BACK IN JAPAN.
SO WE'RE PUTTING TOGETHER A FEATURE!
AND SHE INSISTED...
...THAT WE HIRE YOU AS HER PHOTOGRAPHER.
WE'LL BE DOING THE SHOOT THIS FRIDAY.
I KNOW IT'S SHORT NOTICE... BUT COULD YOU?

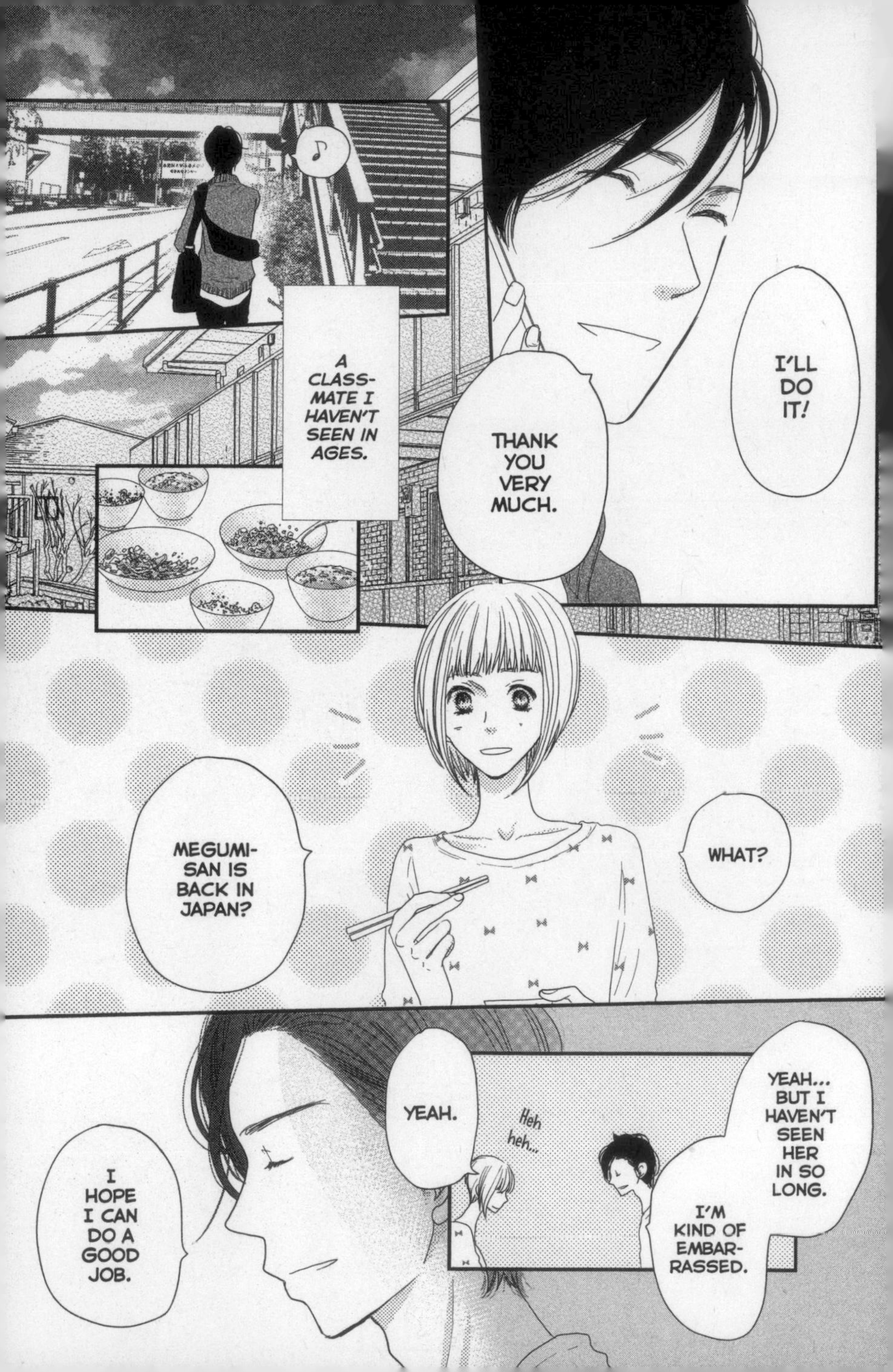
I'LL DO IT!
THANK YOU VERY MUCH.
♪
A CLASSMATE I HAVEN'T SEEN IN AGES.
WHAT?
MEGUMI-SAN IS BACK IN JAPAN?
YEAH... BUT I HAVEN'T SEEN HER IN SO LONG.
I'M KIND OF EMBARRASSED.
Heh heh...
YEAH.
I HOPE I CAN DO A GOOD JOB.

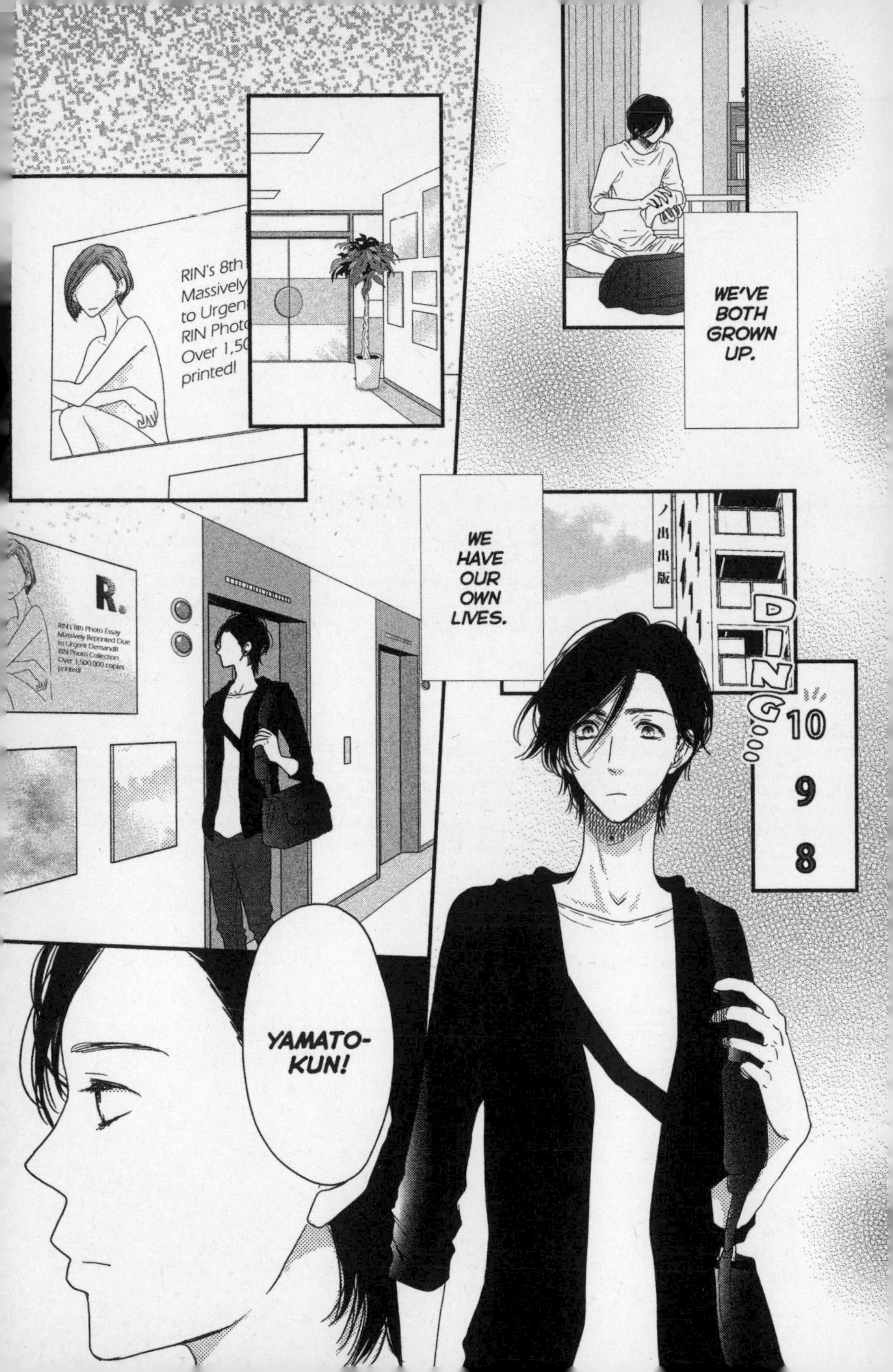
WE'VE BOTH GROWN UP.
WE HAVE OUR OWN LIVES.
DING...
10
9
8
R.
RIN's 8th Photo Essay Massively Reprinted Due to Urgent Demand!! RIN Photo Collection Over 1,500,000 copies printed!
YAMATO-KUN!

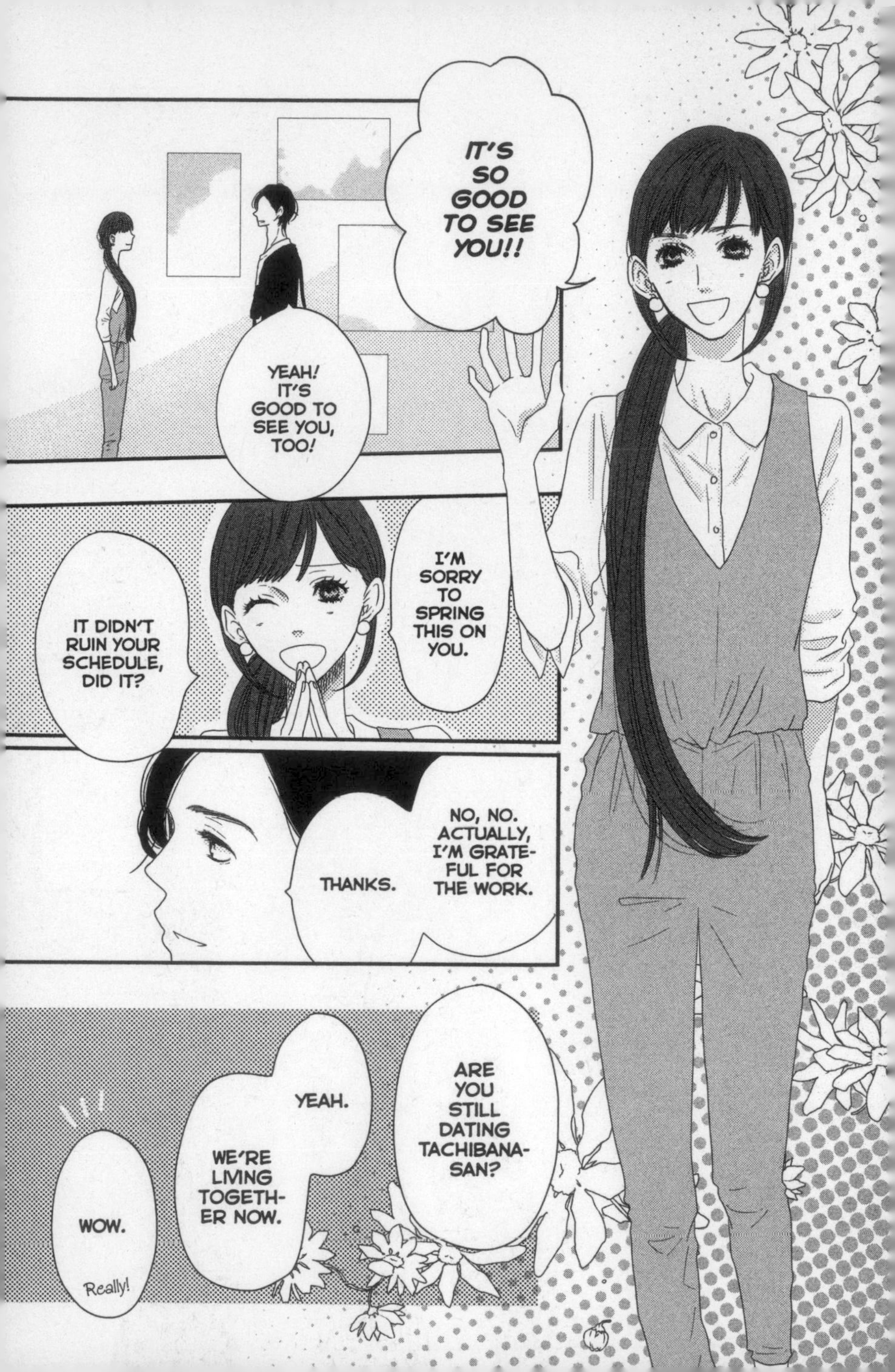
IT'S SO GOOD TO SEE YOU!!
YEAH! IT'S GOOD TO SEE YOU, TOO!
I'M SORRY TO SPRING THIS ON YOU.
IT DIDN'T RUIN YOUR SCHEDULE, DID IT?
NO, NO. ACTUALLY, I'M GRATE-FUL FOR THE WORK.
THANKS.
ARE YOU STILL DATING TACHIBANA-SAN?
YEAH.
WE'RE LIVING TOGETH-ER NOW.
WOW.
Really!

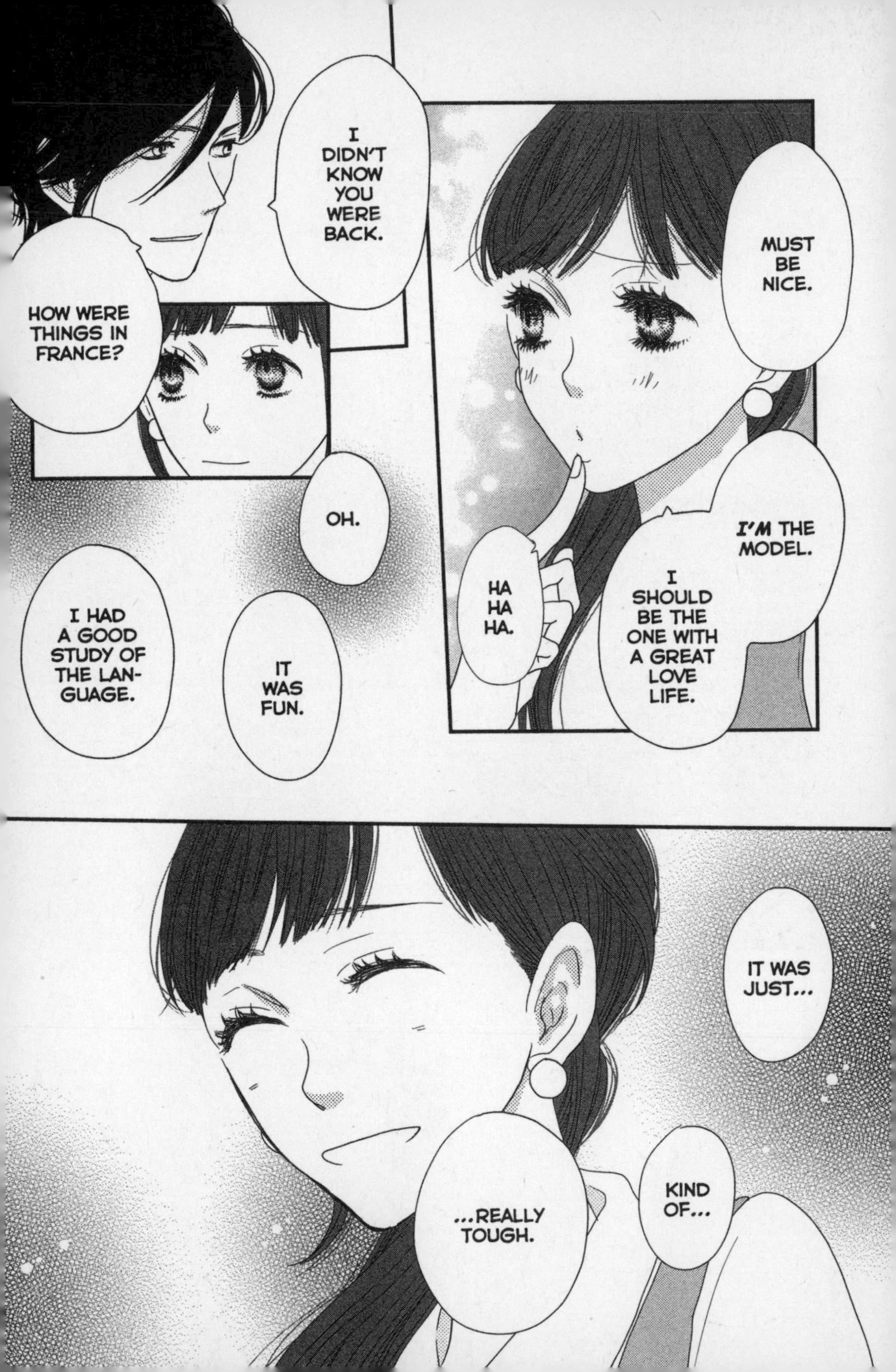
I DIDN'T KNOW YOU WERE BACK.
HOW WERE THINGS IN FRANCE?
OH.
IT WAS FUN.
I HAD A GOOD STUDY OF THE LAN-GUAGE.
MUST BE NICE.
I'M THE MODEL.
I SHOULD BE THE ONE WITH A GREAT LOVE LIFE.
HA HA HA.
IT WAS JUST...
KIND OF...
...REALLY TOUGH.

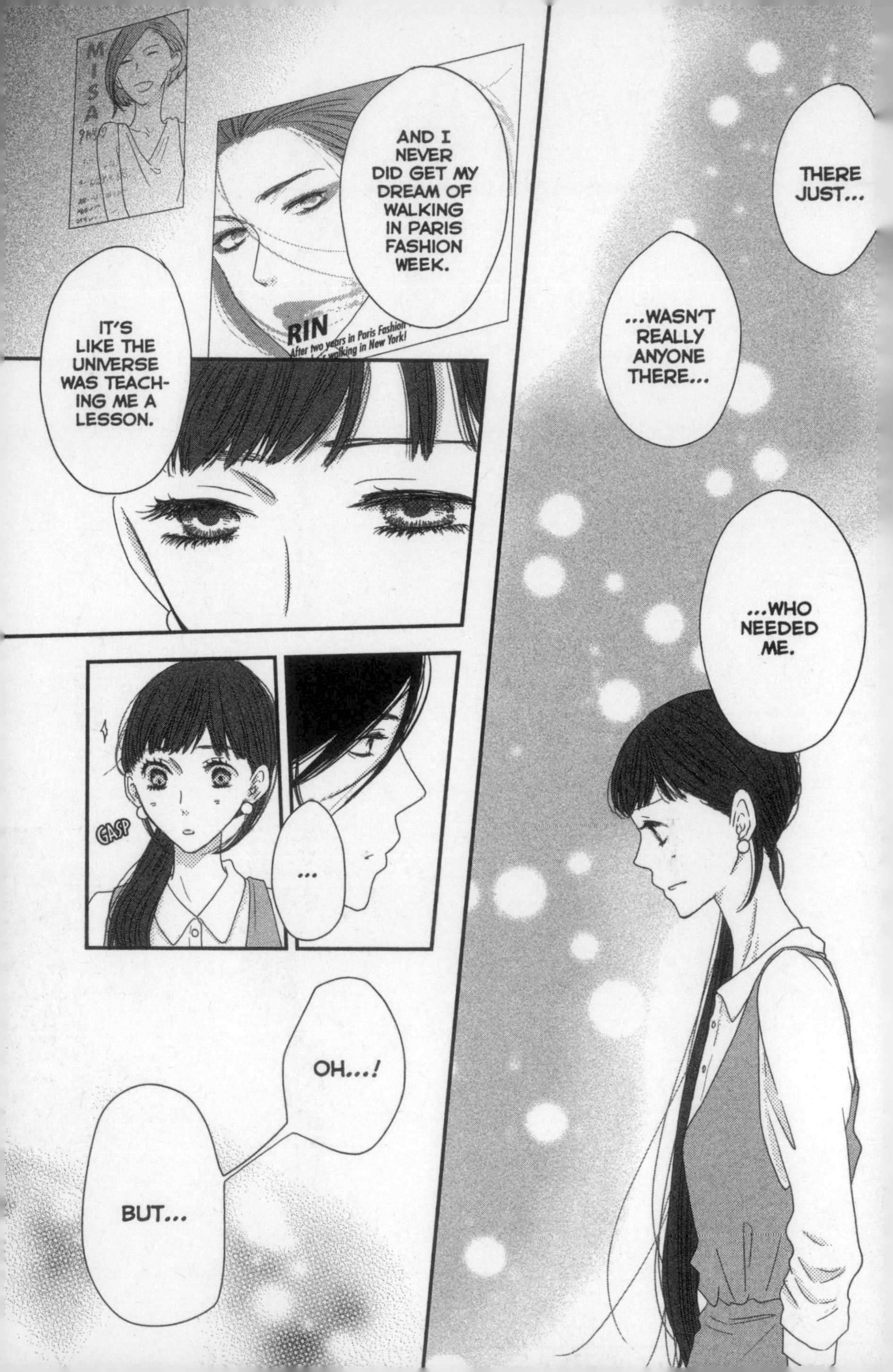
THERE JUST...
...WASN'T REALLY ANYONE THERE...
...WHO NEEDED ME.
MISA
AND I NEVER DID GET MY DREAM OF WALKING IN PARIS FASHION WEEK.
RIN
After two years in Paris Fashion
walking in New York!
IT'S LIKE THE UNIVERSE WAS TEACH-ING ME A LESSON.
...
GASP
OH...!
BUT...

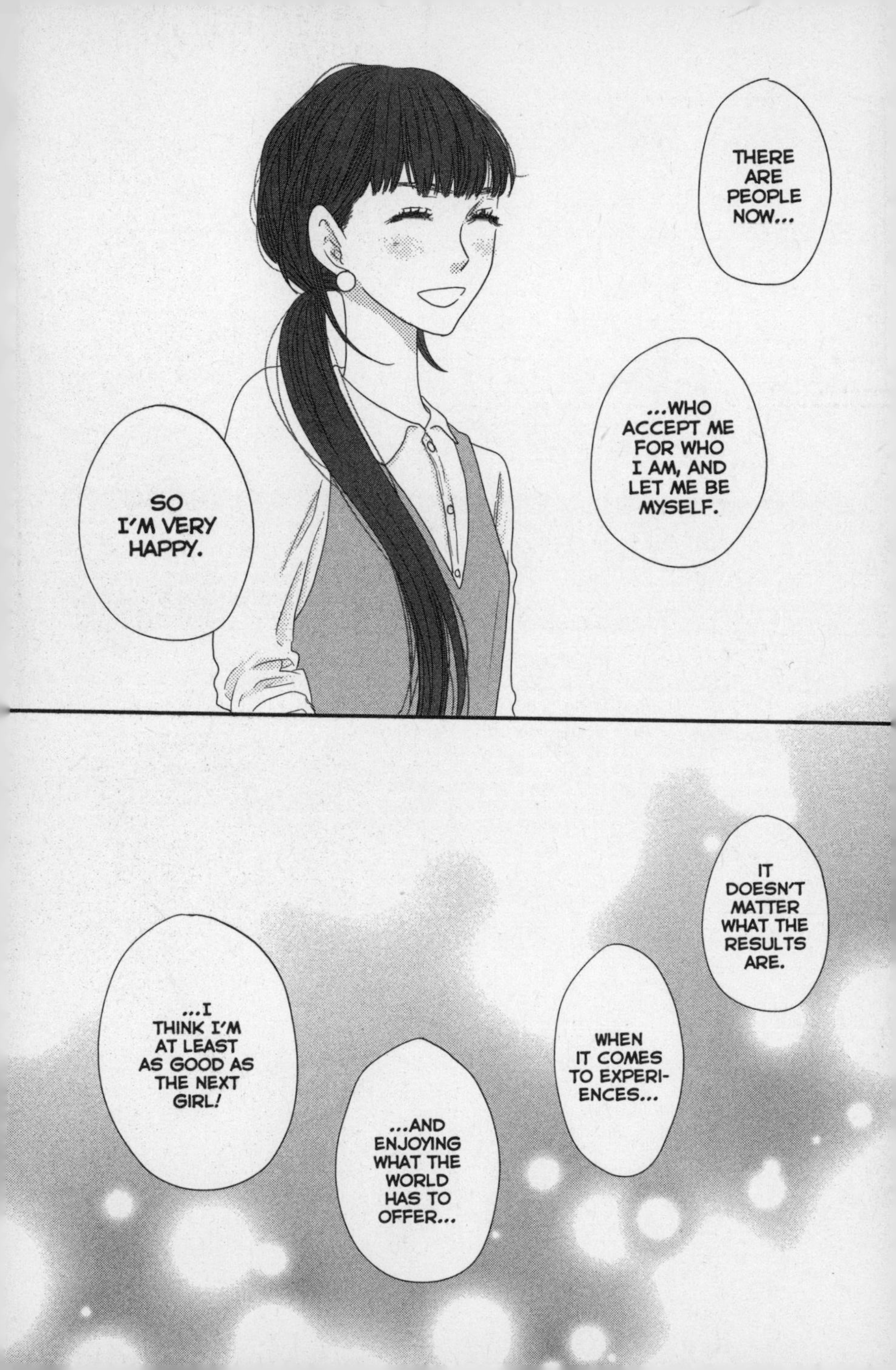
THERE ARE PEOPLE NOW...
...WHO ACCEPT ME FOR WHO I AM, AND LET ME BE MYSELF.
SO I'M VERY HAPPY.
IT DOESN'T MATTER WHAT THE RESULTS ARE.
WHEN IT COMES TO EXPERI-ENCES...
...AND ENJOYING WHAT THE WORLD HAS TO OFFER...
...I THINK I'M AT LEAST AS GOOD AS THE NEXT GIRL!

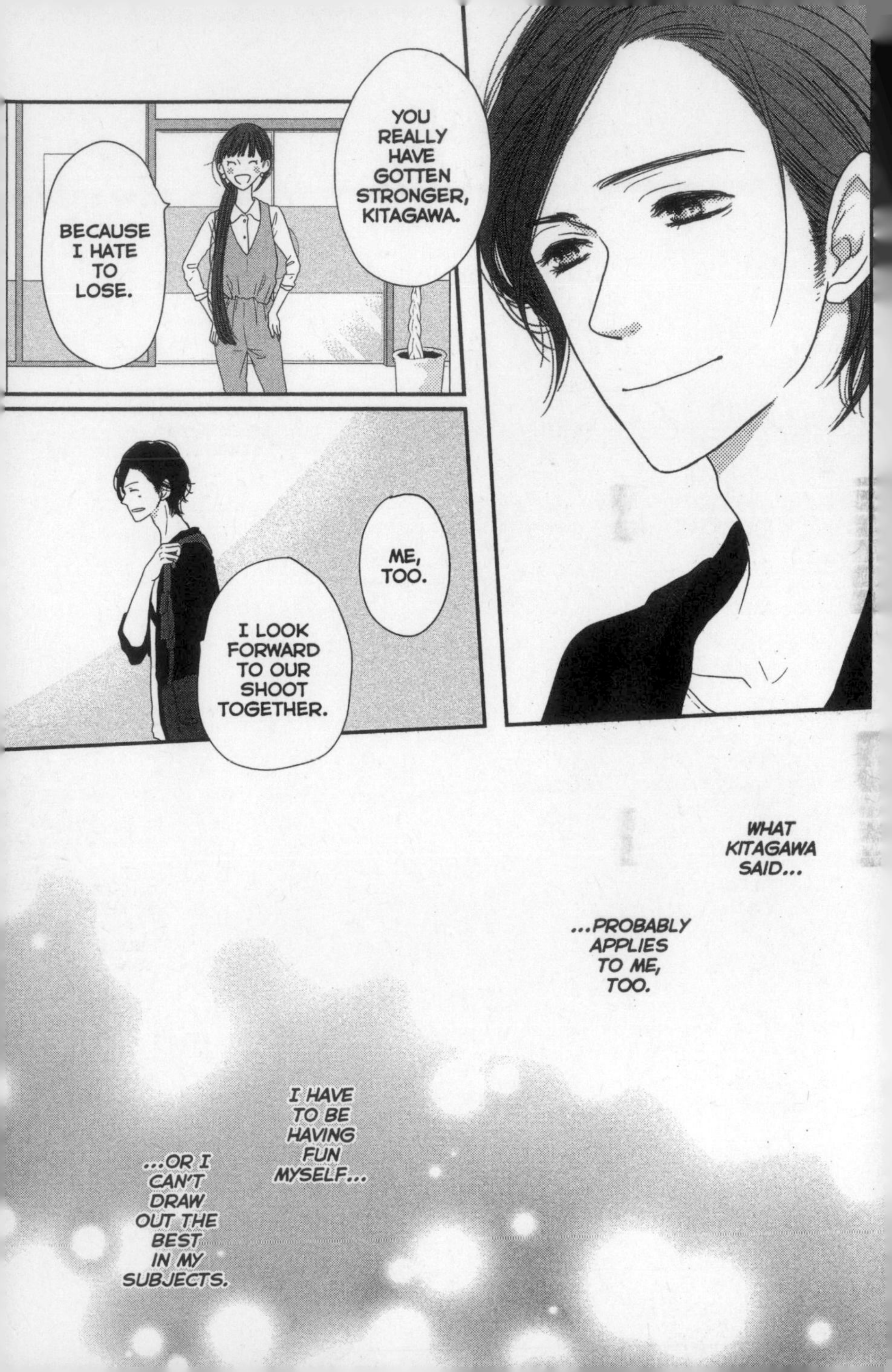
YOU REALLY HAVE GOTTEN STRONGER, KITAGAWA.
BECAUSE I HATE TO LOSE.
ME, TOO.
I LOOK FORWARD TO OUR SHOOT TOGETHER.
WHAT KITAGAWA SAID...
...PROBABLY APPLIES TO ME, TOO.
I HAVE TO BE HAVING FUN MYSELF...
...OR I CAN'T DRAW OUT THE BEST IN MY SUBJECTS.

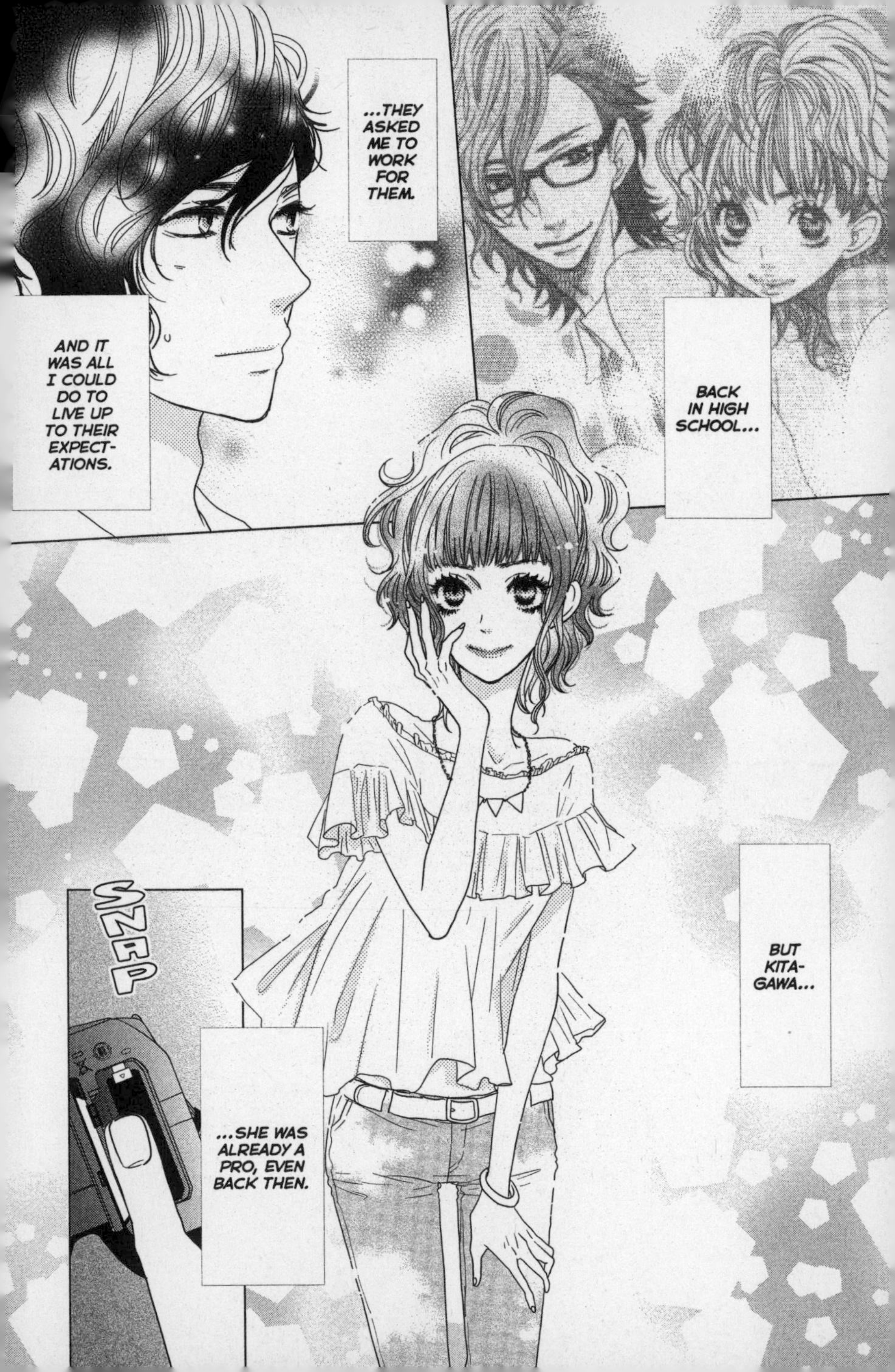
BACK IN HIGH SCHOOL...
...THEY ASKED ME TO WORK FOR THEM.
AND IT WAS ALL I COULD DO TO LIVE UP TO THEIR EXPECT-ATIONS.
BUT KITA-GAWA...
SNAP
...SHE WAS ALREADY A PRO, EVEN BACK THEN.

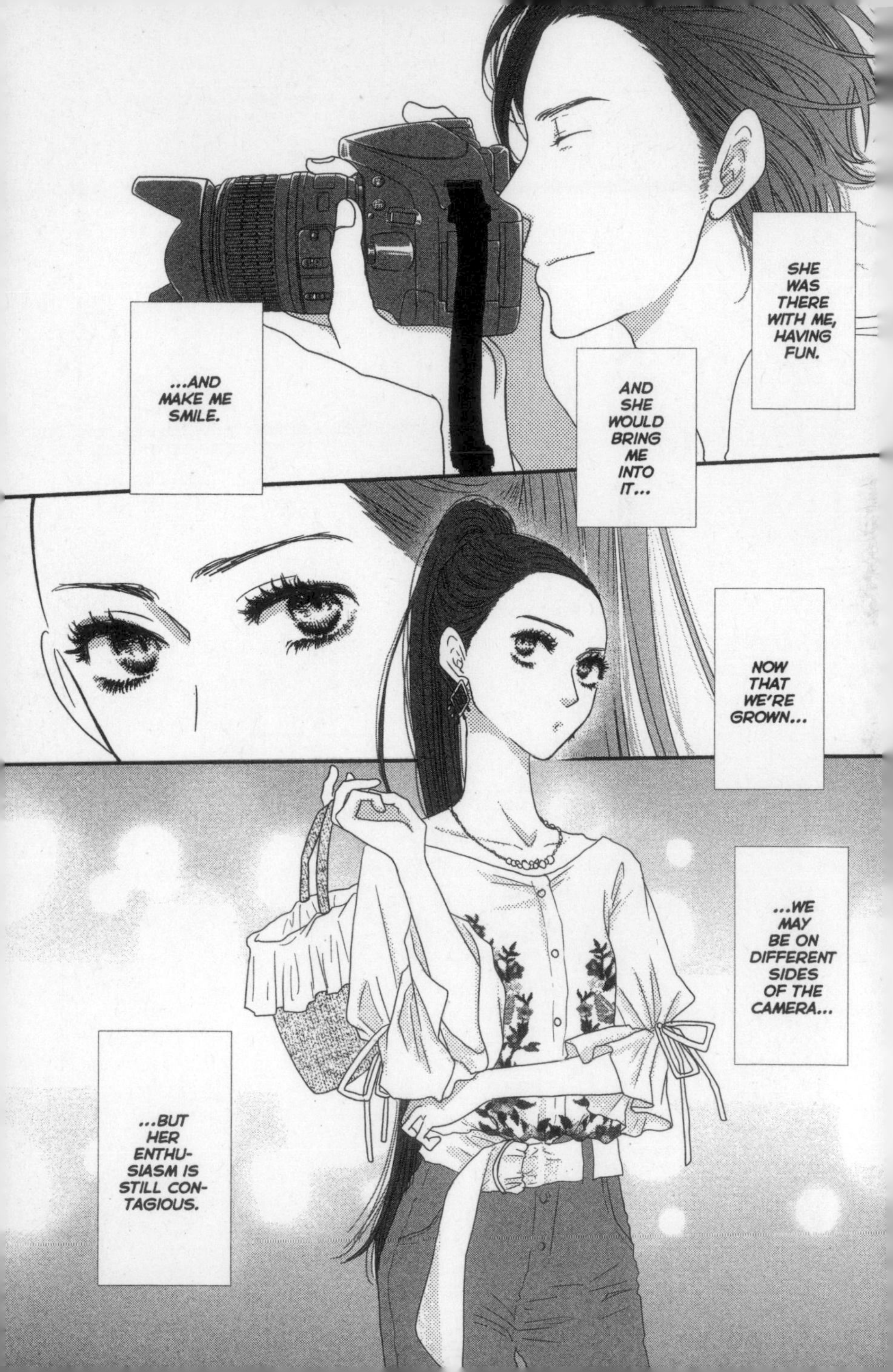
SHE WAS THERE WITH ME, HAVING FUN.
AND SHE WOULD BRING ME INTO IT...
...AND MAKE ME SMILE.
NOW THAT WE'RE GROWN...
...WE MAY BE ON DIFFERENT SIDES OF THE CAMERA...
...BUT HER ENTHUSIASM IS STILL CONTAGIOUS.

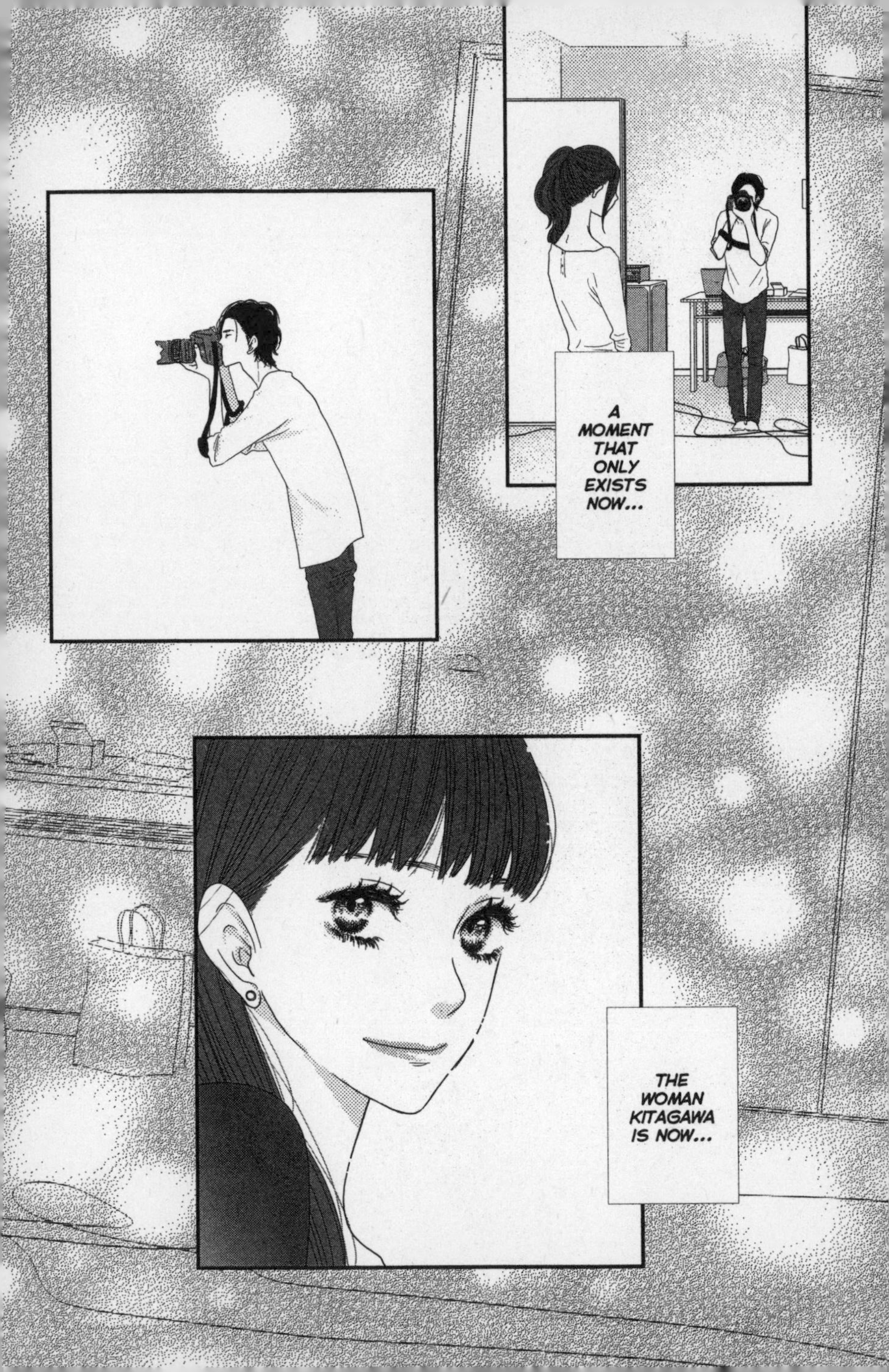
A MOMENT THAT ONLY EXISTS NOW...
THE WOMAN KITAGAWA IS NOW...

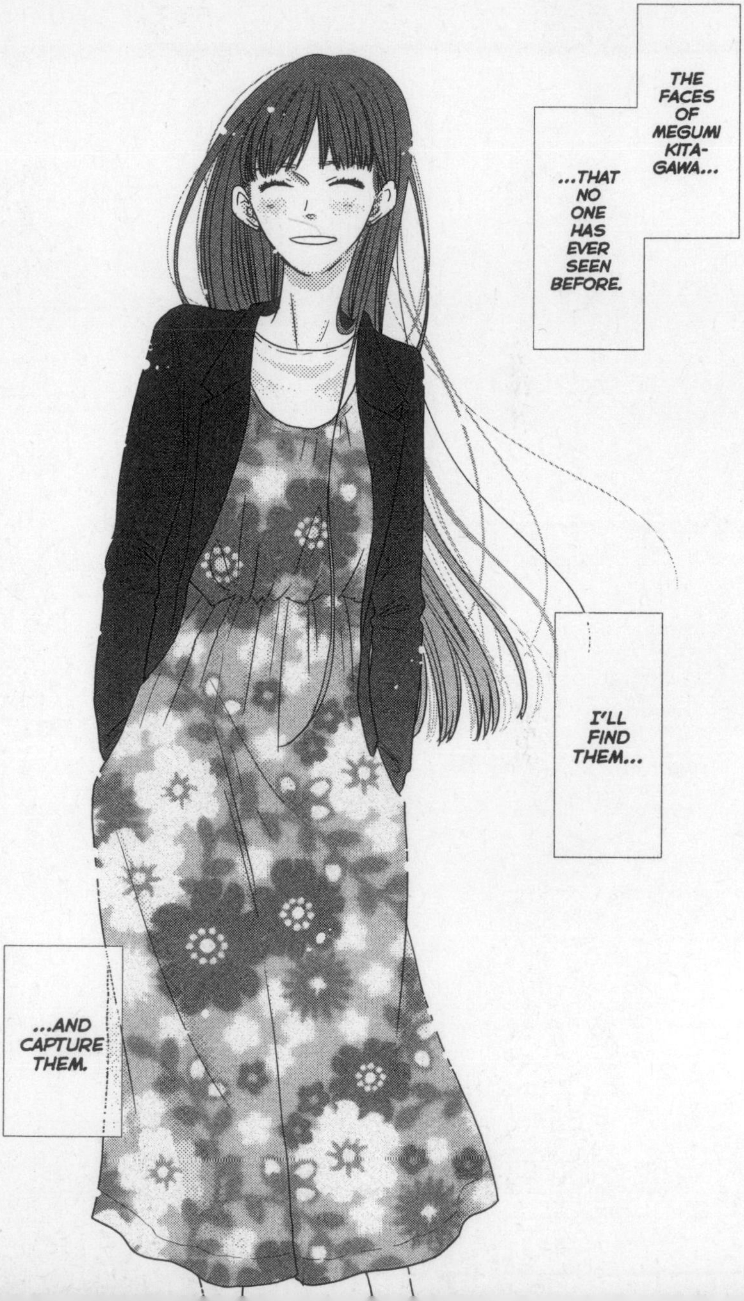
THE FACES OF MEGUMI KITA-GAWA...
...THAT NO ONE HAS EVER SEEN BEFORE.
I'LL FIND THEM...
...AND CAPTURE THEM.

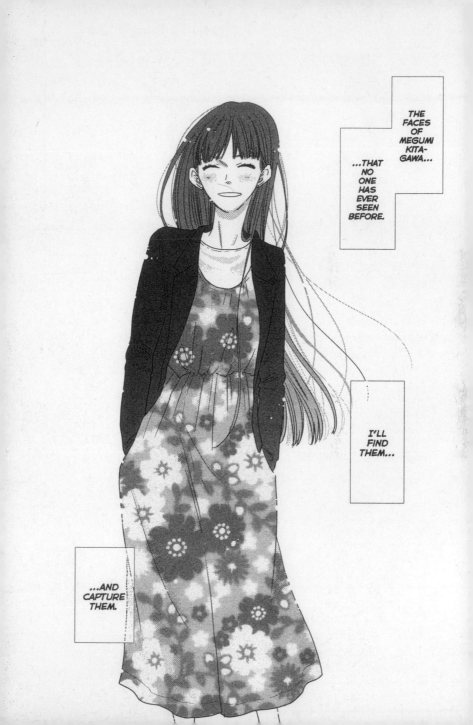

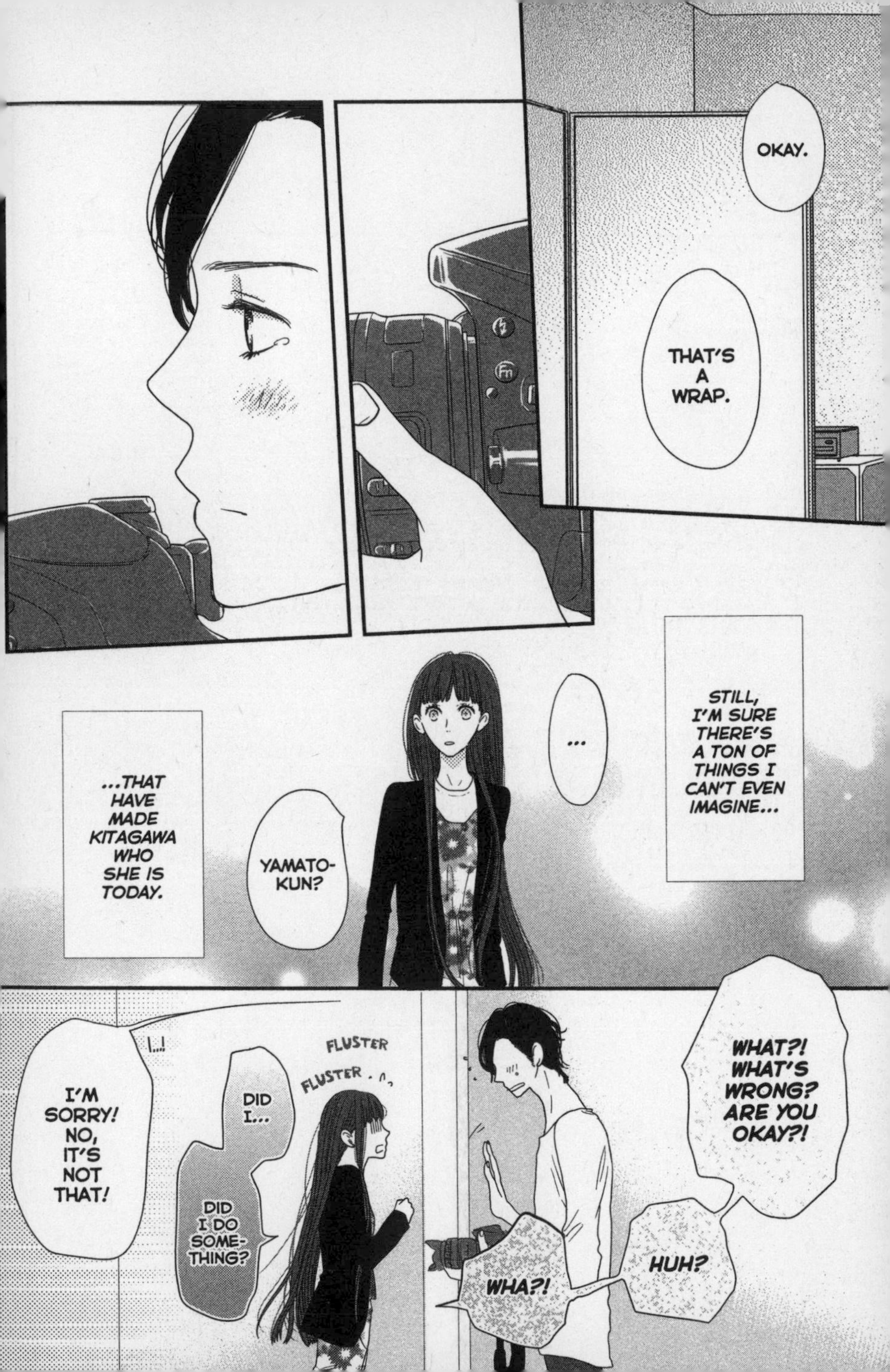
OKAY.
THAT'S A WRAP.
STILL, I'M SURE THERE'S A TON OF THINGS I CAN'T EVEN IMAGINE...
...
YAMATO-KUN?
...THAT HAVE MADE KITAGAWA WHO SHE IS TODAY.
WHAT?! WHAT'S WRONG? ARE YOU OKAY?!
HUH?
WHA?!
FLUSTER
FLUSTER
DID I...
DID I DO SOME-THING?
I'M SORRY! NO, IT'S NOT THAT!

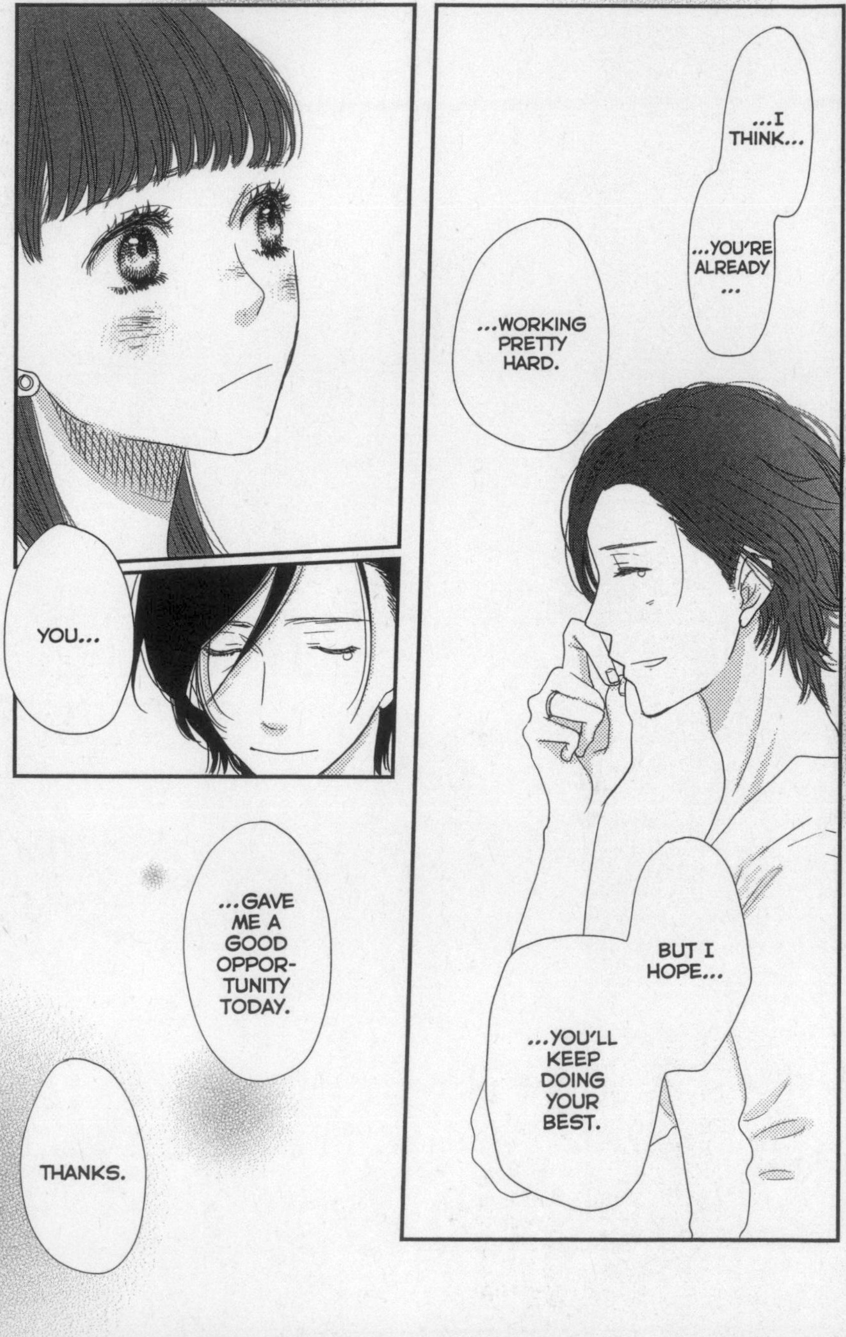
...I THINK...
...YOU'RE ALREADY ...
...WORKING PRETTY HARD.
BUT I HOPE...
...YOU'LL KEEP DOING YOUR BEST.
YOU...
...GAVE ME A GOOD OPPOR-TUNITY TODAY.
THANKS.

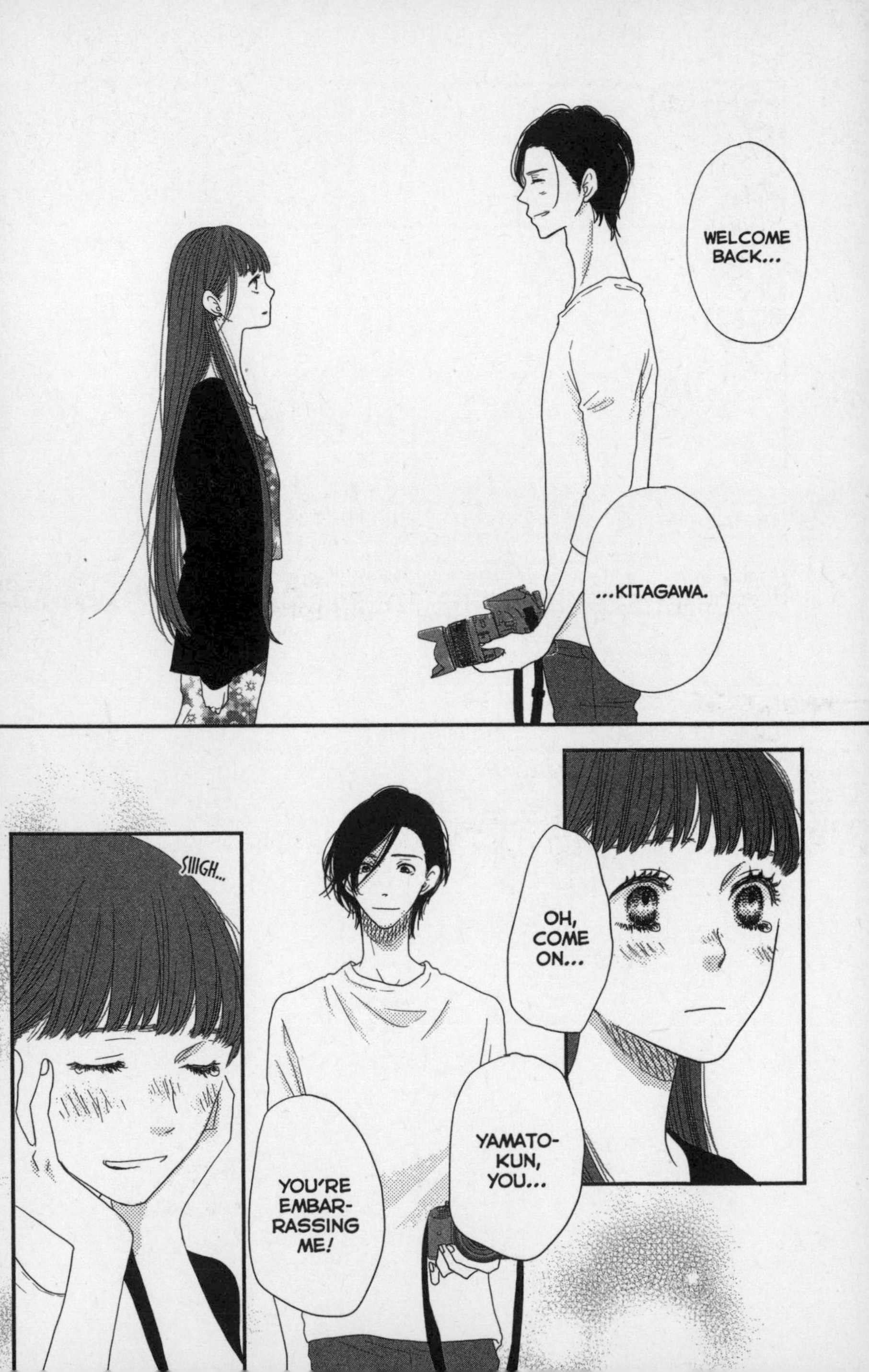
WELCOME BACK...
...KITAGAWA.
OH, COME ON...
YAMATO-KUN, YOU...
SIIIGH...
YOU'RE EMBARRASSING ME!

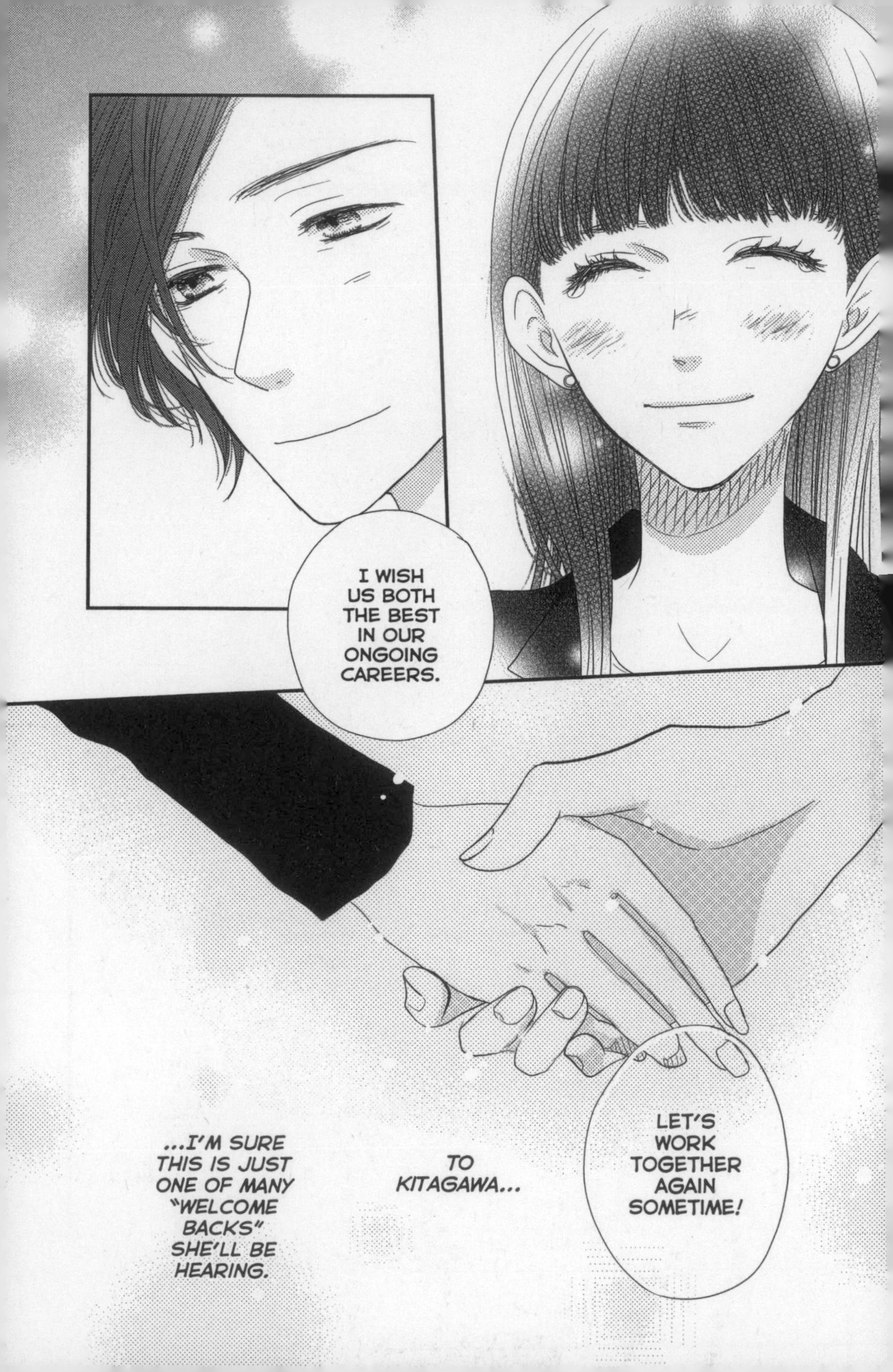
I WISH US BOTH THE BEST IN OUR ONGOING CAREERS.
LET'S WORK TOGETHER AGAIN SOMETIME!
TO KITAGAWA...
...I'M SURE THIS IS JUST ONE OF MANY "WELCOME BACKS" SHE'LL BE HEARING.

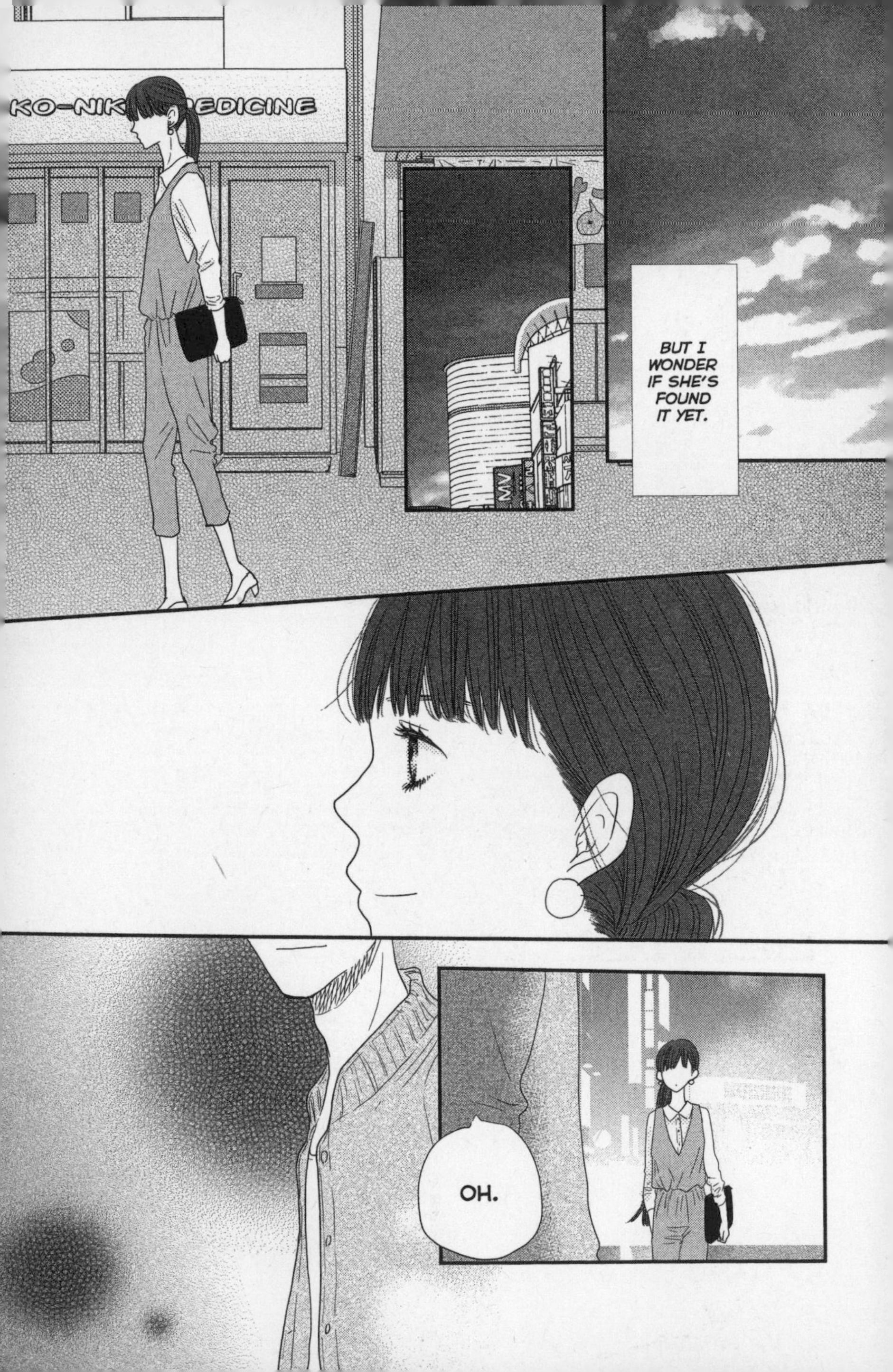

BUT I WONDER IF SHE'S FOUND IT YET.
OH.

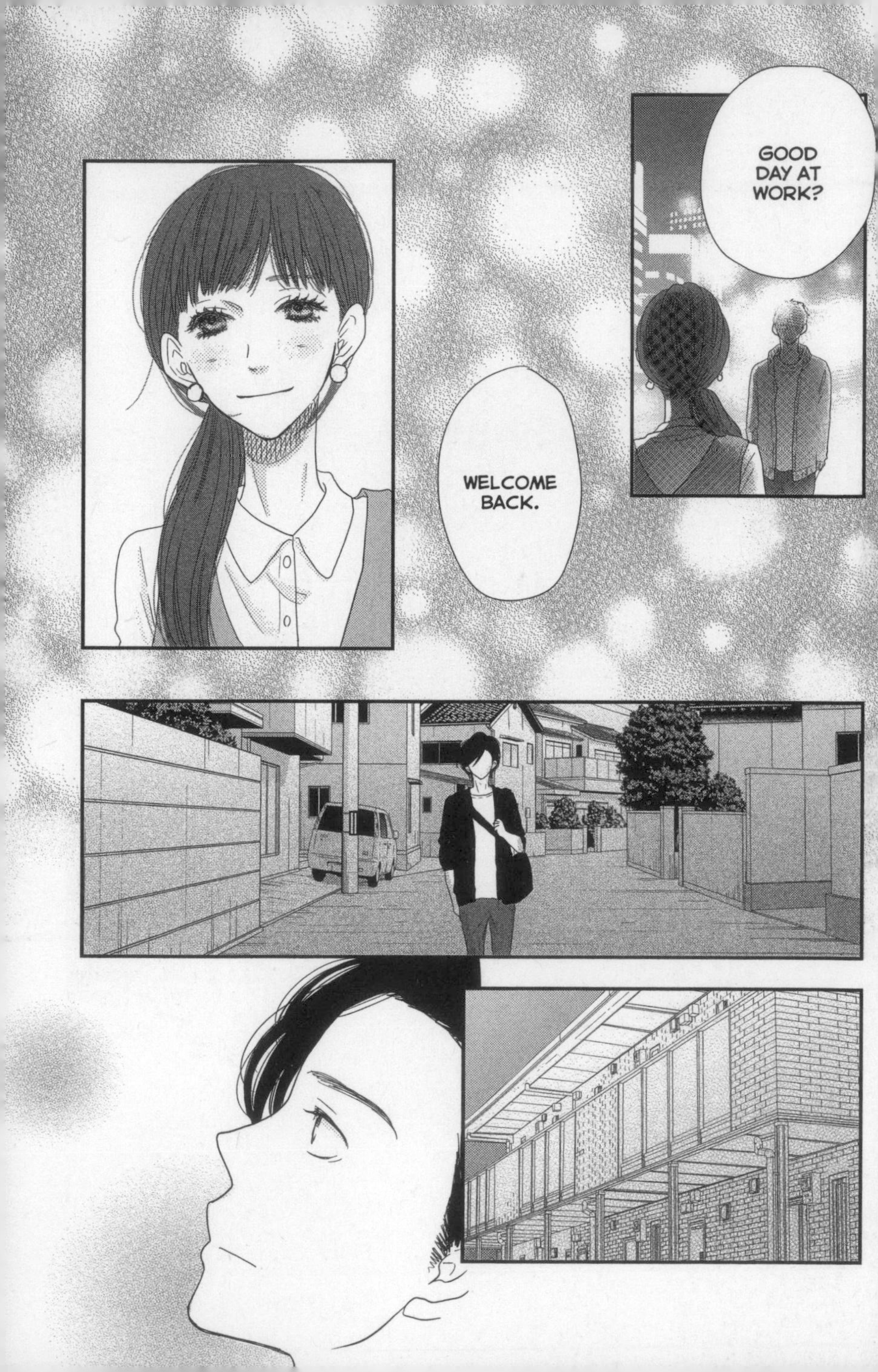
GOOD DAY AT WORK?
WELCOME BACK.

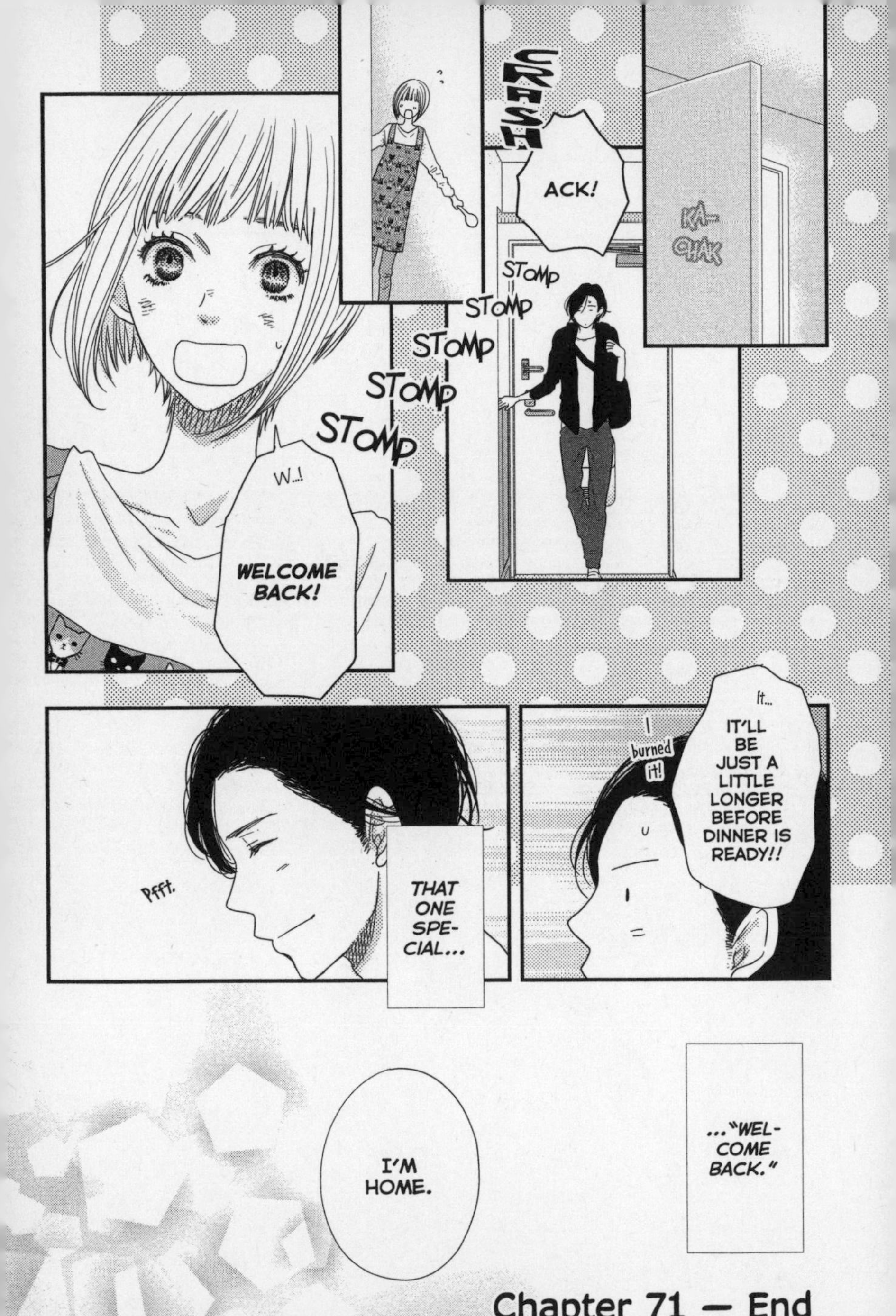
KA-CHAK
CRASH
ACK!
STOMP STOMP STOMP STOMP STOMP
W..!
WELCOME BACK!
It...
IT'LL BE JUST A LITTLE LONGER BEFORE DINNER IS READY!!
I burned it!
THAT ONE SPECIAL...
Pfft.
..."WEL-COME BACK."
I'M HOME.

Chapter 71 — End

Say "I love you".

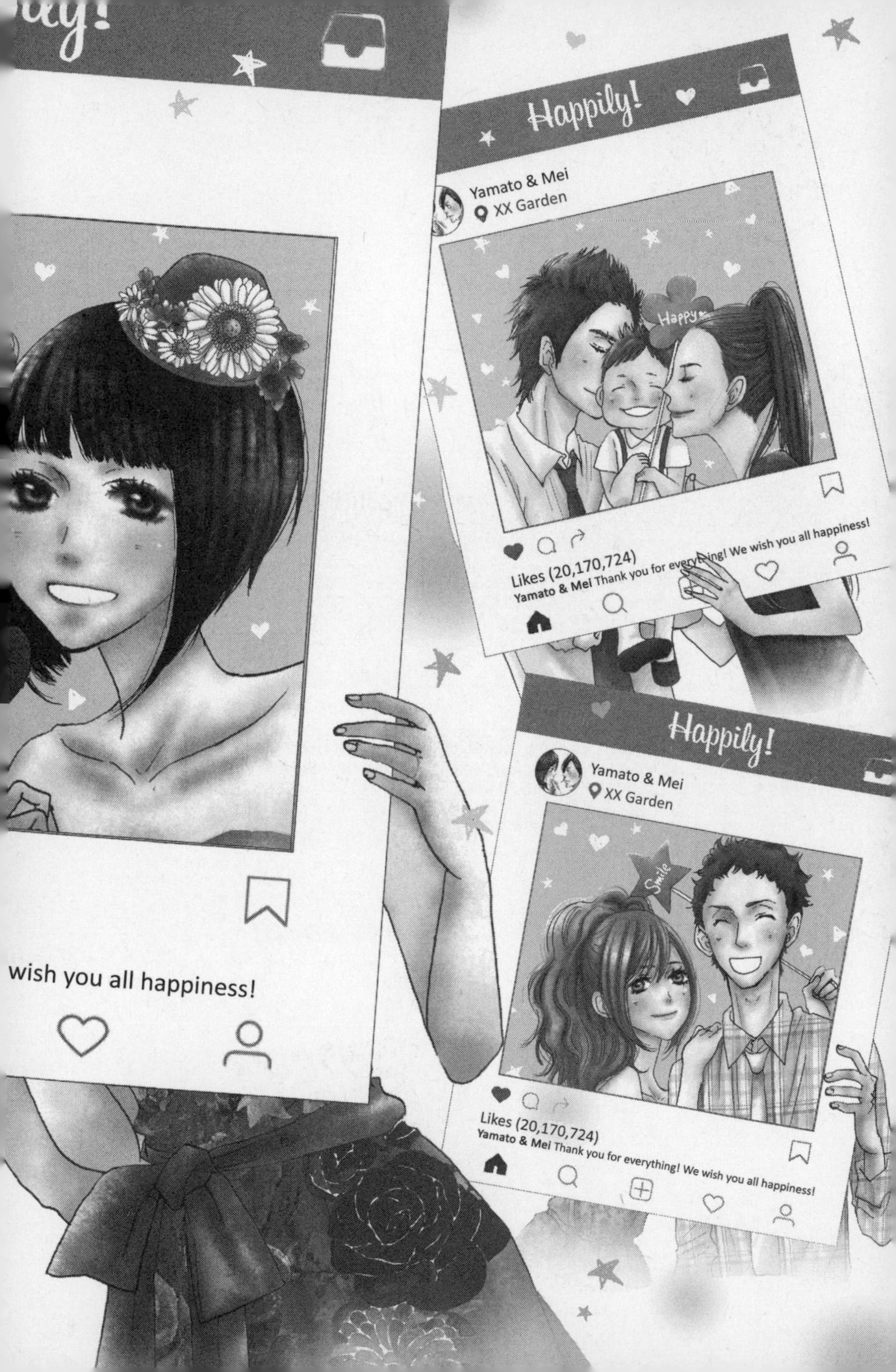

Happily!
Yamato & Mei
XX Garden
Happy
Likes (20,170,724)
Yamato & Mei Thank you for every
ing! We wish you all happiness!
Happily!
Yamato & Mei
XX Garden
Smile
Likes (20,170,724)
Yamato & Mei Thank you for everything! We wish you all happiness!
wish you all happiness!

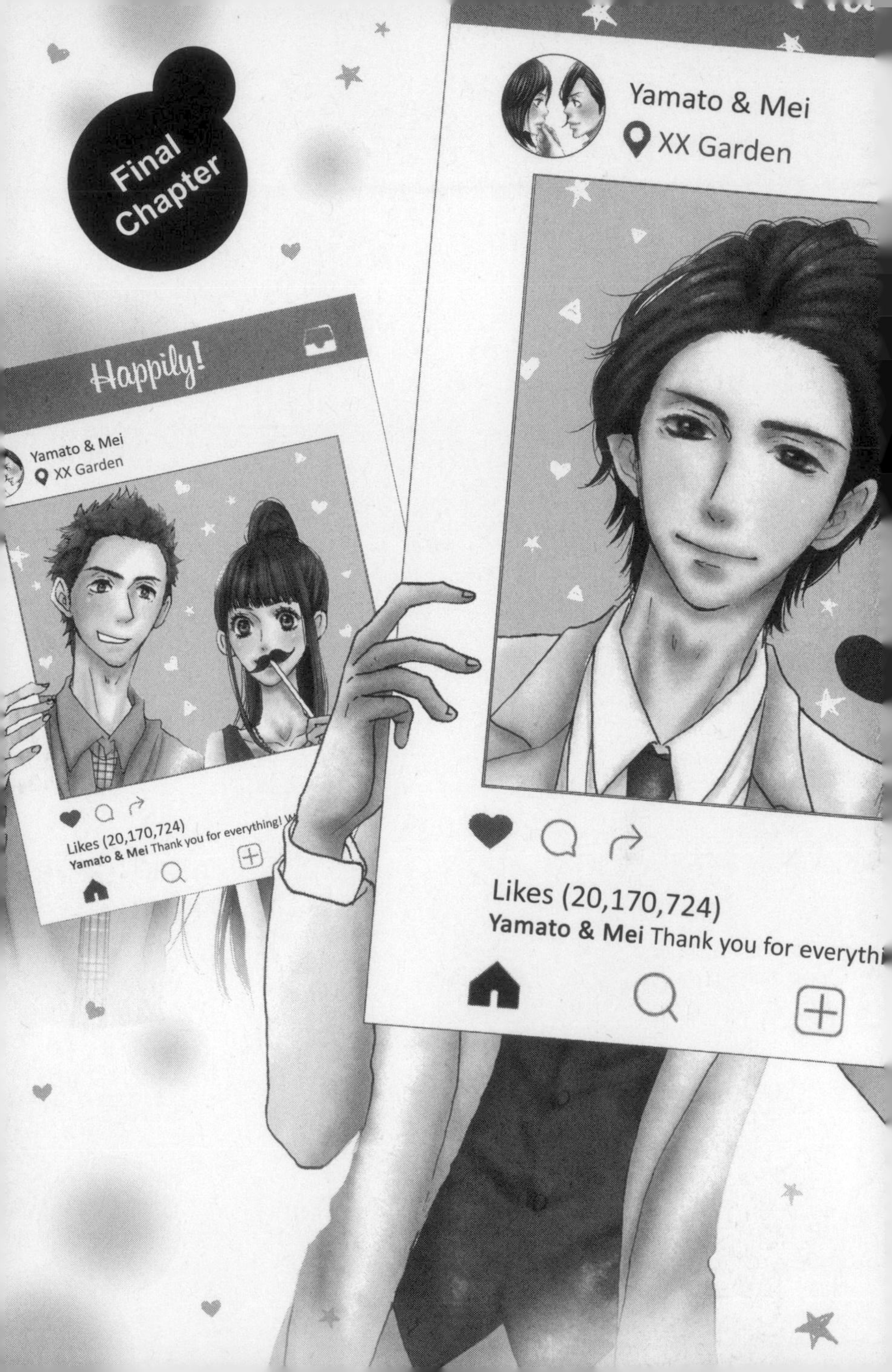
Final Chapter
Yamato & Mei
XX Garden
Likes (20,170,724)
Yamato & Mei Thank you for everythi
Happily!
Yamato & Mei
XX Garden
Likes (20,170,724)
Yamato & Mei Thank you for everything!

Say "I love you".

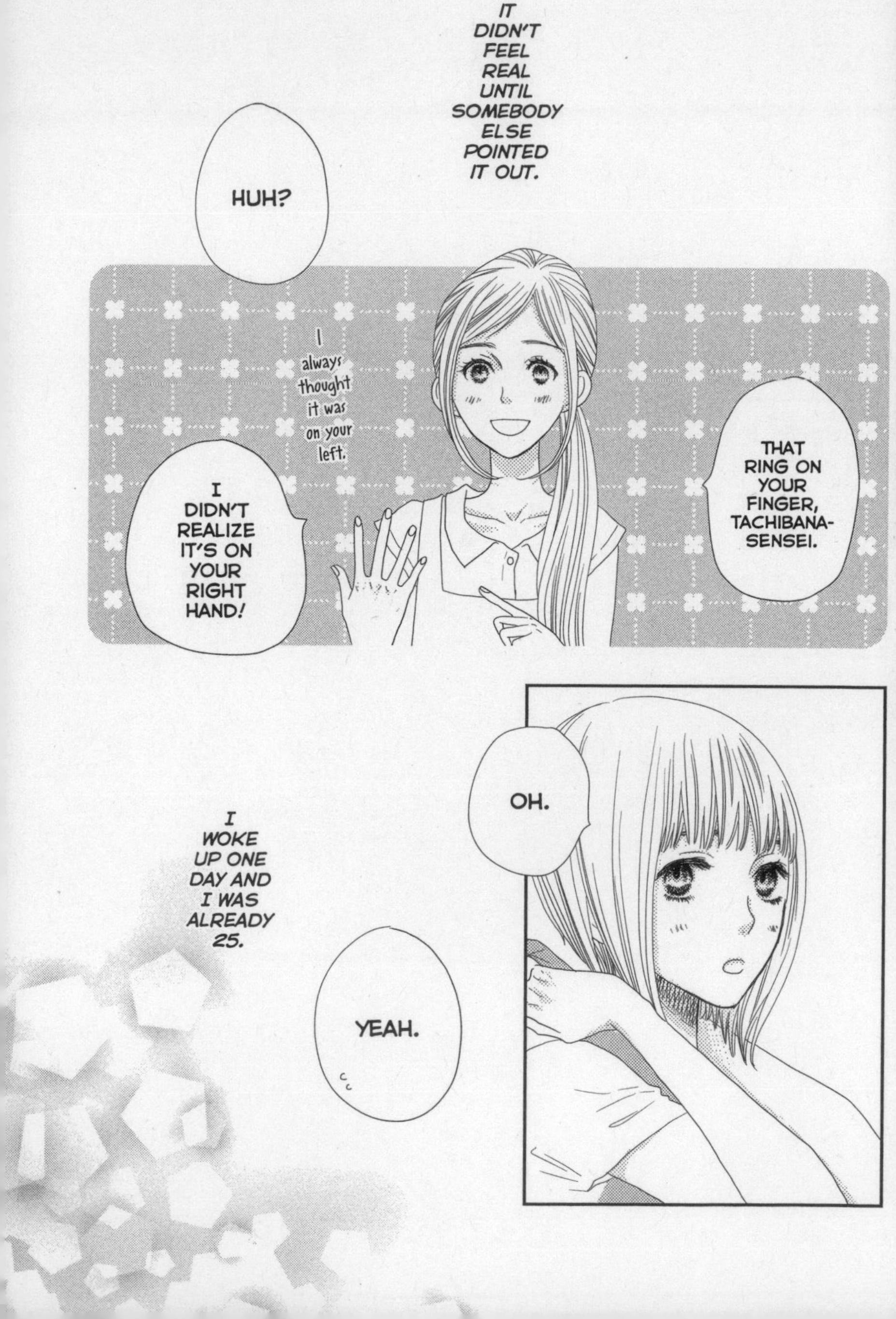
IT DIDN'T FEEL REAL UNTIL SOMEBODY ELSE POINTED IT OUT.
HUH?
THAT RING ON YOUR FINGER, TACHIBANA-SENSEI.
I always thought it was on your left.
I DIDN'T REALIZE IT'S ON YOUR RIGHT HAND!
OH.
I WOKE UP ONE DAY AND I WAS ALREADY 25.
YEAH.

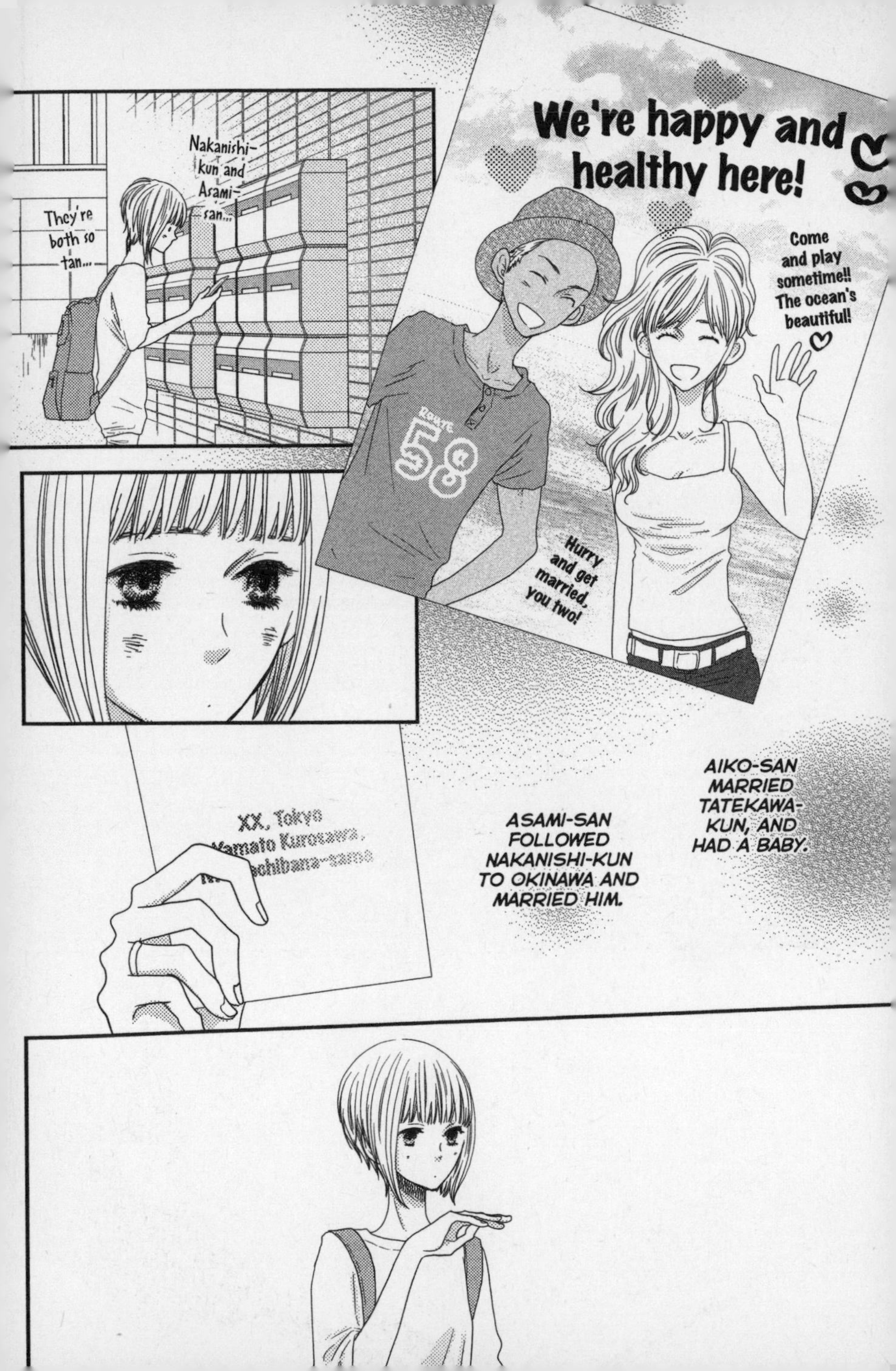
We're happy and healthy here!
Come and play sometime!! The ocean's beautiful!
Hurry and get married, you two!
Nakanishi-kun and Asami-san...
They're both so tan...
XX, Tokyo
Aiko-san married Tatekawa-kun, and had a baby.
Asami-san followed Nakanishi-kun to Okinawa and married him.

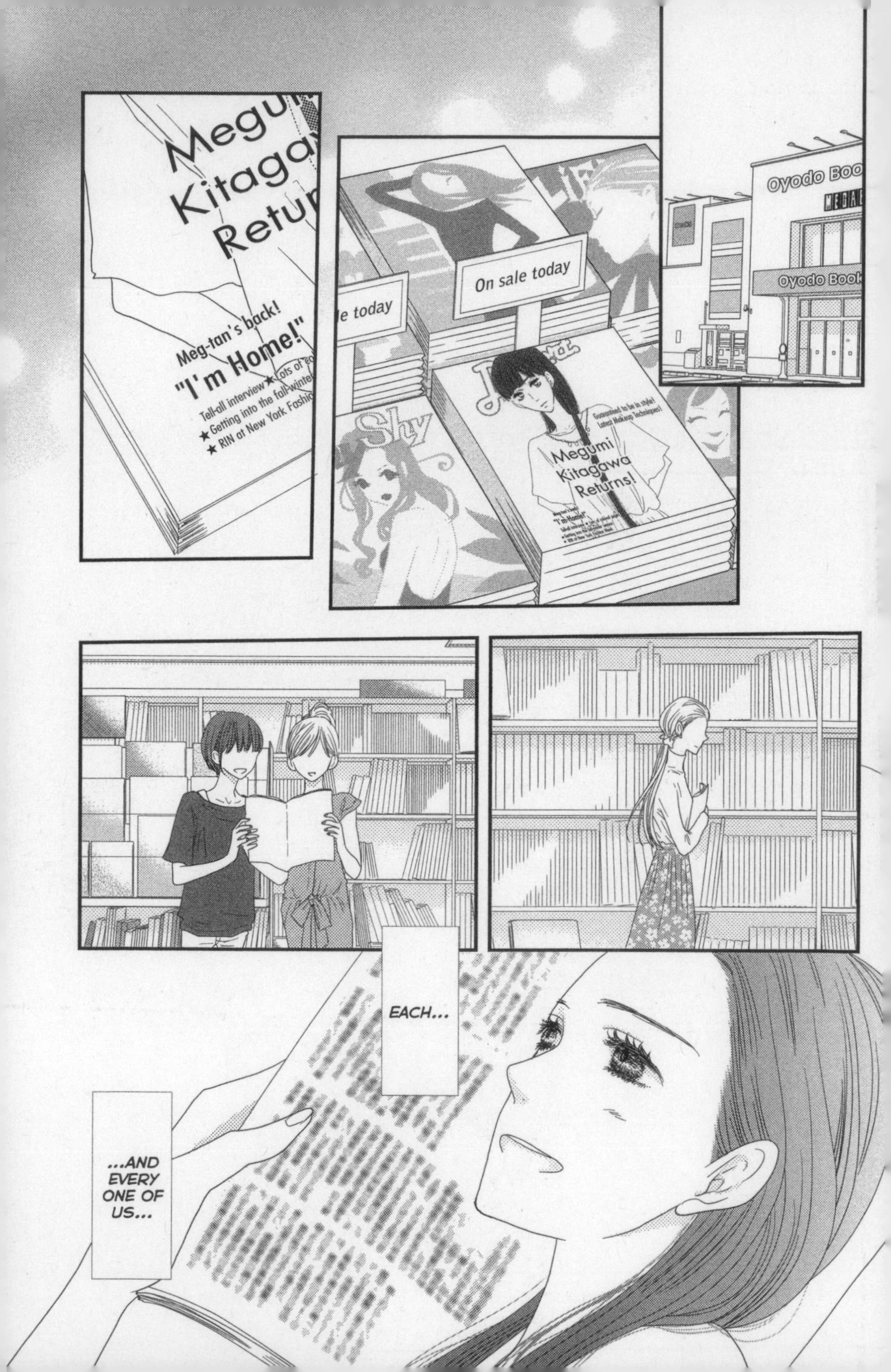

Oyodo Boo
Oyodo Book
On sale today
le today
Guaranteed to be in style! Latest Makeup Techniques!
Megumi Kitagawa Returns!
Shy
Megu Kitaga Retur
Meg-tan's back!
"I'm Home!"
Tell-all interview★Lots of go
★Getting into the fall-winter
★RIN at New York Fashio
EACH...
...AND EVERY ONE OF US...

Hinode
Publishing

Are you in love right now?

Yes, but it's one-sided (ha ha).

We went to the same high school, and now he's a trainer at a gym. It used to be that we'd start arguing as soon as we ran into each other on the street, and I c even stand o look at him.

But no wrong watchin ould e him.

WE'RE
ALL...

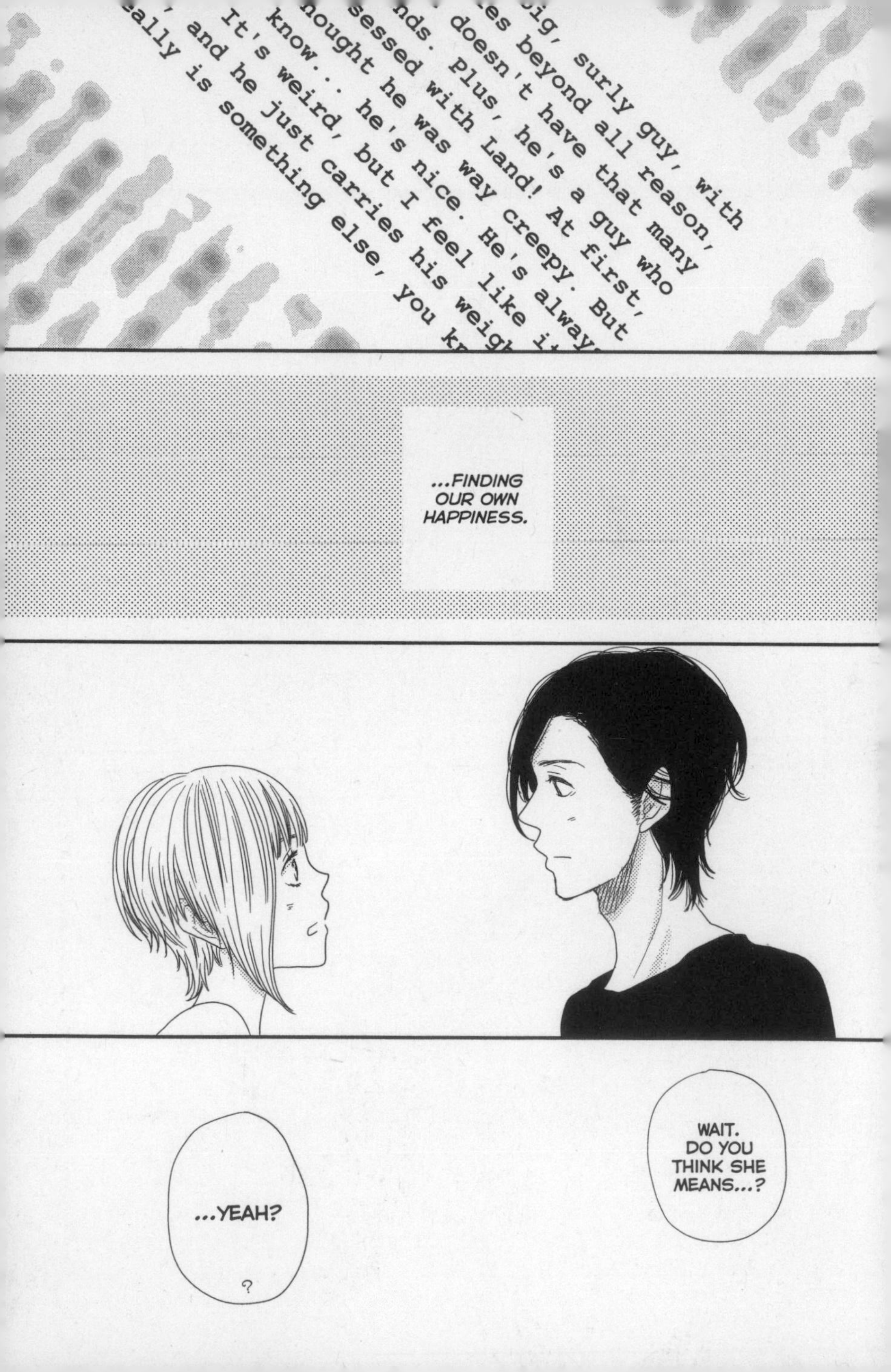
surly guy, with
beyond all reason,
doesn't have that many
Plus, he's a guy who
sessed with Land! At first,
he was way creepy. But
know... he's nice. He's
It's weird, but I feel like
and he just carries his
is something else, you
...FINDING OUR OWN HAPPINESS.
WAIT. DO YOU THINK SHE MEANS...?
...YEAH?
?

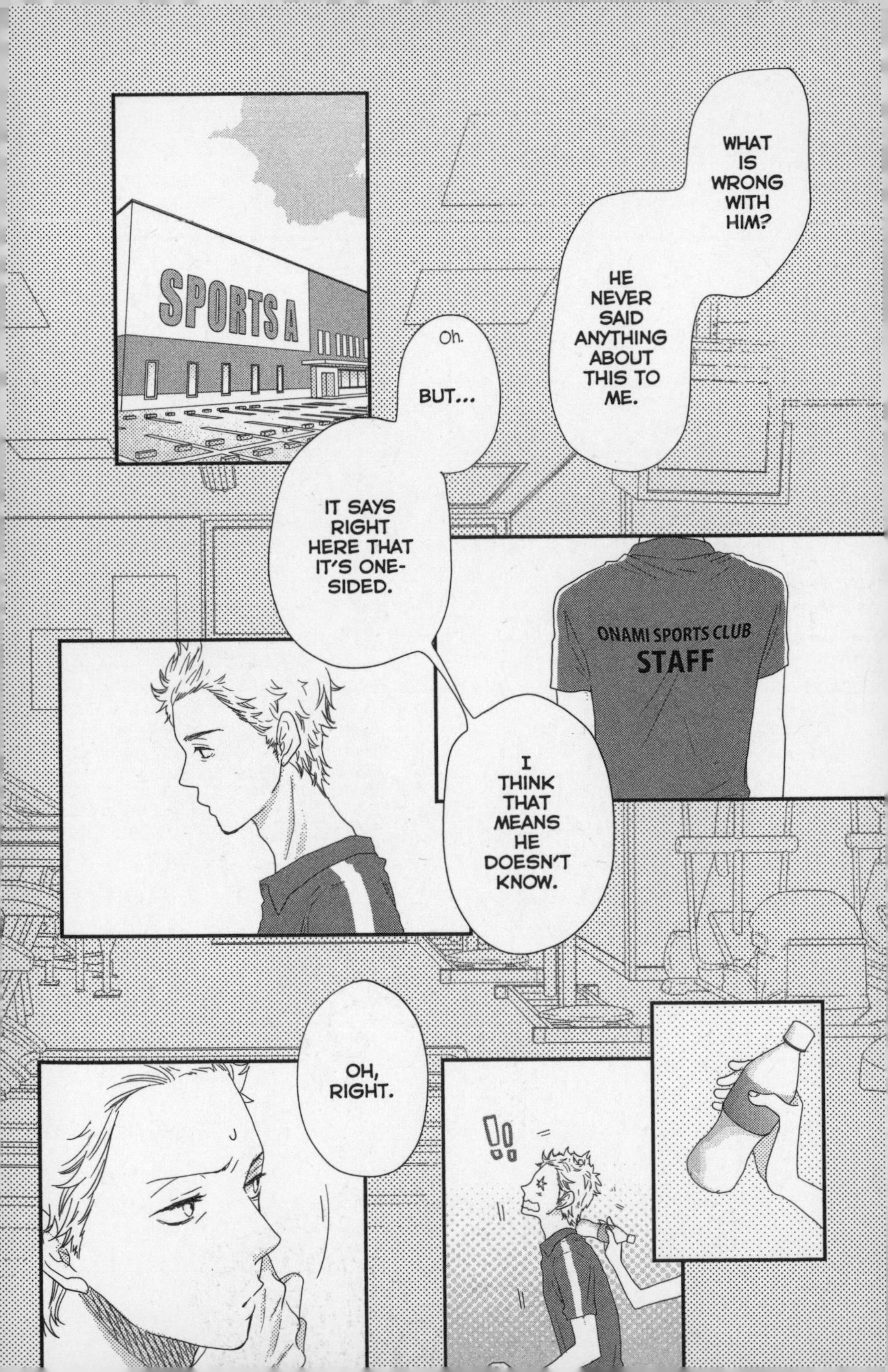
WHAT IS WRONG WITH HIM?
HE NEVER SAID ANYTHING ABOUT THIS TO ME.
SPORTS A
Oh.
BUT...
IT SAYS RIGHT HERE THAT IT'S ONE-SIDED.
ONAMI SPORTS CLUB STAFF
I THINK THAT MEANS HE DOESN'T KNOW.
!!
OH, RIGHT.

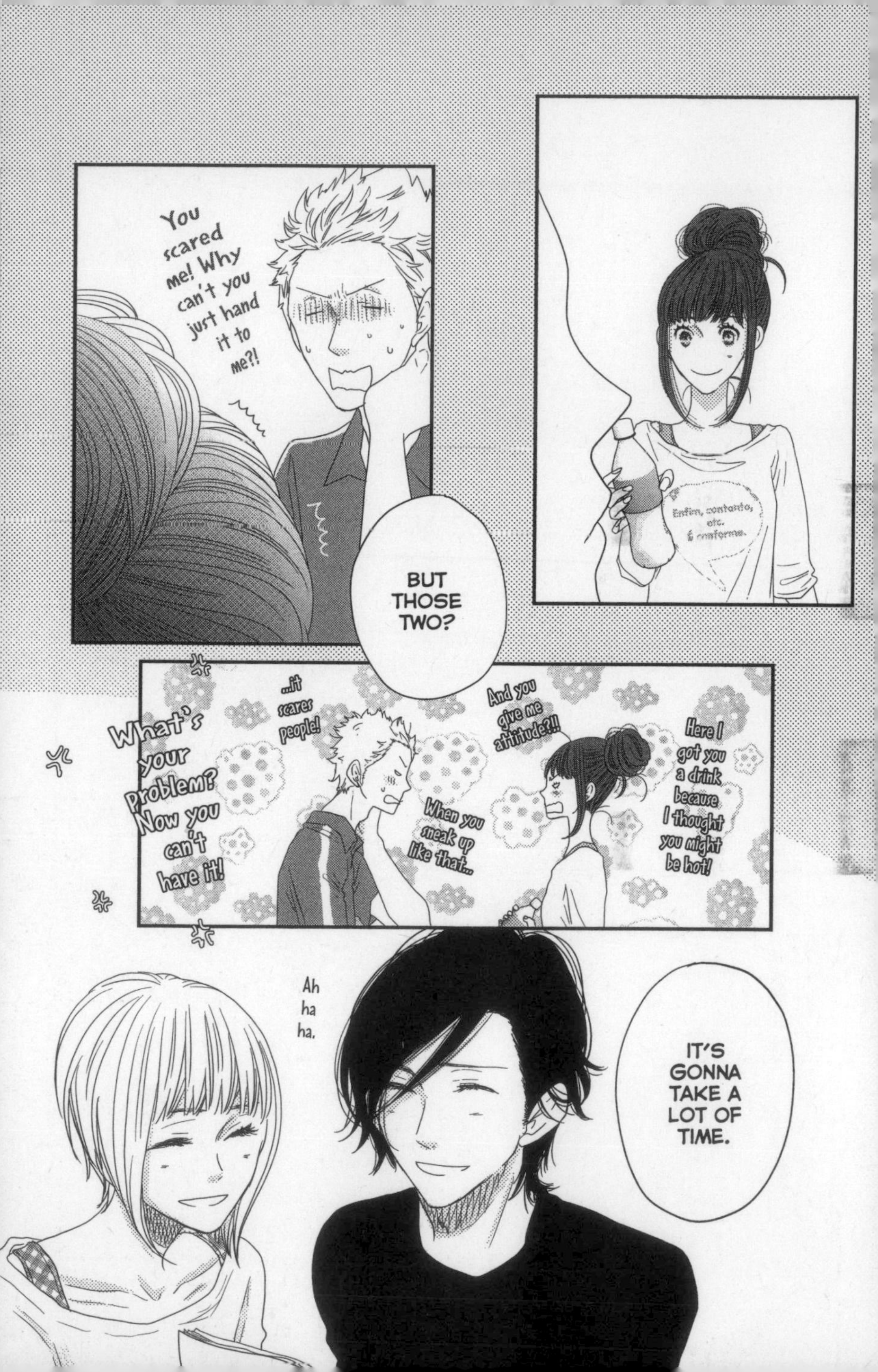
You scared me! Why can't you just hand it to me?!
BUT THOSE TWO?
Here I got you a drink because I thought you might be hot!
And you give me attitude?!!
When you sneak up like that...
...it scares people!
What's your problem? Now you can't have it!
IT'S GONNA TAKE A LOT OF TIME.
Ah ha ha.

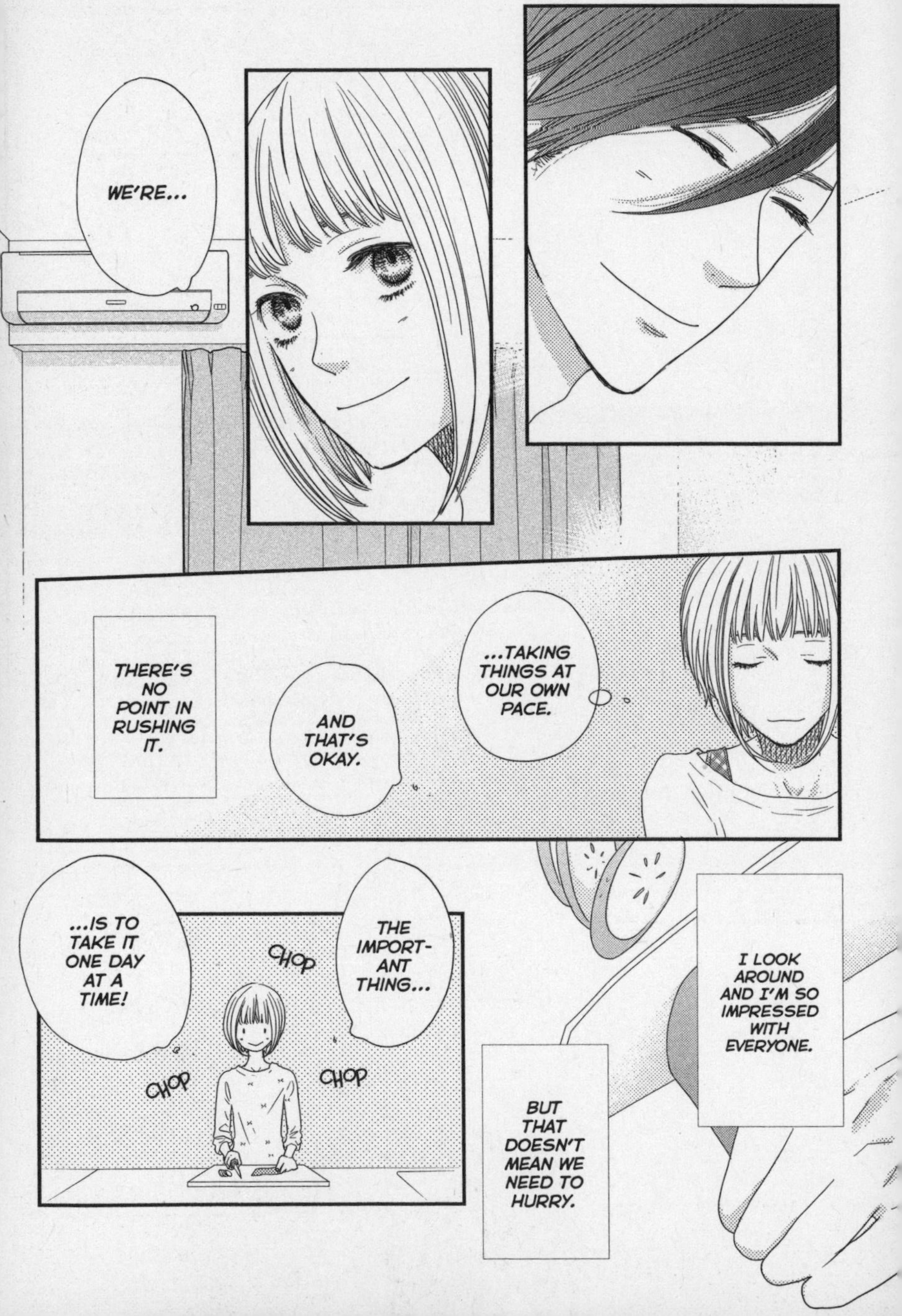
WE'RE...
...TAKING THINGS AT OUR OWN PACE.
AND THAT'S OKAY.
THERE'S NO POINT IN RUSHING IT.
I LOOK AROUND AND I'M SO IMPRESSED WITH EVERYONE.
BUT THAT DOESN'T MEAN WE NEED TO HURRY.
THE IMPORT-ANT THING...
CHOP
CHOP
CHOP
...IS TO TAKE IT ONE DAY AT A TIME!

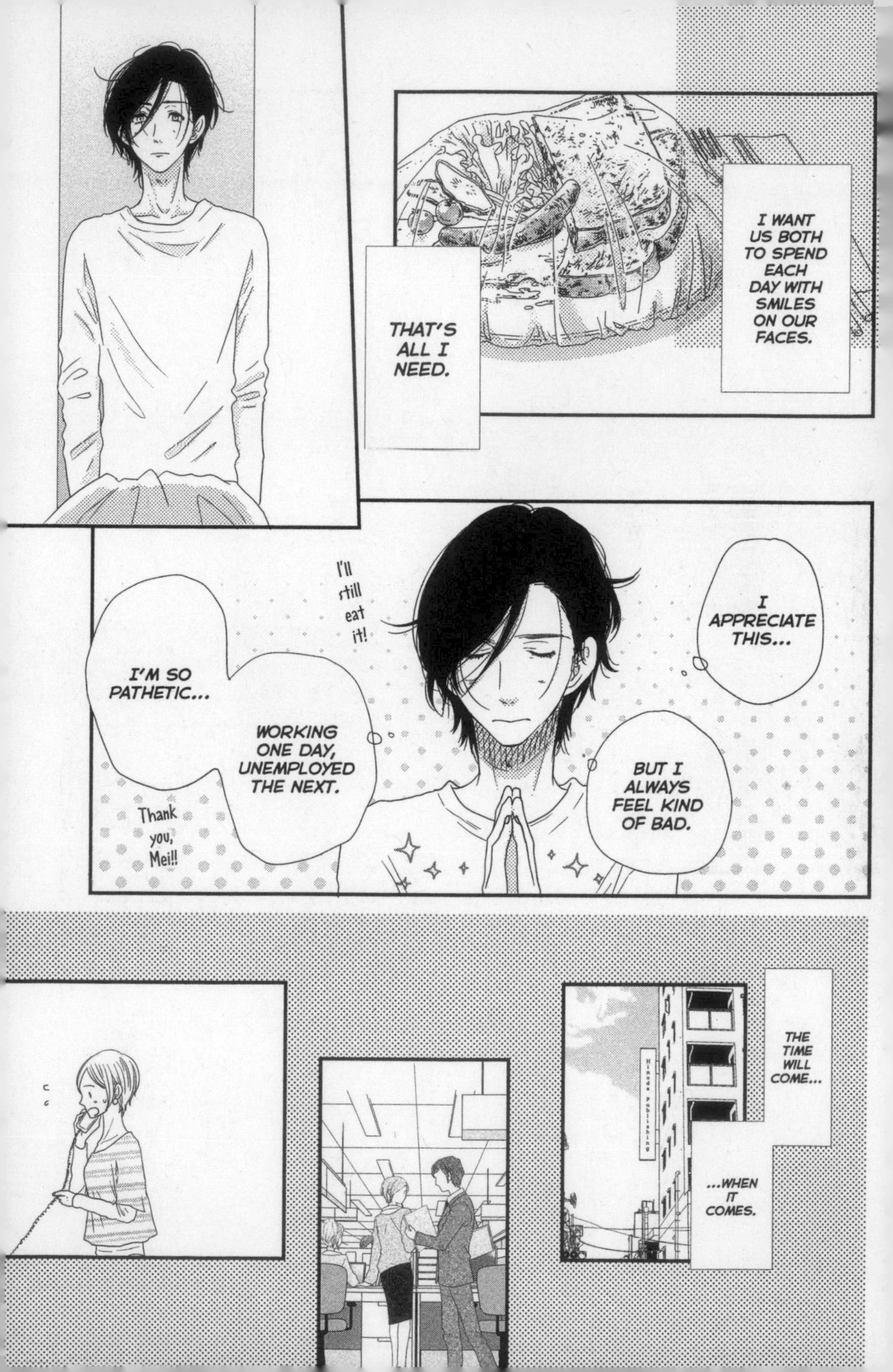
I WANT US BOTH TO SPEND EACH DAY WITH SMILES ON OUR FACES.
THAT'S ALL I NEED.
I APPRECIATE THIS...
BUT I ALWAYS FEEL KIND OF BAD.
I'll still eat it!
I'M SO PATHETIC...
WORKING ONE DAY, UNEMPLOYED THE NEXT.
Thank you, Mei!!
THE TIME WILL COME...
...WHEN IT COMES.

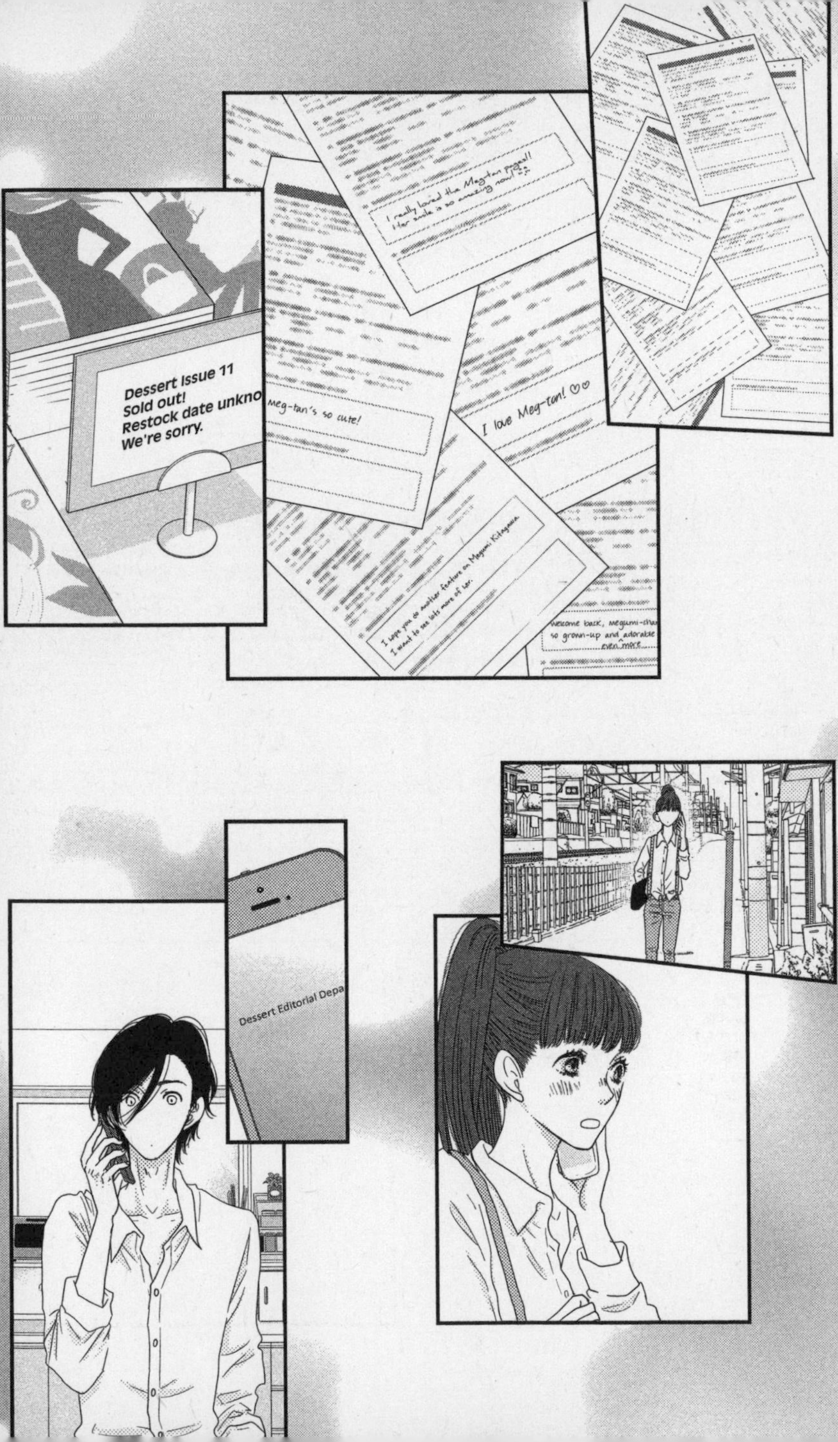
I really loved the Meg-tan pages!!
Her smile is so amazing now!
Meg-tan's so cute!
I love Meg-tan!
I hope you do another feature on Megumi Kitagawa.
I want to see lots more of her.
Welcome back, Megumi-cha
so grown-up and adorable
even more
Dessert Issue 11
Sold out!
Restock date unkno
We're sorry.
Dessert Editorial Depa

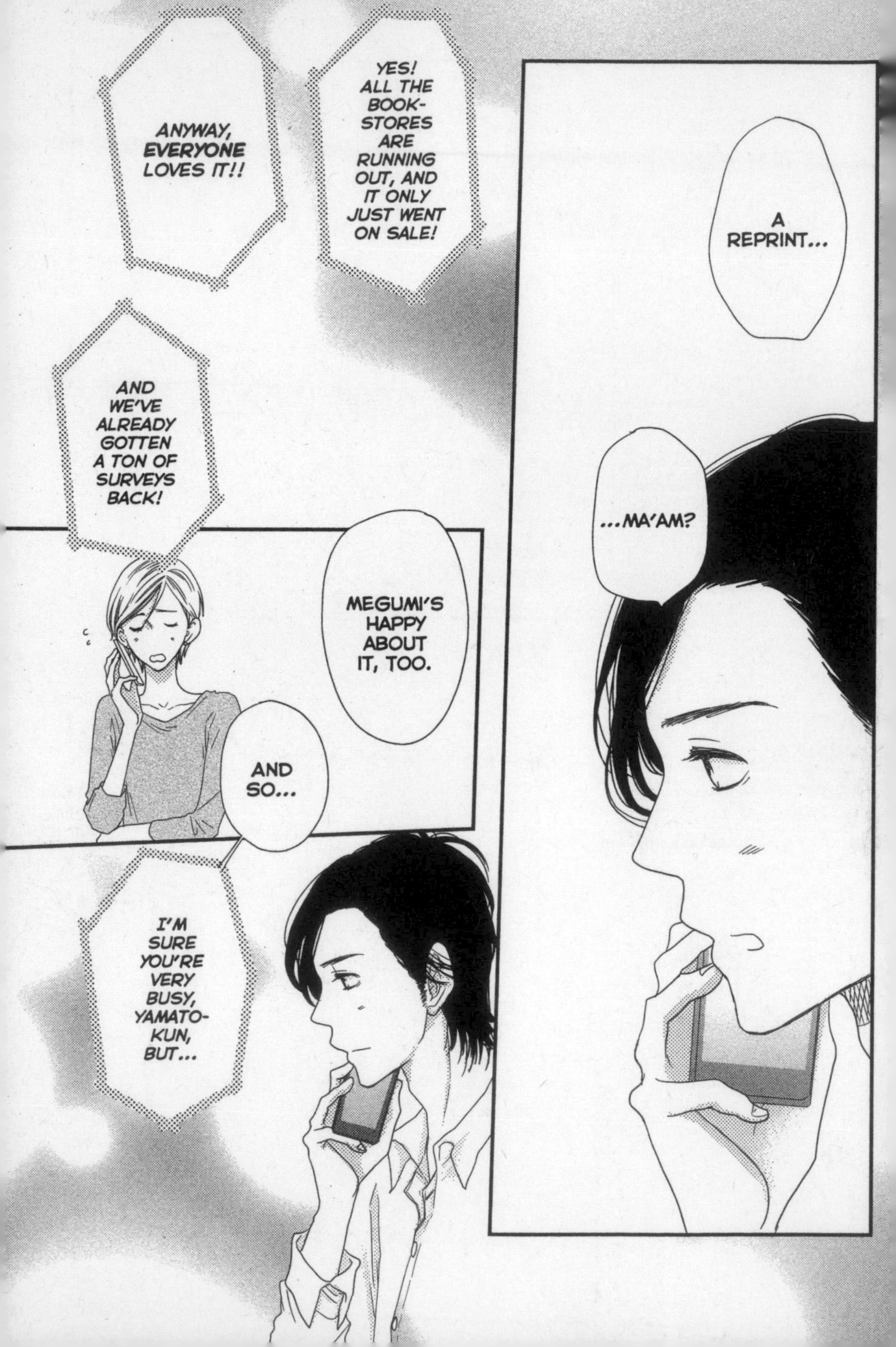
A REPRINT...
...MA'AM?
YES! ALL THE BOOK-STORES ARE RUNNING OUT, AND IT ONLY JUST WENT ON SALE!
ANYWAY, EVERYONE LOVES IT!!
AND WE'VE ALREADY GOTTEN A TON OF SURVEYS BACK!
MEGUMI'S HAPPY ABOUT IT, TOO.
AND SO...
I'M SURE YOU'RE VERY BUSY, YAMATO-KUN, BUT...

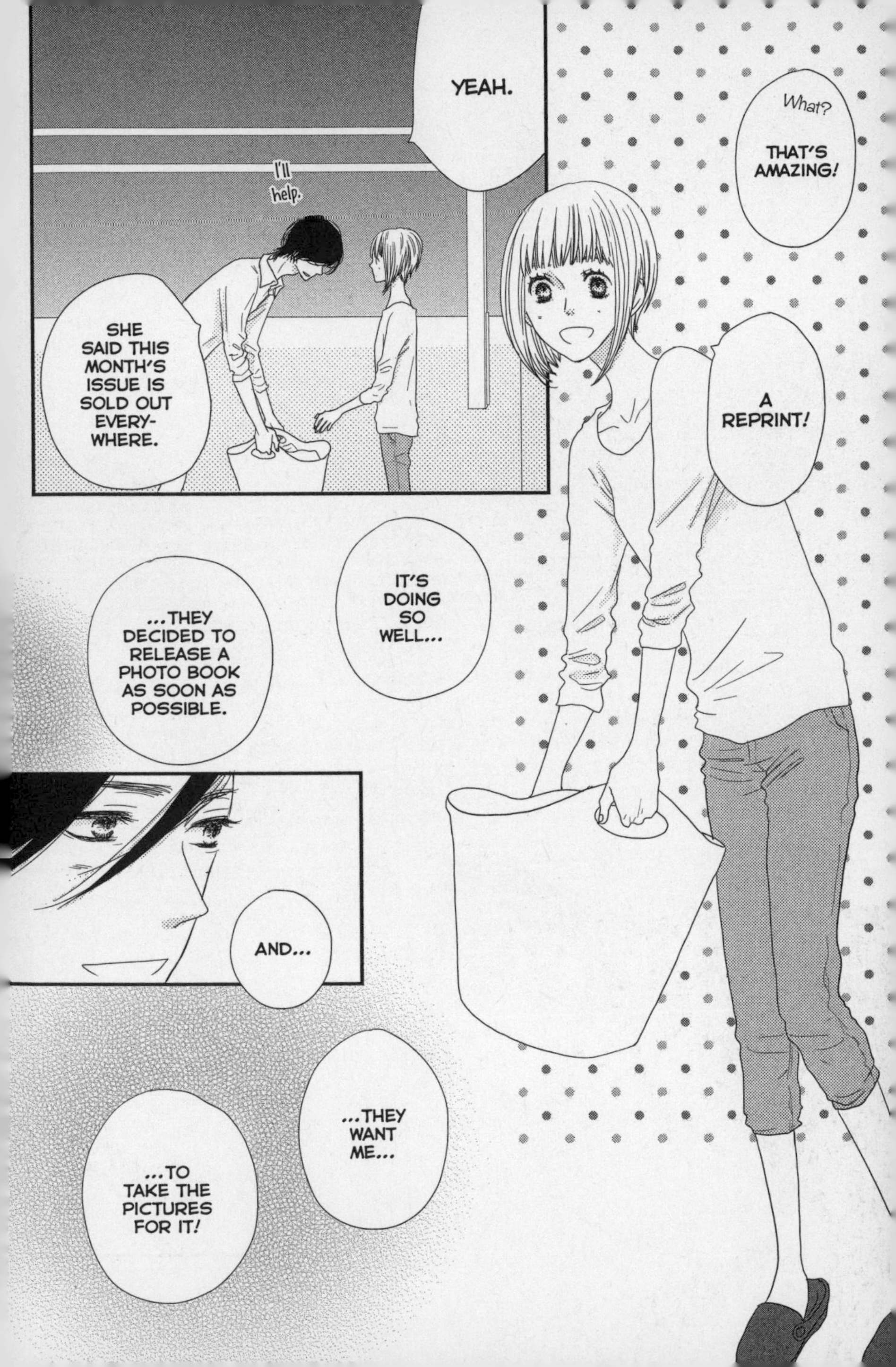
What?
THAT'S AMAZING!
A REPRINT!
YEAH.
I'll help.
SHE SAID THIS MONTH'S ISSUE IS SOLD OUT EVERYWHERE.
IT'S DOING SO WELL...
...THEY DECIDED TO RELEASE A PHOTO BOOK AS SOON AS POSSIBLE.
AND...
...THEY WANT ME...
...TO TAKE THE PICTURES FOR IT!

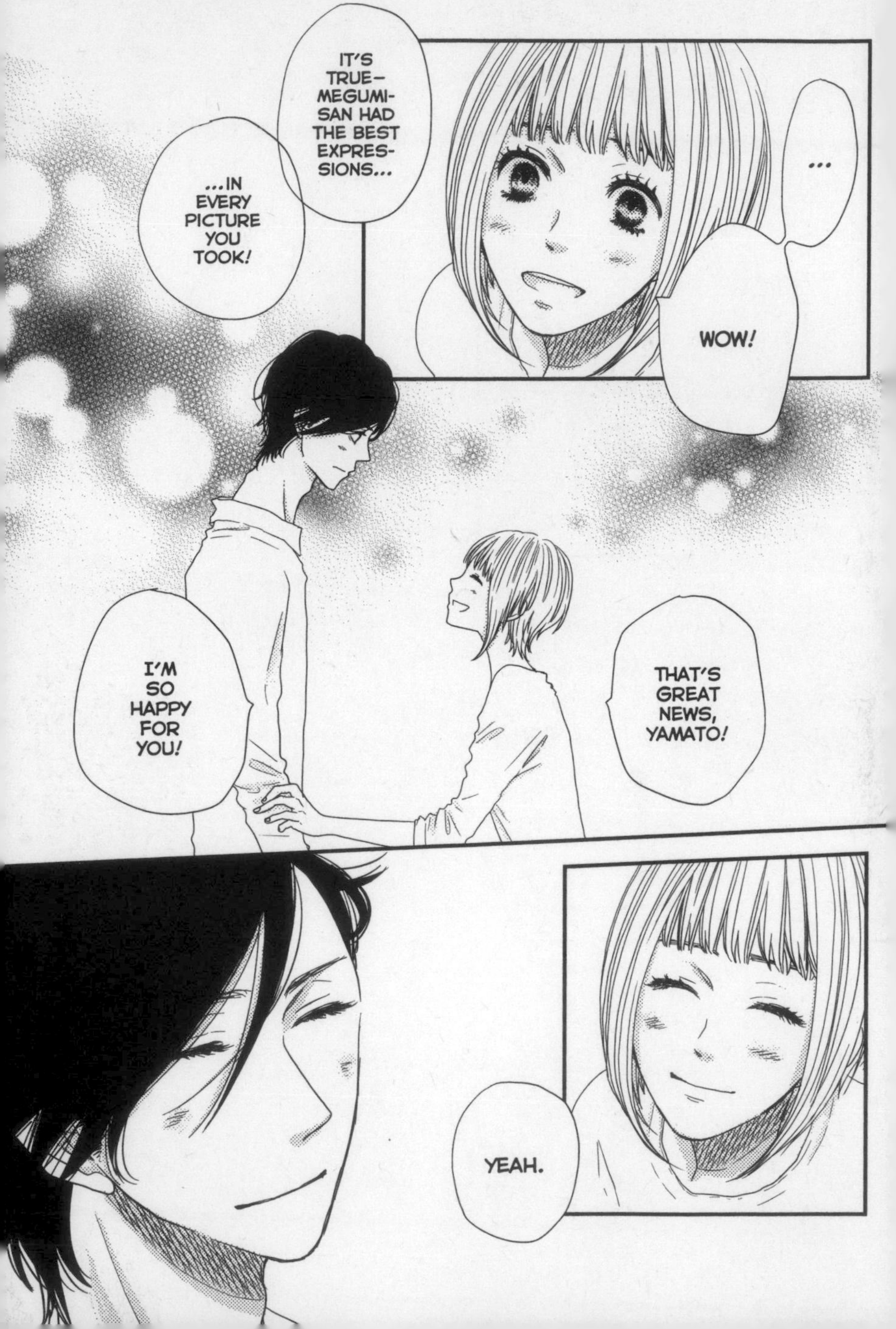
...
WOW!
IT'S TRUE—MEGUMI-SAN HAD THE BEST EXPRESSIONS...
...IN EVERY PICTURE YOU TOOK!
THAT'S GREAT NEWS, YAMATO!
I'M SO HAPPY FOR YOU!
YEAH.

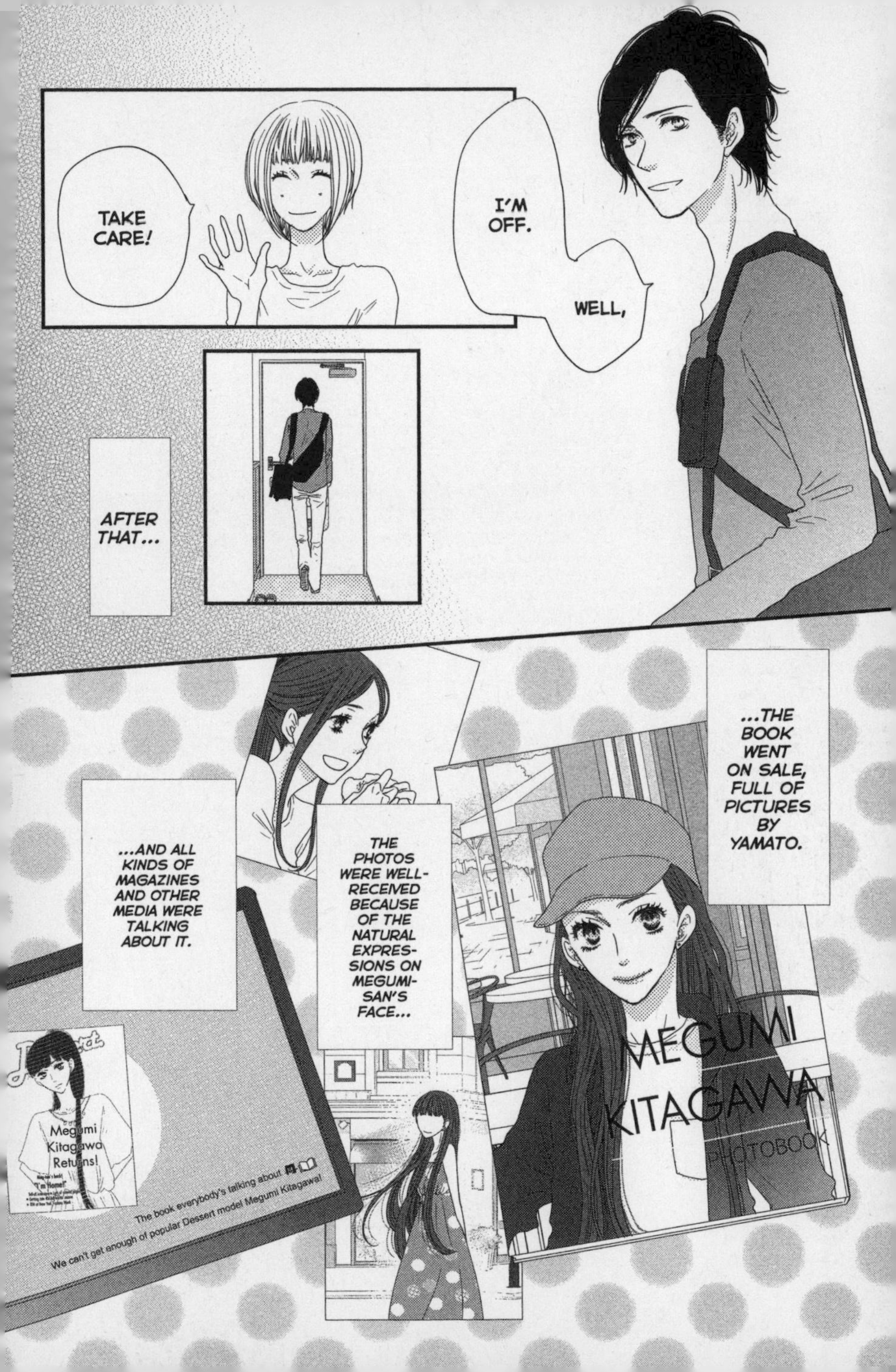
WELL, I'M OFF.
TAKE CARE!
AFTER THAT...
...THE BOOK WENT ON SALE, FULL OF PICTURES BY YAMATO.
THE PHOTOS WERE WELL-RECEIVED BECAUSE OF THE NATURAL EXPRESSIONS ON MEGUMI-SAN'S FACE...
...AND ALL KINDS OF MAGAZINES AND OTHER MEDIA WERE TALKING ABOUT IT.
MEGUMI KITAGAWA
PHOTOBOOK
Megumi Kitagawa Returns!
"I'm Home!"
The book everybody's talking about
We can't get enough of popular Dessert model Megumi Kitagawa!

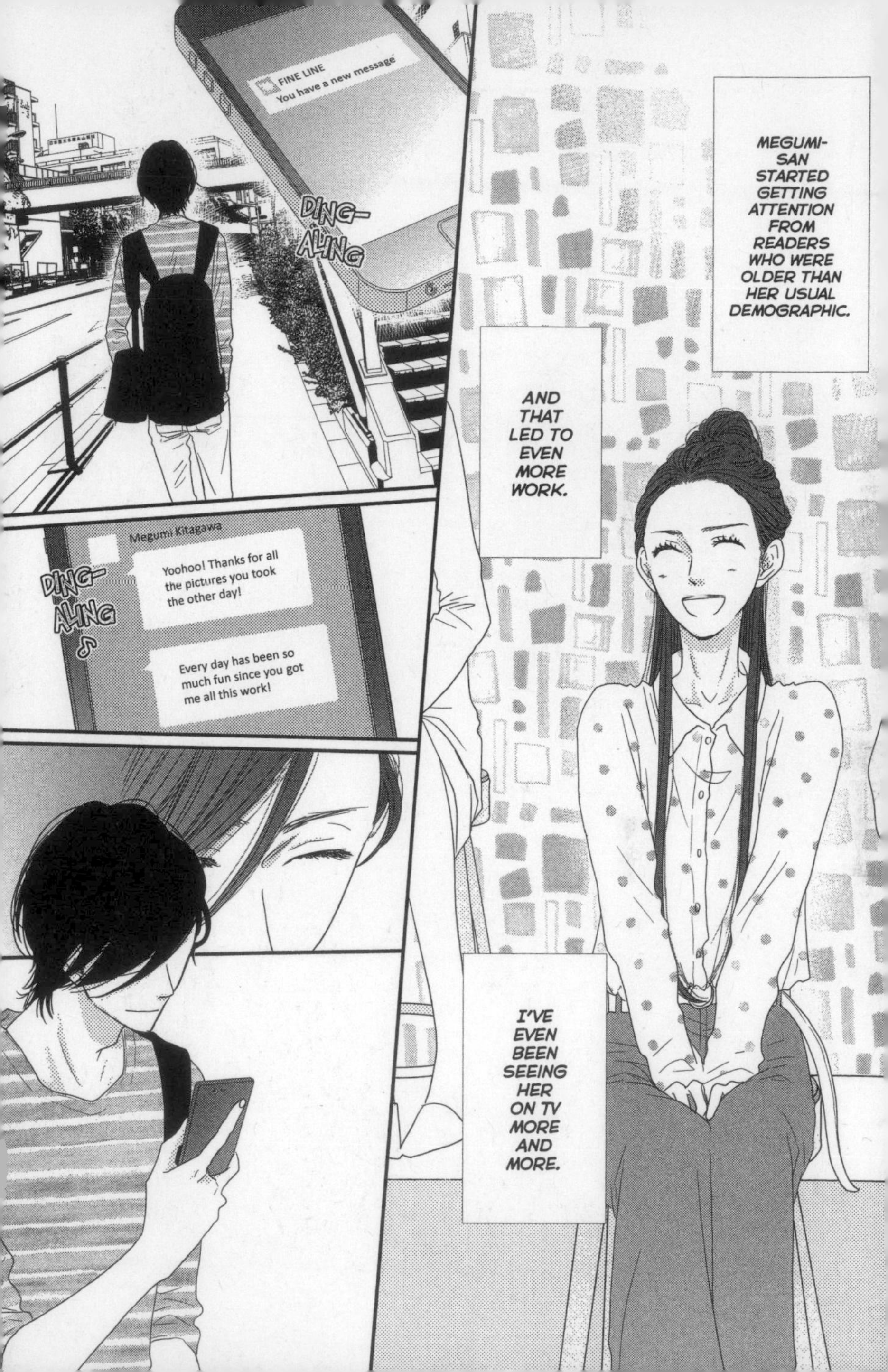
MEGUMI-SAN STARTED GETTING ATTENTION FROM READERS WHO WERE OLDER THAN HER USUAL DEMOGRAPHIC.
AND THAT LED TO EVEN MORE WORK.
I'VE EVEN BEEN SEEING HER ON TV MORE AND MORE.
FINE LINE
You have a new message
DING-ALING
Megumi Kitagawa
Yoohoo! Thanks for all the pictures you took the other day!
Every day has been so much fun since you got me all this work!
DING-ALING ♪

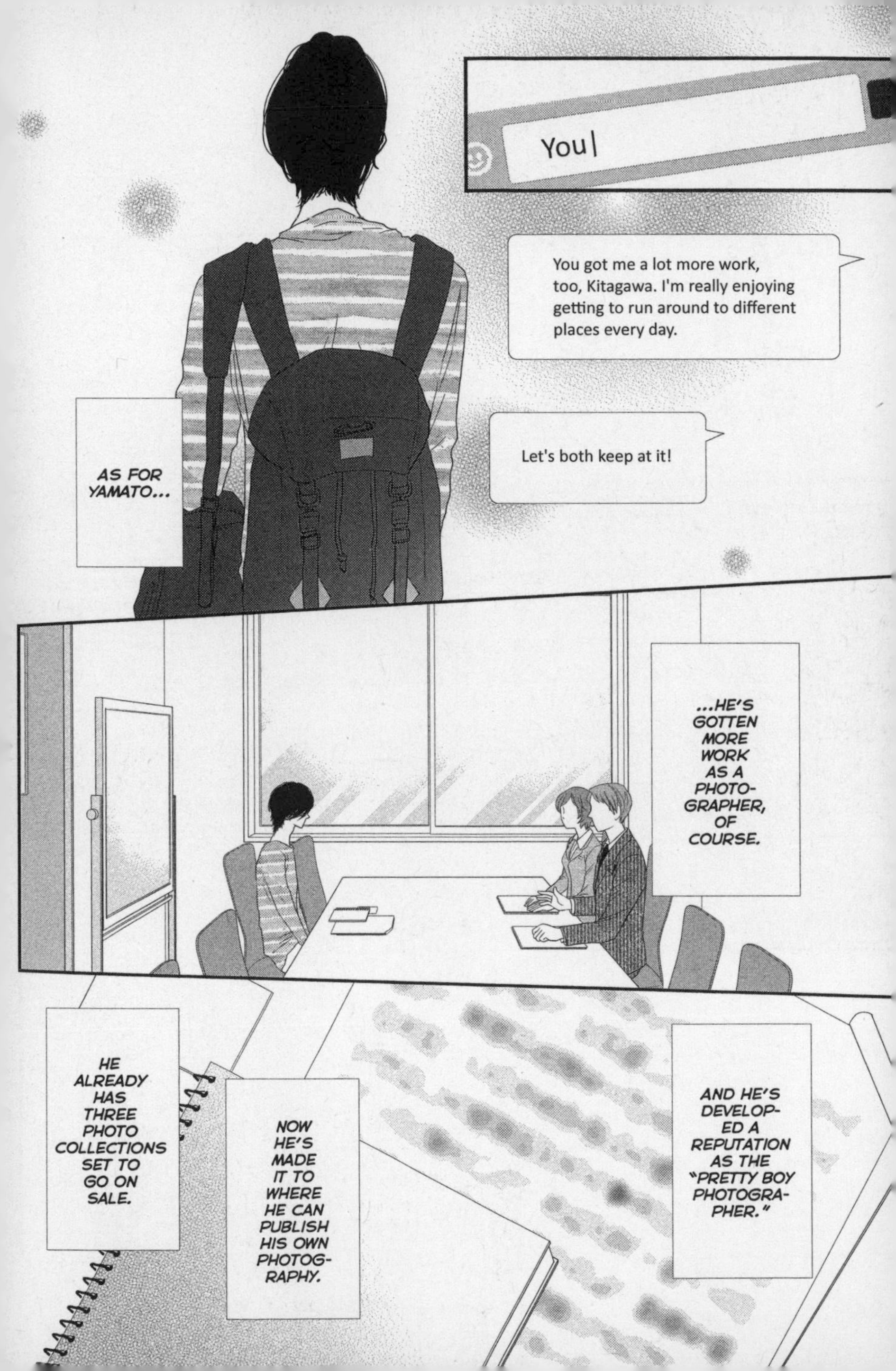
You|
You got me a lot more work, too, Kitagawa. I'm really enjoying getting to run around to different places every day.
Let's both keep at it!
AS FOR YAMATO...
...HE'S GOTTEN MORE WORK AS A PHOTOGRAPHER, OF COURSE.
AND HE'S DEVELOPED A REPUTATION AS THE "PRETTY BOY PHOTOGRAPHER."
NOW HE'S MADE IT TO WHERE HE CAN PUBLISH HIS OWN PHOTOGRAPHY.
HE ALREADY HAS THREE PHOTO COLLECTIONS SET TO GO ON SALE.

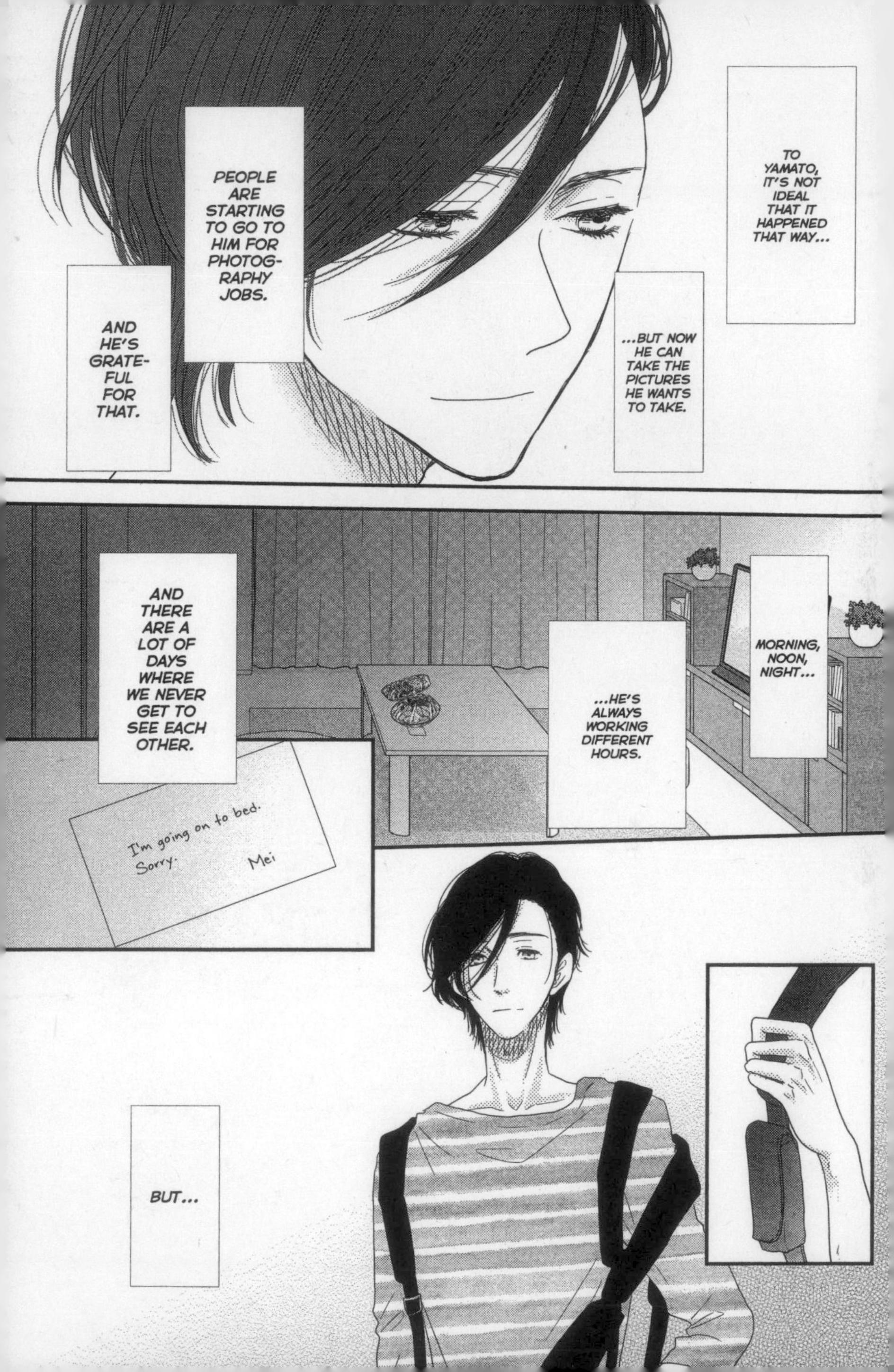
TO YAMATO, IT'S NOT IDEAL THAT IT HAPPENED THAT WAY...
...BUT NOW HE CAN TAKE THE PICTURES HE WANTS TO TAKE.
PEOPLE ARE STARTING TO GO TO HIM FOR PHOTOGRAPHY JOBS.
AND HE'S GRATEFUL FOR THAT.
MORNING, NOON, NIGHT...
...HE'S ALWAYS WORKING DIFFERENT HOURS.
AND THERE ARE A LOT OF DAYS WHERE WE NEVER GET TO SEE EACH OTHER.
I'm going on to bed.
Sorry.
Mei
BUT...

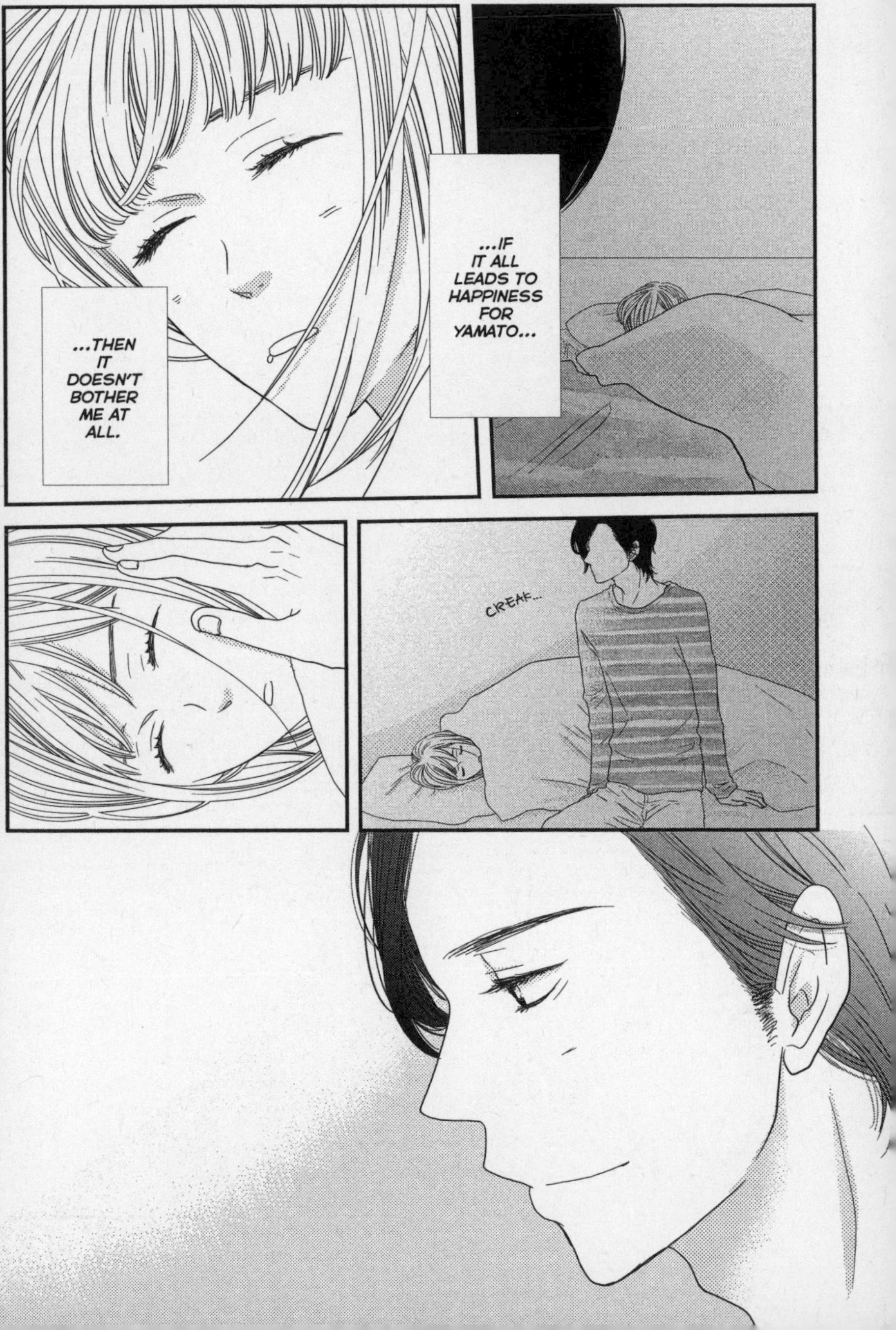
...IF IT ALL LEADS TO HAPPINESS FOR YAMATO...
...THEN IT DOESN'T BOTHER ME AT ALL.
CREAK...

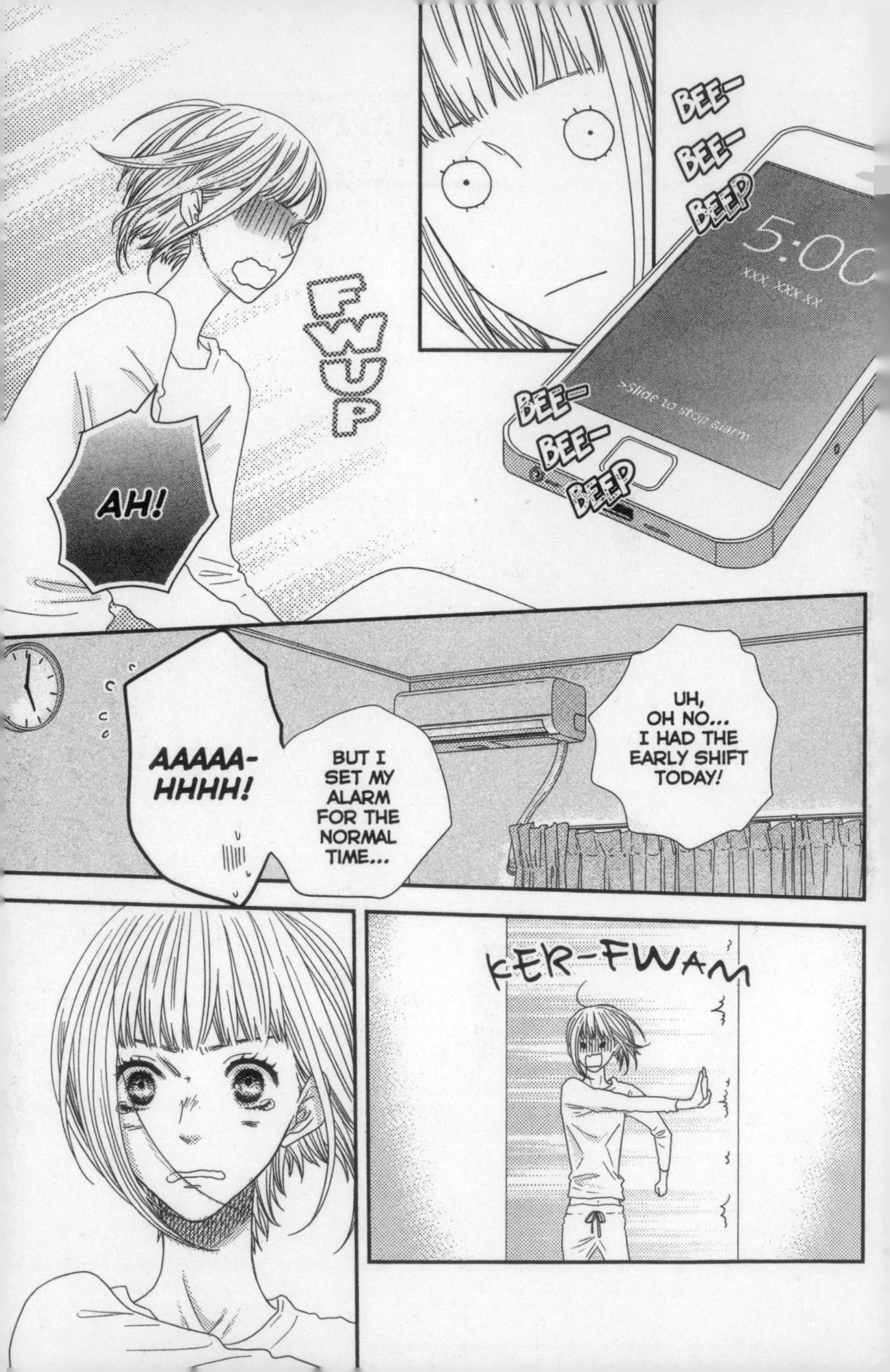
BEE-
BEE-
BEEP
>Slide to stop alarm
BEE-
BEE-
BEEP
FWUP
AH!
UH, OH NO... I HAD THE EARLY SHIFT TODAY!
BUT I SET MY ALARM FOR THE NORMAL TIME...
AAAAA-HHHH!
KER-FWAM

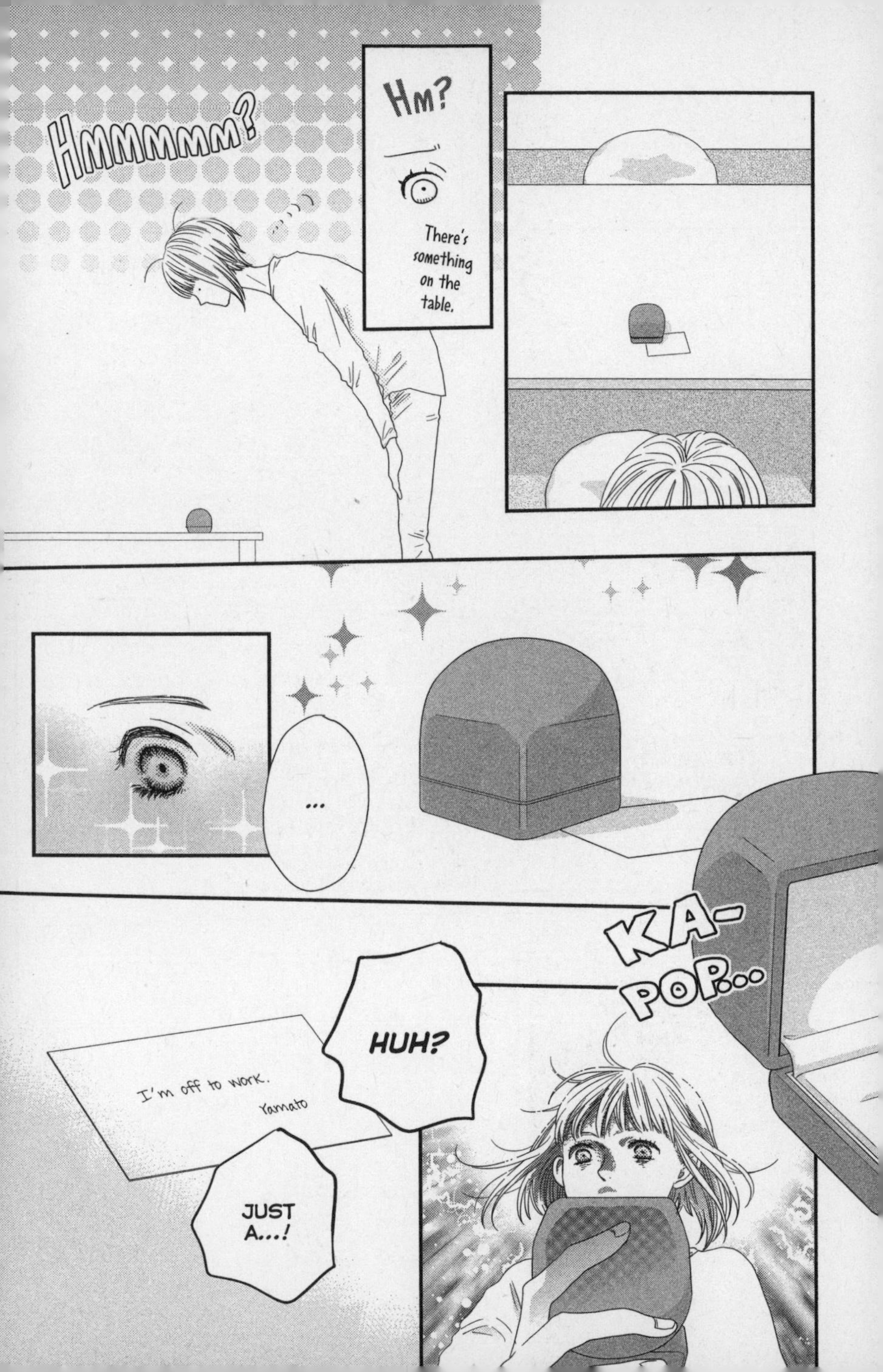
Hm?
There's something on the table.
Hmmmmm?
...
KA-POP...
HUH?
I'm off to work.
Yamato
JUST A...!

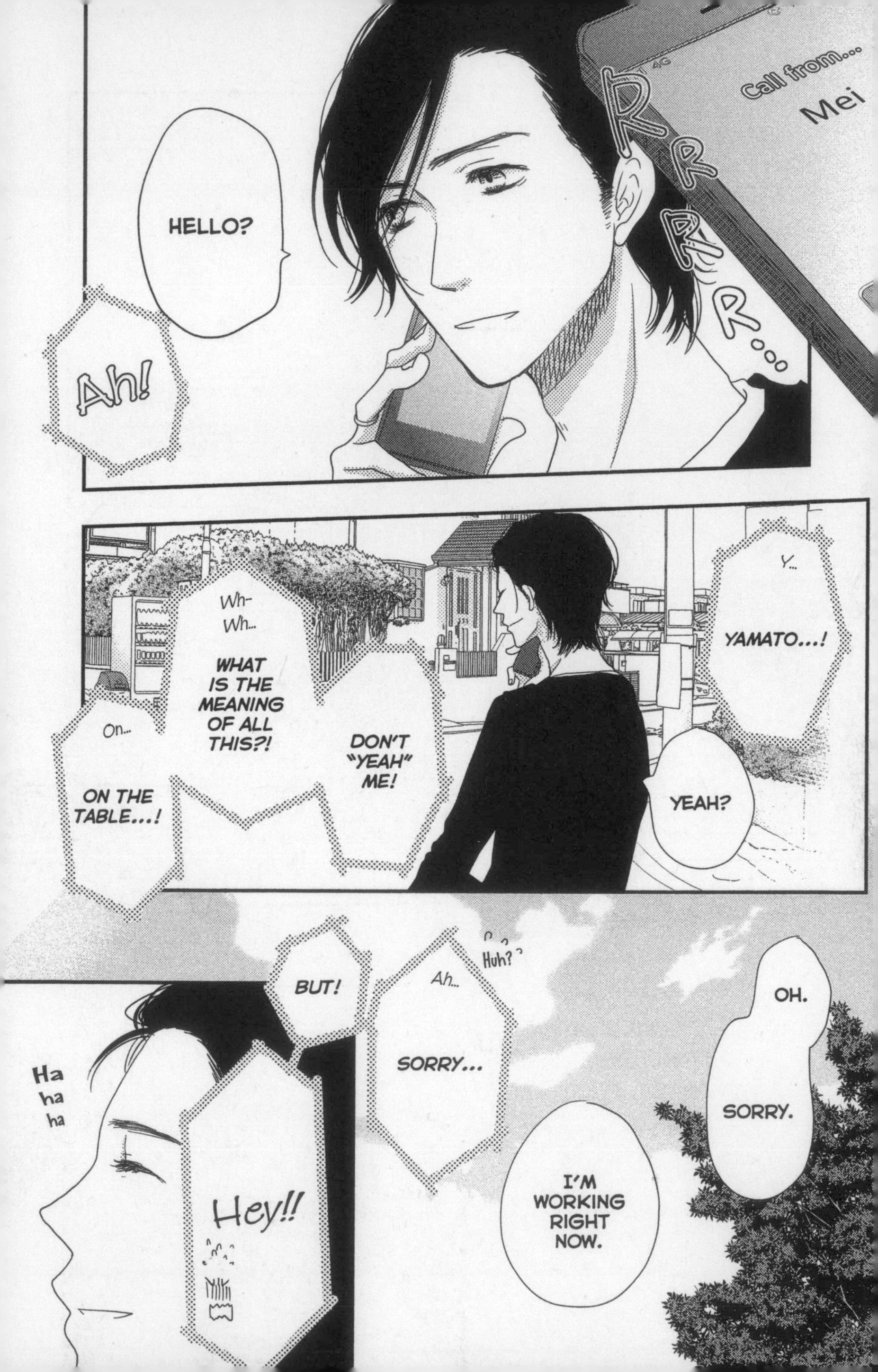
Call from...
Mei
RRRR...
HELLO?
Ah!
Y...
YAMATO...!
YEAH?
DON'T "YEAH" ME!
Wh-
Wh...
WHAT IS THE MEANING OF ALL THIS?!
On...
ON THE TABLE...!
OH.
SORRY.
I'M WORKING RIGHT NOW.
Huh?
Ah...
SORRY...
BUT!
Hey!!
Ha ha ha

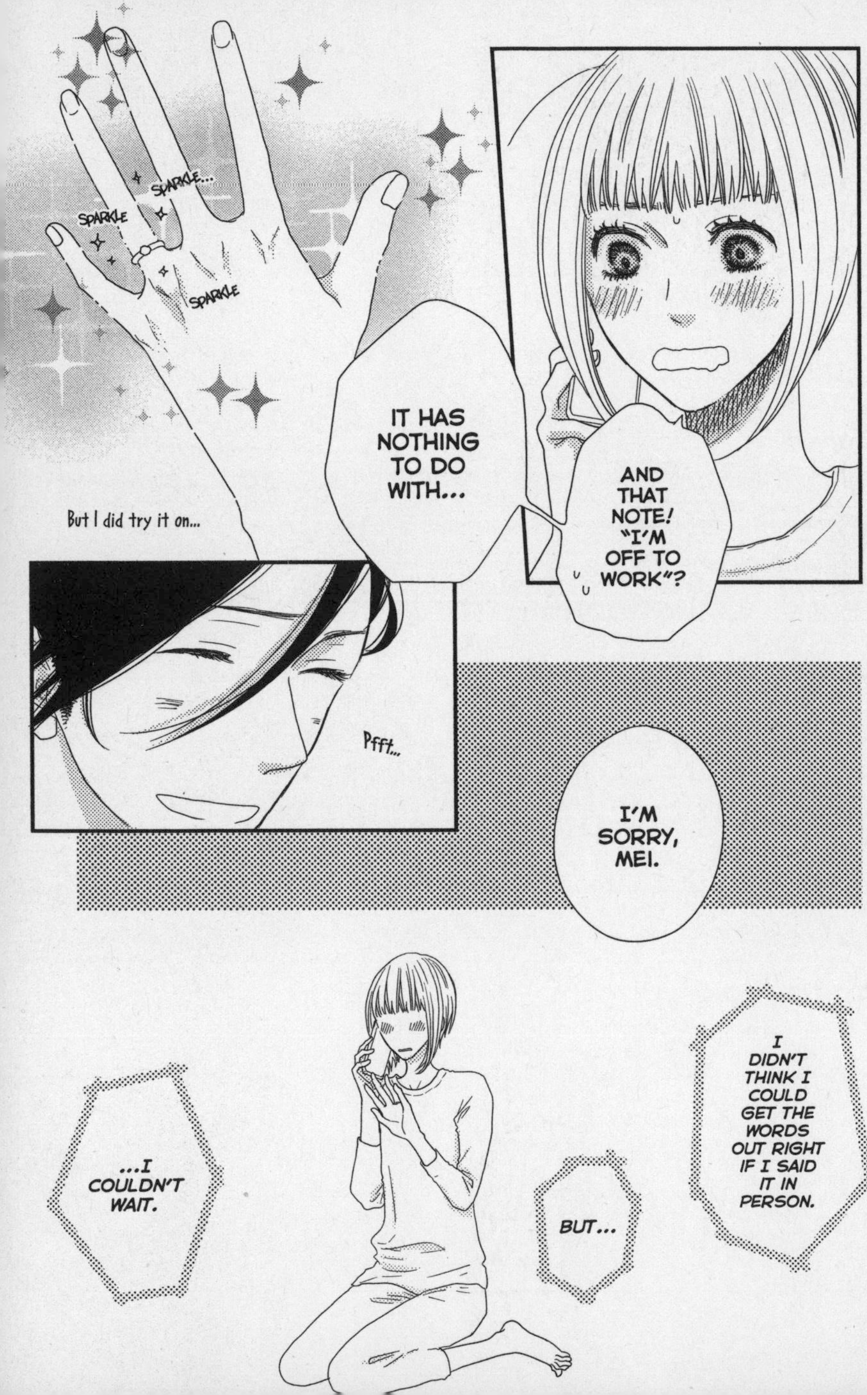
IT HAS NOTHING TO DO WITH...
AND THAT NOTE! "I'M OFF TO WORK"?
SPARKLE...
SPARKLE
SPARKLE
But I did try it on...
Pfft...
I'M SORRY, MEI.
I DIDN'T THINK I COULD GET THE WORDS OUT RIGHT IF I SAID IT IN PERSON.
BUT...
...I COULDN'T WAIT.

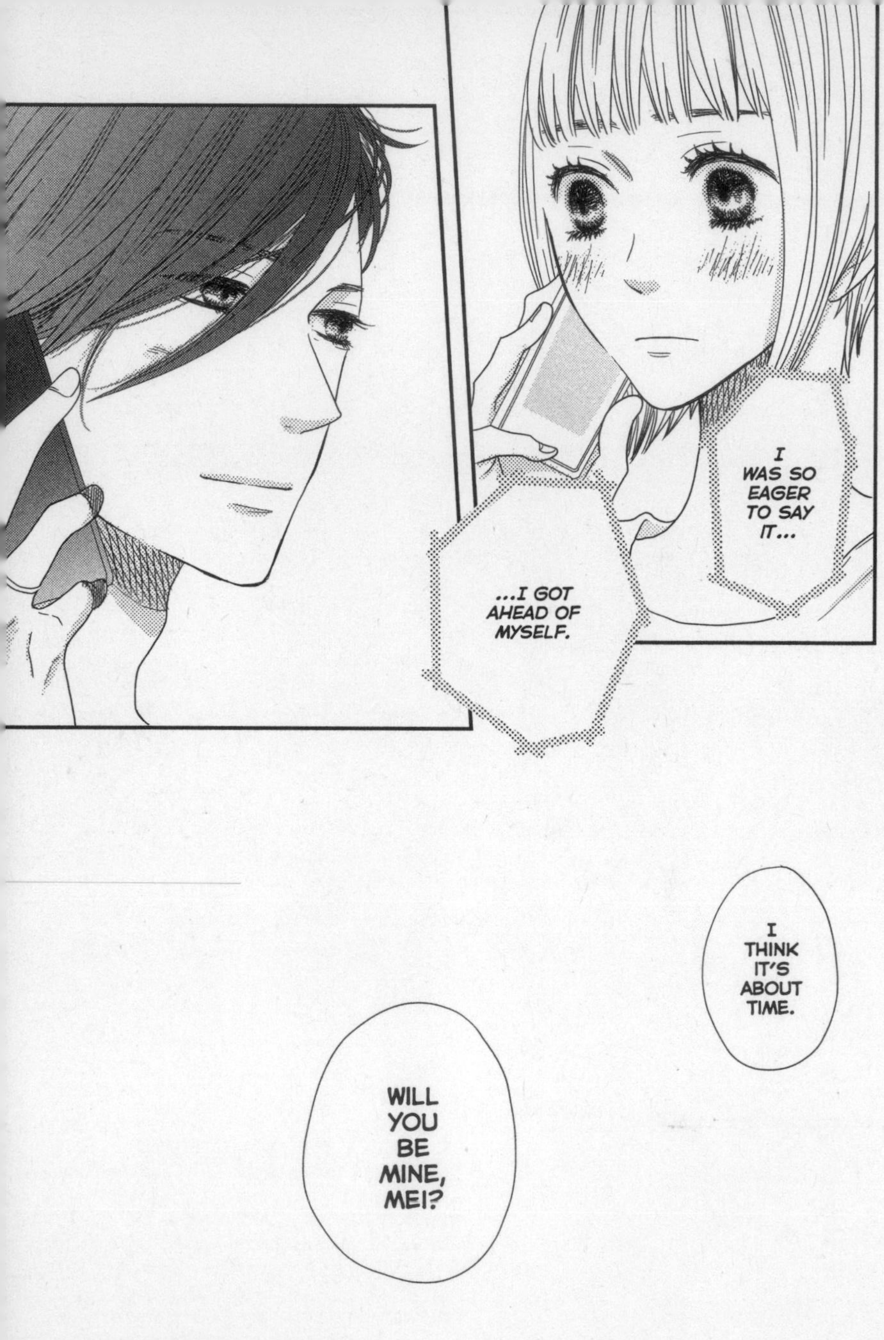
I WAS SO EAGER TO SAY IT...
...I GOT AHEAD OF MYSELF.
I THINK IT'S ABOUT TIME.
WILL YOU BE MINE, MEI?

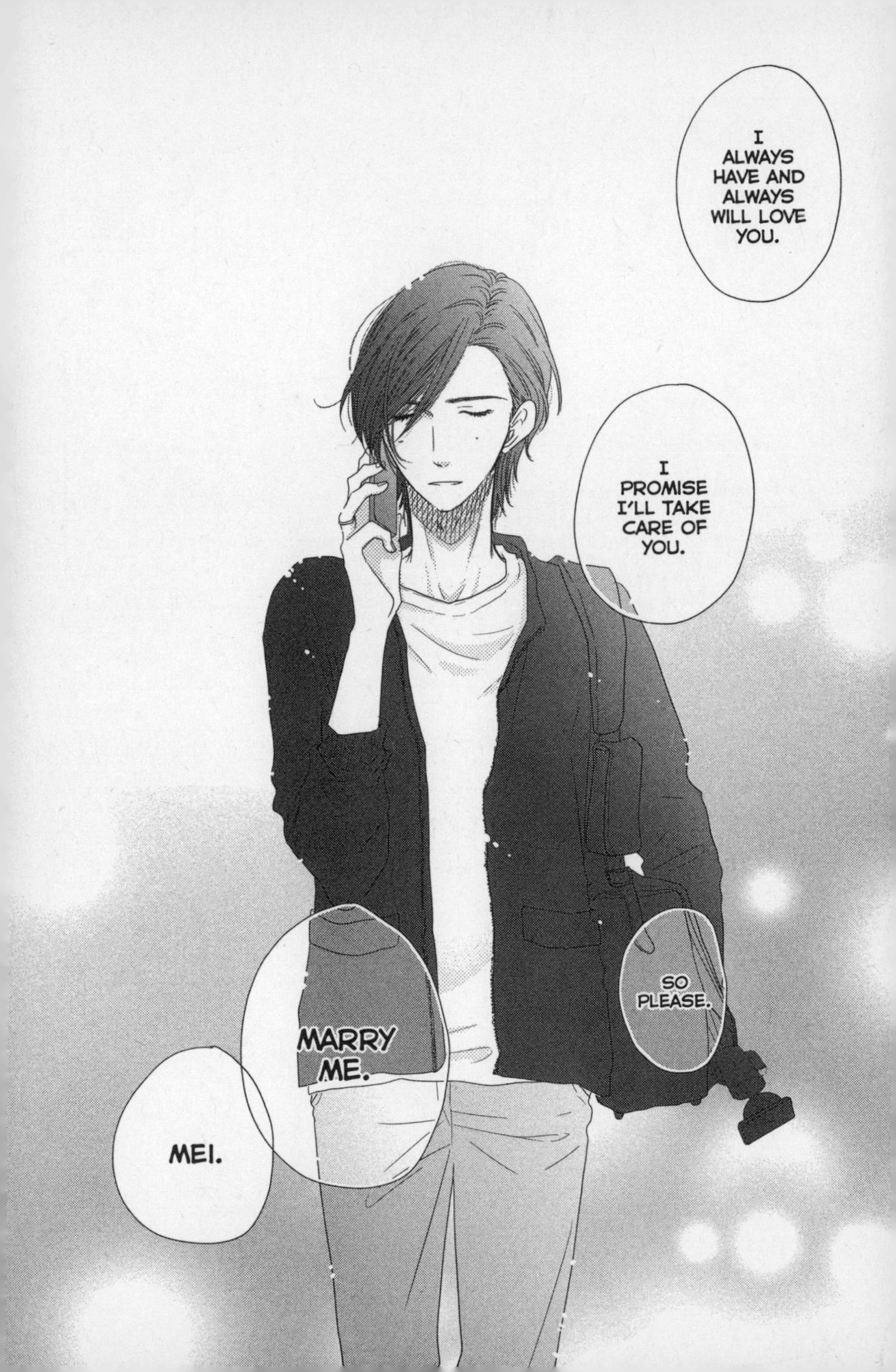
I ALWAYS HAVE AND ALWAYS WILL LOVE YOU.
I PROMISE I'LL TAKE CARE OF YOU.
SO PLEASE.
MARRY ME.
MEI.

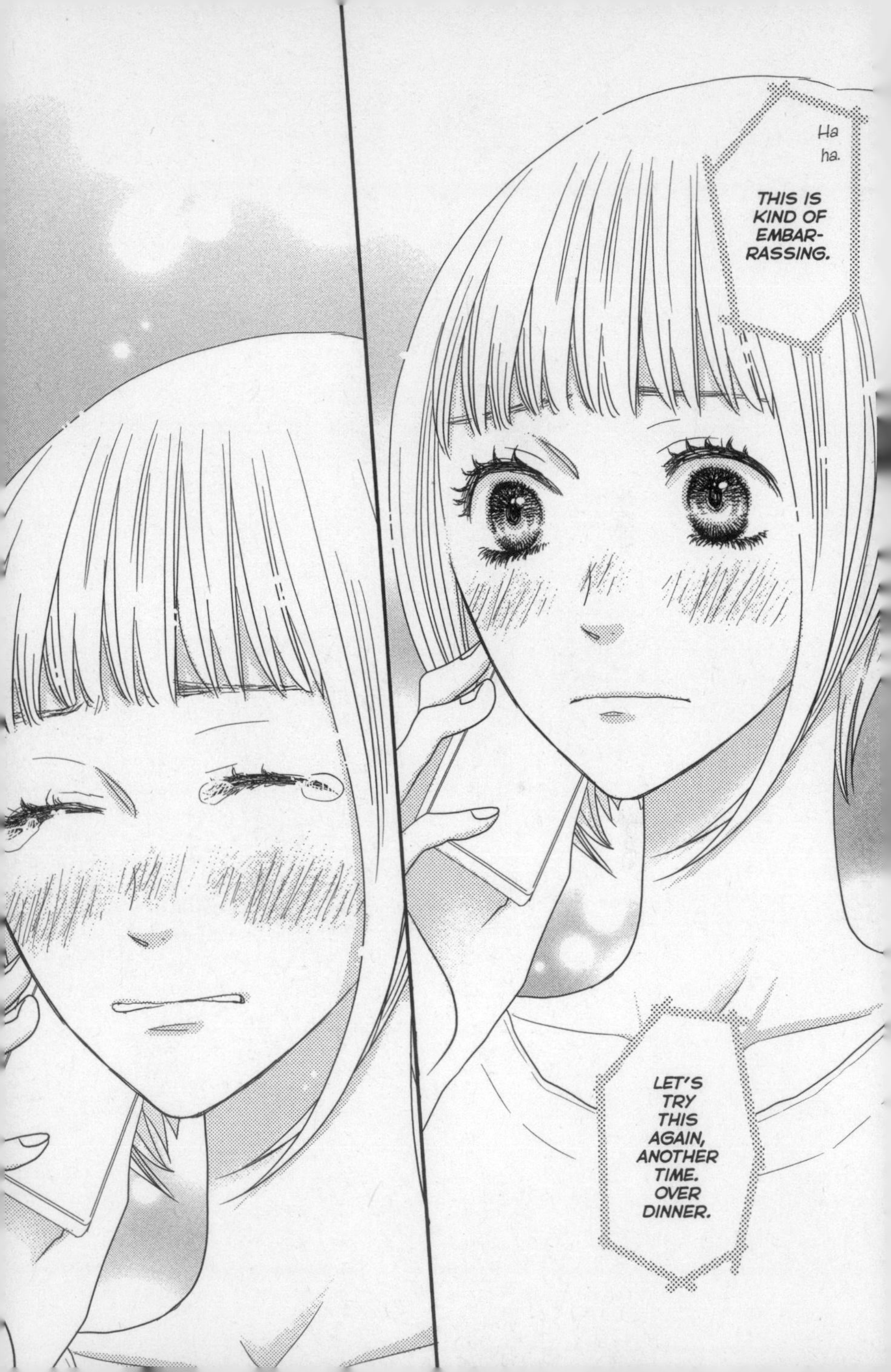
Ha ha.
THIS IS KIND OF EMBARRASSING.
LET'S TRY THIS AGAIN, ANOTHER TIME. OVER DINNER.

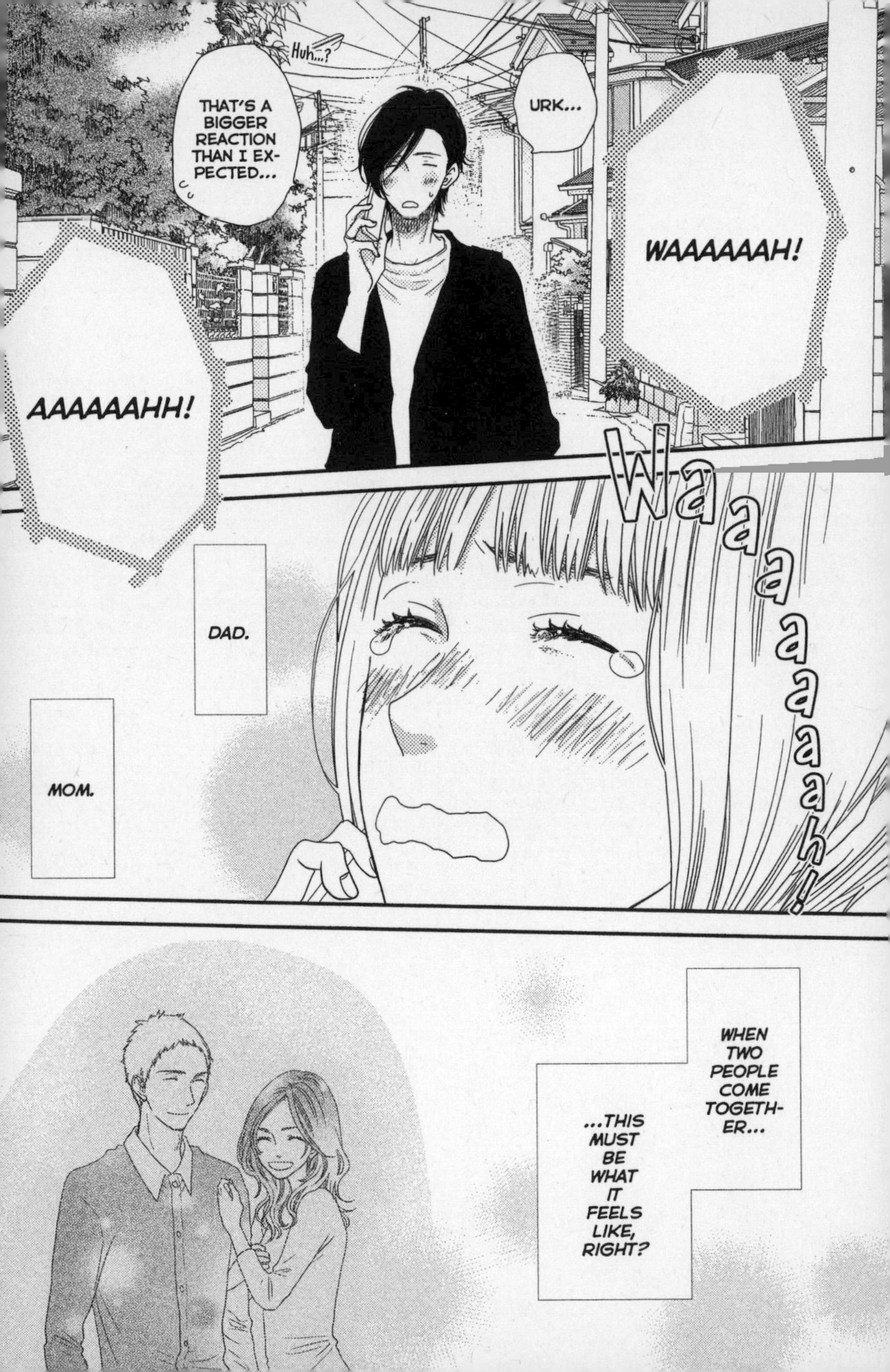
URK...
WAAAAAAH!
Huh...?
THAT'S A BIGGER REACTION THAN I EXPECTED...
AAAAAAHH!
Waaaaaaah!
DAD.
MOM.
WHEN TWO PEOPLE COME TOGETHER...
...THIS MUST BE WHAT IT FEELS LIKE, RIGHT?

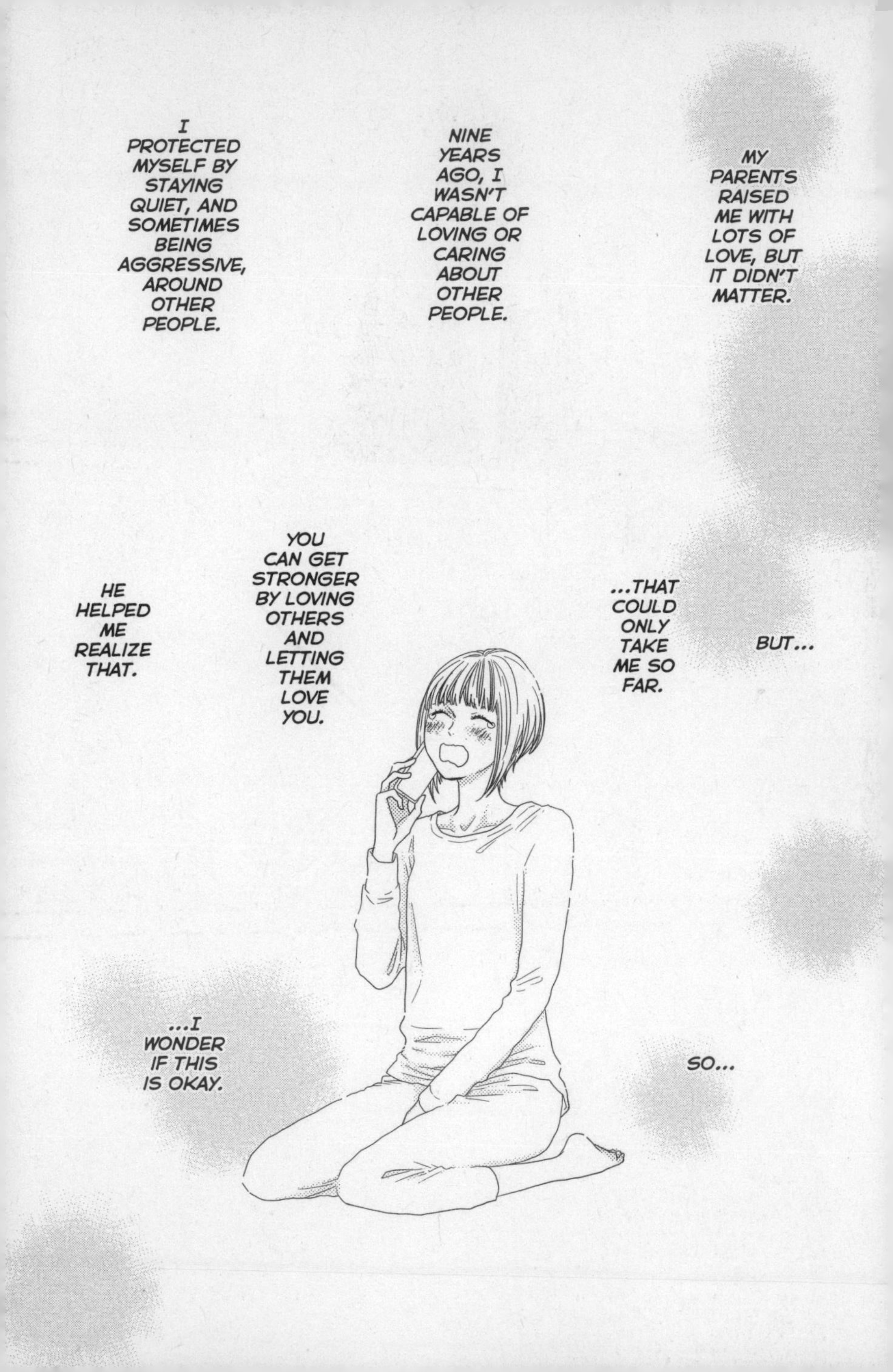
MY PARENTS RAISED ME WITH LOTS OF LOVE, BUT IT DIDN'T MATTER.
NINE YEARS AGO, I WASN'T CAPABLE OF LOVING OR CARING ABOUT OTHER PEOPLE.
I PROTECTED MYSELF BY STAYING QUIET, AND SOMETIMES BEING AGGRESSIVE, AROUND OTHER PEOPLE.
BUT...
...THAT COULD ONLY TAKE ME SO FAR.
YOU CAN GET STRONGER BY LOVING OTHERS AND LETTING THEM LOVE YOU.
HE HELPED ME REALIZE THAT.
SO...
...I WONDER IF THIS IS OKAY.

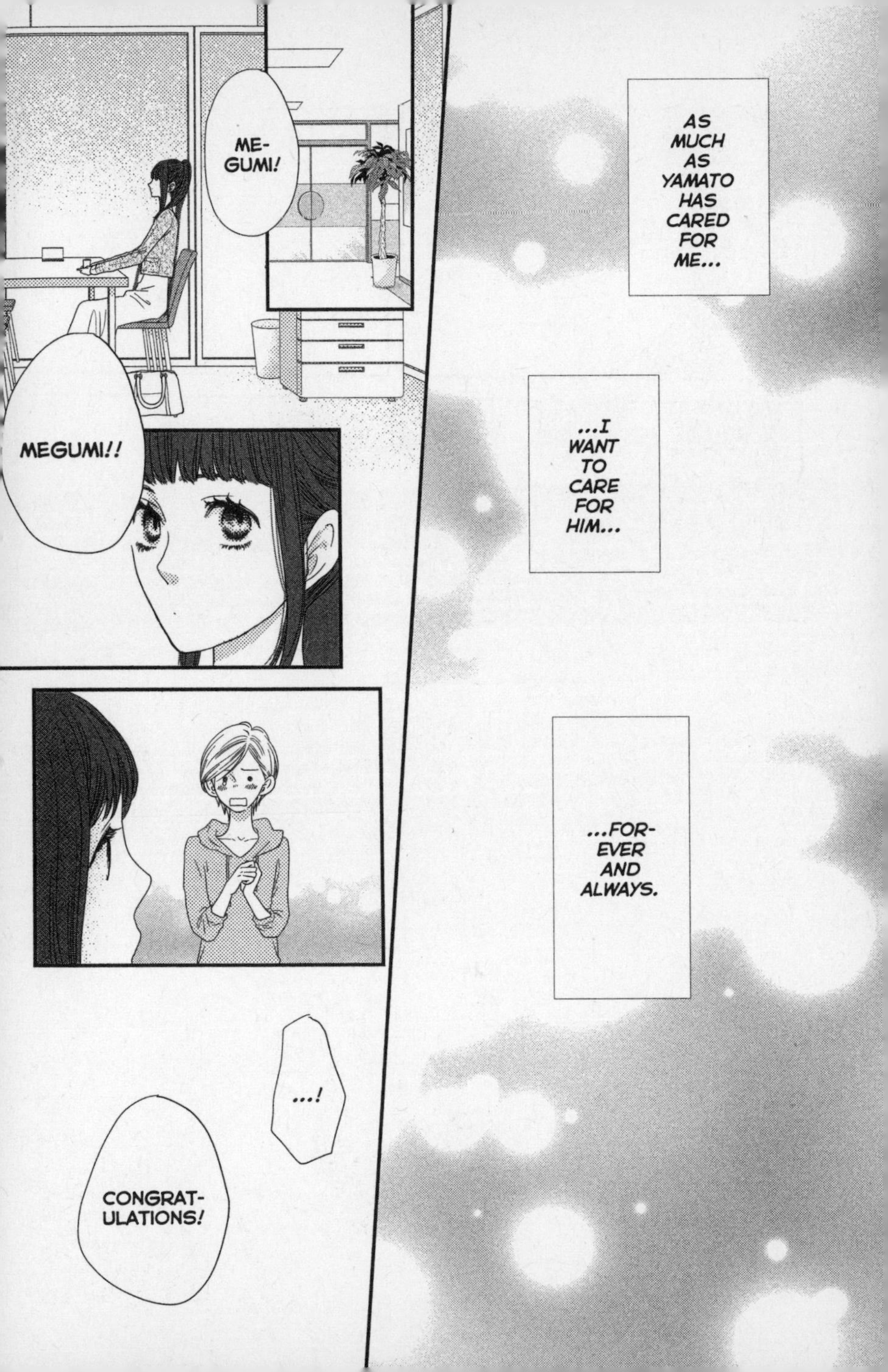
AS MUCH AS YAMATO HAS CARED FOR ME...
...I WANT TO CARE FOR HIM...
...FOR- EVER AND ALWAYS.
ME- GUMI!
MEGUMI!!
...!
CONGRAT- ULATIONS!

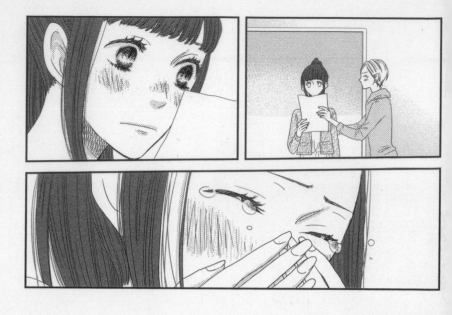

WHEN IT
COMES TO
HAPPINESS...

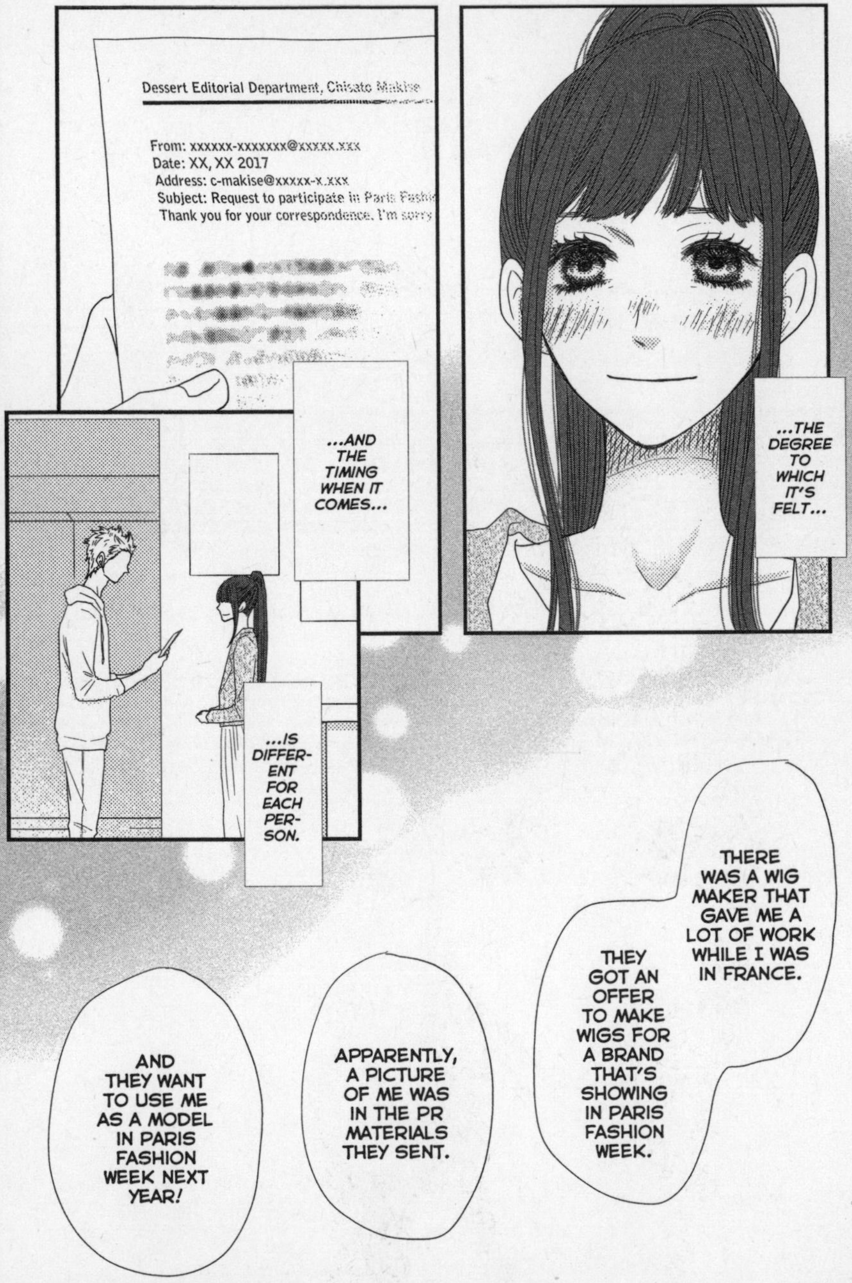
...THE DEGREE TO WHICH IT'S FELT...
Dessert Editorial Department, Chisato Makise
From: xxxxxx-xxxxxxx@xxxxx.xxx
Date: XX, XX 2017
Address: c-makise@xxxxx-x.xxx
Subject: Request to participate in Paris Fashio
Thank you for your correspondence. I'm sorry
...AND THE TIMING WHEN IT COMES...
...IS DIFFERENT FOR EACH PERSON.
THERE WAS A WIG MAKER THAT GAVE ME A LOT OF WORK WHILE I WAS IN FRANCE.
THEY GOT AN OFFER TO MAKE WIGS FOR A BRAND THAT'S SHOWING IN PARIS FASHION WEEK.
APPARENTLY, A PICTURE OF ME WAS IN THE PR MATERIALS THEY SENT.
AND THEY WANT TO USE ME AS A MODEL IN PARIS FASHION WEEK NEXT YEAR!

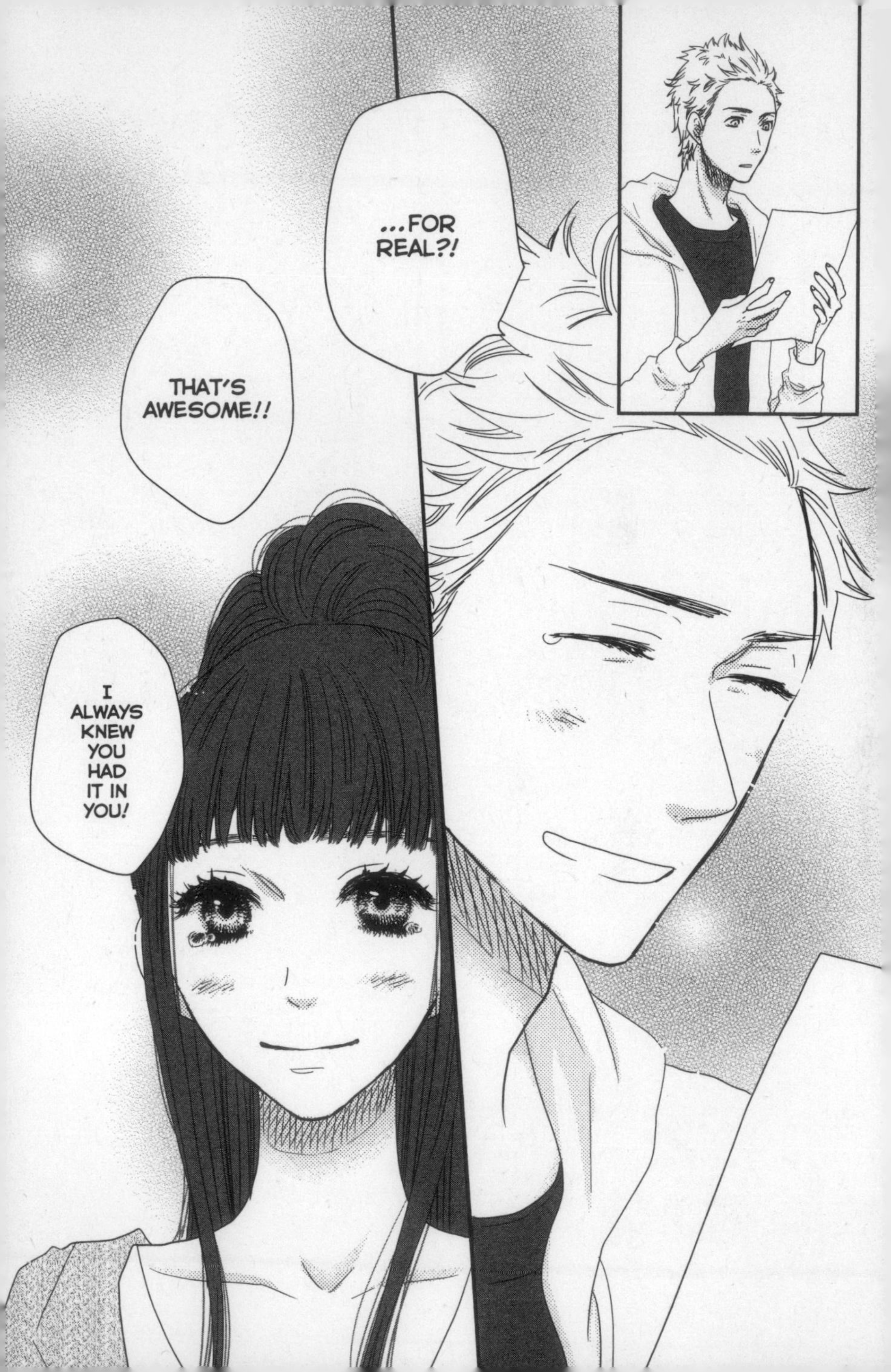
...FOR REAL?!
THAT'S AWESOME!!
I ALWAYS KNEW YOU HAD IT IN YOU!

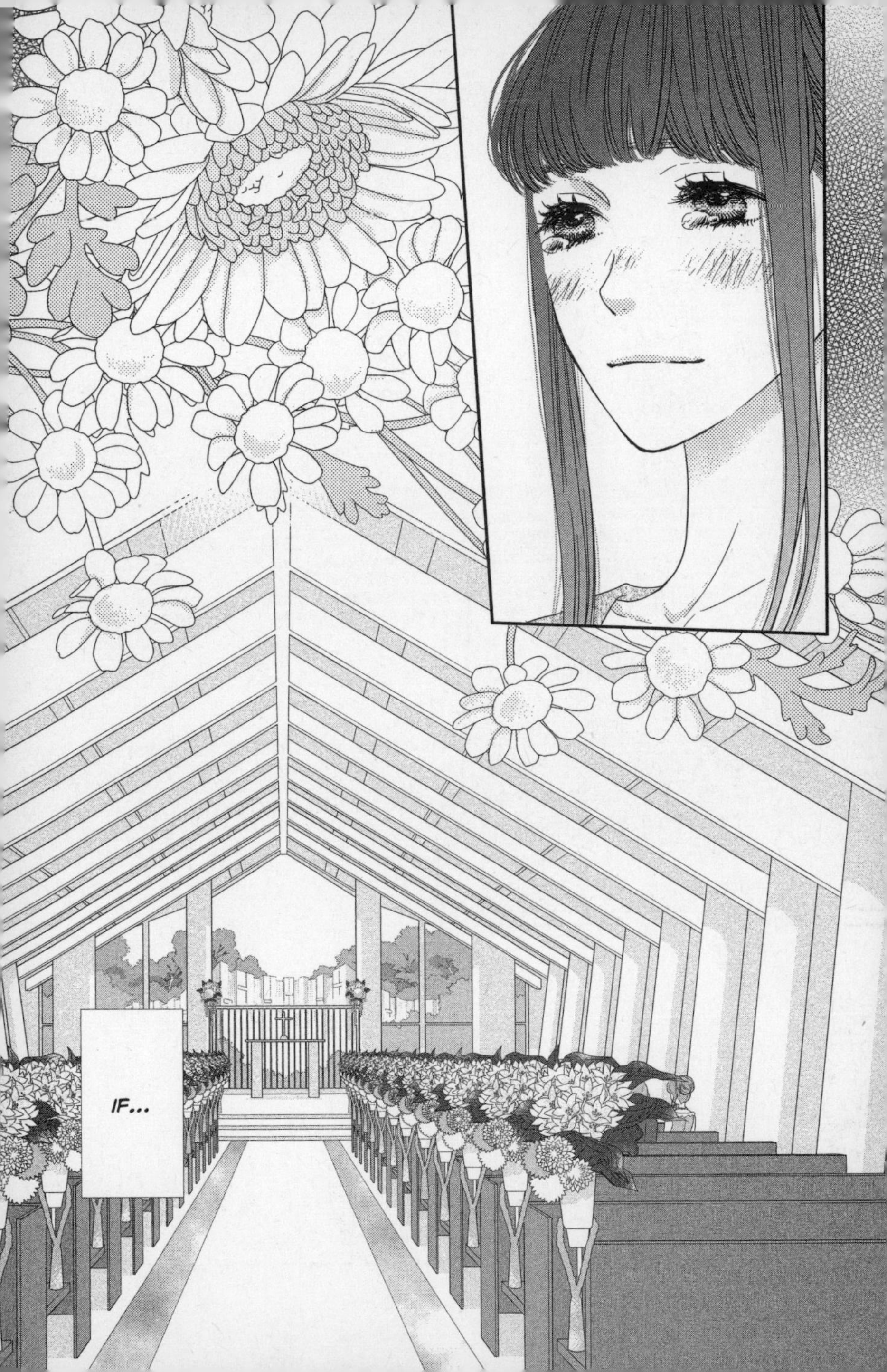
IF...

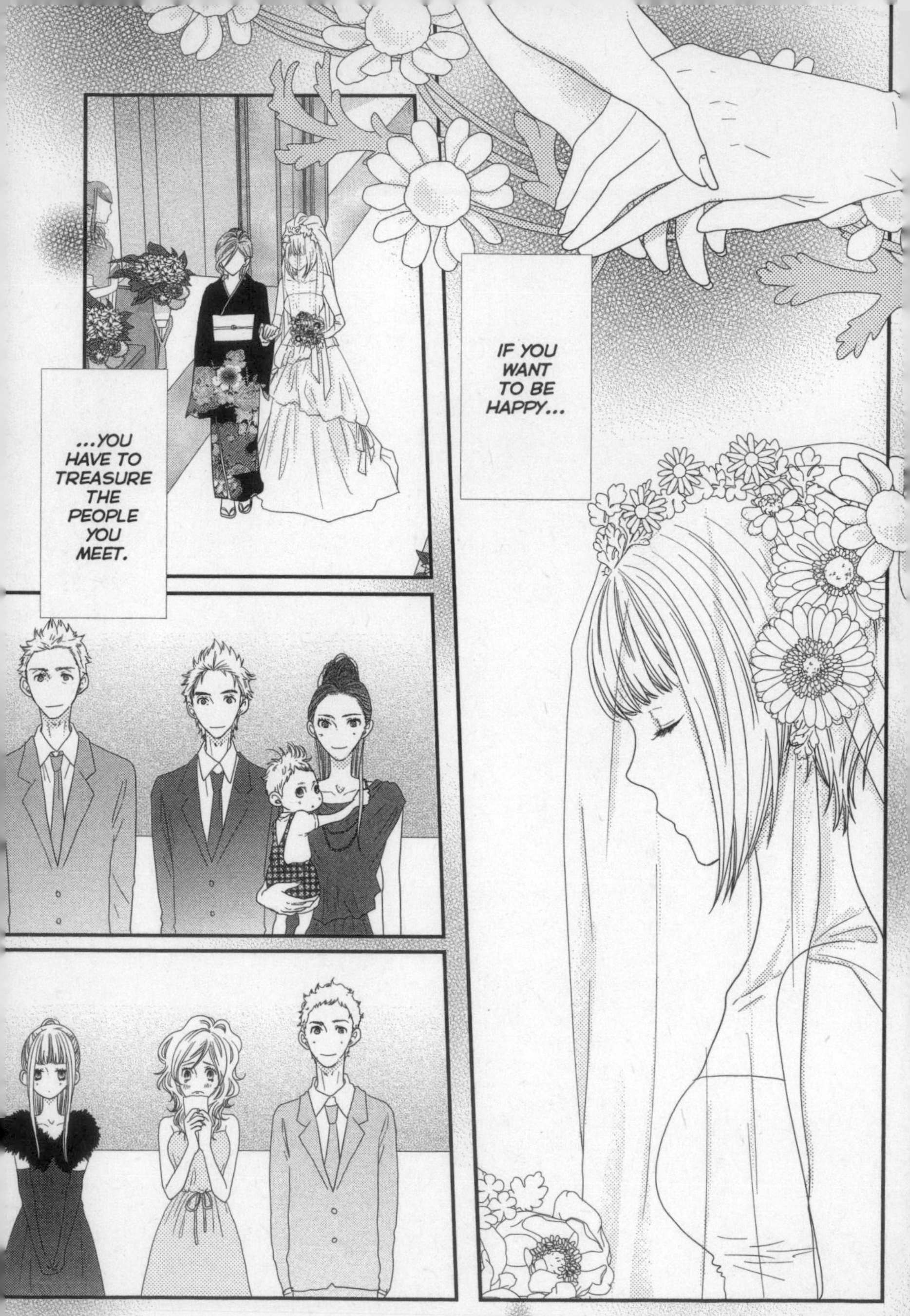
IF YOU WANT TO BE HAPPY...
...YOU HAVE TO TREASURE THE PEOPLE YOU MEET.

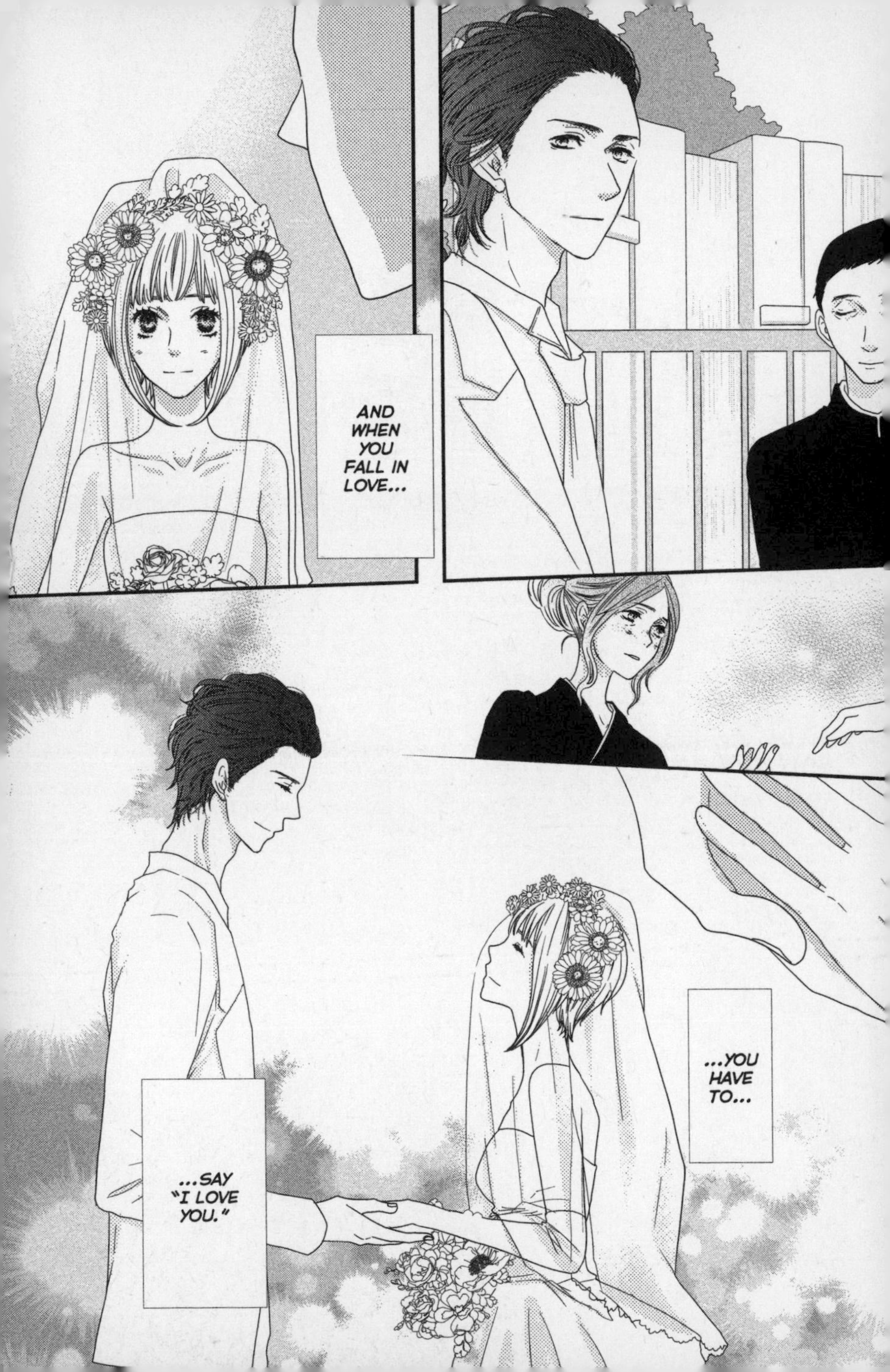
AND WHEN YOU FALL IN LOVE...
...YOU HAVE TO...
...SAY "I LOVE YOU."

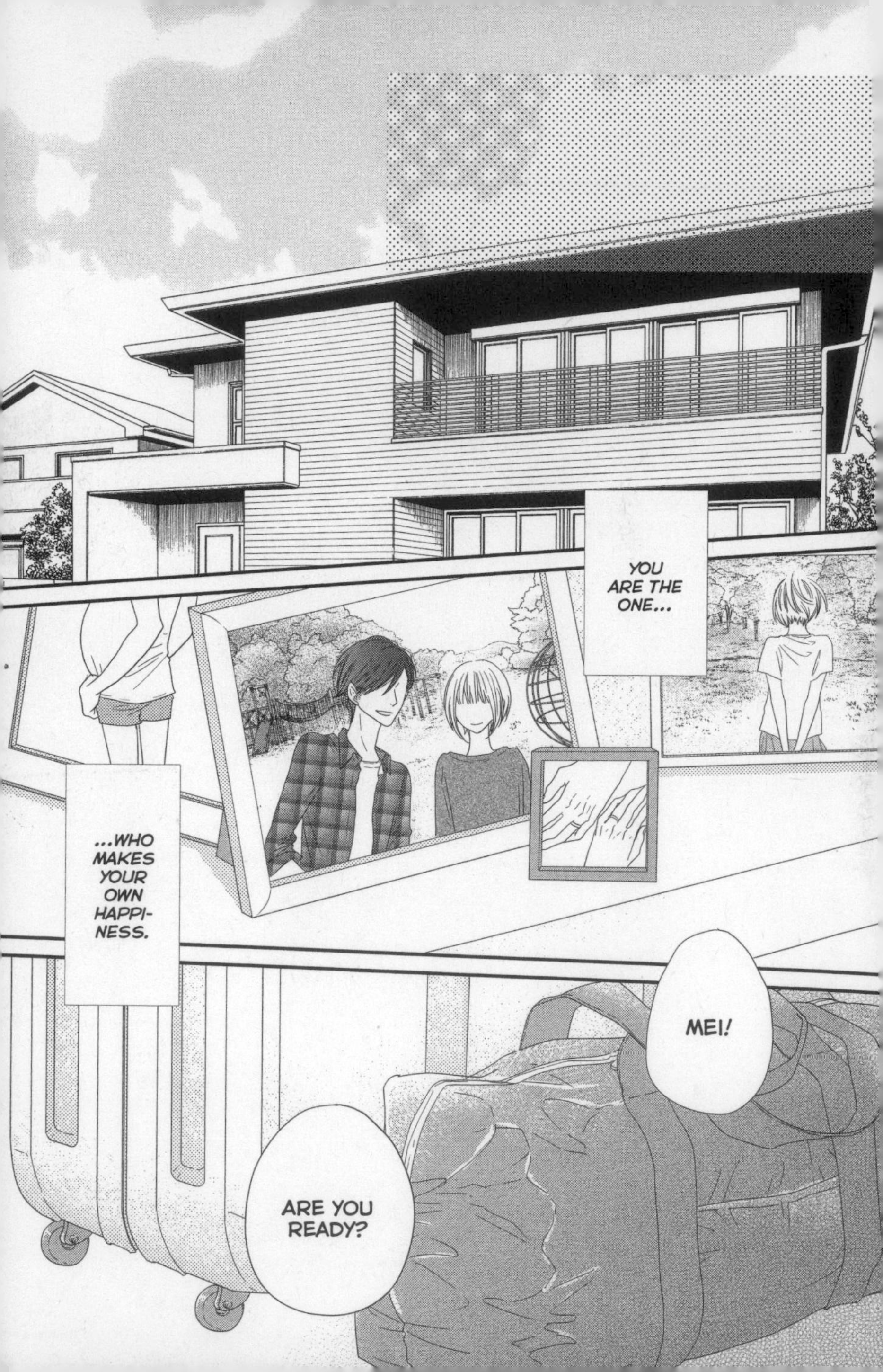
YOU ARE THE ONE...
...WHO MAKES YOUR OWN HAPPI-NESS.
MEI!
ARE YOU READY?

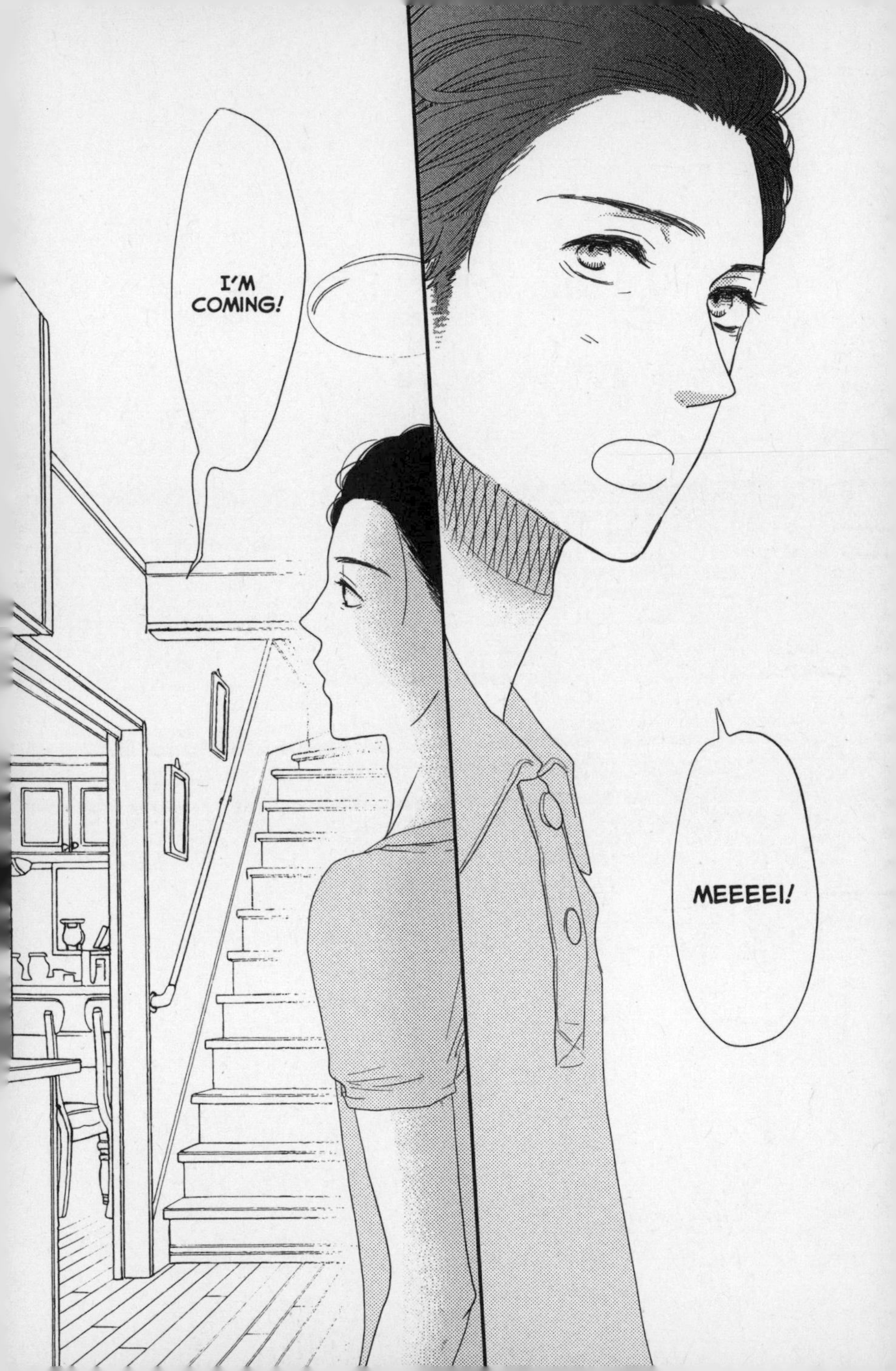
MEEEEI!
I'M COMING!

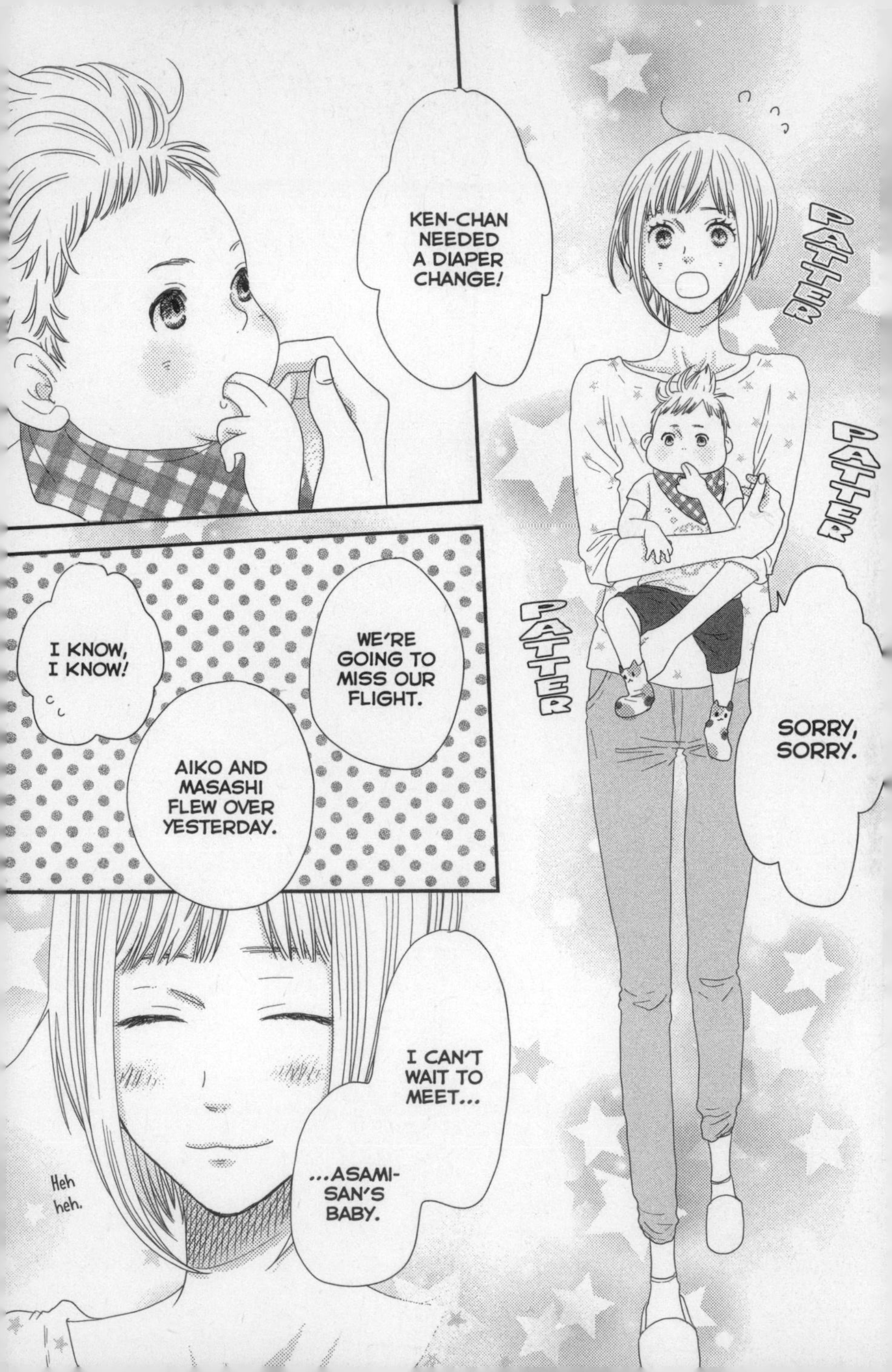
PATTER
PATTER
PATTER
SORRY, SORRY.
KEN-CHAN NEEDED A DIAPER CHANGE!
WE'RE GOING TO MISS OUR FLIGHT.
AIKO AND MASASHI FLEW OVER YESTERDAY.
I KNOW, I KNOW!
I CAN'T WAIT TO MEET...
...ASAMI-SAN'S BABY.
Heh heh.

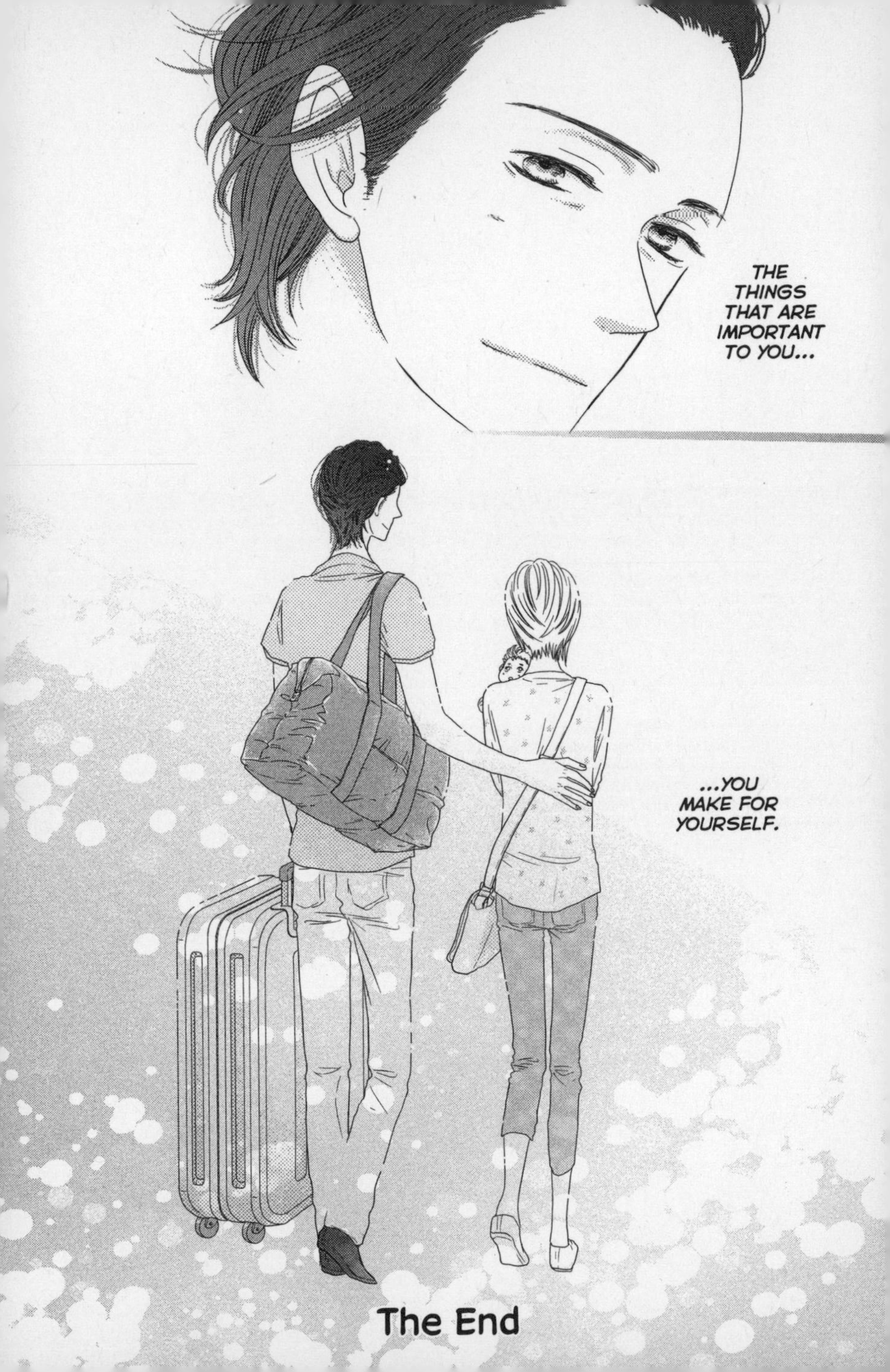
THE THINGS THAT ARE IMPORTANT TO YOU...
...YOU MAKE FOR YOURSELF.
The End

Say "I love you".

Hello. Kanae Hazuki here. And here it is—the final volume.

Nine years...

My first thought is that it went by in a flash, but when I look back, I realize it really has been a long time. I did a few series before this one, but this is the first time I've spent so much time drawing the same characters.

I used to always shamelessly draw whatever I wanted, but when this series turned into a long one, at some point the story material got to be such that I couldn't just scribble it down, and as the volume numbers got higher, "whatever I want"...wasn't enough anymore. And that's how I really feel.

The way my personality works, when I came across something I didn't know, I hated having to look it up in a book (I'm not a fan of print) or going to places for research (I'm the definition of shy), and on top of that I'm just lazy, so as the series got longer and I heard so much from all of you, and with *Dessert* magazine doing such big things to get everyone excited about it...with the whole thing getting bigger and bigger, I would feel like I was in over my head and I'd get depressed and nervous.

But from the very beginning of the series, there was a part of me that thought, "I brought these characters into the world, and I want to make them happy," and your letters and tweets showed me how strongly you readers feel about all of the characters. Now I believe it was those things that helped me to treat the various topics with such care, and to make it to the end of the series (Still, I didn't manage to draw the conclusion of *all* the characters' stories, and for that, I apologize).

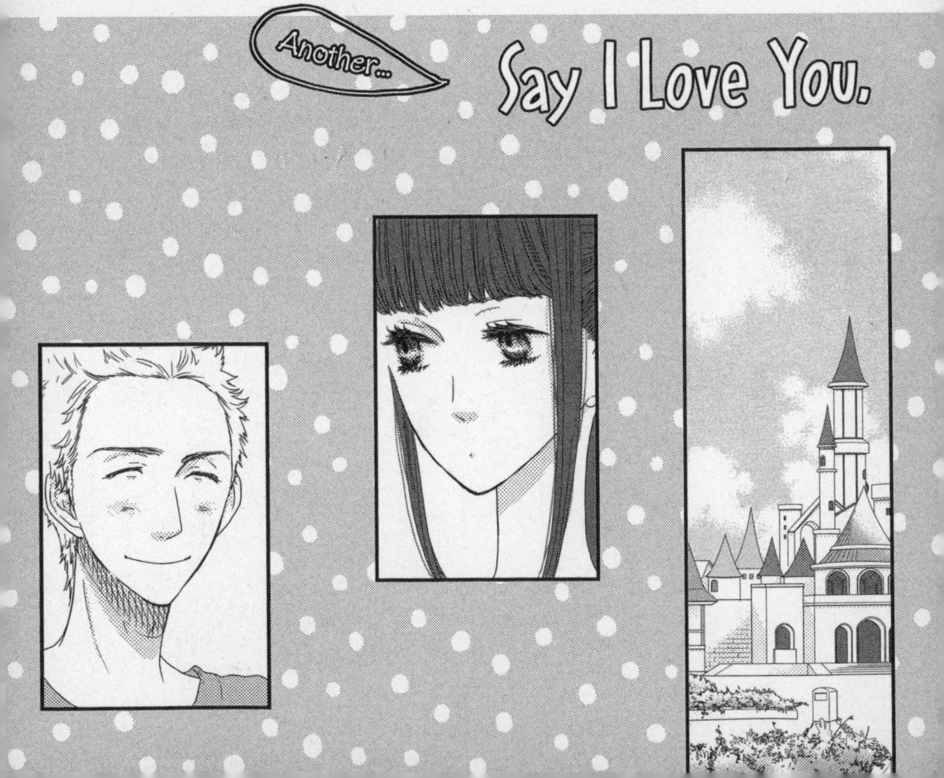
Another...
Say I Love You.

My editor would take me on research trips, and when it was beyond my capacity to research something, my editor would ask either someone from a different department or someone in production, or she'd research it for me...she really did everything for me.

The series was animated, and made into a movie...

These...are all things I never would have imagined, and on one hand I couldn't believe it, but on the other, I was very happy.

Of course, I think this all happened because the people who were involved read my manga and it caught their attention. So part of it is that that convinced me that the thing I drew wasn't a bad thing after all, but most of all, I think it made me happy because of my mother who passed away ten years ago.

Before *Say I Love You.* started, I never had much in savings, so I spent every day panicking, wondering how I would make it through each day, but I kept drawing, just to make sure I wouldn't stop, and my mother just watched over me without a word.

When she got sick and went to the hospital, I felt like I had to work even harder just because she wasn't there for me anymore, so I couldn't even go visit her like I should have, and as I was busy with that, she quietly passed away.

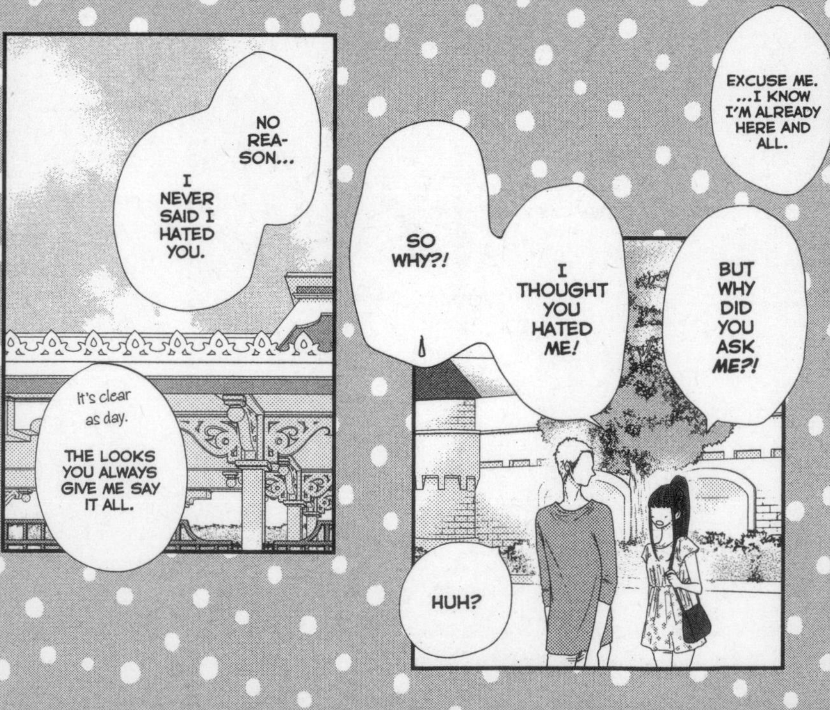
EXCUSE ME. ...I KNOW I'M ALREADY HERE AND ALL.
BUT WHY DID YOU ASK *ME?!*
I THOUGHT YOU HATED ME!
SO WHY?!
HUH?
NO REA-SON...
I NEVER SAID I HATED YOU.
It's clear as day.
THE LOOKS YOU ALWAYS GIVE ME SAY IT ALL.

I have always, always...always regretted that.

I was always too proud to say "thank you" or "I'm sorry" when I should have.

Now, I wish I had said those words so many more times when she was alive. It's true—once they're gone, there is nothing you can do for them. You can't even hold their hand.

As the chapters of *Say I Love You.* kept coming out, the contents of the letters I received would change, and I would learn what was going on in the lives of the people who sent them, and what was worrying them, so I got to see a lot of that kind of thing.

They loved someone but couldn't bring themselves to tell them, they couldn't bring themselves to say thank you to a significant other, they were being bullied, they lost their parents like I did and were living in a home, they couldn't get along with their family...really, all kinds of situations. I was happy to know that these people read my manga and felt strongly enough about it to write me a letter. The people who wrote letters to me mean a lot to me, too.

The one thing I can say is, if there's even one person in your life who means anything to you, I know it's a little embarrassing, but you should make sure to express your feelings in words whenever you get the chance! It doesn't matter if it's late, or if you have to work yourself up to it—just make sure to tell them!

We humans are creatures who only remember the negatives, so whenever you feel grateful, make sure to express it in words, and implant it in our memories!

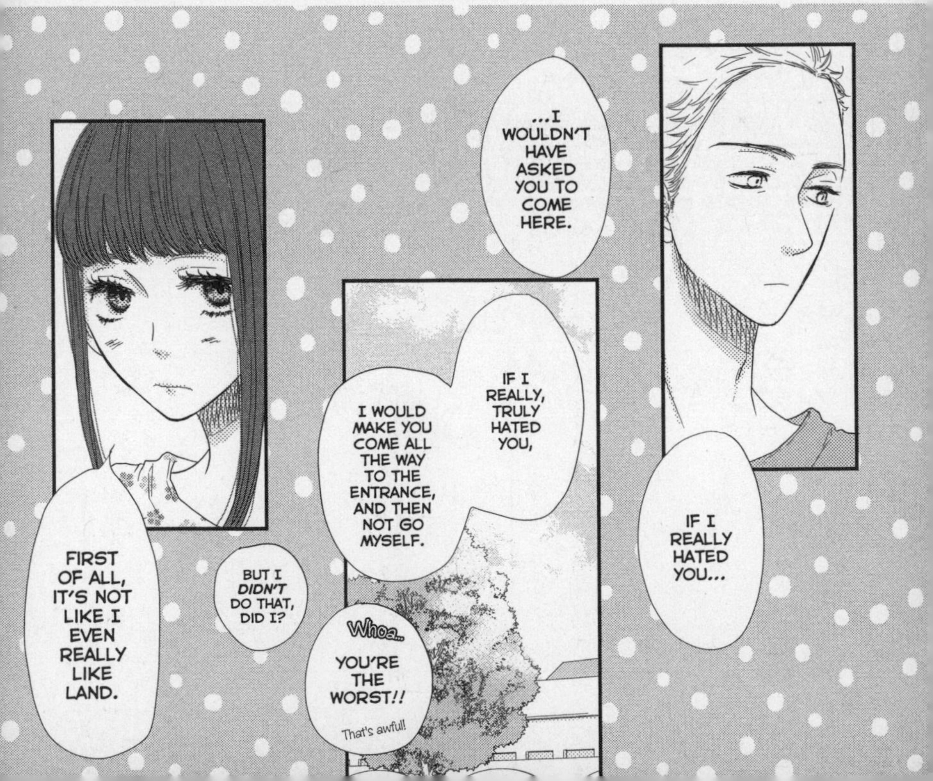
IF I REALLY HATED YOU...
...I WOULDN'T HAVE ASKED YOU TO COME HERE.
IF I REALLY, TRULY HATED YOU,
I WOULD MAKE YOU COME ALL THE WAY TO THE ENTRANCE, AND THEN NOT GO MYSELF.
BUT I *DIDN'T* DO THAT, DID I?
Whoa...
YOU'RE THE WORST!!
That's awful!
FIRST OF ALL, IT'S NOT LIKE I EVEN REALLY LIKE LAND.

I've gotten off track...

I would always draw this series, thinking about how I could convey my gratitude to my mother, and they made it into a movie. That made me so, so happy. Ever since I was a little girl, my mother would watch quietly over me as I drew pictures, and I think maybe I've finally managed to give her something in return.

But more than anything, it's all thanks to you, who allowed this manga to grow and kept reading until that movie offer came.

Really, truly, thank you.

And I won't list any names here, but thank you to everyone who cheerfully allowed me to interview them for my manga research.

Say I Love You. is ending now, but for me this is a new beginning.

I hope that if you spot another manga from me somewhere that you'll pick it up and read it. Thank you so, so much for reading this far!

Kanae Hazuki

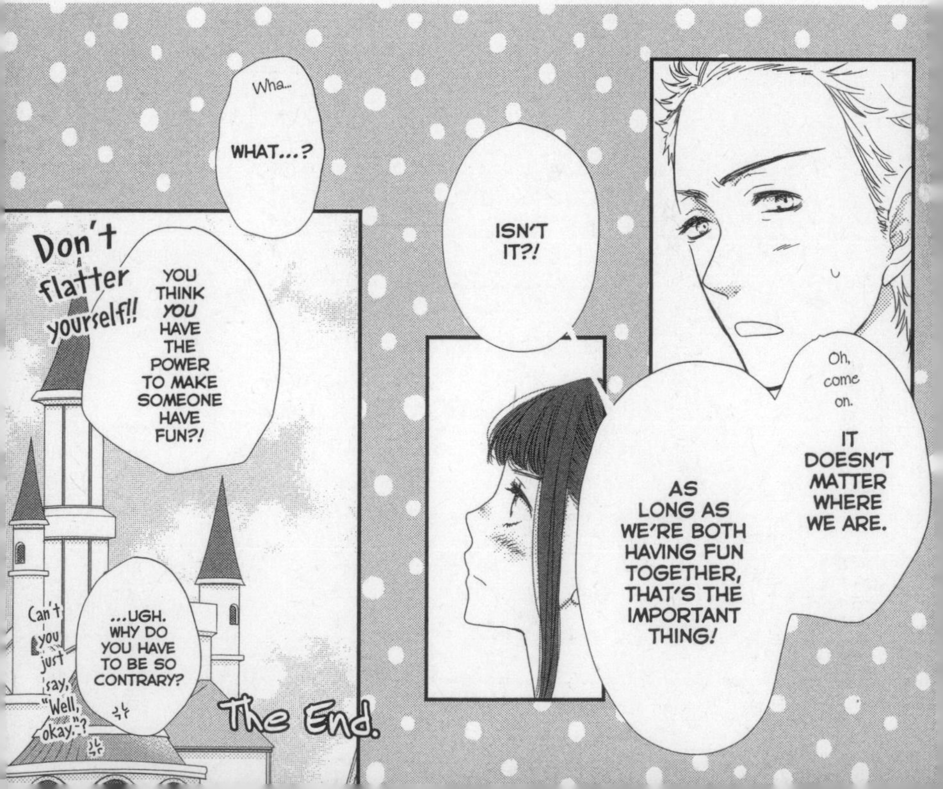
Oh, come on.
IT DOESN'T MATTER WHERE WE ARE.
AS LONG AS WE'RE BOTH HAVING FUN TOGETHER, THAT'S THE IMPORTANT THING!
ISN'T IT?!
Wha...
WHAT...?
YOU THINK *YOU* HAVE THE POWER TO MAKE SOMEONE HAVE FUN?!
Don't flatter yourself!!
...UGH. WHY DO YOU HAVE TO BE SO CONTRARY?
Can't you just say, "Well, okay."?
The End.

TRANSLATION NOTES

WHEN HE STARTED CRYING, I TRIED TO GIVE IT BACK.

BUT THEN YUKI-SENSEI CAME.

SHE'S ALWAYS GETTING MAD. I HATE HER.

Yuki-sensei

Yūki-kun and Yuki-sensei, page 10
At first glance, it may seem like the child and the teacher have the same name (and the similarity, no doubt, is why Yuki-sensei seems to be playing favorites), but they are slightly different. The line over the U in Yūki-kun is called a macron, and in the case of Japanese words, it indicates that the vowel is longer than one without a macron. The name Yūki has three beats (yu-u-ki), while Yuki only has two (yu-ki).

YEAH... IT COST A LOT TO RENT THE SPACE...

BUT I WAS HOPING IT COULD GIVE ME SOME GOOD EXPOSURE.

THAT'S ALL.

Ha ha.

Rental galleries, page 48

Though Japan does have formal art galleries that work on commission and museums for displaying the works of established artists, a great number of art galleries in Japan fall under the category of *kashi-garō*, or rental galleries. Rental galleries are spaces that allow anyone to display their art as long as they pay to rent the gallery space. The fee usually covers just the space and listings in mailers and/or websites—everything else is at the exhibiting artist's expense. In Japan, where the barrier of entry for prestigious galleries and museums is extremely high, rental galleries are the easiest way for up-and-coming artists to get attention for their works, and this is exactly what Yamato did to bring more attention to his photography.

aving lost his wife, high school teacher Kōhei Inuzuka is doing his best to raise his young
aughter Tsumugi as a single father. He's pretty bad at cooking and doesn't have a huge
ppetite to begin with, but chance brings his little family together with one of his students, the
onely Kotori. The three of them are anything but comfortable in the kitchen, but the healing
ower of home cooking might just work on their grieving hearts.

This season's number-one feel-good anime!" —Anime News Network

A beautifully-drawn story about comfort food and family and grief. Recommended." —Otaku
SA Magazine

sweetness & lightning

By Gido Amagakure

KC
KODANSHA
COMICS

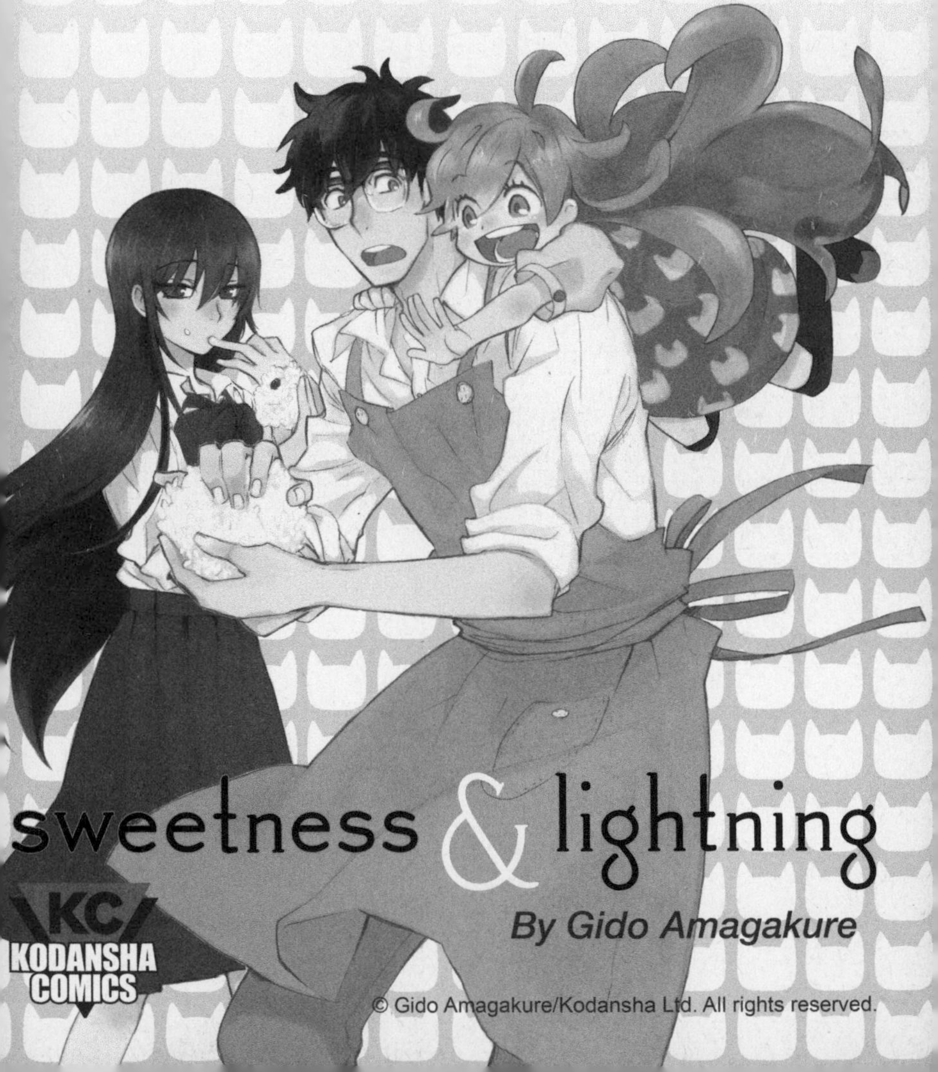

The prince in his dark days

By **Hico Yamanaka**

A drunkard for a father, a household of poverty... For 17-year-old Atsuko, misfortune is all she knows and believes in. Until one day, a chance encounter with Itaru–the wealthy heir of a huge corporation–changes everything. The two look identical, uncannily so. When Itaru curiously goes missing, Atsuko is roped into being his stand-in. There, in his shoes, Atsuko must parade like a prince in a palace. She encounters many new experiences, but at what cost...?

Based on the critically acclaimed classic horror manga

The first new *Parasyte* manga in over 20 years!

NEO PARASYTE f

BY ASUMIKO NAKAMURA, EMA TOYAMA, MIKI RINNO, LALAKO KOJIMA, KAORI YUKI, BANKO KUZE, YUUKI OBATA, KASHIO, YUI KUROE, ASIA WATANABE, MIKIMAKI, HIKARU SURUGA, HAJIME SHINJO, RENJURO KINDAICHI, AND YURI NARUSHIMA

A collection of chilling new *Parasyte* stories from Japan's top shojo artists!

Parasites: shape-shifting aliens whose only purpose is to assimilate with and consume the human race... but do these monsters have a different side? A parasite becomes a prince to save his romance-obsessed female host from a dangerous stalker. Another hosts a cooking show, in which the real monsters are revealed. These and 13 more stories, from some of the greatest shojo manga artists alive today, together make up a chilling, funny, and entertaining tribute to one of manga's horror classics!

KC
KODANSHA
COMICS

KODANSHA COMICS

Japan's most powerful spirit medium delves into the ghost world's greatest mysteries!

Story by Kyo Shirodaira, famed author of mystery fiction and creator of *Spiral*, *Blast of Tempest*, and *The Record of a Fallen Vampire*.

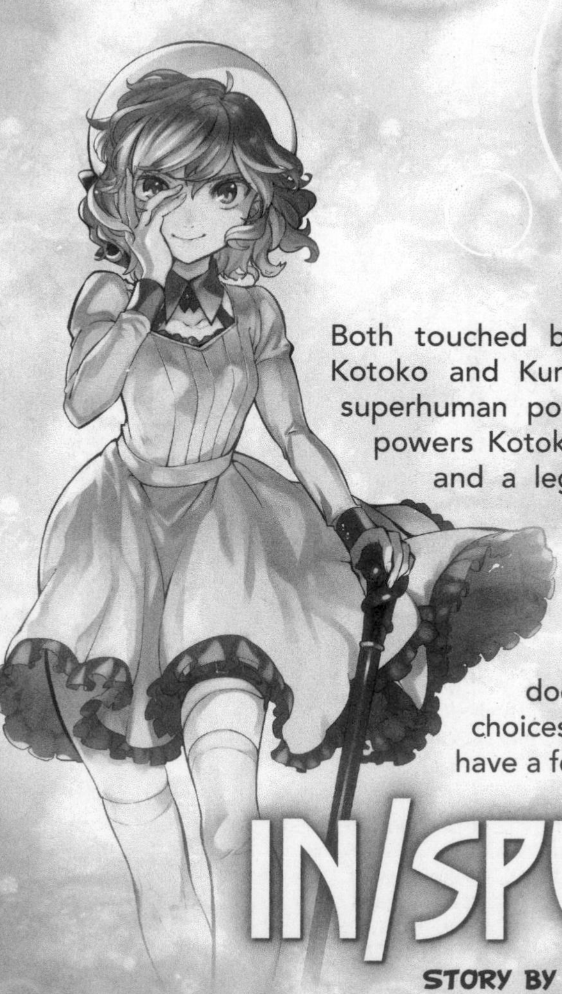

Both touched by spirits called yôkai, Kotoko and Kurô have gained unique superhuman powers. But to gain her powers Kotoko has given up an eye and a leg, and Kurô's personal life is in shambles. So when Kotoko suggests they team up to deal with renegades from the spirit world, Kurô doesn't have many other choices, but Kotoko might just have a few ulterior motives...

IN/SPECTRE

STORY BY KYO SHIRODAIRA
ART BY CHASHIBA KATASE

My Little Monster

OPPOSITES ATTRACT...MAYBE?

Haru Yoshida is feared as an unstable and violent "monster."
Mizutani Shizuku is a grade-obsessed student with no friends.
ate brings these two together to form the most unlikely pair. Haru
rmly believes he's in love with Mizutani and she firmly believes
e's insane.

KC
KODANSHA
COMICS

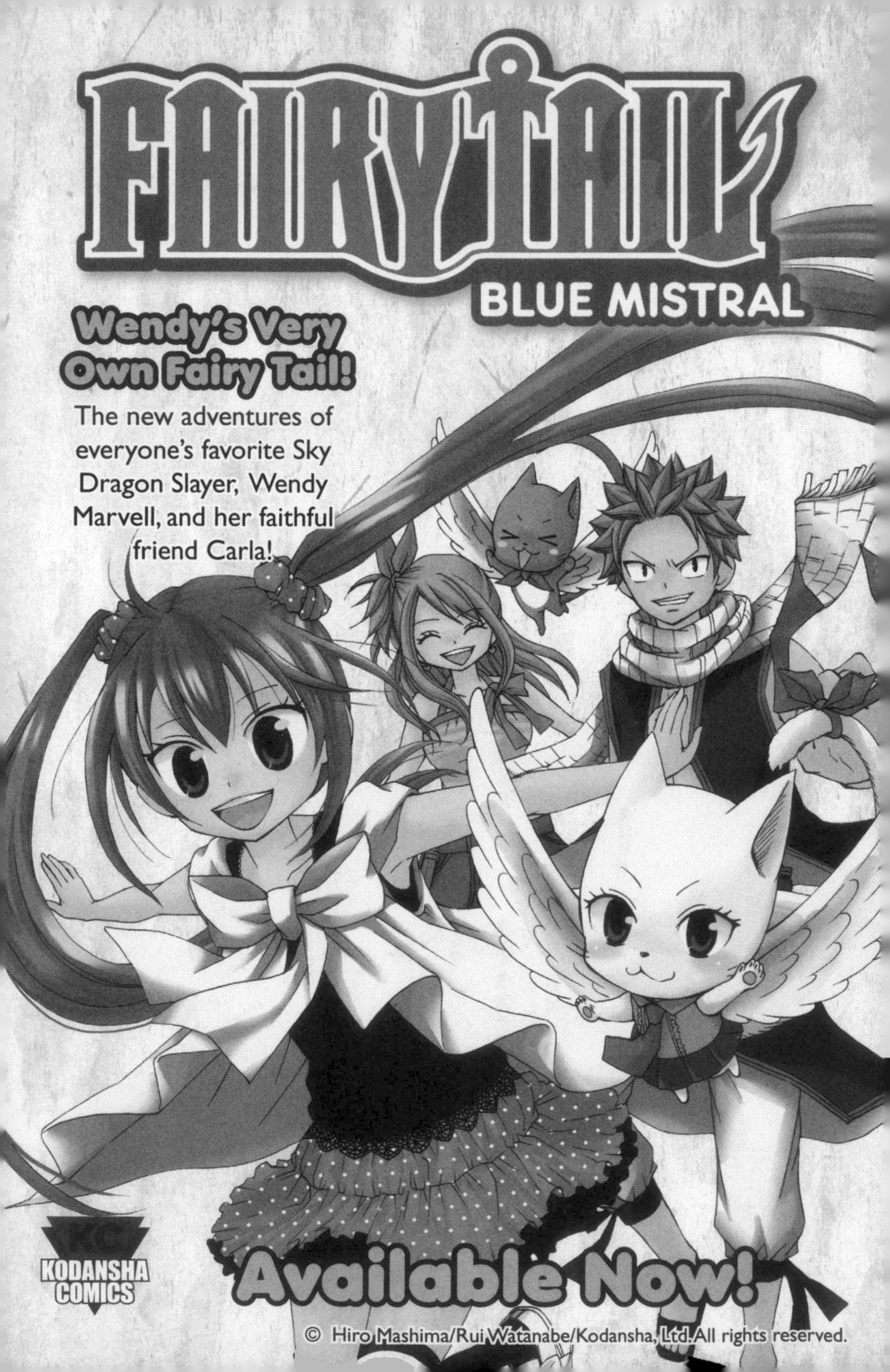
FAIRY TAIL
BLUE MISTRAL
Wendy's Very Own Fairy Tail!
The new adventures of everyone's favorite Sky Dragon Slayer, Wendy Marvell, and her faithful friend Carla!
KODANSHA COMICS
Available Now!
© Hiro Mashima/Rui Watanabe/Kodansha, Ltd. All rights reserved.

"An emotional and artistic tour de force! We see incredible triumph, and crushing defeat... each panel [is] a thrill!"
—Anitay

"A journey that's instantly compelling."
—Anime News Network

WELCOME TO THE BALLROOM

By Tomo Takeuchi

Feckless high school student Tatara Fujita wants to be good at something—anything. Unfortunately, he's about as average as a slouchy teen can be. The local bullies know this, and make it a habit to hit him up for cash, but all that changes when the debonair Kaname Sengoku sends them packing. Sengoku's not the neighborhood watch, though. He's a professional ballroom dancer. And once Tatara Fujita gets pulled into the world of ballroom, his life will never be the same.

A Kodansha Comics Trade Paperback Original
Say I Love You. volume 18 copyright © 2017 Kanae Hazuki
English translation copyright © 2017 Kanae Hazuki

Published in the United States by Kodansha Comics, an imprint of Kodansha USA Publishing, LLC, New York.

Publication rights for this English edition arranged through Kodansha Ltd, Tokyo.

First published in Japan in 2017 by Kodansha Ltd., Tokyo as *Sukitte iinayo.* volume 18.

ISBN 978-1-63236-441-8

Printed in the United States of America.

www.kodanshacomics.com

9 8 7 6 5 4 3 2 1
Translation: Alethea and Athena Nibley
Lettering: Jennifer Skarupa
Editing: Ajani Oloye
Kodansha Comics edition cover design: Phil Balsman

You're Reading in the Wrong Direction!!

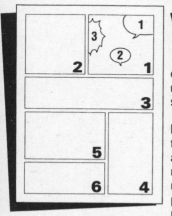

Whoops! Guess what? You're starting at the wrong end of the comic!

...It's true! In keeping with the original Japanese format, **One Piece** is meant to be read from right to left, starting in the upper-right corner.

Unlike English, which is read from left to right, Japanese is read from right to left, meaning that action, sound effects and word-balloon order are completely reversed...something which can make readers unfamiliar with Japanese feel pretty backwards themselves. For this reason, manga or Japanese comics published in the U.S. in English have sometimes been published "flopped"– that is, printed in exact reverse order, as though seen from the other side of a mirror.

By flopping pages, U.S. publishers can avoid confusing readers, but the compromise is not without its downside. For one thing, a character in a flopped manga series who once wore in the original Japanese version a T-shirt emblazoned with "M A Y" (as in "the merry month of") now wears one which reads "Y A M"! Additionally, many manga creators in Japan are themselves unhappy with the process, as some feel the mirror-imaging of their art skews their original intentions.

We are proud to bring you Eiichiro Oda's **One Piece** in the original unflopped format. For now, though, turn to the other side of the book and let the journey begin...!

–Editor